THE SOCIAL AND ECONOMIC
DEVELOPMENT OF CREWE
1780-1923

THE

SOCIAL AND ECONOMIC

DEVELOPMENT OF CREWE

1780-1923

BY

W. H. CHALONER

[1950]

AUGUSTUS M. KELLEY PUBLISHERS

MANCHESTER UNIVERSITY PRESS

© 1950 W. H. Chaloner.

First Published 1950 by
Manchester University Press

Reprinted 1973 by
Manchester University Press
316-324 Oxford Road
Manchester M13 9NR England

ISBN 0 7190 0545 0

Augustus M. Kelley Publishers
305 Allwood Road
Clifton New Jersey 07012 U. S. A.

Library of Congress Cataloging in Publication Data

Chaloner, William Henry.
    The social and economic development of Crewe,
1780-1923.

    Original ed. issued as no. 14 of Economic
history series.
    Bibliography: p.
    1. Crewe, Eng.--Social conditions. 2. Crewe,
Eng.--Economic conditions. I. Title. II. Series:
Economic history series, no. 14.
[HN398.C7C48 1973]   309.1'427'1   73-1616
ISBN 0-678-00754-3

PRINTED IN THE UNITED STATES OF AMERICA
by SENTRY PRESS, NEW YORK, N. Y. 10013

CONTENTS

To
MY FATHER
and
MY MOTHER

TABLE OF APPENDICES AND ILLUSTRATIONS

APPENDICES

ILLUSTRATIONS

ERRATA

Page xiii, middle of page, entry for Owen, G.
        For Methodistaeth read Methodistiaeth

Page 97, line 5 from bottom of main text
        For Macclesfields read Macclesfield

Page 160, line 23 down   For 1887 read 1886
        line 24 down   For 1888 read 1887

BIBLIOGRAPHY

ORIGINAL MANUSCRIPT AND UNPUBLISHED MATERIAL

1. *Coppenhall Parish Registers* (1653 to date), in possession of the Rector of Coppenhall, Crewe, Cheshire.
2. *Register of Burials* (Church Coppenhall), 1857 *sqq.*, in possession of Crewe Corporation.
3. *Register of Burials* (Crewe Burial Board), 1872 *sqq.*, in possession of Crewe Corporation.
4. *Coppenhall Parish Book* (1816–99), containing vestry minutes, churchwardens' accounts and miscellaneous reports on parish matters—in possession of the Rector of Coppenhall, Crewe, Cheshire.
5. *Town Book of Monks Coppenhall* (1792–1850), containing accounts of the surveyors of highways, overseers of the poor and petty constables for the township for various periods between these dates—in possession of Crewe Corporation.
6. *Poor Rate Book, Monks Coppenhall* (1837–44, 1867), in possession of Crewe Corporation.
7. *Monks Coppenhall (later, Crewe) Local Board* (1860–77), minutes of board and committee meetings—in possession of Crewe Corporation.
8. *Nantwich Board of Guardians* minute books (1837–80), in Nantwich Workhouse.
9. *Crewe Town Council* (1877–1923) minutes of council and committee meetings. Abstract of Accounts of Crewe Corporation (1877–8, 1879–81, 1882 to date).
   Annual Reports of Crewe Borough Medical Officer of Health (1893 to date).
10. *Church Coppenhall Parish Council* minutes (Dec. 4, 1894, to 1936), in possession of Crewe Corporation.
11. *Grand Junction Railway Company Board* minutes (1835–46) and directors' reports to the shareholders (1833–46).
12. *London and North-Western Railway Board* minutes of full board and committees.
13. *Crewe Co-operative Friendly Society* minutes of committee of management 1856–80—in possession of the Society.
    Annual Reports 1849–50, 1852–3.
    Rules of 1845 to date (in Registry of Friendly Societies, London).
14. *Crewe Mechanics' Institution* (1845–1912).
    Crewe Newsroom and Library Committee minutes 1844–5.
    Minutes of council of Institution 1845–50.
    Minutes of Mechanics' Institution sub-committee 1845–8.
    Annual Reports of council 1845–1912.
    Rules of 1845.
    Catalogue of the library of the Crewe Mechanics' Institution, containing revised rules (1848)
    (the above are in the possession of the Institution).
15. *Crewe Engineering Society* (1879–84) minute books.
16. *Crewe Scientific Society* (1898–1902) minute books (the records of the above two societies are in the possession of the Crewe Mechanics' Institution).
17. *Public Record Office*: census enumerators' manuscript returns for Monks and Church Coppenhall townships in 1841 and 1851.
    Home Office correspondence, 1848.

18. *Land Tax Returns* (1781–1832) for townships of Monks and Church Coppen-hall in County Record Office, Chester (the returns for 1782, 1788, 1800 and 1801 are missing).

19. *Birmingham Public Reference Library :*
    (*a*) Notice issued March 17, 1826, on behalf of the Liverpool and Bir-mingham Railway Committee, listing parishes on the proposed route.
    (*b*) Case in support of the Birmingham and Basford Railroad Bill, March, 1831.

20. Monumental masonry in Coppenhall churchyard, Crewe Cemetery, Wis-taston churchyard and Crewe Market Hall.

NEWSPAPERS AND PERIODICALS

Cassier's Magazine, 1903.
Chambers' Edinburgh Journal, 1846, 1850, 1889.
Cheshire Observer, 1861–4, 1867.
Chester Chronicle.
Chester Courant.
Chester Record, 1860.
Christian Socialist, 1850–1.
Co-operative News.
Co-operator, 1860–71.
Coppenhall Parish Magazine.
Crewe Chronicle (founded March 21, 1874)—in British Museum from April 17, 1875.
Crewe Guardian (founded August 29, 1863)—in British Museum from Sep-tember 25, 1869.
Economic History Review, vol. xvii, no. 1 (1947), pp. 27–44 (article by M. and J. B. Jefferys : " The Wages, Hours and Trade Customs of the Skilled Engineer in 1861 ").
Farmer and Stockbreeder, 1909.
Friends' Historical Journal, 1922.
Herepath's Railway Magazine, 1835–9.
Illustrated London News.
Index to London Gazette, 1830–80.
Journal of Association, 1852.
Liverpool Courier.
Liverpool Daily Post, 1912.
Manchester City News.
Manchester Daily Examiner.
Manchester Guardian.
Nantwich Guardian.
Primitive Methodist Magazine, 1855.
Proceedings of the Institution of Civil Engineers.
Proceedings of the Institution of Mechanical Engineers.
Public Administration, April, 1937.
Railway Gazette (supplement of September 16, 1938).
Staffordshire Advertiser.
Stockport Advertiser.
The Times (London)—various ordinary issues and supplements.
Warrington Guardian, 1868.

DIRECTORIES

S. Bagshaw : *Directory of Cheshire*, 1850.
F. White : *ibid.*, 1860.
Kelly : *ibid.*, 1857, 1865, 1878.
Morris : *ibid.*, 1864, 1874.
I. Slater : *ibid.*, 1883.
W. Eardley : *Crewe Almanack* (issued annually 1869–1917, but copies for 1869–72,
    1874, 1876–7, 1879–82, 1884, 1886 were not available).
F. Porter : *Directory for Crewe*, etc., 1887, 1895.
Postal Directory for Crewe, etc., 1913.
I. Slater : *Directory of Lancashire*, 1871–2.

GOVERNMENT PUBLICATIONS

Census of Great Britain, 1801–1931.
Education Enquiry, vol. i, 1833 (abstract of answers and returns relating to the
    numbers of schools).
Journals of the House of Commons, 1824–31.
Minutes and reports of the Committee of the Privy Council on Education, various
    dates.
*Minutes of Evidence . . . in support of the Cheshire Junction Railway Bill before
    the Committee of the House of Lords in the Session of 1836* (Manchester Public
    Reference Library).
Minutes of Evidence, Select Committee on Railway Labourers (1846).
Reports of the Local Government Board.
Return of Owners of Land, 1873, vol. i (1875).
Returns of Industrial and Provident Societies, 1863–7, 1870–5.

PUBLISHED MATERIAL RELATING MAINLY TO CHESHIRE AND CREWE

*Act for enclosing lands in the manor and township of Church Coppenhall . . . in the
    county of Chester*, 54 Geo. III, cap. 166, R.A., June 17, 1814, pp. 16.
Caine, Rev. C. : *History of Wesleyan Methodism in the Crewe Circuit* (1883).
Caunt, W. H. : *Official Souvenir of the Annual General Meeting of the Delegates
    of the National Union of Railwaymen, July 2–7, 1923, held in the Town Hall,
    Crewe* (1923).
Chaloner, W. H. : *History of the Cotton Manufacture in Nantwich, 1785–1874*
    (1938).
—— *History of the Crewe Congregational Church, 1841–1947* (1947).
—— " The Worsdells and the Early Railway System " (*Railway Magazine*,
    Oct., 1938).
—— " Reminiscences of Richard Lindop (1778–1871), farmer, of Church
    Coppenhall " (*Trans. Lancs. and Ches. Antiq. Soc.*, vol. lv).
Cheshire County Council : *Alphabetical list of Deposited Plans at the County
    Record Office, Chester Castle, regarding Railways, 1806–1946* (1947).
Anon. : *Christ Church, Crewe, a Short History*, n.d.
Anon. : *Description of the new Engineering Laboratories at the Crewe Technical
    Institute* (1915).
Disbrowe, E. J. W. : *History of the Volunteer Movement in Cheshire, 1914–1920*
    (1920).
Earwaker, J. P. : *Local Gleanings*, vol. i (1879–80).
Anon. : *Fasciculus Cestriensis in Honour of Sir William Hodgson* (1934).

Gladden, W. : *Cheshire Folk* (1932).

Hall, J. : *History of Nantwich* (1883).

Hinchliffe, Rev. E. : *Barthomley* (1856).

Holland, H. : *General View of the Agriculture of Cheshire* (1808).

Johnson, J. : *Fifty years 1882–1932, . . . an account of the Baptist Church, Union Street, Crewe* (1932).

Anon. : *Jubilee of Crewe* (1887)—reprinted from the *Crewe Guardian.*

Lake, C. S. : *Reorganisation of Crewe Locomotive Works, L.M.S.R. Co.,* 1929.

Lucas, G. D. : *History of the Crewe Co-operative Friendly Society, 1845–1929* (1929).

Anon. : *Official description of the London and North-Western Railway Company's Works at Crewe* (1903, 1913).

Ormerod, G. : *History of the County Palatine and City of Chester,* vol. iii (2nd ed., 1882—T. Helsby).

Pegler, Rev. G. : *The Crewe Waters* (1914)—reprinted from the *Crewe Guardian.*

Pocock, T. I., and others : *The Geology of the Country around Macclesfield, Congleton, Crewe and Middlewich* (Memoirs of the Geological Survey, 1906).

Powicke, F. J. : *History of the Cheshire County Union of Congregational Churches, 1806–1906* (1906).

Report of the mid-Cheshire Joint Town Planning Advisory Committee (1929).

Rules of various Crewe co-operative societies (Registry of Friendly Societies, London).

Slater, G. : *Chronicles of Lives and Religion in Cheshire* (1891).

Terry, A. : *Historical Records of the 5th Administrative Battalion of the Cheshire Rifle Volunteers* (1879).

Timperley, P. : *Brief History of the Crewe Memorial Cottage Hospital* (1922).

Tomkins, C. : *Crewe and its Industrial Advantages* (n.d. ? 1934).

Urwick, W. : *Historical Sketches of Nonconformity in the County Palatine of Chester* (1864).

Wedge, T. : *General View of the Agriculture of Cheshire* (1794).

Whittle, R. : *Recollections of Events during my connection with the [Crewe Co-operative Friendly] Society* (1876).

OTHER PRINTED MATERIAL USED

Ackworth Old Scholars' Association, *35th (1916)* and *39th (1920) Annual Reports.*

Ackworth Scholars' List, 1779–1879 (1879).

Adamson, J. W. : *English Education, 1789–1902* (1930).

Amalgamated Society of Engineers : *Annual Reports, 1861–70.*

—— *Jubilee Souvenir* (1901).

Bessemer, Sir H. : *Autobiography* (1905).

Burke's *Peerage* (1934, 1937).

Burn, D. L. : *Economic History of Steelmaking, 1867–1939* (1940).

Caird, J. : *English Agriculture in 1850–51* (1852).

Clapham, Sir J. H. : *Economic History of Modern Britain,* vols. i and ii (1930, 1932).

Co-operative Congresses, *Annual Reports.*

Co-operative Wholesale Society's *Annual,* various dates.

Crosland-Taylor, W. J. : *Crosville* (1948).

Crutchley, E. T. : *G.P.O.* (1938).

Darroch, G. R. S. : *Deeds of a Great Railway, a Record of the Achievements and Enterprise of the London and North-Western Railway Company during the Great War* (1920).

Dickinson, H. W., and Titley, A. : *Richard Trevithick* (1934).

Dictionary of National Biography.
Ensor, R. C. K. : *England, 1870–1914* (1936).
Freeling, A. : *Grand Junction Railway Companion* (1837).
Hambleton, F. C. : *John Ramsbottom, the Father of the Modern Locomotive* (1937).
Hampson, T. : *The Whittles of Horwich* (1884).
Head, Sir F. B. : *Stokers and Pokers* (1st ed. 1849).
Hovell, M. : *The Chartist Movement* (2nd ed. 1925).
Hudson, J. W. : *History of Adult Education* (1851).
Hughes, J. : *Liverpool Banks and Bankers* (1906).
Jefferys, J. B. : *The Story of the Engineers, 1800–1945* (1946) (published for the Amalgamated Engineering Union on the twenty-fifth anniversary of the foundation of the Union).
Lardner, D. : *Railway Economy* (1850).
Lewin, H. G. : *Early British Railways to 1844* (1925).
—— *The Railway Mania and its Aftermath, 1845–1852* (1936).
Lewis, S. : *Topographical Dictionary of England*, 4th ed. atlas (1840), 7th ed. vol. i (1848).
McDermot, E. T. : *History of the Great Western Railway Company*, vol. i (1936).
Marshall, C. F. D. : *Centenary History of the Liverpool and Manchester Railway* (1930).
—— *History of British Railways down to the year 1830* (1938).
Mills, I. : *Threads from the Life of John Mills, Banker* (1899).
Nicholson, J. : *A Hundred Years of Vehicle Building (1834–1934)* (1934).
Osborne, E. C. and W. : *Guide to the Grand Junction Railway* (2nd ed., 1838).
Owen, G. : *Hanes Methodistaeth Sir Fflint* (1914).
Phillips, J. : *General History of Inland Navigation* (4th ed., 1803).
Priestley, J. : *Historical Account of the Navigable Rivers, Canals and Railways of Great Britain* (1831).
Prospectus of the Union of Lancashire and Cheshire Institutes (1936–7).
Redfern, P. : *Story of the C.W.S.* (1913).
Redlich, J. and Hirst, F. W. : *Local Government in England*, 2 vols. (1903).
Robson, W. A. (ed.) : *Public Enterprise* (1937).
Roscoe, T. : *History of the London and North-Western Railway* (1847).
Rules of the Journeyman Steam Engine Makers' Society (1843).
Saunders, A. M. Carr-, and others : *Consumers' Co-operation in Great Britain* (1938).
Smiles, S. : *Lives of the Engineers, George and Robert Stephenson* (1904 ed.).
Steel, W. L. : *History of the London and North-Western Railway* (1913).
Stretton, C. E. : *History of the Amalgamation of the L.N.W.R. Co.* (2nd ed., 1901).
—— *History of the Chester and Crewe Railway* (1890).
—— *History of the Grand Junction Railway* (1901).
—— *History of the Manchester and Birmingham Railway* (1901).
Stuart, J. : *Reminiscences* (1912).
—— *Six Lectures to the Workmen of Crewe* (1869).
Touzeau, J. : *Rise and Progress of Liverpool*, vol. ii (1910).
Unwin, G., and others : *Samuel Oldknow and the Arkwrights* (1924).
Webb, S. and B. : *Consumers' Co-operative Movement* (1921).
—— *History of Trade Unionism* (2nd ed., 1920).
—— *Parish and County* (1906).
—— *Statutory Authorities for Special Purposes* (1922).
Who was Who, 1896–1916.

MAPS

1. Photograph of MS. map of the Crewe area, 2 inches to 1 mile, 1831 (Ordnance Survey).
2. Plan of Crewe, 1 foot to 1 mile (Crewe Works, April 7, 1868).
3. Tithe Commutation maps of Monks and Church Coppenhall (1839 and 1840 respectively), (in possession of the Rector of Coppenhall).
4. Ordnance Survey of Crewe, Nantwich and surrounding district (1874–6), sheet lvi, 6 inches to 1 mile (1882).
5. Ordnance Survey of Crewe (1874), 1 inch to 41·66 feet, or 10·56 feet to 1 mile.
6. Crewe Station in 1837 and 1917, 40 feet to 1 inch (Municipal Buildings, Crewe).

ACKNOWLEDGMENTS

I MUST thank the former L.M.S. Railway Company, the members and officials of Crewe Corporation, Crewe Co-operative Friendly Society, the Council of the Crewe Mechanics' Institution and the former Rector of Coppenhall, the Rev. Canon J. Beddow, for access to and the provision of original records. In addition, I have received valuable help and the loan or gift of books and documents relating to Crewe from the late Mrs. A. G. Hill, Mr. F. Froggatt, the late Mr. E. Derbyshire, Mr. J. Rhodes, Mr. J. H. Ravenscroft, Mr. H. Sheen, Mr. J. L. Nickalls (Librarian, Friends' House, London), Messrs. G. F. & H. Wordsell, Mr. G. D. Lucas, Mr. F. C. Mather and Miss E. Sudlow, for which I am most grateful.

I am indebted also to Mr. Henry R. Ball for the drawings of the maps and diagrams, to the Borough of Crewe for the Map of Street development in Crewe up to the 1930's, and to Mr. H. M. McKechnie, Secretary of Manchester University Press for technical help while the book has been going through the press. Mr. Geoffrey R. Axon, A.L.A., very kindly made the index.

ABBREVIATIONS USED IN THE FOOTNOTES

Abst. Accts.	Abstract of Accounts of Crewe Corporation.
Ann. Rep. C.C.F.S.	Annual Report of the Crewe Co-operative Friendly Society.
A.R.C.M.I.	Annual Reports of the Crewe Mechanics' Institution.
Bagshaw	S. Bagshaw's *Directory of Cheshire*, 1850.
C.C.F.S.	Crewe Co-operative Friendly Society.
C.Ch.	*Crewe Chronicle* newspaper.
C.G.	*Crewe Guardian* newspaper.
Ch.C.P.C.	Church Coppenhall Parish Council Minutes.
Church Ctee.	Crewe Church Committee, Grand Junction Railway Board.
C.L.B.M.	Monks Coppenhall (later Crewe) Local Board Minutes.
C.M.	Crewe Mechanics' Institution Council Minutes.
Coun.	Full meeting of Crewe Town Council.
C.P.B.	Coppenhall Parish Book.
C.P.R.	Coppenhall Parish Registers.
Crewe Ctee., L.N.W.B.	Crewe Committee, London and North-Western Railway Board.
Ctee. of Coun.	Committee of Crewe Town Council.
D.N.B.	*Dictionary of National Biography*.
E.A. 98, 02, etc.	Wilmot Eardley's *Crewe Almanack* for 1898, 1902, etc.
Econ. and Ret.	Economy and Retrenchment Committee, Crewe Town Council.
Educ. Ctee.	Education Committee, Crewe Town Council.
E.L.	Electric Lighting (later Supply) Committee, Crewe Town Council.
Elect. Div. Ctee.	Electoral Divisions Committee, Crewe Town Council.
Estate Ctee., L.N.W.B.	Estate Committee, London and North-Western Railway Board.
Exec. Ctee., L.N.W.B.	Executive Committee, London and North-Western Railway Board.
Farm Ctee.	Farm Committee, Crewe Town Council.
Fce.	Finance Committee, Crewe Town Council.
Gen. and Loco. Ctee., L.N.W.B.	General Stores and Locomotive Expenditure, London and North-Western Board.
G.J.B.M.	Grand Junction Railway Board minutes.
G.J.B. Rep.	Grand Junction Railway Board report to shareholders.
G.P.C.	General Purposes Committee, Crewe Town Council.
Health Ctee.	Health Committee, Crewe Town Council.
Housing Ctee.	Housing Committee, Crewe Town Council.
I.L.N.	*Illustrated London News*.
Ind. Sites Ctee.	Industrial Sites Committee and sub-committee, Crewe Town Council.

Kelly, 1857, etc. . . .	Kelly's *Directory of Cheshire*, 1857, etc.
L.N.W.B.	London and North-Western Railway Board minutes.
Mat. and C.W. Ctee. .	Maternity and Child Welfare Committee, Crewe Town Council.
M.I.	Crewe Mechanics' Institution sub-committee minutes.
Mkt. Ctee.	Market, Cemetery and Water Committee, Crewe Town Council.
M.O.H.	Annual Reports, Crewe Borough Medical Officer of Health.
Morris, 1864, 1874 . .	Morris' *Directory of Cheshire*, 1864, 1874.
Municipal Housing Ctee.	Municipal Housing Committee, Crewe Town Council.
Nat. Reg. Ctee. . . .	National Registration Committee, Crewe Town Council.
N.R.	Crewe News Room and Library Committee minutes.
Porter, 1887, 1895 . .	Porter's *Directory of Cheshire*, 1887, 1895.
P.R.B.M.C.	Poor Rate Book, Monks Coppenhall.
Proc. Inst. C.E. . . .	*Proceedings of the Institution of Civil Engineers.*
Proc. Inst. Mech. Eng. .	*Proceedings of the Institution of Mechanical Engineers.*
P.R.O.,H.O.	Public Record Office, Home Office Papers.
S.A. Ctee.	School Attendance Committee, Crewe Town Council.
Slater	Slater's *Directory of Cheshire*, 1882.
T.B.M.C.	Town Book of Monks Coppenhall.
White	F. White's *Directory of Cheshire*, 1860.
Works Ctee.	Works Committee, Crewe Town Council.

INTRODUCTION

" Community building is the most important aspect of history, but as it is also the most difficult aspect it is the one that has been least studied."— GEORGE UNWIN and others : *Samuel Oldknow and the Arkwrights*, p. 159.

MODERN town planning owes more to the early Victorian period than is generally imagined. The two decades between 1830 and 1850, it is true, saw the final collapse, for reasons which are still obscure, of the Georgian manner in urban architecture and town planning. The collapse was succeeded by the flood of tasteless vulgarities which characterised the high Victorian epoch. Yet all was not lost. The early years of Victoria's reign saw the creation of at least three planned urban communities in the great British tradition of New Lanark, Mellor, Saltaire, Styal, Bournville and Port Sunlight. On the London and North-Western Company's iron road the Grand Junction's model town of Crewe was balanced by the London and Birmingham Company's Wolverton, while the Great Western Railway boasted its model colony of New Swindon.

It is the foundation of the railway colony at Crewe, and its subsequent history, with which we are concerned. Visitors to early Victorian Crewe were impressed by its air of neatness and regularity. They departed loud in their admiration of the community-building efforts of what was then Britain's greatest railway company. They noted particularly Crewe's comparatively wide, regular streets, built for the most part at right-angles to each other, and its model railway company's cottages.

Early Crewe owed its existence as a community to the public spirit of that famous group of railway capitalists known as " The Liverpool Party." The members of the " Party " have left their stamp on Crewe even in the town's oldest street-names —Lawrence Street, Moss Square and Earle Street. Even today it can be said that the only narrow and unsatisfactory highways in the older part of the town are either those which follow the line of the ancient township roads or those built by early non-railway enterprise. The houses built on the railway company's estate were grouped round a social centre housed in Moss Square and Prince Albert Street. This area contained the Town Hall, the Mechanics' Institution, the railway company's National schools, and, dominating all, Christ Church. In the early period of the town's history the care of the railway directors for the moral welfare and the economic efficiency of their workmen led to a ban on the building of public-houses on the company's estate and a careful watch on the number of such establishments over the frontier.[1] Later this temperance campaign was taken up with great energy by the Nonconformist and Liberal elements in the town, with important results for the national and local politics of Crewe.

It has been asserted, with literary exaggeration, that the railway company introduced a " feudal system . . . with modifications," and the works have been compared to a feudal castle. There is an element of truth in the observation, even though the relations between the artisans and the works officials seem to have been free and easy in the early period of the town's history. The directors felt that they had certain obligations towards their employees, " for even a railway company has bowels of compassion, although they are not on public exhibition." On the other hand, the men, working for the company in the production of a new and revolutionary method of transport, felt that their labours had a social purpose, a sentiment which has largely vanished in these days of more impersonal railway organisation, when the steam locomotive no longer possesses the romantic fascination attached to it by the men of the early railway age. Again, if the industrious engineer-apprentice of the London and North-Western Railway at Crewe could not marry his master's daughter, he could often do the next best thing, which was to marry his foreman's daughter.[2]

The historical records of Crewe throw much light on the question of " the condition of the people " in the nineteenth century, although the scene was not always so idyllic as it appeared to one observer in 1850 :—

" Six o'clock strikes and the work ceases. In walking leisurely to the station I saw many of the workmen digging in their little gardens,

---

[1] *E.g.* in 1855 the directors resolved that the attention of the local magistrates should be called to the inconveniences arising from " the large number (33) of public and beer houses in Crewe."

[2] W. Gladden : *Cheshire Folk* (1932), pp. 8–14, 70, 91.

' bringing themselves,' as Emerson phrases it, ' into primitive relations with the soil and nature ' ; others were reading the papers of the day at the Mechanics' Institution ; others strolling among the green fields round the town ; and others walking to a classroom to hear a teetotal lecture ; while some were proceeding to recreations of a very different kind." [1]

In spite of ugly revelations of promiscuous overcrowding in the least-respectable quarters of the town in the 1870's, the inhabitants of Crewe were fond of flinging the taunt " We have no slums in Crewe " at the inhabitants of historic Chester and Nantwich.[2] On the whole, the boast was justified. The history of the friendly society movement in the town provides ample material for exact study in an important but inadequately explored corner of social and economic history. The first branch of Oddfellows in Crewe dates from 1842, one year before the official inauguration of the railway colony, and the first local branches of the Foresters and the Druids were founded in 1843. Thirty years later the various friendly society branches in the town filled nearly two pages of Wilmot Eardley's *Crewe Directory*. In addition, the individual shops in the railway works usually had sick-clubs of various ages and varying financial stability. This does not take into account the widespread friendly society activities of Crewe's trade union branches.[3]

The " respectable artisan " could be as land-hungry as the squirearchy and middle classes with whom he was soon to share political power ; the means at his disposal were more limited, but by dint of quiet saving in good times he performed feats that looked imposing when taken collectively. Speaking at Crewe in 1861, a railway foreman said

". . . the subscriptions of the men at the Works to friendly societies [were] £1,500, and their investments in building societies £1,200, per annum . . . the company's servants at Crewe were owners of property in the town and neighbourhood to the value of more than £14,000." [4]

---

[1] *Chambers' Edinburgh Journal* (1850), vol. xiii, pp. 391–2.
[2] Gladden : *op. cit.*, p. 10 ; *C.Ch.*, 1.5.75, 5.9.75 ; *C.G.*, 21.3.74.
[3] *C.G.*, 11.2.71, 7.10.71, 16.3.72, 4.1.93, 13.12.93, 10.6.96, *E.A.* 73, pp. 23–4 ; *C.W.S. Annual* 1884, p. 320.
[4] *I.L.N.*, Jan. 19, 1861, p. 64.

An examination of the poor's rate book for the township dated 1867 suggests, however, that this was a somewhat optimistic estimate, although the freeholds were certainly divided among a large number of persons.[1]

Benevolent company paternalism could not last for ever; one by one the directors of the old Grand Junction Board retired from the seats of power on the London and North-Western, the building efforts of the railway company slackened, and the tradesmen of both the older and newer portions of the town, often Radicals, joined to demand more efficient and responsible forms of local government. In the earlier period the Radical reputation of the inhabitants did not lead them to oppose the company; rather, their political animosities were directed against the surrounding Tory landowners, parsons and farmers. With the establishment of the Local Board in 1860 began a process which entailed the gradual abandonment by the company of its self-imposed tasks of government in favour of a corporate organisation, and if the powerful personality of Francis William Webb might later attempt to set up through the town council a quasi-dictatorship in the interests of the railway authorities and the local Conservative Party, such an interference with public control and political opinions could only end, and did indeed end, in a bitter storm of recrimination and party strife. This led to its eventual collapse. After the overwhelming victory of the Radicals, and amidst their necessary reforms, came the rise of the Labour Party, which was finally able, in 1930, to wrest control of the town council from a coalition of the two older parties. The railway company did not, however, sink to the position of being merely the largest ratepayer, and continued to exercise a benevolent influence on the town by methods less controversial in character. The attainment of a separate corporate life by the community of Crewe measures the success of the founders of the colony.

---

[1] *Cf.* speech by the Earl of Derby in 1872 : " He entirely disbelieved the truth of the popular notion that small estates were undergoing a gradual absorption in the larger ones. It was true that the class of peasant proprietors . . . was tending to disappear. . . . In the place of that class, however, there was rapidly growing up a new class of small proprietors, who, dwelling in or near towns or railway stations, were able to buy small freeholds " (*Return of Owners of Land, 1873*, vol. I, pp. 3–4).

CHAPTER I

THE CREWE DISTRICT OF CHESHIRE IN THE CANAL ERA AND THE EARLY RAILWAY AGE

THE district now called Crewe, which includes the ancient parish of Coppenhall and portions of the surrounding townships, consists of drift deposit boulder clay of the glacial period, superimposed on a deep hollow in the hills and valleys of the Keuper marl. The Valley Brook appears to have cut down to this clay formation within the borough. The depth of the clay belt varies ; for example, at Sydney, which lies on the site of a pre-glacial river valley excavated when the land stood several hundred feet higher than at present, these deposits have a maximum depth of 320 feet, thus going down at least 160 feet below the present sea level. A boring a little north of Crewe showed 142 feet of clay, including some of the laminated variety. Near the gasworks in Wistaston Road, a boring showed 162 feet of clay, partly glacial and partly Keuper red marl with gypsum. The laminated clays closely resemble these other clays, but are stratified deposits, and were evidently formed in still water, most probably in glacial lakes.[1] These clays are intersected on the surface by occasional lines and pockets of sand and gravel, the remains of the old river and brook courses. The most important of these is a line of running sand which extends through the parish from north to south *via* Hightown and Flag Lane. This has caused much damage at various times to building and sewerage operations. The belt of drift sand underlying the clay rises to the surface in a bay-like curve in the outlying villages of Wistaston, Shavington, Weston, Crewe Green and Haslington. The lowest part of the town is to the west of Queen's Park (113 feet above sea level), and the highest on the north side of St. Paul's Church, Hightown (200 feet). Brine

---

[1] The succession of strata from the surface downwards appears to be :— boulder clay, laminated clay, drift sand, Keuper marl, red marl with gypsum, rock salt and thin sandstone, Keuper sandstone, red and white sandstone, Bunter sandstone, pebbly sandstones and red mottled sandstones. For the geology of the Crewe district, see T. I. Pocock and others : *The Geology of the Country around Macclesfield, Congleton, Crewe and Middlewich* (1906).

lies underneath Crewe, and was first discovered in the early 1840's during boring operations for water on the site of Christ Church and in Wistaston Road during the 1860's, when the railway company, fearing subsidence, put an end to the experiment. In 1874 boring operations in Church Coppenhall led to the finding of "medicinal waters" and to Henry Platt's unfortunate project for making Crewe the Harrogate of Cheshire, by means of the Coppenhall Spa Pump. Subsidence from the pumping in the mid-Cheshire salt-field was first noticed at Sydney, Church Coppenhall, about 1910, and by 1920 the total subsidence amounted to 6 feet; it was then estimated to be continuing at the rate of 3 inches per annum.[1] Peat is found on Coppenhall Moss. The whole district is generally flat, except for local glaciation hummocks.

The ancient parish of Coppenhall is traversed by two east-to-west streams, the Leighton (or North) Brook and the Valley (or South) Brook. The Valley Brook, sometimes dignified into the River Waldron or Wulvern, is the more important of the two, and drains an area of about 30 square miles. It rises in the hills near Talke, Staffs, and is a tributary of the River Weaver. From 1843 to the 1860's it formed at once both the chief source of water for the town and its main outlet for sewage. The Leighton Brook is a small, unimportant stream; it also is a tributary of the Weaver, but does not join the Valley Brook.

The Cheshire Plain provides through the Midland Gate a natural route between London and the Midlands on one hand, and the Irish Sea, Lancashire and North Wales on the other. Nantwich and Crewe command the northern side of the Midland Gate (the relatively narrow plain between the South-West Pennines and the Shropshire hills), as Stafford commands the southern side.

In the sphere of agriculture, South Cheshire is a dairy-farming, rather than an arable, region. James Caird, writing of Cheshire in the early 1850's, noted as "a somewhat anomalous circum-

---

[1] *C.G.*, 11.7.74 to end of 1876 *passim*, 29.9.77 ; Works Ctee., 10.12.12 ; M.O.H., 1902, p. 7. ; 1920, pp. 9–10 ; private information. It has been suggested that, as the heavy clay belt gives a firm foundation for workshops, this may have been one of the reasons why the Grand Junction Railway directors and engineers decided to locate the Edgehill Works at Crewe. No positive evidence for this exists.

stance" that "the less fertile parts of the county—the poor cold clays for a circuit of some miles round Nantwich—are said to produce the best quality of cheese." [1]   It is therefore not surprising to find, besides salt-boiling, important tanning and shoe-making industries in eighteenth- and nineteenth-century Nantwich, the great road centre of South Cheshire, 4 miles south-west of Crewe.   In the mid-eighteenth century, however, a good deal of the land traffic between the growing Lancashire towns and the Midlands appears to have passed through Cranage, near Holmes Chapel, 10 and 14 miles north-east of Crewe and Nantwich respectively.   William Harrison wrote as follows in 1886 :—

" Formerly ... and down to the middle of last century, it [Cranage] occupied a position analogous in some respects to that of Crewe at the present day.   It was close to the junction or parting of the ways, the spot where travellers who had journeyed together from the metropolis must say good-bye, if they were destined, the one for Manchester, and the other for Liverpool, Warrington or the north."

During the eighteenth century, Nantwich had been linked to wider markets not only by turnpike legislation, commencing in the case of South Staffordshire and Chester between 1729 and 1744, in the case of North Staffordshire (Newcastle-under-Lyme) in 1766, but also by various artificial waterways.   The first of these was the Chester to Nantwich canal, constructed between 1772 and 1779.   Later this line of communication had been extended from Nantwich to Whitchurch in Shropshire and thence to mid-Wales by another company.   The two undertakings were amalgamated in 1813 as the "United Company of Proprietors of the Ellesmere and Chester Canals."   In 1826 a body of local capitalists obtained an Act of Parliament for cutting a canal from the Ellesmere and Chester canal at Nantwich to Tettenhall in Staffordshire, for the purpose of linking the Liverpool and Birmingham areas.   The undertaking, the last of the canal era's great engineering triumphs, owed its origin to the various railway projects of the mid 1820's.   Alarmed by the threat from the new method of locomotion, men interested in canals desired a quicker route between the two great industrial areas of South Lancashire and the Black Country.   This Birmingham and Liverpool Junction canal was constructed between

[1] *English Agriculture in 1850–51* (1852), p. 254.

1828 and 1831. Four miles to the north-east of Crewe ran the famous Grand Trunk canal which since its completion in 1777 had linked the Trent to the Mersey, the North Sea to the Irish Sea. In 1827 the proprietors of the Ellesmere and Chester canal obtained powers to construct a branch from Wardle Green, a few miles north-west of Nantwich, to the Grand Trunk at Middlewich. This section, opened in 1831, and still known to bargees as "The New Cut," completed the canal network of South Cheshire.[1]

Anciently, Cheshire was well-wooded and there is some evidence which suggests that oak trees from the clayey soil of Coppenhall went to feed the salt-pans and tanneries of Nantwich, in the shape both of timber and of bark.[2] The scattered cottages and farm-houses of Coppenhall were of the famous black-and-white type characteristic of the Cheshire plain. Here again the local raw materials could be used—heavy oak beams jointed together in squares formed the frames of the buildings and the squares were filled in with wattle and daub. Two examples of this black-and-white architecture survived within the borough boundary until the 1920's—Thomas Beech's Hillock House and William Roylance's farm-house of 1639.

The ecclesiastical parish of Coppenhall had at an early date been divided into the civil townships of Church Coppenhall and Monks Coppenhall. In 1816 an Act of Parliament (56 Geo. III, c. xv) set up a turnpike from Nantwich to the Grand Trunk canal at Wheelock Wharf, and this improved road passed through the southern extremity of Monks Coppenhall, which is equidistant from these two places. The Middlewich to Nantwich highway, turnpiked in 1835, skirts Monks Coppenhall to the west. Church Coppenhall lies to the north of Monks Coppenhall and contains the ancient parish church of St. Michael.

---

[1] For the Cheshire turnpike system, with map and list of acts, see W. Harrison's two articles in *Trans. Lancs. and Ches. Antiq. Soc.*, vol. iv, pp. 80–92, esp. p. 84, and vol. x, pp. 237–48. The origins of the Nantwich to Wheelock Wharf turnpike may be studied in *Chester Chronicle*, Sept. 2, 1814, May 31 and July 12, 1816. For the Nantwich canals, see J. Phillips : *General History of Inland Navigation*, 4th ed. (1803) ; J. Priestley : *Historical Account of the Navigable Rivers, Canals and Railways of Great Britain* (1831), pp. 74–7, 233–46 ; J. Hall : *History of Nantwich*, pp. 227, 243, 357.

[2] Ormerod: *Hist. Ches.*, 2nd ed., vol. iii, pp. 326–7 ; *Local Gleanings*, ed. J. P. Earwaker, vol. i (1879–80), pp. 302–3.

Monks Coppenhall was smaller, less populous and less fertile than Church Coppenhall, but was destined to contain the nucleus of the modern town of Crewe. The respective areas were 1,336 and 1,535 acres. The boundaries of the municipal borough of Crewe were until 1892 those of the ancient township of Monks Coppenhall ; from that date they included portions of Wistaston, Church Coppenhall and Shavington-cum-Gresty townships, which increased the area of the borough of Crewe to 2,193 acres. A further extension under the Ministry of Health's County of Chester Review Order, 1936, took in the remainder of Church Coppenhall, together with portions of the other adjacent townships, and increased the borough's area to 4,144 acres. Modern Crewe takes its name from the railway station of Crewe, which was from 1837 situated in the old *township* of Crewe, adjacent to Monks Coppenhall, and quite distinct from the *municipal borough* of Crewe. The actual railway station of Crewe was therefore outside the borough area from its incorporation in 1877 until the extension of 1936. This township of Crewe contains the ancestral home and park of the Crewe family. John, second Baron Crewe (1772–1835), was forced to allow the railway line to impinge on his estates, but his successor, Hungerford, third baron (1812–94), drew the line at locomotive works. He is said to have planted clumps of trees at strategic points along the roads passing through his estate to the new settlement, in order to hide the railway colony from his view. " Anywhere but the new town " was his traditional reply to the coachman who enquired the destination of his lordship's daily drive. This placing of the railway works to the west of the station rather than to the east meant that the new town, called Crewe for convenience, grew up in the township of Monks Coppenhall and gave rise to the local proverb " The place which is Crewe is *not* Crewe ; and the place which is not Crewe *is* Crewe." [1]

At the opening of the nineteenth century the two Coppenhalls were typical Cheshire townships containing a number of scattered farmsteads and labourers' cottages. No trace has been found

[1] For the Crewe family see Ormerod, vol. iii, pp. 313–14 ; Burke's *Peerage* (1937), pp. 663–4 ; *Times*, Jan. 15, March 14, 1936 (sale of estate to Duchy of Lancaster) ; private information ; *Census 1881*, vol. ii, p. 457 ; for the earlier history of Coppenhall, see Ormerod, vol. iii, pp. 324–9.

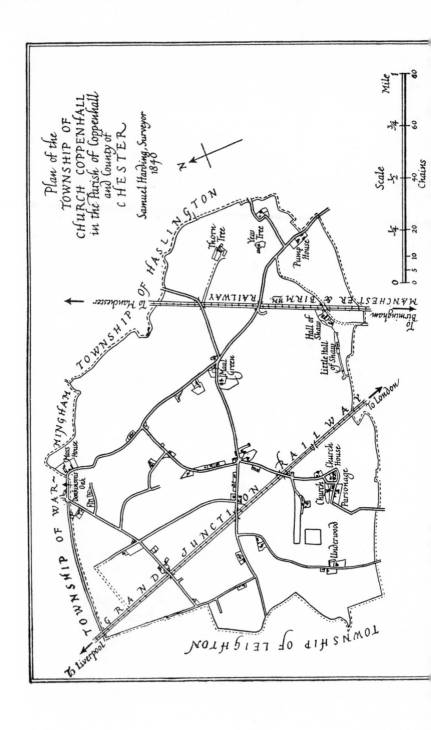

Plan of the
TOWNSHIP OF
CHURCH COPPENHALL
in the Parish of Coppenhall
and County of
CHESTER

Samuel Harding, Surveyor
1840

N

Scale

0 5 10   20   40   60   80
                    Chains
          ¼   ½   ¾   1
                    Mile

TOWNSHIP OF HASLINGTON

TOWNSHIP OF WAR~MINGHAM

TOWNSHIP OF LEIGHTON

To Manchester

MANCHESTER & BIRM.th RAILWAY

To Birmingham

GRAND JUNCTION RAILWAY

To Liverpool

To London

Thorn
Tree

Yew
Tree

Pump
House

Hall of Shaw

Little Hall
of Shaw

Mill
Green

Mass House

Dickinson's
Oak

Church
House

Church

Parsonage

Underwood

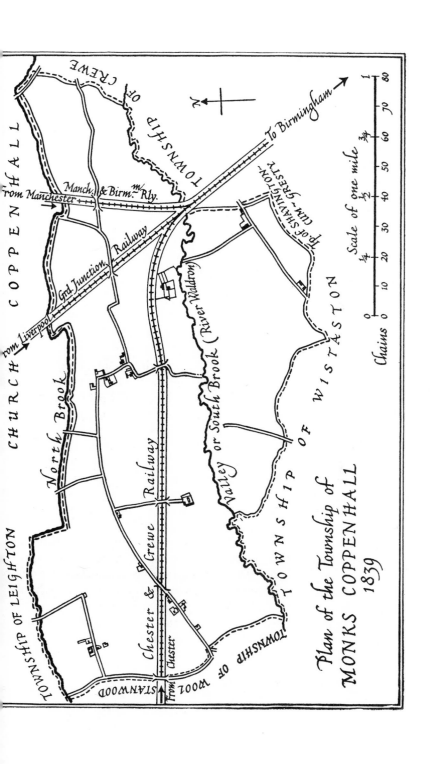

Plan of the Township of
MONKS COPPENHALL
1839

of any nucleated village settlement or of the open-field system of agriculture typical of Southern England and the Midlands, although there was a perceptible thickening of the density of human settlement in the area surrounding Cross Green in Church Coppenhall. The census returns for the Coppenhalls from 1801 to 1831 show an appreciable increase in the case of Church Coppenhall, but only a small one in the case of Monks Coppenhall :—

	Population.			
	1801	1811	1821	1831
Monks Coppenhall	121	114	146	148
Church Coppenhall	241	266	366	350
Total for whole parish . . .	362	380	512	498 [1]

In the case of the parish as a whole the population increased by 37·5 per cent. between 1801 and 1831. In the same period the population of England increased by over 55 per cent., so that the population of Coppenhall was not increasing as fast as that of the nation as a whole.

From the annual land-tax returns for the period 1781–1832,[2] the enumeration officer's return for Monks Coppenhall for the 1831 census, the Monks Coppenhall rate-book of 1837–44 and the original census returns for both townships preserved in the Public Record Office, it is possible to obtain a detailed picture of the social and economic conditions in the area in the years immediately preceding the railway age. Richard Sherwin's census return of 1831 for the township of Monks Coppenhall shows that there were then 27 families or householders, composed of 11 farmers, 11 labourers, 3 shoemakers, 1 tailor and 1 school-mistress. The 3 shoemakers can be accounted for only on the supposition that they were employed by the master shoe-manufacturers of Nantwich, an example of work being " put out " from a town into a nearby village. No similar information

---

[1] *Census* 1851, part I, vol. ii, div. viii, pp. 20–3.

[2] The returns for both townships are preserved in the County Record Office, Chester Castle ; those for 1782, 1788, 1800 and 1801 are missing.

is available for Church Coppenhall, but in the 1841 census 32 persons in that township called themselves farmers.[1]

The picture presented by the early records of the Coppenhall area is therefore that of an overwhelmingly rural society, but not of a society remaining unchanged from decade to decade. When Henry Holland reported to the Board of Agriculture in 1808 that the character of the small landowners of Cheshire had been " very much altered of late years " he was merely indicating a tendency which had been in operation, as far as Coppenhall was concerned, throughout the eighteenth century. It seems to have affected all grades of landowners and not merely the small ones.[2] Apart from the changes in tenancy and ownership made necessary by death there existed a brisk traffic in farms and small freeholds and a still brisker coming and going of tenant farmers, so that even at ten-yearly intervals the names on the land-tax returns show considerable alteration. There is little evidence that the pace of this turnover underwent any considerable quickening during the period of the French Wars and their aftermath.[3]

Most of the land in the two townships was owned by absentee landlords throughout the period ; *e.g.* in 1799 there were 24 persons owning land or rights over land in Monks Coppenhall, of whom only two, Thomas Galley and Charles Hassall, were actually resident in the township, and even they rented the bulk of their farms from other landowners. By 1837, 29 persons held land in the township, and after the arrival of the railway colony this number increased rapidly. Owing to encroach-

[1] Return of 1831 printed in *C.G.*, 19.11.04 ; P.R.O.,H.O. 107/116.

[2] H. Holland : *General View of the Agriculture of Cheshire* (1808), p. 79. Holland went on : " From the advantages which have been derived from trade, and from the effects of the increase of taxes, which have prevented a man from living with the same degree of comfort on the same portion of land he could formerly, many of the old owners have been induced to sell their estates ; and new proprietors have spread themselves over the county, very different in their habits and prejudices."

[3] Richard Lindop of Church Coppenhall considered that there had been a quickening, especially after the roadmaking activities of the Rev. J. S. Cattlow in 1806–7, but Lindop's long memory reached back well into the mid-eighteenth century, and he tended to post-date the changes. (See his interesting but incomplete list of changes of estate-ownership in Church Coppenhall during this period, printed in *Trans. Lancs. and Ches. Antiq. Soc.*, vol. lv, pp. 119–21.)

ments on the common land of the township, the number of owner-occupiers was much larger in Church Coppenhall, where one-third of the 45 landowners occupied their own properties in 1799. Their holdings, however, were on the average smaller than those of the absentees and together amounted to less than one-sixth of the total assessed value of the township to the land-tax. Just as little difference in social status can have existed between the larger owner-occupiers and the tenant farmers, so there was little to choose between the farm-worker possessing a minute freehold and the landless labourer. In spite of the rigid classification into " farmer " and " labourer " met with in the census returns, the impression received from a study of the remaining material, especially that relating to Church Coppenhall (where some of the freeholds had an annual value of only £1 2s. 6d.), is that of a community whose members shaded imperceptibly in economic status from subsistence level to modest wealth.[1]

Contrary to the popular belief, the years between 1799 and 1830 showed a definite, if small, increase in the number and importance of owner-occupiers in the local rural economy.[2] The process can also be traced whereby prosperous tenant farmers like George Vernon, John Scragg and Peter Holland, senior, quietly bought up small freeholds as they came on the market, while here and there substantial owner-occupiers such as Joseph Stokes, Peter Walker and Thomas Beech kept alive the tradition of the yeomen of England.[3]

The absentee landlords between 1781 and 1841 presented a considerable diversity of social types. They included great land-owners like the Duke of St. Albans, Sir John Chetwode, 4th bart.

[1] The annual rentals of holdings in Monks Coppenhall in 1795 ranged from £2 10s. to £91.

[2] *E.g.* from two to five in Monks Coppenhall. For Church Coppenhall the evidence from the land-tax returns is less complete, as between 1799 (when the tax was made perpetual) and 1802 several acts of Parliament were passed which made it possible for landowners to commute their annual payments for a lump sum. About 25 per cent. by value of the Church Coppenhall estates therefore disappeared from the returns, but in the case of Monks Coppenhall the holdings of those who had commuted continued to be entered up by the township assessors and collectors.

[3] Peter Holland, senior, tenant farmer in Monks Coppenhall, leased out his freehold in Church Coppenhall, and so comes under the classification of absentee landlord in that township.

(1764–1845), the Rev. Sir Thomas Broughton, 6th bart. (d. 1813), and Sir John Delves Broughton, 7th bart., his successor as lord of the manor of Church Coppenhall, representatives of the smaller gentry such as George Wilbraham, John Bloor, younger son of Sir John Bloor, Peter Walthall of Derbyshire, the Church Norcops and Thomas Heath (1722–1802), who was also a chain-factor of Warrington, and no less than six clergymen, including Dr. Whittington Landon, Dean of Exeter and Provost of Worcester College, with a sprinkling of lawyers and widows; a considerable number of the latter appear to have married again.

An interesting feature of the land-tax returns is the evidence they yield of a considerable investment of capital in agricultural land by merchants and lawyers from Nantwich ; *e.g.* in 1790–1 George Garnett, a Nantwich cheese-factor, purchased a Church Coppenhall estate, assessed to the poor-rate at £55 per annum, while Thomas Ellison, a Nantwich liquor merchant, purchased two estates in the same township with an assessed value of £148 per annum between 1825 and 1829. The most famous of these Nantwich investors, however, was a solicitor named Richard Edleston (1781–1839). He commenced operations between 1811 and 1816 by acquiring the Oak farm and the Hall o'Shaw farm in Monks Coppenhall, together with a smaller estate ; in 1819–20 he extended his purchases to Church Coppenhall and bought the Underwood farm from Sir John Delves Broughton, together with the lordship of the manor. The assessed value of these estates totalled £106, and in 1822–3 he and Thomas Hilditch became joint owners of the Dairy House farm, Monks Coppenhall, with an annual assessed value of £36. His purchases of land in Coppenhall are said to have amounted to about a hundred Cheshire acres, each acre containing 10,240 square yards. It is possible that in the course of these operations he also acquired the lordship of the manor of Monks Coppenhall, which in 1817 was vested in William Massey.[1]

[1] Land Tax Returns (Monks and Church Coppenhall), 1781–1832 ; Poor Rate Book, Monks Coppenhall, 1837–44 ; *Return of Owners of Land, 1873*, vol. 1 (Cheshire) ; Burke's *Peerage* (1937), pp. 530–1 ; *C.G.*, 29.9.77 ; will of Thomas Heath ; *E.A.* 02, pp. 21–3, 29 ; private information from Rev. J. Beddow, Rector of Coppenhall, and C. M. McHale, Esq., solicitor to the Edleston Trustees ; Ormerod : *op. cit.*, vol. iii, p. 329. Edleston is said to have paid £35 per acre for his first purchase of 60 (statute) acres (*Chambers' Edinburgh Journal*, Jan. 31, 1846, p. 77).

About the character of the agricultural production there exists a certain amount of scattered information. Caird's remarks about the pre-eminent quality of the cheese produced by the clayey belt round Nantwich are confirmed in a manuscript, now lost, by the daughter of an early nineteenth-century rector of Coppenhall. She wrote of that period :—" The parishioners of Coppenhall then were small farmers and labourers, the farmers working upon their land and their wives and daughters making cheese and some of the best Cheshire cheese was then made in Coppenhall."

With the coming of the railway settlement a fresh impetus was given to dairy farming, and by 1850 there were 12 farmers in Monks Coppenhall, in spite of the diminution of the land available for pasture. A thriving trade was done in dairy produce, and two at least of the farmers of Monks Coppenhall are spoken of as carrying on a retail milk trade in the town.[1] Yet even on the poor soil of Coppenhall wheat seems to have been grown in considerable quantities in the first half of the nineteenth century, and towards the end of the Napoleonic Wars " so high was the price obtained from it . . . that the living of Coppenhall went up in value " to £500 per annum, as it depended chiefly on the produce of tithes and the two portions of glebe land in the parish. Such was the fall in prices during the twenty years after Waterloo that on the commutation of tithes, between 1836 and 1840, the value of the living fell to £275 per annum.[2] The grain surpluses of the local farmers flowed to the wholesale market through the agency of corn dealers or millers known as " swealers," who called periodically upon them to ascertain if any foodstuffs were on sale. We hear of one farmer in the 1840's, William Astbury of Hightown, who stored away the wheat from a succession of harvests into every available room of his dwelling in the expectation of a considerable increase in the price. Traditionally, the cultivation of wheat in the district is said to have ceased soon after the repeal of the Corn Laws in 1846. Before this event Astbury had introduced the first steam threshing-machine to operate in the locality.[3]

[1] *C.G.*, 31.8.78 ; *E.A.* 02, pp. 21–3, 33 ; Bagshaw 1850, p. 367.
[2] *Coppenhall Par. Mag.* 1906 ; *C.G.*, 12.9.23 (speech by Rev. W. C. Reid, Rector).
[3] *E.A.* 02, pp. 21–3.

From 1806 onwards the roads in Coppenhall were much improved. Richard Lindop, a local farmer of the time, tells us in his charming *Reminiscences* that, as a result, "many sought the opportunity for investment in the neighbourhood on account of the suitableness of the soil for cheese-making."[1] This movement, and the high price of grain, led to the enclosure by a private Act of Parliament (54 Geo. III, c. 166, 1814) of Coppenhall Moss and Mapeley's Moss in Church Coppenhall. The enclosure affected 157 acres, or about one-tenth of the land in the township, and, when the project was first mooted by the larger landlords, "the race of tenants demurred greatly," because of the threatened loss of peat, fuel and free pasture which would ensue. The promoters, however, bought off the rector, and the opposition was satisfied on condition that "a sufficient breadth of turbary" and 40 acres remained unenclosed.[2] The land-tax returns for Church Coppenhall throw no light on the enclosure of 1814–16, but they illustrate the process whereby landless labourers squatted on the common waste of Coppenhall Moss and Mapeley's Moss, built cottages thereon, and fenced in small pieces of land with the acquiescence, if not the formal agreement, of the lord of the manor. The returns of the early 1780's show these "enclosiers," of which there were more than a dozen, as freeholds in the occupation of the squatters (one of whom had actually leased his portion). From 1786 onwards, however, the lord of the manor, the Rev. Sir Thomas Broughton, is shown as the ground landlord of these tenements, and this continued to be the case until 1799, when 14 of these enclosures are again noted in the return as freeholds belonging to the squatters. They remained so until the returns ceased to be deposited in the county archives in 1832. It is impossible to say from the evidence available whether the period 1786–99 witnessed an unsuccessful attempt to reassert the lord's manorial rights, or whether the squatters came to some financial arrangement with Broughton's agent. In the early 1830's this shrunken Coppenhall Moss was cut into

---

[1] *Trans. Lancs. and Ches. Antiq. Soc.*, vol. lv, p. 119.
[2] *Ibid.*, p. 121. Although Joseph Hill was named sole Commissioner in the Church Coppenhall Enclosure Act, the person who acted as Commissioner was Joseph Remer, member of a progressive farming family in the adjacent township of Warmingham (Holland : *op. cit.*, pp. 115, 131, 162 ; *Chester Chronicle*, Nov. 17, 1815).

two portions by the Grand Junction Railway and passed into private ownership.[1]

In 1832 the Crewe district, with its economic dependence on Nantwich and its heavy clay soil, was an unremarkable corner of rural England, in spite of the improvements in land and water transport which had been made in the neighbourhood since the 1770's. Into this quiet township, in the course of the 1830's, came the railways with their surveyors, contractors and navvies. The advance guard was followed in the early 1840's by a second wave of immigration, this time of skilled craftsmen for the workshops of the Grand Junction line.

Railway projects in South Cheshire began as a supplement to the existing canal network. In 1806 a scheme was put forward for horse-railways or tramroads to link the Chester–Nantwich canal with the collieries and ironworks near Newcastle-under-Lyme in North Staffordshire. The completion of the plan would have entailed the construction of two lines, the first one westwards from the Newcastle-under-Lyme canal at Newcastle to Silverdale ironworks, whence it was to run in a north-westerly direction. The second railroad also ran westwards, from the northern end of Sir Nigel Gresley's canal at Apedale. This canal connected the Apedale coalmines and ironworks to Newcastle-under-Lyme, and had been constructed under the powers of an Act of Parliament passed in 1775 (15 Geo. III, c. 16). The two proposed lines of railway were to unite about a mile south-west of Audley, on the Cheshire-Staffordshire border, and to go *via* Balterley Hall, Gorsty Hill, Weston Hall and the Hough, *i.e.* south of Crewe, to Nantwich along a route which lay for the most part along the southern edge of the Nantwich–Newcastle turnpike road. Arrived at Nantwich, the railway was to skirt the southern side of the town to join the Chester canal near Dorfold Hall. This interesting project, however, seems to have gone no further than the deposit of a plan with the Clerk of the Peace for the county palatine of Chester, as

---

[1] *Trans. Lancs. and Ches. Antiq. Soc.*, vol. lv, pp. 122–4. Crewe Corporation now owns the north-eastern portion, amounting to 15 acres, recovered by the generous action of Alderman C. H. Pedley and his brother G. A. Pedley, whose father, Alderman Richard Pedley, had purchased it some years after the auction of the Underwood farm held on the death of R. H. Edleston in 1886.

no trace of it is to be found in the *Journals of the House of Commons*.[1]

During the company-promotion boom of 1824–5 projects began in earnest. After preliminary publicity in the local press during November, 1824, a petition was presented to the House of Commons on February 18, 1825, from interested persons in Warwickshire, Staffordshire, Shropshire, Cheshire and Lancashire setting forth the advantages of making "a railway or tramroad, for the transit of waggons and other carriages to be propelled thereon, by locomotive or moveable steam engines, or other sufficient power" from Birmingham, *via* Acton, near Nantwich, and Chester, to "the Royal Rock Ferry" on the River Mersey in Cheshire, "with the requisite vessels to transport the said waggons and other carriages, or the lading and burden thereof, across or along the River Mersey to Liverpool." The petitioners craved leave to bring a Bill into Parliament for this ambitious train-ferry scheme, which included three branches from the main line, the most important being that from Ravensmoor, near Nantwich, to Lane End in Stoke-on-Trent, North Staffordshire.[2] Their request, however, was rejected owing to non-compliance with Parliamentary standing orders. There had also been considerable opposition from interested landowners, and very little influential outside support.[3]

This first failure did not deter a section of the promoters, who reintroduced "in substance the same" scheme, shorn of its branches, into Parliament on February 15, 1826. In its second form "proper wharfs, docks, basins, quays, warehouses and other works" were to be constructed at Rockferry, and the train-ferry was apparently intended to serve other ports in the Mersey besides Liverpool. The Bill reached its second reading (February 22), but there were heavy complaints from disgruntled persons in the Potteries who had been subscribers to the original

[1] *Plan of the Proposed Railways from the Chester Canal to the Collieries near Newcastle* (County Record Office, Chester); Cheshire County Council: *Alphabetical list of deposited plans regarding railways*, p. 1; J. Priestley: *Historical Account of the Navigable Rivers, Canals and Railways of Great Britain* (1831), pp. 324–5, 470–1.

[2] A plan for this branch had been deposited with the Clerk of the Peace in 1824 (Cheshire County Council: *op. cit.*, p. 1).

[3] *Journals of the House of Commons*, vol. 80 (1825), pp. 84, 117, 146, 159, 203, 213, 234, 304.

scheme in 1824, on the grounds that the new line of railway was " through many parts of the country totally different " from that proposed in the previous session of Parliament, and omitted altogether " any communication with the Staffordshire Potteries, in consequence of which communication the petitioners originally became subscribers to the undertaking."

In spite of wide support from merchants and manufacturers in towns.so far apart as Kidderminster, Nantwich and Glasgow, to name only a few, from the coal, iron and pottery trades of Staffordshire and from the Eastern branch of the Montgomery-shire Canal Company, the Bill was shelved on May 5, 1826.[1]

After the failures of 1824–6 there was a lull until the early 1830's, and when the revived project for a railway between Birmingham and Liverpool reached its Parliamentary stage in February, 1831, there were considerable differences both in the route and the methods proposed to achieve the great object of establishing " a cheap, certain and more expeditious communication between the important manufacturing towns of Birmingham and Wolverhampton, the iron manufactories and mining districts of Staffordshire, the saltworks of Cheshire and the town and port of Liverpool."

One section, 46 miles long, was to be built, chiefly with Black Country capital, from Birmingham *via* Wolverhampton, Chebsey and Whitmore across Staffordshire to the township of Basford, in the parish of Wybunbury in Cheshire, a few miles south of Coppenhall. From this point of junction a separate company of proprietors, composed almost entirely of Liverpool men, was to construct and operate the second portion, 39 miles long, of the proposed line. This ran across Cheshire from Chorlton township through Crewe, Monks and Church Coppenhall, Warmingham, Hartford and Preston-on-the-Hill to Norton, where it was to be carried over the Mersey by a bridge to Cuerdley in Lancashire and so to Liverpool. Over large sections of the line this followed the route finally chosen for the Grand Junction Railway of 1833.

The Birmingham and Basford Railway Bill received its first reading in the Commons on February 28, 1831, and in spite of

---

[1] *Journals of the House of Commons*, vol. 81 (1826), pp. 49, 67, 79–80, 87, 90–2, 230, 326–7 ; Birmingham and Liverpool Railway statutory notice to parishes along route, March 17, 1826 (Birmingham Public Reference Library).

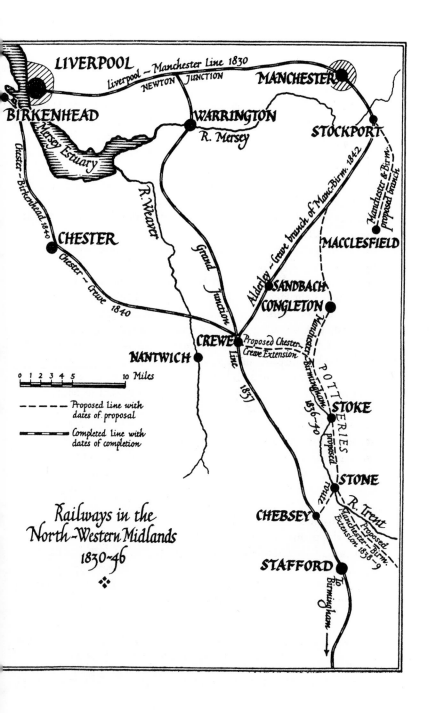

Railways in the
North-Western Midlands
1830-46

certain infractions of Parliamentary standing orders was allowed
to proceed to a second reading on March 8, although strong
opposition had developed from interested landowners and from
the Birmingham, the Birmingham and Worcester, the Staffordshire and Worcestershire, and the Wyrley and Essington Canal
Companies by the time Parliament was dissolved.   In the new
Parliament of June, 1831, the Bill soon reached its second reading
(June 28), but after it had been sent to committee the Bill as
deposited in the Private Bill Office on July 2 was found to cover
only the Birmingham to Wolverhampton section (13 miles), and
had thus been " altered in a manner unparalleled in Parliamentary
usage."   Under these circumstances it is not surprising that
the Committee on the Bill was discharged and the Bill itself
withdrawn (July 6).

The Liverpool to Chorlton Railway Bill was read for the first
time on February 22, 1831.   Considerable opposition soon
developed, not only from landowners and tenants in Chorlton,
Basford, Crewe, Church Coppenhall and Warmingham, *i.e.* at
the vital point of junction (February 28), but also from the
established transport undertakings in the area whose interests
would be threatened by railway construction.   The River
Weaver Navigation trustees, the proprietors of the Mersey and
Irwell Navigation and "several owners and masters of flats,
boats, and other vessels trading . . . on the River Weaver . . .
between Northwich and Liverpool, and on the River Mersey
between Liverpool and the Sankey Brook Navigation above
Runcorn," joined the Grand Jury of the county palatine of
Chester and the Cheshire magistracy in Easter Quarter Sessions
assembled, in petitioning against the Bill (March 1–April 15).
Notwithstanding this opposition and the dissolution of Parliament, the promoters were not discouraged and reintroduced the
measure in the new Parliament (June, 1831), but it disappears
from the Journals of the House after its second reading on July 1,
presumably as a result of the withdrawal of the complementary
Birmingham and Basford Railway Bill.[1]

From purely physical considerations the ancient community of

[1] *Journals of the House of Commons*, vol. 86 (1830–1, part i), pp. 260–508,
passim ; vol. 86 (1830–1, part ii), pp. 531–99, *passim* ; case in support of
the Birmingham and Basford Railway Bill, March, 1831, with map of proposed
line from Birmingham to Liverpool (Birmingham Public Reference Library).

Nantwich, commanding the north side of the Midland Gate and only 4 miles from the Crewe district, would have made a better railway centre than Monks Coppenhall. Nantwich was already the road centre of South Cheshire, and by 1831 possessed canal communication with every part of England and Wales. Until 1830 the early projects for a railway from Liverpool to Birmingham generally included Nantwich in their route, but the final Grand Junction Act of 1833 (3 Wm. IV, c. 34), which gave Parliamentary sanction for the scheme, steered clear of the place. The actual line was cut through the townships of Crewe, Monks Coppenhall and Church Coppenhall.

The reasons for this decision, important as it later became for the district, are by no means clear, as no manuscript or printed reference to the cause of the alteration in the route has been found. Many suggestions have been put forward in explanation, the two most likely being the opposition of the Nantwich landowners, and the lower price of land in a purely agricultural district as compared with urban Nantwich. Samuel Smiles tells us that about 1823–6, when engaged on making the survey, George Stephenson

" called upon some of the landowners in the neighbourhood of Nantwich to obtain their assent, and was greatly disgusted to learn that the agents of the canal companies had been before him, and described the locomotive to the farmers as a most frightful machine, emitting a breath as poisonous as the fabled dragon of old ; and telling them that if a bird flew over the district where one of these engines passed, it would inevitably drop down dead." [1]

In all probability, these agents were connected with the Birmingham and Liverpool Junction canal, the proprietors of which, alarmed at the progress of railways, were in the 1820's cutting their waterway, as straight as a Roman road and unequalled in the magnitude of its earthworks, across the Cheshire Plain and through the Midland Gate, to link up these two important centres.

There was great opposition to any railway passing through the district, and a farmer named Willett of Shavington, near Crewe, " undertook the herculean task of sending a circular and a letter to every member of the House of Commons and the House of Lords, asking them to use every endeavour to oppose

[1] *Lives of the Engineers : George and Robert Stephenson*, ed. 1904, p. 278.

the passage of the measure " of 1833, as the railway would ruin the local estates.   After the cutting of the railways, Willett sold his farm lands, for which he had paid £4,000, for over £10,000. On the other hand, Thomas Beech, senior, and his son, farmers of Monks Coppenhall, did all in their power to assist the passing of the Bill, and later placed their local knowledge and even their farm horses at the disposal of Locke and Errington, the engineers of the Grand Junction Company.[1]   The man who supplied all the land required in Monks Coppenhall by the Grand Junction and Manchester and Birmingham Railways was Richard Edleston, the Nantwich lawyer.   His lands lay in the eastern portion of the township, and as the railway works and colony expanded, the railway company and persons desiring to build had to purchase further portions at gradually rising prices.   It was perhaps natural in such circumstances that the local legend of a cunning lawyer making large profits for himself and his descendants from an intelligent anticipation of the railway mania should arise and gain wide circulation.   Unfortunately for this legend, it appears from the evidence quoted above that Richard Edleston had purchased his Coppenhall estates before the railway mania reached the Crewe district and at a time when the route of the projected Liverpool to Birmingham line ran through Nantwich and not Crewe.   Further, there is a tradition in the Edleston family that Richard Edleston himself was opposed to railways invading his rural estate.   On his death in 1839, his eldest son, R. C. Edleston (1816–71), also a Nantwich lawyer, became lord of the manor.   On his death the now empty title passed to his nephew R. H. Edleston (1851–86).   The Edleston lands were vested in the Edleston Trustees in 1839, where what is left of them remains to this day.[2]

The actual operation of constructing the railways in Coppenhall seems to have aroused a certain animosity among some of the local inhabitants.   Richard Lindop, whose land was intersected by the Manchester to Crewe line, complained quaintly :—

" The makers of railways, masters and men, acted as though it was

---

[1] *C.G.*, 5.10.78.
[2] *C.G.*, 25.11.71, 16.9.27 ; *Crewe and its Industrial Advantages* (n.d. ? 1934), p. 3 ; G.J.B.M., July 1, 1840 ; Crewe Ctee., L.N.W.B., July 27, Sept. 22, 1847 ; tombstones of Edleston family in Coppenhall Churchyard.

their interest to outwit and oppress all that stood below the standard
of power to stand up for themselves. A railway company with an
Act of Parliament was not to be approached indignantly by a tenant
farmer without an Act of Parliament. Though the law is the law
for both sides, yet the executive power belongs to the higher order of
society. . . ."

Yet even Lindop, looking back to the idyllic age before the
coming of the iron monster, was obliged to admit that " nothing
could stand before the imagery presented by railways." [1]

The Grand Junction line, the first railway to pass through
Crewe, was financed by the " Liverpool Party " which had
turned the Liverpool and Manchester Railway into a successful
speculation. The merchants and industrialists of Birmingham
appear to have played an unimportant part in the project. The
" Party " included such men as John Moss, a Liverpool banker,
Sir Hardman Earle, Robert Gladstone, Charles Lawrence, Joseph
Sandars, J. C. Ewart, the Croppers, Robert Barbour and Charles
Tayleur.[2] In 1835 the Grand Junction absorbed the Warrington
and Newton Railway, a short line connecting the Grand Junction and the Liverpool and Manchester tracks, and communication between Birmingham, Manchester and Liverpool became an
accomplished fact when the Grand Junction line itself was opened
for traffic on July 4, 1837. It paid well from the beginning, and
was so busy in the first months that it could afford to neglect
the carriage of goods until February 1, 1838. Its prospects and
importance were further enhanced when, on September 17, 1838,
the opening of the London and Birmingham Railway made it
possible to travel from London to either Manchester or Liverpool
by rail. The strategic position of the Grand Junction Railway
as a link between the north and south of England made it, in the
hands of the " Party," an admirable weapon for shaping the railway system of the area through which it passed to the wishes of
the Liverpool interest.[3]

[1] *Trans. Lancs. and Ches. Antiq. Soc.*, vol. lv, pp. 126–7.
[2] W. L. Steel : *History of the L.N.W.R.*, p. 91 ; preambles to 7 Geo. IV,
c. 49 ; 3 Wm. IV, c. 34 ; 3 Wm. IV, c. 36 ; and 9 & 10 Vict., c. 204 ;
J. Hughes : *Liverpool Banks and Bankers*, pp. 197–8 ; *Times*, Jan. 27, 1877.
[3] 5 & 6 Wm. IV, c. 8 ; *Railway Magazine*, July, 1837, p. 56 ; Aug., 1837,
p. 127 ; Feb., 1838, p. 132 ; Oct., 1838, pp. 343–5 ; H. G. Lewin : *Early
British Railways*, p. 23.

The business men of Manchester soon found the Grand Junction route to London *via* Warrington an inconvenient one, since they had first to go west to Newton Junction, then south to Birmingham and then almost due east to Rugby. From Liverpool, the route was sufficiently direct, and it was not until the completion of the railway bridge over the River Mersey at Runcorn in 1869 that it was in any way abbreviated, but between Birmingham and Manchester the long detour increased the distance to 99 miles as against 82 by a more direct route. As early as 1834, meetings were held in Manchester complaining of this state of affairs, and the " Manchester Party " resolved to cut a line of its own. All were agreed on the Manchester–Stockport section, but " as to the direction to be followed south of Stockport the promoters became divided in their opinions." [1] One party desired a link-up with the Grand Junction Railway at Crewe, because it would be the shortest line to construct (30 miles), run over fairly level country, and would give direct communication with the Chester and Crewe line, which was also first proposed in 1834–5. A second party desired a line from Manchester to Norton Bridge, near Stafford, to join the Grand Junction there. A third party " would not hear of any proposal to form a junction with the Grand Junction Company at any point," and desired a line from the Churnet Valley, ending in a forked junction with one arm to Tamworth and the other to Burton-on-Trent. The fourth party desired a line from Stockport to Stoke and thence to Stone, Colwich, Lichfield, Tamworth and Nuneaton to Rugby.[2]

The Grand Junction directors could not look on these proceedings with indifference, and in December, 1835, they promised the Manchester and Cheshire Junction Provisional Committee (*i.e.* the promoters of the first, cheapest and most practicable route) every assistance in the scheme to join the Grand Junction line in the neighbourhood of Crewe. At the same time, the third and fourth bodies of Manchester opinion united to promote the Manchester and South Union Railway, which was to run

---

[1] C. E. Stretton : *History of the Manchester and Birmingham Railway*, p. 4 ; *Manchester City News*, April 15, 1882.

[2] Stretton : *op. cit.*, pp. 4–5 ; Lewin : *op. cit.*, p. 67 ; *Railway Magazine*, Feb. 1836, pp. 359–61.

via the Potteries to Tamworth, whence the Birmingham and Derby Company was to promote a line to Rugby. This would cut out the Grand Junction from the Manchester traffic altogether, and was opposed by both the Grand Junction and the Manchester and Cheshire Junction interests. Bills for the South Union and the Cheshire Junction were introduced into Parliament in 1836, but failed to pass.[1]

A digression is here necessary to trace the history of the Chester and Crewe Railway, apparently first projected in 1835 by local capitalists at Chester. It attracted the attention of the Grand Junction directors in September, and later in the same year Herepath, quoting the *Chester Chronicle*, said :—" The superiority of a line terminating at or near Crewe, over either of the two other and shorter ones proposed, must now be obvious. . . . It would, in fact, be in the nature of a continuation of the Manchester and Cheshire Junction line. . . ." [2]

The proposed line was 20½ miles long and ran across the flat Cheshire countryside ; no tunnels would be needed and the cost would be comparatively low. Its construction would give Chester communication by rail with Manchester, Birmingham, Liverpool and London. It might even serve to revive Chester's former prosperity, lost by the silting-up of the River Dee and the rise of Liverpool and Holyhead. Estimates showed that it would be a cheap line—£11,622 a mile—and this was probably one of the reasons for the selection of Crewe as its termination. Members of the Chester and Crewe Railway Provisional Committee gave evidence in support of their scheme before the House of Lords in 1836 and incidentally threw some light on the choice of Crewe as the point of junction. George Stephenson, it appeared, had surveyed the Chester and Crewe and alternative routes in 1826 and 1836. His partiality for the easiest route, even at the expense of a detour, and his abhorrence of " bad " gradients, secured his verdict for the Chester to Crewe line, as against a shorter line (12 miles) from Chester to the Weaver viaduct. The shorter line would have gone over Delamere Forest and entailed several heavy climbs. The first

[1] G.J.B.M., Dec. 30, 1835 ; Feb. 3, May 18, June 15 and 29, July 13 and 27, Sept. 16, 1836 ; Lewin : *op. cit.*, p. 67 ; *Railway Magazine*, Dec., 1836, pp. 473–4.
[2] *Railway Magazine*, Dec., 1835, pp. 271–2.

line gave quicker access to London and Birmingham.[1] The Crewe route gave the best of all worlds, indeed :—

" Q. Would not the utility of a line from Chester to Crewe be very much diminished if the communication from Crewe to Manchester was withdrawn ?

" *A.* Yes." [2]

From the evidence of Joseph Locke, engineer to the Grand Junction, we learn more. Asked whether Crewe would be a good point of junction, he replied that " Crewe was fixed upon as the point to connect Manchester before the Manchester and Cheshire Junction was ever thought of." [3]

In 1837 the provisional committees of the Manchester and Cheshire Junction and the Manchester and South Union railways, *i.e.* the two rival bodies of Manchester projectors, composed their differences and fused their interests. In spite of opposition from the Grand Junction they obtained the Manchester and Birmingham Railway Act (1 Vict., c. 69) on June 30, 1837.[4]

Meanwhile, in spite of lack of support from the Grand Junction directors, the Chester and Crewe Railway promoters had also obtained their Act (1 Vict., c. 63) on the same day. They hoped that the new Manchester and Birmingham Company would soon construct its promised branch from Manchester to Crewe. By 1839, however, owing to difficulties in raising money, the Chester and Crewe directors were trying to get rid of their line in its unfinished state and by 3 & 4 Vict., c. 49 (May 19, 1840) the Chester and Crewe Company was incorporated in the Grand Junction. Public traffic on this line commenced on October 1, 1840, and the Grand Junction thus strengthened its hand in view of approaching competition.[5] One by one the causes were beginning to operate which had as their final result the establishment of, firstly, an important railway junction, and secondly, a railway engineering works, at Crewe.

[1] *Railway Magazine*, Oct., 1837, p. 243.

[2] *Extracts from the Minutes of Evidence . . . in support of the Cheshire Junction Railway Bill*, 1836, p. 23.

[3] *Ibid.*, p. 2.

[4] *Railway Magazine*, June, 1837, p. 414 ; Stretton : *op. cit.*, p. 5 ; Lewin : *op. cit.*, pp. 67–70.

[5] *Railway Magazine*, Dec., 1838, p. 469 ; Stretton : *History of the Chester and Crewe Railway*, p. 6.

The Manchester and Birmingham Railway had a longer independent existence than the Chester and Crewe line. Negotiations beforehand with the Grand Junction Board ensured the new company every facility for working their traffic over the Grand Junction line from the point of union down to Birmingham, but the point of union itself was moved south to Chebsey in Staffordshire.[1] The new main line was to go through the Potteries. There were to be branches from Alderley to Crewe (16 miles), and from Stockport to Macclesfield (11 miles). The directors of the Grand Junction consoled their shareholders with the " sour grapes " plea that there was really very little Manchester to Birmingham traffic.[2]

Quarrels soon broke out between the two Boards. The Grand Junction directors opposed bitterly a subsidiary company promoted in 1838–9 by the Manchester and Birmingham directors and designed to filch the remainder of the Manchester–Birmingham traffic from the Grand Junction. The Bill for this subsidiary company was thrown out of Parliament in 1839 after a terrific struggle, and its rejection marked a substantial victory for the " Liverpool Party." Meanwhile, the Manchester and Birmingham directors pushed on energetically with the construction of their line, and the section from Manchester to Stockport was opened on June 4, 1840. Yet even twelve months before this event the Manchester and Birmingham Company had begun to find difficulty in raising money, owing to the commercial depression and financial stringency which prevailed between 1839 and 1842, and had reached an agreement with the Grand Junction, in 1839, to abandon all its schemes except the Stockport–Alderley–Crewe branch. The agreement was not divulged to the shareholders for a year ; the commercial and industrial interests of the Potteries were furious when they learnt of their " betrayal." The Grand Junction, with luck and superior financial resources, had at last attained its object by resurrecting the " Manchester and Cheshire Junction " of 1836.[3]

The Manchester and Birmingham Board now concentrated on the Stockport–Crewe section, but the " Liverpool Party "

[1] Lewin : Dec., 1838, pp. 67–70.
[2] *Railway Magazine*, Oct., 1837, p. 273.
[3] Stretton : *Manchester and Birmingham Railway*, pp. 5–6 ; *Railway Magazine*, Aug., 1838, pp. 101–7 ; Lewin : *ibid.*, pp. 126–8.

was taking no chances and, although the line was ready for opening by April, 1842, it made use of legal quibbles to extract better terms from its humbled rival. Finally, the attenuated Manchester and Birmingham Company waived all right to work over the Grand Junction track ; the Grand Junction took charge of all traffic south of Crewe and gave the Manchester and Birmingham 30 per cent. of the proceeds. On August 10, 1842, the final section, from Sandbach to Crewe, was opened, and Manchester got its first shorter route to the south. The Manchester and Birmingham Railway Company became almost an appanage of the Grand Junction–Liverpool and Manchester–Chester–Crewe system, and an attempt in 1845-6 to assert its independence was one of the reasons for the great amalgamation which brought the London and North-Western Railway into existence in 1846.[1]

Crewe was thus by 1842 the focus of four lines of railway. The existence of this junction tended to attract further lines to it with cumulative force. In 1848 the Crewe and Kidsgrove Junction branch of the North Staffordshire Railway was opened, and in 1858 a branch of the London and North-Western Railway from Shrewsbury, *via* Nantwich, completed the number of lines which ran into Crewe. The two last lines gave Crewe access to the coalmines and the Potteries of North Staffordshire and to Central and South Wales respectively.[2]

PARISH AND TOWNSHIP GOVERNMENT, 1792–1860

The system of local government in the parish and townships of Coppenhall before 1860 conformed in type to that existing chiefly in the North of England and Wales, where " the jurisdiction of particular Constables, Overseers of the Poor, and Surveyors of Highways was determined, unlike that of their Churchwardens, not by the boundaries of the parish, but by those of the separate . . . townships within the parish." [3] In theory, therefore, the government of the twin townships of Monks and Church Coppenhall was distinct, except in the case

[1] Stretton : *ibid.*, pp. 6–8.
[2] Bagshaw 1850, p. 23 ; Lewin : *Railway Mania and its Aftermath*, p. 391 ; Hall : *History of Nantwich*, pp. 247–8.
[3] S. and B. Webb : *The Parish and the County*, p. 11.

of the churchwardens, but there are certain indications which suggest that in practice the same vestry meetings of ratepayers served for the business of both townships, possibly for the selection of nominees for township offices and certainly for the passing of the surveyor's accounts. This lack of sharp distinction was further emphasised by the fact that some of the ratepayers, and especially the Rector of Coppenhall, were qualified to take part in the government and vestry meetings of both townships.[1]

From the early part of the eighteenth century until 1806 the Rectors of Coppenhall were absentees and pluralists. Even the curates for the most part lived at a distance.[2] In 1806, however, a newly-appointed rector, the Rev. J. S. Cattlow, took up permanent residence in the parish and played an active and reforming part in local government. Since then every Rector of Coppenhall has been resident.[3]

Separate account books for the two sets of township officials were kept, and investigation of the local government of pre-railway Monks Coppenhall is made possible by the survival of the " Town Book of Monks Coppenhall," which contains the names and some of the accounts of the Overseers of the Poor (1792–1844), the Supervisors (*i.e.* Surveyors) of Highways (1792–1850) and the Constables (1792–1843). In the case of Church Coppenhall township no such document can be traced, but the Coppenhall Parish Book has survived ; this contains the Churchwardens' accounts for both townships from 1816 onwards, together with reports of vestry meetings of the whole parish for various purposes. It appears that until 1805, when the Rev.

[1] C.P.B., April 21, 1840 ; June 17, 1848 ; June 8, 1848 ; and *passim* ; T.B.M.C., *passim* ; occasionally separate meetings of the parishioners of Monks Coppenhall did take place, *e.g.* on July 12, 1797 " at Daniel Clowes's," and July 9, 1841 (T.B.M.C.).

[2] With the honourable exception of the Rev. William Harding, whose curacy, at £50 per annum, lasted from 1729 to 1775. He and Elizabeth his wife had seven children baptised at Coppenhall. His family worked in different ways in the parish, Mrs. Harding as a monthly nurse, while her daughter kept a little shop in one end of the rectory dining-room ; the other end was used as the village school, which was kept by the curate's son. This son, John Harding, became clerk of the parish and landlord of the Blue Bell Inn, hard by the church (*Trans. Lancs. and Ches. Antiq. Soc.*, vol. lv, p. 128).

[3] *Ibid.*, pp. 112, 116–18.

J. S. Cattlow first took office as surveyor, it was the practice in Monks Coppenhall for one individual to hold the three offices of surveyor, constable and overseer, but after that year it became customary for the surveyorship to be held as a separate office, with an exception in 1815–16, while the offices of overseer and constable still continued, with a few exceptions, to be held by the same person.

The churchwardens for the parish were two in number ; one of these, called the People's Warden, was elected by the vestry meeting and handled all business connected with Monks Coppenhall. The other, chosen by the Rector, and therefore called the Rector's Warden, handled Church Coppenhall matters. These two officers kept the church fabric and graveyard in repair, paid out so much per dozen for sparrows' heads and, to pay their expenses, levied a church-rate. Church Coppenhall paid 14 twenty-sixths of these expenses and Monks Coppenhall 12 twenty-sixths, levied by two separate rates. The churchwardens had charge of the financial details in connection with the building of the new Coppenhall Church in 1821–2, when, in spite of £400 raised by two briefs, a debt of £600 was incurred, which was not paid off until the financial year 1832–3.[1]

The growth of the new railway town of Crewe in Monks Coppenhall broke up the religious homogeneity of the district, already attacked from 1806 onwards by the Primitive Methodist movement. By 1850 the Crewe district contained a mixed population of many sects. As early as November 23, 1843, a Mormonite workman, assisted by two co-sectaries, had caused the death of his wife by baptising her in the Valley Brook.[2] There were many militant Dissenters among the mechanics and tradespeople of Crewe. They objected to vestry government and church-rates on religious grounds, while others were contemptuous of the ancient system's limited powers and efficiency. Some went further ; at a well-attended vestry meeting on November 4, 1858, Messrs. John Eaton, Allen Priest, Samuel

---

[1] The Town Book of Monks Coppenhall is in the possession of Crewe Corporation, the Coppenhall Parish Book in the custody of the Rector of Coppenhall ; see also *Trans. Lancs. and Ches. Antiq. Soc.*, vol. lv, pp. 124–6, 129–30.

[2] *Chester Courant*, Dec. 5, 1843 ; C.P.R., Nov. 26, 1843—burial of Sarah Cartwright, "drowned by Mormonite immersion."

TIMBER-FRAME PARISH CHURCH OF ST. MICHAEL'S, COPPENHALL, DEMOLISHED 1821

(courtesy Lancashire and Cheshire Antiquarian Society)

Heath, Peter Cork and others, all prominent Dissenters and Radicals, together with Patrick Walsh, a Catholic, carried an amendment " that no rate be granted for Church purposes." A poll was taken in the Town Hall later in the month, but the Church party carried the day. We are told elsewhere that Samuel Heath " paid the penalty of his convictions by being summoned for the non-payment of church-rates," an echo of this epic battle in the annals of the parish.[1] The inseparable connection of the ancient system of local government with the Established Church, and the consequent sectarian strife thereby engendered, formed one of the chief causes making for the super-session of the vestry by a secular Local Board of Health for Monks Coppenhall in 1860.

Soon after the foundation of the new railway town of Crewe, the Grand Junction directors erected Christ Church in Monks Coppenhall for the spiritual welfare of their workmen. The building was consecrated on December 18, 1845, at which date it already possessed two churchwardens. For some time the new church remained a chapel-of-ease to St. Michael's, Coppenhall, until in 1846 a vicar was appointed and the ecclesiastical parish created ; it was not until 1855, however, that the exact boundary delimiting " The District Chapelry of Christ Church, Crewe," within the old parish was fixed.[2] The Coppenhall churchwardens continued to levy church-rates in both Monks and Church Coppenhall until 1866 and 1868 respectively.

The constables' accounts for the township of Monks Coppenhall start in 1793 and come to an end in February, 1837, although the list of constables appointed continues until 1843. As distinct from the other township officials the petty constable was exclusively the Justices' man, and the ratepayers had no say in the choice of the officer who did most of the legal business of the district (serving warrants and summonses, seizing law-breakers, representing the township at presentments of defective parish roads and bridges at Quarter Sessions, taking in lists of free-holders, jurymen, lunatics, public-houses and men liable to serve in the militia). After being sworn in at the Hundred Court at

[1] Rev. J. Beddow : *History of the Heath Family* (unpublished MS) ; *E.A.* o2, p. 63.
[2] Anon : *Christ Church, Crewe, a Short History* (n.d.) ; *London Gazette,* Feb. 13, 1855, pp. 546–7.

Nantwich by the High Constable or his representative, the petty constable had to attend " monthly meetings " of the Justices of the Peace at Nantwich, Bridgemere and Wybunbury on legal business.   Another sphere of his activity was in county finance, and he made four payments per annum (" quarterly pays ") as the township's contribution towards county expenses.   In 1793–4 these payments amounted to £8 16s., but in 1833–4 a levy of more than £29 was made ; this was by no means exceptional. To recoup himself the constable levied a separate rate in the township until 1815 ; after this date the overseer of the poor performed this operation and paid the needful sums over to the constable.   From their beginning in 1793, the year in which the war against Revolutionary France began, the constables' accounts show the importance of militia business, but it was not until 1801 that any appreciable increase in its volume occurred. On October 15, 1801, the following entry occurs :—" To going round the township to take an account of persons' properties and likewise what sort of arms each person would choose to carry " ; and as the possibility of an invasion by Napoleon Bonaparte increased, so did the preparations for the " Army of Defence." In 1802–3, the peak period of exertions in this direction, the accounts show great activity in balloting for the militia, swearing the men in, hiring militia men to represent the township, and taking a census of the waggons and carts in the township.   After 1806 there was some slackening, although the militia business remained important long after Waterloo ; as late as May, 1828, 4 guineas were paid by the ratepayers of Monks Coppenhall " towards a substitute for the militia."   After the Reform Act of 1832, the compilation and presentment of lists of voters loomed larger than militia men in the township work, and the local armed forces are not mentioned in the last set of accounts. In 1829, the Cheshire Police Act (10 Geo. IV, c. xcvii) set up the rudiments of the first paid county police force in the United Kingdom.   It enabled " the magistrates of the county palatine of Chester to appoint special high constables for the several hundreds . . . and assistant petty constables for the several townships."   As a consequence of this measure the opening years of the 1830's saw great activity on the part of these deputy High Constables.   For a year, in 1832–3, an assistant petty constable named Simson was appointed for Monks Coppenhall in addition to the regular petty constable, and received £4 12s. for his services.[1]

Other duties performed by the constable included that of relieving poor travellers equipped with begging passes. These were very numerous in 1812–13, and appear to have been chiefly soldiers and sailors. Again, the constable was put to a great deal of trouble in 1814–15, when the overseer of the poor refused to accept office, while between 1815 and 1817 a great deal of activity was displayed in the erection of a new pinfold for cattle. After 1843 the only township constable of whom we have record is Richard Stockley, who served in that capacity for some years and " had supplied to him the recognised staff and handcuffs." Later he was employed in a similar capacity by the railway company —" the last of an interesting line of almost prehistoric preservers of the peace." [2]

The accounts of the supervisors or surveyors of the highways for Monks Coppenhall exist from 1802 to 1850, with gaps between 1813 and 1819, and 1848 and 1849. The office of surveyor, like those of constable and overseer, was unpaid, although small perquisites were admitted in the accounts. Therefore, in spite of the control over the appointment legally given to the Justices, it is probable that the nominee of the retiring surveyor, or a name on the list presented by the local vestry, was usually accepted without demur.[3] As in the case of the constables, the surveyors of Monks Coppenhall were without exception substantial local farmers and men of substance. In the case of the surveyors of highways, the accounts for Monks Coppenhall are supplemented by a literary description of the roads in Church Coppenhall about the same time. Richard Lindop (1778–1871) lived in Coppenhall from infancy until advanced old age, with only five years' absence. Of the condition of the roads before 1806 he wrote :—

" The roads were made of three-feet wide pavements with gobs of earth on each side to prevent carts from passing, preserving them for horse and foot passengers. Near six miles of these roads were in actual service in this township, obtained at enormous toil and

---

[1] S. and B. Webb : *op. cit.*, pp. 25–9, 297–8, 407–8, 502 ; *Annual Register*, 1829, appendix to Chronicle, p. 281.

[2] *E.A.* 02, p. 25.

[3] S. and B. Webb : *op. cit.*, pp. 29–30.

expense. Besides these there were stepping-stones about eighteen inches apart, and if the unwary passenger missed his footing, woe to him. His foot fell ankle deep in the mud. The carts' roads, if roads they may be called, were of very ancient date . . . as no trace of anything like material was to be seen." [1]

The ruts were "excessive deep," and Lindop claimed that this caused " the nave of the wheel to draw along the mud lifted out [of the channel] by the passing wheel." This so hindered transport that sometimes nine horses, one behind the other, would be required to pull "a narrow wheeled wagon with little more than one ton of coal in it" along the miry lanes of Coppenhall. Lindop also refers to the statute labour of six days per annum on the roads, which was supposed to be exacted from every inhabitant of a township until it was abolished by the Highways Act of 1835 :—

" At a convenient time the surveyor gave the [parish] clerk orders to publish for a day's work in the highways. On the next Sunday the clerk, rushing out of the church at the end of the service in the afternoon, cries ' Oyez ! Oyez ! this is to give notice that the inhabitants of Church Coppenhall are requested to meet at Cross Green on Wednesday morning at 8 o'clock with picks and shovels in order to repair the highways. God save the King.' " [2]

In 1806 the Rev. J. S. Cattlow, who had been appointed Rector of Coppenhall and surveyor of highways for Monks Coppenhall in 1805, came to live in the parish and, according to Lindop, took up the work of improving the roads of the two townships with enthusiasm. During his two years of office as

[1] *Trans. Lancs. and Ches. Antiq. Soc.*, vol. lv, p. 112. We are also told that for several years at the beginning of the nineteenth century " the residents of Coppenhall could not drive to Nantwich over Beam Heath in the winter, but had to go round by Crewe Green, a distance of about seven miles " (*ibid.*, p. 129).

Concerning Lindop's " pavements " and " gobs of earth," Holland mentioned " a circumstance almost peculiar to the county of Cheshire, which is, that in every by-lane, where carts can scarcely force their way, a narrow paved causeway is provided for the accommodation of horse and foot passengers, along which they may travel with expedition and safety at every season of the year. These causeways are usually defended by posts, or by a copse, from the injuries they might otherwise sustain, in the passing of carts " (Holland : *op. cit.*, p. 304).

[2] *Ibid.*, p. 113.

surveyor the magistrates helped " as far as they durst, for road-making in these parts was quite a new thing." Cattlow also obtained access to a bed of excellent gravel ; his energy

" bore down all before it ; also it spread into other townships and parishes, so that by the time of ten or twelve years there was miles of new roads made in the middle of the county of Cheshire. These were days worth living to see, for those that could not obtain access to our bed of gravel fled to Winsford for cinders." [1]

Owing to the loss of the records, it is impossible to give exact information of his work in Church Coppenhall, but during his second year of office in Monks Coppenhall the amount expended on the roads had more than doubled as compared with 1804–5. Although expenditure was not maintained at this level after 1807, in the average year more was spent on the roads after 1807 than before 1805. The abolition of statute labour in 1835 led to an immediate quadrupling of road expenses to over £50 for the year ending March, 1837. The coming of the railway colony was reflected in a further increase to over £91 in the year 1841–2. This unprecedented sum was soon surpassed, however, in 1843–4 when £261 was needed to meet the high-way expenses of the new town. An interesting but solitary entry in the Town Book of Monks Coppenhall gives an account of the meeting of an otherwise unknown " Road Committee " in August, 1849, which, with the surveyor, Samuel Heath, in the chair, decided to widen Small Lane (Hungerford Road) by 4 feet, and to levy a rate of 4d. in the pound.

The materials used for repairing the roads were chiefly gravel,

---

[1] *Trans. Lancs. and Ches. Antiq. Soc.*, vol. lv, pp. 118–19 ; according to other evidence from a trustworthy source (Cattlow's daughter), his interest in road improvement was not entirely unselfish :—" When the Rev. Mr. Cattlow came to Coppenhall he set up a gig. . . . The roads of Coppenhall were all clay in the middle with a causeway of pavement at the side for foot passengers and horses. During the first winter the Rev. Mr. Cattlow's gig was left at a farm-house about a mile and a half from the rectory and the family walked to it and left it there on returning home. Half a mile of road having been mended before the second winter, the gig was left at a house only a mile from the rectory, and the third winter the gig was brought to the Rectory " (*Trans. Lancs. and Ches. Antiq. Soc.*, vol. lv, p. 129). Holland, writing in 1808, considered that the Cheshire roads generally were " greatly better than they were twenty years ago " and in " a state of progressive improvement " (*op. cit.*, p. 302).

cinders and sand, with occasional loads of stone from Mow Cop in Staffordshire. The chief farmers of the township contributed their carts and teams in place of the statute labour of the poorer inhabitants, and one of the changes made by the Act of 1835 was that the work of these carts and teams was henceforward paid for, while the owners paid an increased rate. Even in the early railway colony the profession of public works contractor had not evolved, and the farmers continued to supply this necessary equipment.[1] From 1838 onwards it became customary to appoint two surveyors, only one of whom presented the accounts. In the general decay of township government in Monks Coppenhall, which took place after 1843, the accounts of the surveyors from 1848 to 1860 have been lost, and even the very names of these officials are practically untraceable during that period, with the exception of Samuel Heath (1849–50) and Thomas Bromfield (1859–60). The latter, when superseded by the new Monks Coppenhall Local Board, yielded up the balance of the last of the old highway rates in 1860. During his year of office Samuel Heath is reputed to have " transformed the main thoroughfare of this township from the veriest quagmire into a respectable roadway extending from the Royal Hotel . . . to Merrill's Bridge." [2] For the township of Church Coppenhall, however, surveyors of highways or " waywardens," as they were more commonly called, continued to be appointed until 1894, to represent the district on the Nantwich Highway Board, set up in 1863 under the Highways Act of 1862 (25 & 26 Vict., c. 61). This body, on which 25 townships and places in the Nantwich district were represented, controlled all rural highways in the area not under the jurisdictions of the county and the Monks Coppenhall and Nantwich Local Boards ; it was not abolished until the setting up of the Nantwich Rural District Council and the Church Coppenhall Parish Council in 1894.[3]

The overseer of the poor for Monks Coppenhall was appointed by two Justices of the Peace from among the " substantial householders " ; he possessed two functions, firstly, to relieve the poor

[1] *E.A.* 02, p. 19.

[2] *C.G.*, 17 and 31.10.85 ; C.L.B.M., July 6, 1860, and June 25, 1861 ; White 1860, p. 349.

[3] *London Gazette*, March 13, 1863, pp. 1476–80 ; *Public Administration*, April, 1937, pp. 215–26 ; Ch.C.P.C., Dec. 4, 1894 ; *C.G.*, 6.1.94.

and unemployed and secondly, to lay and collect rates to meet the expenses involved in this work and in the activities of the surveyor and constable. The accounts of the overseers of Monks Coppenhall are extant from 1795 to 1837, when they handed over the duty of administering the Poor Law to the new Nantwich Board of Guardians set up under the Poor Law Amendment Act of 1834. The overseer for Monks Coppenhall was, from 1805 onwards, with few exceptions, also the constable for the township, so that he was therefore the officer with whom the inhabitants came into most frequent and intimate contact. For example, in 1801–2, when the population numbered only 121, no less than 12 individuals and families in the township received relief in different forms. The amounts varied from £13 3s. to 5s. 6d., while the total disbursements totalled over £73, at a time when the rateable value of the township was only £588. This year and the preceding one were exceptional, and the usual figure was in the region of £50. From 1813 onwards, however, the cost of relief rose sharply, and remained around £90 per annum until the mid-1820's, when it fell slightly to between £70 and £80. The steady rise in the cost of relief during the 1830's can be attributed to the increase of population during that period. The overseers' accounts are by far the most interesting of those which have survived. Relief took various forms, the most common being that of a weekly payment ranging from 1s., in the case of children, to a maximum of 5s., in the case of adults, although 2s. and 3s. per week were the usual figures. Besides this direct monetary payment, pensioners and others might receive the rents of their cottages or potato patches, seed potatoes, bottles of medicine, clothes, shoes, pieces of cloth, loads of coal, coffins, " bread and ale at the funeral " (1801–2), maternity benefits, or the services of a midwife or doctor. The wives of the militia men had to be supported while the bread-winner was away from the township drilling, and the men themselves received payments. The overseer often had to attend the Justices' meeting at Nantwich to " father the child " of some erring woman, and, when the father had been discovered, to obtain an affiliation order against him. In addition to this, the overseer had to collect the father's affiliation payments, and see that the child benefited from them ; the overseers also boarded out in the parish both illegitimate and pauper children, usually with substantial farmers, who received a weekly payment of 1s. or 1s. 6d. in return.   The township did not possess a "poor's house," but the cottages for which the overseer paid the rent, year after year, fulfilled this need.   On July 10, 1819, overseer William Davies went to Middlewich about "the condition of the poor house" there, and again in 1821 overseer William Roylance made the same journey "to enquire the rates of the poor house for Samuel Charlesworth."   In 1827, 1828 and 1829, the township paid a subscription of 2 guineas as an entrance fee to the Middlewich Workhouse in order to obtain the right to nominate an inmate.   The determination of the precise "settle-ment" of anyone in receipt of relief formed a considerable part of the overseer's duties and often involved journeys to other parts of the county.   The general impression is gained that a considerable degree of mobility within the county existed among even the poorest strata of the population.   Only on one occasion did the Monks Coppenhall overseer bind a pauper's son appren-tice to a trade other than that of labourer in husbandry.

Poor Law reformers of the early nineteenth century alleged that flagrant abuses occurred in the indiscriminate administration of relief by overseers.   Whatever may have been the situation in other parts of the country, such abuses appear to have been absent in the case of Monks Coppenhall.   There is no evidence that agricultural wages were subsidised from the poor-rate, and most of the cases relieved were old people or genuine paupers. Occasionally a man would receive relief when out of work, *e.g.* Thomas Greenwood received £6 4s. in the winter of 1831-2. Nevertheless, there was apparently little reluctance to receive money and goods from the township and little stigma attached to poor relief.   It is interesting to observe the preparations for the change to the régime of Guardians of the Poor, at a time when the overseer's task of rate-collecting was becoming an increas-ingly onerous one.   Several letters from the Poor Law Com-missioners arrived in Coppenhall during 1836-7, and a copy of the Act of 1834 was purchased for 1s. 6d.   The overseer went with the surveyor to Nantwich in June, 1836 to attend a meeting " on the Commissioners," and in the following November met the Assistant Poor Law Commissioner there.   A few months later preparations were made for the removal of two aged and infirm paupers, Thomas Greenwood and Thomas Kirk, from

HILLOCK HOUSE, HIGHTOWN, CREWE. THOMAS BEECH'S TIMBER-FRAME FARM-HOUSE

their rent-free cottages in Monks Coppenhall to Nantwich Work-house, and when, on February 20, 1837, the Nantwich Board of Guardians held its first meeting there, the Rev. Robert Mayor, Rector of Coppenhall, and Edward Jackson attended as the first Guardians of the Poor for Monks and Church Coppenhall respectively.[1] Relieved of the business of poor-law administration, the overseers were now able to concentrate their energies on the collection of rates and the compilation of the voters' list. Fortunately the poor-rate book for Monks Coppenhall from 1837 to 1844 has survived, and an examination of it shows an unpaid overseer struggling with an ever-increasing number of separate amounts to be collected. In 1838 the rate was signed for the first time by two overseers, and this became the fixed custom for Monks Coppenhall until the ancient office was abolished in 1929. Between 1837 and 1844 the J.P.s who allowed assessments were usually local clergymen (the Rev. T. Brooke, Rector of Wistaston, the Rev. E. Hinchcliffe, Rector of Mucklestone, and the Rev. R. H. Gretton, Rector of Nant-wich); local landowners (J. W. Tollemache and J. W. Hammond of Wistaston Hall) appear less frequently. In 1843 it became necessary for the two overseers to appoint a paid deputy, John Pointon. In 1849 we find Samuel Heath acting as assistant over-seer and surveyor of highways, and when Thomas Bromfield gave up his office as surveyor in 1860 he continued to hold that of assistant overseer. The office had become a permanent part of local government machinery in the town.[2]

Of the other parish officers, the only one traceable in Coppen-hall is the parish clerk, who was nominated by the Rector of Coppenhall. From 1805 to 1843 the office was held by William Roylance, farmer of Monks Coppenhall (1786–1871), who was responsible for the copper-plate writing in the parish and town-ship records during his term of office. He not only held all the township offices several times, but also taught as village school-master. It was in the years immediately after his tenure of office as clerk that any orderly township records ceased to be kept in Monks Coppenhall.[3]

[1] Nantwich Board of Guardians, Minute Book, 1837.
[2] Poor-rate Book, Monks Coppenhall, 1837–44; *C.G.*, 17.10.85, *E.A.* 73, p. 29; Ormerod, vol. iii, pp. 304, 348.
[3] *C.G.*, 18.3.71; S. and B. Webb: *op. cit.*, pp. 33–4; *E.A.* 02, p. 23.

The census figures of 1841 gave some indication that Crewe had become an important railway junction and that the Grand Junction Board was busy constructing workshops and cottages for its mechanics, who were to be transferred thither in March, 1843 :—

	Population.	
	1831	1841
Monks Coppenhall . . .	148	203
Church Coppenhall . . .	350	544
Totals for parish . .	498	747

i.e. an increase of exactly 50 per cent. During the same period the population of England as a whole increased by only 14·5 per cent. Inhabited houses in Monks Coppenhall increased from 26 to 33 only. An examination of the census enumerators' returns for 1841 from Coppenhall disclosed the presence of a sprinkling of Irish labourers, besides an influx of agricultural and other labourers not born in the county of Chester. There are other indications that many of the labourers attracted to the vicinity by the buildings and excavations lodged in the farm labourers' cottages in the townships surrounding Monks Coppenhall, for their populations show a sudden jump between 1831 and 1841, followed by stagnation or decline during the decade 1841–51 :—

	Population.		
	1831	1841	1851
Church Coppenhall	350	544	495
Crewe	295	396	365
Haslington	1,028	1,146	1,153
Wistaston	350	355	298
Warmingham	372	420	423 [1]

The rateable value of Monks Coppenhall in 1795 was £588, while that of Church Coppenhall stood at more than double

[1] *Census* 1851, part i, vol. ii, div. viii, pp. 20–3 ; P.R.O.,H.O. 107/116.

this amount—£1,290. This emphasises the difference in the agricultural fertility of the land in the two townships, since the difference in acreage between them was only 15 per cent. A complete change in the relative position took place after the establishment of the Grand Junction railway works in 1841–3 :—

	Rateable Value.		
	1838	1847	1859
Church Coppenhall	£3,100	£3,700	£3,825
Monks Coppenhall	£1,842	£5,720	£11,494 [1]

The rôle of the vestry in the government of the township between 1843 and 1860 should not be exaggerated, for although in these years it was still the only legal body, there had grown up in Monks Coppenhall an extra-legal system whereby the new town of Crewe was ruled more efficiently than it could have been by the decaying township pattern of government. This system was the creation of the Grand Junction and London and North-Western Railway directors, acting through their Crewe Committee, set up in its final form in 1845 " to take charge of . . . the general management of the town of Crewe." [2]

[1] T.B.M.C., *passim* ; C.P.B., March 26, 1838, Easter Monday, 1847, Sept. 29, 1859 ; Poor-rate Book, Monks Coppenhall, 1837–44 ; White 1860, pp. 342–3.
[2] G.J.B.M., June 14, 1845.

CHAPTER II

THE SOCIAL POLICY OF THE RAILWAY COMPANY
AT CREWE, 1841–1919

" But nobody seemed to think of going away from the Station ; indeed, the only mode of exit and entrance was through a close-shut iron gate, beside which stood a policeman looking with enviable coolness on all the bustle around him. . . .

' Where is Crewe ? ' I said to the guardian of the iron gate.

' Cross the bridge, go straight on, and turn to the right,' was the concise reply.

So I crossed the bridge, and found myself in a pleasant country road. The flat, rich fields of Cheshire extended on the left and to the right, at the distance of about half a mile appeared the square massive tower of a church, surrounded by long ranges of low buildings like workshops, and rows of buildings evidently quite new. Some neat cottages lined the sides of the road, and there were two or three inns, all bearing the signs of youth. . . . Turning to the right [1] I passed a Methodist chapel, bearing the date of its erection, 1848 ; a new flour-mill driven by water ; a new inn with a brave new sign-board ; and crossing the boundary made by the Chester line, I arrived in Crewe."

—From " A Day at Crewe," in *Chambers' Edinburgh Journal*, vol. xiii (new series), 1850, pp. 391–2.

BEFORE the removal of the Grand Junction Railway Company's locomotive and rolling stock works to Crewe can be dealt with, the reasons which made all the large railways undertake the direct manufacture of engines, waggons and coaches, must be considered. Most of the early railway companies had originally been, like their predecessors the canal companies, merely the passive owners of a system of transport open to the use of all on payment of a toll. In some cases the right to work the line was leased to a few private individuals, but complaints of inefficiency and the danger of accidents gradually forced the vast majority of companies to work the lines themselves. Even then, they often contracted with engineering firms for a supply of locomotives and the services connected with the running and staffing of trains. These arrangements also proved unsatisfactory, and the final development was the direct manufacture by the companies of the necessary locomotives and rolling stock.[2]

[1] down Mill Street.

[2] D. Lardner : *Railway Economy* (1850), pp. 107–8 ; see also C. F. Dendy Marshall : *History of British Railways down to . . . 1830* (1938).

In the case of the Grand Junction, complaints about the insufficiency of locomotive power began almost as soon as the line was opened. Early in 1838 ten more engines were badly needed on account of the severe weather, which had increased the traffic and also damaged the locomotives. Later in the year, it was officially disclosed that some of the company's engines were so unsuitable for constant and heavy traffic " that some have been almost rebuilt." [1] Joseph Locke (1805–60), chief engineer to the Grand Junction from 1835 to 1846, said :—

" At an early period, the Grand Junction Company bought all their locomotives from manufacturers. . . . But the engines were, necessarily, in need of constant repair, and an establishment was formed for that purpose at Crewe. Then arose the question, whether this establishment could not be advantageously used, not only for the repair, but also for the construction, of engines. The plan was tried . . . and the cost was found to be much less than the price they had formerly paid." [2]

The sudden demand for locomotives during the railway booms was also a factor increasing the desirability of direct construction. The demand came not only from Britain but from Europe, and it was to the inability of British steam-engine manufacturers to satisfy it that Dr. Lardner attributed the decision of the larger railway companies " to erect extensive works for the manufacture of engines . . . at convenient points upon the principal lines." [3] The same reasoning was applicable to the manufacture of carriages and waggons : the advantage of large-scale organisation, a minute division of labour, and uniformity of pattern and parts, could all be obtained. It must be remembered that in the 1840's the spectacle of a joint-stock company entering upon intricate manufacturing operations was an unusual one. The one-man business or small partnership was regarded as the normal type of industrial organisation, and there were some who foretold disaster, among them no less an authority than Robert Stephenson. He may, however, have been biased by the fact that he was himself a private manufacturer of locomotives.[4] Captain Mark Huish, secretary and general manager of the Grand

---

[1] *Railway Magazine*, April, 1838, p. 268 ; Sept., 1838, p. 189.
[2] *Proc. Inst. C.E.*, vol. xi, 1851–2, pp. 466–7 ; *D.N.B.* (Locke).
[3] Lardner : *op. cit.*, pp. 107–8.
[4] *Proc. Inst. C.E.*, vol. xi, 1851–2, pp. 461–3, 468.

Junction and London and North-Western Railways from 1841 to 1858, spoke of the inevitable tendency of a railway company " to extend the principle of doing as much as possible for themselves, especially when they found that they could rely upon the quality of the articles which they had hitherto manufactured." [1]

This principle was carried out to its fullest extent at Crewe by F. W. Webb, Chief Mechanical Engineer, L.N.W.R., 1871–1903, who prided himself on producing everything required for the manufacture of locomotives in the Crewe Works.[2] About 1908 began an agitation for the application of " scientific management " to the various railway workshops in Great Britain, with a view to eliminating waste, and a movement (widely supported by interested private manufacturers) was started, which had as its object the curtailment of manufacturing by railway companies. There was some criticism of Crewe Works at the meeting of L.N.W.R. shareholders in February, 1912, to which Sir Gilbert Claughton, the chairman, replied :—

". . . if he were not the chairman of the company, he would be one immediately to make a ring against them if they were dependent on outside firms for everything they required and the rate of speed they required it. Everything, however, that was done at Crewe was subjected to the most minute estimates, and if in any case it was found that the company could not make at or under market terms, outside firms were invariably asked to tender." [3]

The engine sheds and the repair shops of the Grand Junction were, until 1843, situated near those of the Liverpool and Manchester Railway at Edgehill, Liverpool, but it is doubtful whether any locomotives were ever manufactured there. When William Buddicom and Alexander Allan were appointed Superintendent and Assistant Superintendent respectively of the company's locomotive department in 1840, the stock of engines consisted of 56 of the " Planet " class by various makers. Great changes were in progress at the time and the two men carried out many improvements to locomotive design at Edgehill. In 1841

[1] *Proc. Inst. C.E.*, vol. xi, 1851–2, p. 473.

[2] *C.G.*, 6.10.77 ; *Cassier's Magazine*, Sept., 1903, pp. 393–407 ; Oct., 1903, pp. 519–33 ; see chap. iv *infra*.

[3] *Times* (*Finance Suppt.*), Feb. 17, 1912 ; see also *ibid.*, Aug. 23, 1911.

Francis Trevithick (1812–77), son of the great Richard Trevithick, was appointed superintendent of the locomotive power department, in succession to Buddicom, on the recommendation of Locke.[1]

From 1837 until 1840 Crewe was merely a station on the Grand Junction line, and differed little from Whitmore or Hartford. The first train of a regular public service reached Crewe from Liverpool at 8.45 a.m. on July 4, 1837 ; after a stay of eleven minutes it departed and " ascended the Madeley bank to Whitmore " on its journey to Birmingham.[2] The station at Crewe was " of the first class " and situated on the Nantwich to Wheelock turnpike road, 4 miles from Nantwich and 6 miles from Sandbach. This road fed the railway, for the " Crewe Railway Coach, from Macclesfield through Congleton and Sandbach, to Crewe," ran twice daily to meet the trains, while a coach to and from Whitchurch and " an Omnibus from Nantwich to Crewe to meet all the trains and convey passengers to Nantwich," were also running. They usually found sufficient employment. There was also a minor station at Coppenhall, about a mile to the north, but it was closed down later in the century.[3] The Crewe station was described in 1838 as follows :—" There is a convenient and lofty brick house built here in Modern Gothic style for an inn ; a very neat house for the clerk of the station, and an engine-house with a spare engine . . . always ready for use."[4]

In 1850 a shrewd observer visited the new railway town of Crewe, and seeing its lack of raw materials and the great display of cattle-auction announcements, summed up in a phrase which still holds true :—" Crewe is but a mechanical settlement in an agricultural district."[5]

[1] *C.G.*, 17.10.82 ; C. F. Dendy Marshall : *Centenary History of the Liverpool and Manchester Railway*, pp. 120–2 ; G.J.B.M., July 21, 1841 ; H. W. Dickinson and E. R. Titley : *Richard Trevithick*, 1934, pp. 284–5.

[2] A. Freeling : *Grand Junction Railway Companion*, 1837, pp. 56–9 ; Stretton : *History of the Grand Junction Railway*, p. 4. The formal opening of the line had taken place on July 3, 1837, when the directors and their friends took a trip down the line to Birmingham.

[3] E. C. and W. Osborne : *Guide to the Grand Junction Railway*, 1838, 2nd ed., pp. 68, 216–17 ; Freeling · *op. cit.*, p. 57.

[4] Osborne : *op. cit.*, pp. 216–17 ; Lord Crewe had built the inn (T. Roscoe : *History of the L.N.W.R.*, 1847, pp. 74–5).

[5] *Chambers' Edinburgh Journal*, vol. xiii (new series), 1850, pp. 391–2.

The Crewe district had no appreciable water-power, no iron-ore deposits, no coal-mines. The decision to remove the loco-motive, coach and waggon departments of the Grand Junction Railway from Edgehill to the deep rural surroundings of Crewe must have been dictated mainly by its central position on a rail-way network. The Edgehill Works were at a remote angle of the system, which after May, 1840, included the Chester to Crewe line, and was soon to include the Manchester to Crewe branch of the abortive Manchester and Birmingham line. The imperative necessity of enlarging the works and locomotive stock, and the cheapness of land near Crewe, must each have had its share in determining the choice of site. The lack of coal deposits and other raw materials, such as timber and iron, could be partly met by the fact that a railway company could transport them cheaply in slack periods ; after 1848 the opening of the Crewe to Kidsgrove branch of the North Staffordshire Railway made available coal supplies from the pits of the North Stafford-shire field.

The earliest positive evidence of an intention to remove to Crewe dates from June 10, 1840, and proves that the matter had been under consideration for some time before this. On June 20 and July 1, 1840, the Grand Junction Board ordered the purchase of a considerable quantity of land " at the junction of Crewe." On the latter day Locke was requested to prepare " plans, drawings and estimates for an establishment at Crewe ; which shall include the shops required for the building and repairs of carriages and waggons as well as engines." [1] In 1841 the con-tract for the erection of these works, as well as about 200 cottages, was given to a firm of Liverpool builders. An entry in the poor-rate book of Monks Coppenhall under September 10, 1841, concerning " the land that they are building on," shows that at least eighteen months elapsed before works and cottages were ready for occupation.

Early in 1842 a goods station had to be opened at Crewe, and the plans of the directors for the new colony expanded. Soon the building of cottage property and workshops was involving

---

[1] G.J.B.M., *loc. cit.*, and Feb. 26, April 7 and 21, 1841. At the same time Buddicom was instructed " to prepare a list of tools, etc., required for the new works . . . and obtain proposals from the manufacturers of tools of the best description " (G.J.B.M., May 19, 1841).

CREWE STATION ABOUT 1848

them in problems of sewerage and water-supply. The same day's proceedings saw the first steps taken in the direction of a social policy (January 5, 1842) :—

" A letter from the Revd. John Cooper (Rector of Coppenhall) to the Chairman was read, calling the attention of the Directors to the fact that the existing church accommodation at Coppenhall was too little for the population and was 1½ mile from the Company's depot, and hoping that the Board would provide in some way for the spiritual wants and education of the numerous workmen and their families about to be brought there." [1]

Locke was therefore asked to leave space for a church and school when laying out the town. The problems of local government and social welfare had forced themselves upon the Board, and it set to work to solve them. Railway companies were notoriously unmindful of the welfare of the temporary labourers who constructed their lines, but they took up a different attitude towards the comparatively highly paid skilled mechanics and workers in their permanent establishments.[2] The Grand Junction Board was compelled by a mixture of principle, self-interest and necessity to adopt what may be termed a social policy towards its employees in the new colony at Crewe ; in the absence of any efficient old-established system of government and urban economic organisation in the hitherto rural township of Monks Coppenhall, the company was obliged to undertake the task of building up a new community itself. It was not that the task was a new one : Robert Owen's work at New Lanark, Samuel Oldknow's at Mellor, the experiments at Styal and Saltaire were all symptoms of the same complex social changes taking place at the time, although they might differ in detail. As Unwin expressed it :—

" The workers drawn together in the earliest factories set up in country districts had at first no organised or traditional community

---

[1] G.J.B.M., Jan. 5, 1842 ; see also Nov. 17 and 24, Dec. 15, 1841, Jan. 28, 1842.

[2] There was a sharp distinction between the two classes, well brought out in 1846 before the Select Committee on Railway Labourers :—" *Question* 2112 (Sir Thomas Acland) :—Had not the Great Western Railway taken considerable pains at Swindon for the accommodation and convenience and improvement of the labourers there ? *Answer* (I. K. Brunel) :—Yes ; but those are labourers brought together permanently " (p. 146).

life of their own, and were thus thrown into greater dependence on the social initiative of their employer, who if he responded to the call might become in a very real sense a founder of a new community." [1]

The following pages may serve to give some indication of how the " Liverpool Party " fulfilled its task with regard to the new settlement in South Cheshire.

The Census of 1841 showed that the population of Monks Coppenhall was 203 ; at the end of 1842 the township contained about 1,000 inhabitants, according to a reliable estimate. Before the arrival of the mechanics and their families from Edgehill the place must have presented the appearance of a new town of the same period in the U.S.A., except that the resources of civilisation were a little nearer. The Grand Junction directors appointed an architect, John Cunningham, in 1842 " to superintend the whole of the buildings . . . the drainage also and every other matter connected with the proper completion of the buildings, cottages and other erections at Crewe." He held the post until 1850 at the considerable salary of £300 per annum. Thirty-two of the new Grand Junction cottages were occupied by November, 1842. [2]

The increasing volume of work led to the constitution, in February, 1842, of a committee of four, including the Chairman of the company, John Moss, to superintend the new colony, and, as reconstituted in 1845, " to take charge of . . . the general management of the town of Crewe." This body became responsible for the municipal affairs of the community. [3] In February, 1843, the cottage department at Crewe was placed under R. S. Norris, the resident engineer, while the workshops and yards were placed under Trevithick. The long-awaited transfer from Edgehill was about to begin ; the men chose their cottages, while arrangements were made to transport their families free of charge. This mass migration meant that from 750 to 900 persons living in different parts of Liverpool were suddenly uprooted from familiar surroundings and placed

[1] G. Unwin and others : *Samuel Oldknow and the Arkwrights*, pp. 159–60.

[2] *Chester Courant*, Dec. 12, 1843 ; G.J.B.M., Jan. 5 and 21, 1842 ; Crewe Ctee., L.N.W.B., Jan. 24, 1850 ; P.R.B.M.C., Nov. 25, 1842.

[3] G.J.B.M., Jan. 21, 1842 ; June 14, 1845. The minutes of the Crewe Ctee. for 1842–6 are missing.

Birmingham and Liverpool Railway.

NOTICE IS HEREBY GIVEN,

THAT a Bill hath been brought into the Honourable the House of Commons for making, carrying, and maintaining a Railway or Tram-road from the Town of Birmingham, in the County of Warwick, to the Royal Rock Ferry, on the western side or shore of the River Mersey, in the County Palatine of Chester; and that a printed Copy of such Bill, together with a Map or Plan annexed thereto, will be deposited with the Parish Clerk of the several and respective Parishes of Birmingham, St. Martin and St. Philip in Birmingham, Harborne, West Bromwich, Hales Owen, Rowley Regis, Tipton otherwise Tibbington, Sedgley, Wednesbury, Darlaston, Wolverhampton, Bushbury otherwise Byshbury, Wombourn, Brewood, Shareshill, Penkridge, Bradley, Lapley, Church Eaton, Gnosall, Norbury, High Offley, Adbaston, Cheswardine, Market Drayton otherwise Drayton in Hales, Adderley, Audlem, Wrenbury, Acton, Baddiley, Bunbury, Tattenhall, Tarvin, Waverton otherwise Wharton, Christleton, Chester, Saint Oswald, Saint John, The Holy and undivided Trinity, Shotwick, Burton, Neston, Eastham, Brombrorough otherwise Bromborrow, and Bebington, in the several Counties of Warwick, Stafford, Salop, Chester, and the County of the City of Chester, on or before the 30th day of March instant. Dated the 17th day of March, 1826.

Geo Barker

SOLICITOR.

THE ROUTE PROPOSED IN 1826

together in the semi-rural district of Crewe. By 1844, 217 of
the company's cottages and houses were occupied. The actual
removal took place in March, 1843, and according to one account
the exact date was March 18.[1]

The directors, fully aware of the difficulties, gave Locke wide
powers

" not only to give minute and specific directions on all the details,
fix the new rates of wages etc., but personally to superintend the
organisation of the new establishment so that in this important change
the basis of an economical system for all time coming may be settled." [2]

The total cost of establishing the new colony and works was
estimated to be almost £110,000, which included the cost of a
gasworks.[3]

The finishing touches were given to the workshops in
November, 1843, and " a grand dinner, tea and ball " were given
" to the superintendents, clerks, and workmen, as well as their
wives, families and acquaintances," on December 2, 1843, to
celebrate the occasion ; in its account of this the *Chester Courant*
newspaper of December 12 gave the following description of
the town, the earliest known :—

" About two years ago only, the site could boast of but a few
detached farm houses. The Company (and a few others) have
imparted to it a very different aspect. Their own land . . . is about
30 acres, and the whole is laid out in streets, and nearly covered with
comfortable cottages in varied and distinctive styles uniform in the
several streets. . . .   There are also schools, an assembly room, committee room for magistrates, etc. The Company have fitted up a
portion of their buildings as a temporary Church of England, and
have appointed their own chaplain." [4]

The railway works, as " the grand manufactory of the whole
line " were pronounced to be " the finest and most expensive
workshops in the world." Such was the beginning of the new
community and in his appropriate speech on the occasion John

[1] G.J.B.M., Feb. 3, 8, 22, 1843 (221 houses and cottages built) ; P.R.B.M.C.,
June 2, 1843 ; *C.G.*, 8.6.78.
[2] G.J.B.M., Feb. 22, 1843.
[3] G.J.B.M., May 10, 1843. By July, 1845, £130,340 had been expended
on land, works and machinery at Crewe (G.J.B. Rep., Aug. 1, 1845).
[4] Reproduced with added woodcuts in the *Illustrated London News* of
Dec. 23, 1843.

Moss, chairman of the directors, noted the problems of social readjustment created and the solutions planned by the Board :—

". . . the company had found it advisable to remove their great works for the whole line to that place ; . . . the men around him had, no doubt, by coming there, dissevered many ties of kindred and affection and deprived themselves of many of the enjoyments of more populous localities ; but . . . he and his brother directors were anxious to make them as comfortable as lay within their power."

I. The Housing Policy of the Company

With regard to the housing accommodation provided, its cheapness and careful arrangement according to the economic resources and social rank of the occupants made a favourable impression on contemporary observers. Two of the accounts, dating from 1846 and 1850 respectively, are worth reproduction :—

" The dwelling-houses arrange themselves in four classes : first, the villa-style lodges the superior officers ; next a kind of ornamented Gothic constitutes the houses of the next in authority ; the engineers domiciled in detached mansions, which accommodate four families, with gardens and separate entrances [these are the famous ' block-houses '] ; and last, the labourer delights in neat cottages of four apartments, the entrances within ancient porches. The first, second and third, have all gardens and yards ; the fourth has also gardens. . . . The rooms are all capacious ; the ground-floors are tiled, and, as the back and front are open, ventilation is perfect. Each house is supplied with gas ; the water is always on at present in the street, but is to be immediately introduced into the houses. The engineers . . . pay 3s. 6d. per week, the labourers 2s. For water there is no charge, but for gas they pay in winter twopence per week for each burner. The fittings cost them nothing.[1]

" The general appearance of Crewe is very pleasing. The streets are wide and well-paved ; the houses are very neat and commodious, usually of two stories, built of bricks, but the brick concealed by rough-cast plaster, with porches, lattice windows, and a little piece of garden ground before the door. . . . The accommodation is good, and it would be difficult to find such houses at such low rents even in the suburbs of a large town." [2]

---

[1] *Chambers' Edinburgh Journal*, Jan. 31, 1846, p. 78, copied by S. Lewis : *Topographical Dictionary of England*, ed. 1848, vol. I, p. 725.

[2] *Chambers' Edinburgh Journal*, vol. xiii (1850), pp. 391–2.

The company first decided to fix the rents of the cottages and houses on the principle that the company would obtain 5 per cent. net on capital, plus 1¼ per cent. for repairs and depreciation, but after a short trial it was found that rents fixed on this basis were too high and the following prices were adopted in April, 1843. They included a charge of 6*d*. per week for parish rates, water and lighting (9*d*. per week in the case of Class 4—the " lodges " for the superior officers).

Class.	Number.	Total Rent per Week.	Cost of Building.
1	40 at	2*s*. 9*d*.	£125
2	64 ,, 28 ,,	3*s*. 9*d*. 4*s*. 0*d*.	£144
3	20 ,, 60 ,,	4*s*. 0*d*. 4*s*. 3*d*.	£167
4	9 ,,	7*s*. 0*d*.	£303

Even these revised scales seem to have proved too much for the employees, for a year later the rents of the first three classes were again reduced by 9*d*. per week, which meant that the cheapest were 2*s*.[1] A strict watch was kept on " filthy and disreputable " tenants, and any company's servant who was caught " bringing discredit on the establishment and endangering the health of the town " was liable to dismissal.[2]

These are the houses which did not need investigation by the public and private sanitary reformers of the 1840's; their existence therefore tends to be overlooked by the pessimist school of economic historians when investigating the so-called " Bleak Age."

In 1846 a review of the cottage department showed that, with the exception of Class 1 (4 per cent.), the cottages gave a return on capital of about 5 per cent., excluding the cost of the land. Besides cottages, the company had as early as 1842 considered the provision of shops for the colony, although none is

[1] G.J.B.M., Feb. 22, April 19, 1843 ; June 26, 1844.
[2] G.J.B.M., Sept. 20, 1843.

listed in the rate-book in April, 1844.   However, Sir F. B. Head
mentioned shops built by the company as existing in 1848,
probably on Coppenhall Terrace and the north side of the
Market Square.[1]   By January, 1846, Crewe's estimated population was 2,000 and between 1845 and 1847 fresh accommodation
remained an urgent necessity for the mechanics and coach-
builders, as well as for " Enginemen, Guards, Porters, Cokemen,
etc."   In the course of 1848, however, the railway depression,
linked with the general decline in business activity, made itself
felt in Crewe and ended the first hectic period of building.   Dismissals took place from the works, some of the houses fell empty,
and were let " to respectable tenants, whether connected with
the works or not."   In times of depression it was the custom of
the company's estate agent to make all workmen owning their
own houses and living in them move into houses owned by the
company if no other means of filling them could be found.   As
repairs in the early days were not carried out on a regular basis,
many cottages suffered during the local depression, which lasted
until 1851.[2]   The total number of houses built by the company
during the first period (1842–8) was 520 of all classes, and the
number built by private persons about 300.   At the time of the
1851 census, Monks Coppenhall contained 825 inhabited, 27
uninhabited and 8 unfinished houses, which meant an average
of 5·5 persons per house.[3]

By this time the depression had begun to lift and 1852 saw an
acute housing shortage.   Great complaints came from the workmen, and the years from 1853 to 1857 saw the second great spurt
of building activity, made especially necessary by the establishment in the town of the company's new rail-rolling mill in 1853.
Prosperity brought with it a desire for higher standards in
accommodation, for in 1854 not only did 8 works foremen
prevail on the directors to build them a better class of house at
£280 each (rent £14 per annum), but there were in addition
numerous demands from ordinary workmen " requesting that

[1] G.J.B.M., April 27, 1842 ;   April 9, 1845 ;   Crewe Ctee., L.N.W.B.,
Sept. 8, 1846 ;   Dec. 4, 1849 ;   P.R.B.M.C., April 23, 1844 ;   Sir F. B. Head :
Stokers and Pokers, 1849, p. 110.

[2] Crewe Ctee., L.N.W.B., Sept. 22, 1847 ;   Jan. 17, March 22, 1848 ;
Feb. 13, 1849 ;   Oct. 8, 1850 ;   July 11, 1854 ;   private information.

[3] Crewe Ctee., L.N.W.B., April 5, 1852 ;   Bagshaw 1850, p. 367 ;   *Census
1851*, part 1, vol. 2, div. viii, pp. 20–3.

their parlours may be lobbied off and the floors boarded." By 1857, 732 company's houses had been built. When, in 1859–60, practically the whole of the coach-making department, then employing 700 men, was removed from Crewe, an exchange of houses with immigrants from the uprooted Wolverton loco-motive department was effected.[1]

The company played a minor part in the building booms of the succeeding decades, and the history of later housing develop-ment in Crewe lies scattered in the archives of private builders, house title-deeds, the minute books of the building societies and the proceedings of Local Board and Town Council. Several further blocks were constructed by the company, but the number owned by it has probably never been much in excess of 845, whereas by the census of 1881 the houses in Crewe numbered 4,864. There was a loss of interest in the layout of the town among the directors and officials of the company, an example of which was the conversion of Dorfold, Betley and Tollitt Streets into dark and depressing cul-de-sacs by the erection of the new general offices of the Locomotive Department in 1876.[2]

The company acted as a pioneer and set standards for the private builder which were not always reached. Forty years after the first company's houses had been erected, a student of working-class housing wrote of them :—" As to the houses . . . they are excellent. . . . I only wish all working people were as well housed as those employed by our best-known railway company." [3]

As the town grew, it was found that some of the company's cottages in the centre of Crewe were occupying sites of com-mercial importance and in the 1870's a slow process of demolition began which replaced them by shops and offices. The first period of change came to an end in 1915, but in the early 1930's

[1] Crewe Ctee., L.N.W.B., June 29, July 13, Nov. 1 and 16, 1852 ; Feb. 15, 1853 ; Jan. 10, March 21, July 11, 1854 ; Gen. and Loco. Ctee., L.N.W.B., March 11, 1853 ; Jan. 24, 1854 ; July 14, 1854 ; Jan. 25, 1860 ; Sub-Ctee., L.N.W.B., April 17, 1854 ; Exec. Ctee., L.N.W.B., Oct. 23, 1857 ; Jan. 7, 1858 ; Kelly 1857, pp. 103–5.
[2] Official Guide to the L.N.W.R. Works at Crewe, 1903, p. 5 ; Census 1881, vol. 1, p. 31 ; C.G., 6.10.77 ; Works Ctee., 11.9.00.
[3] Rev. P. Dean, quoted in C.Ch., 2.9.82 ; John Allman said in 1871 :— " there had come into the town certain builders that . . . had perhaps built a class of property . . . that was not very creditable " (C.G., 2.9.71).

a second period of building activity started in the same district and will be carried further when the policy embodied in the Crewe Corporation Act of 1938 can be carried out. This provides the powers whereby 173 company's houses on the west side of the Market Square may be demolished to relieve traffic congestion by providing a site for a 'bus station and a car park. Meanwhile, Crewe is still peculiar among English towns of comparable size in that there is a considerable amount of small cottage property in the centre of the town. Although it is old and increasingly inadequate according to modern housing standards, it has rarely been empty on account of the low rents charged.[1]

II. The Company's Public Utilities

Steam engines, stationary or locomotive, require abundant water, and it is therefore not surprising to find Crewe Works established close to the Valley Brook. The company's engineers adapted the waterworks which supplied the engineering shops to supply the new colony, and the Brook became the sole source of water, apart from rain-tubs and wells, until 1864. The search for water began in 1841, when Locke sank a well near Christ Church. Brine flowed, and the boring had to be abandoned. Instead, the flour mill and dam in Mill Lane (now Mill Street) were purchased, and a reservoir constructed further upstream in 1842.[2] Sir F. B. Head paid great attention to the water-supply in 1848 :—

" Close to the entrance of the Locomotive Department stands . . . a steam pump, which, besides supplying the engine that propels the machinery of the workshops, gives an abundance of water to the locomotives at the station, as also to the new railway town of Crewe. . . . This pump lifts about eighty or ninety thousand gallons of water per day from a brook below into filtering beds, whence it is again raised about forty feet into a large cistern, where it is a second time filtered through charcoal for the supply of the town." [3]

At first, only the better-class houses received a supply from taps. The inhabitants of the cottages had to go with buckets

[1] 1 & 2 Geo. VI, June 23, 1938 ; *C.Ch.*, Oct., 1938–Jan., 1939, *passim*.
[2] *C.G.*, 29.9.77 ; G.J.B.M., Jan. 5, 1842.
[3] *Op. cit.*, pp. 100–1. The " cistern " still stands.

to tanks erected in various parts of the town for their water. In the first years of the colony the combined charge for light and water was included in the rent. The first recorded complaint about bad quality and insufficient supply occurs in 1854, the precursor of many which were to be made later in the century. Dr. Richard Lord, first M.O.H. for the town, who came to Crewe in 1856, said of the first eight years of his residence :— " I am bound to mention that the water supplied then was execrable . . . it did sometimes happen that the tap got stopped up with something other than fish. Mere mud was hardly noticed, much less talked about." [1]

This state of affairs, and the rapidly-increasing needs of both town and works, set the company looking for a supplementary supply. In 1862, Professor Hull, a geologist, reported that an artesian supply could be obtained from the red sandstone at Whitmore in Staffordshire, and borings were commenced. A spring at Madeley in the same county was also laid under contribution about 1873. The first domestic supplies from Whitmore seem to have reached the town in 1864.

The enlightened action of the company in providing public baths made a great impression in the 1840's, when personal cleanliness was not regarded as a strict social necessity even by those who could afford soap. The first Crewe public baths, built in 1845, were under the care of a sub-committee of the council of the Mechanics' Institution until 1862. They consisted of " eight common baths, with hot, cold and shower to each, and one vapour bath." Sir F. B. Head has left us an interesting and amusing description of them as they appeared on his visit in 1848.[2] The charge for a bath was only $1\frac{1}{2}d.$, but the council of the Institution complained in 1850 and 1851 that they " continued deficient of that support expected from a population of 5,000 in Crewe." [3] Doubtless many of the artisans possessed private tin baths and wooden tubs which they used in preference, especially when water began to be laid on by tap.

---

[1] C.G., 7.8.78 ; see also G.J.B.M., Dec. 14, 1842 ; Feb. 22, April 19, 1843 ; Crewe Ctee., L.N.W.B., Jan. 24, 1854 ; Bagshaw 1850, p. 368 ; *Chambers' Edinburgh Journal*, vol. xiii (1850), p. 391.
[2] *Op. cit.*, p. 109 ; see also A.R.C.M.I., 1849, 1852, 1855 ; C.M., Sept. 13, 1845 ; Bagshaw 1850, p. 368.
[3] A.R.C.M.I., 1850, 1851.

By 1857 the works had expanded until the baths were nearly in the centre of them and "almost inaccessible to the public." The company accordingly built a second suite of public baths in Mill Street. These were opened in 1866 and contained a swimming-pool. From 1899 onwards it became apparent that they were quite inadequate for a town of over 40,000 inhabitants. In that year Crewe Town Council was told, in reply to a request that they should be enlarged, that the directors "thought the time had arrived when the Corporation should themselves provide the necessary bath accommodation." [1] The question continued to be considered half-heartedly until 1919, when C. J. Bowen Cooke, Chief Mechanical Engineer, London and North-Western Railway, 1909–20, and Mayor of Crewe, 1918–19, brought forward a scheme for the erection of a combined social centre and public baths by the company as Crewe's War Memorial. Owing to post-war economic conditions, and their effect on the railways, this scheme was abandoned. Meanwhile, the old baths continued to be used until March 31, 1936, and from that time until November 6, 1937, when the Corporation's public baths in Flag Lane were opened, Crewe presented the unusual spectacle of a modern community containing nearly 50,000 souls, but without public baths within its boundaries. Many Crewe people, even before 1914, used the baths in Nantwich, Winsford and the Potteries.[2]

The first gasworks in Crewe, erected by the Grand Junction Company in 1842–3, stood in Lockitt Street. There is a tradition that in the beginning the directors intended the gas for the use of the works only, but soon after the foundation of the colony "the inhabitants petitioned the company to supply them with gas, which the company did." [3] In 1850–1, the directors decided to supply gas to all applicants in Crewe at a charge of 10s. per light per annum, and not merely to their own cottages. Braithwaite Poole claimed about this time that the L.N.W.R. could sell gas in Crewe at 2s. 6d. per 1,000 cubic feet, a very low

[1] Mkt. Ctee., 20.6.99, 17.10.99 ; C.L.B.M., May 25, 1865 ; Kelly 1857, pp. 103–5 ; Morris 1864, p. 75 ; A.R.C.M.I., 1851–63 ; E.A. 73, p. 19 ; M.O.H. 1900, p. 6.

[2] Crewe Town Council proceedings, 1910–14, 1919–20, *passim* ; C.G., 3.3.06, 14.11.06, 7.11.08, 11.11.10, 9.12.10, 11 and 14.7.19, 19.3.20, 6.1.22, 3.2.22 ; C.Ch., 13.11.37.

[3] C.G., 29.9.77.

price, but when extensions to the mains were made in 1857 the directors resolved to charge 7s. per 1,000 cubic feet to persons not in the employ of the company, and two years later the charge to the tenants in Crewe was doubled. At the same time a watch was kept on the consumption of each block of houses, and persons using the gas at night "at improper hours" were to be cut off. It is evident that the early terms had been too generous. Soon after the establishment of the steelworks, in 1864, and the consequent development of the west end of the town, a new gasworks was built in Wistaston Road. Great extensions took place in 1882–6, and this plant now supplies the whole of Crewe.[1]

III. Sewage- and Refuse-Disposal, 1843–61

The method of sewage-disposal adopted at Crewe in the early years was the one most in vogue at the time, *viz.* the sewage flowed down to the Valley Brook and polluted it, while drinking water was obtained from a point higher up the stream. Communities lower down the stream were left to take their chance. The company's cottages were fitted with privies and cesspools ; we are told that the company ". . . formed for their property an outfall into the Mill dam, situated on Mill Lane, and the effluent found its way into the brook." The sewage of the other property found its way into the brook in the best way it could.[2]

The company emptied ash-pits, cesspools and privies, and performed scavenger work in its own streets. Immediately after the transfer from Edgehill an outbreak of sickness occurred among the men at Crewe and the Board set up a committee to consider the establishment of a dispensary and hospital. In 1844 Edwin Edwards (d. 1865) was appointed first company's surgeon at Crewe, with a salary of £50 per annum.[3] The company

---

[1] G.J.B.M., Nov. 9, 1842 ; Feb. 22, April 19, 1843 ; Crewe Ctee., L.N.W.B., Nov. 20, 1849 ; Jan. 14, 1851 ; Exec. Ctee., L.N.W.B., Aug. 7, Dec. 12, 1856 ; Gen. and Loco. Ctee., L.N.W.B., July 27, Aug. 11, 1859 ; Works Ctee., 4.4.82, 1.5.84 ; C.G., 11.11.85 ; Bagshaw 1850, p. 368 ; *Proc. Inst. C.E.*, vol. xi, (1851–2), p. 465.

[2] C.G., 6.10.77 ; see also G.J.B.M., Dec. 15 and 22, 1841 ; Jan. 21, 1842 ; Crewe Ctee., L.N.W.B., April 5, 1852.

[3] G.J.B.M., Oct. 4 and 18, 1843 ; Oct. 23, 1844 ; L.N.W.B., Nov. 14, 1857.

supplied a surgery, and a scheme of health insurance was worked out :—

" To a medical man the Company gives a house . . . in addition to which he receives from every unmarried workman 1*d*. per week ; if married, but with no family 1½*d*. per week ; if married, and with a family 2*d*. per week ; for which he undertakes to give attendance to whatever man, woman or children or babies of the establishment may require them." [1]

After 1848 these fees were deducted by the company from the men's wages ; the scheme was later narrowed down to an accident levy of ½*d*. per week, and commuted for a fixed salary in 1889. The hospital question was considered again in 1854, but postponed. Meanwhile, bad accident cases were sent to Chester Infirmary in a brake van ; deaths occurred so frequently under this system, however, that about 1860 a cottage in Lockitt Street was fitted up as a hospital. Then a house at the corner of Moss Square came into use for some ten years, and a supplementary one was utilised at the corner of Lyon and Liverpool Streets from about 1874. This remained in use until the provision of the present hospital in Mill Street, opened in 1900 at a cost of £7,000. Dr. James Atkinson, second company's surgeon and first Mayor of Crewe, was Edwards' assistant before succeeding him in 1866. Atkinson, a close personal friend of F. W. Webb, could rest assured of every reasonable provision in medical matters. He had an extensive private practice and retired from the post in 1909, to be succeeded by his assistant, Dr. J. Lawrence. [2]

In the first years of the colony the Council of the Mechanics' Institution petitioned the directors in matters of public health, and there is some evidence to show that at this period the Council was regarded as a representative committee of the workmen acting under the Crewe Committee of directors for the better management of the town. It protested vigorously but unsuccessfully in 1846 against a proposal of the directors to have the land round Christ Church consecrated for a cemetery. In

---

[1] Head : *op. cit.*, pp. 109–10.
[2] Crewe Ctee., L.N.W.B., Oct. 3, 1848 ; March 31, 1854 ; *C.G.*, 20.10.88, 7.12.89, 17.1.00, 20.2.01, 29.6.01 ; *C.Ch.*, 10.3.17 ; Kelly 1865, p. 134 ; Ordnance Survey Map of Crewe (1874).

1849 the Council, on account of the great cholera epidemic at Nantwich, requested police-constables Murphy and Blinkhorn to prevent Irish and other beggars from the " low haunts " of that town from entering Crewe. By 1852 the results of imperfect sewerage made themselves felt and much draining of cesspools and privies occurred. A good system of pipe-drainage was necessary in view of the heavy clay soil, and surgeon Edwards attributed " the serious increase of sickness in the town " to the lack of what had only become possible with the invention of a cheap method of making earthenware pipes in the 1840's. A year later the by-laws of the General Board of Health were enforced to prevent overcrowding ; Edwards and Murphy acted as unofficial nuisance inspectors, but neither they nor the company could interfere with nuisances existing on property in private hands.[1]

By 1860, privately-owned buildings and houses were becoming the rule rather than an adjunct to the company's efforts. This was one of the main reasons for the constitution of the Local Board in that year, when the company's municipal functions began to pass slowly from joint-stock to public control.

IV. The Highways and Streets of Monks Coppenhall

The arrival of the railway colony placed a strain on the township's highway administration which it had never been designed to stand, and the roads outside the company's estate went from bad to worse. A person resident in Crewe from 1845 onwards said of this early period that High Street often stood " knee deep in clay," and was a place in which it was " quite common for foot travellers to lose their shoes." In Earle Street " it was a very common occurrence for carts to get up to the axle-tree in clay." [2] With these township roads the company had little to do, except that the surveyors bought cinders and taps from the railway works. Coppenhall's only turnpike road, administered by the Nantwich and Wheelock Turnpike Trustees set

---

[1] Head : *op. cit.*, pp. 109, 112 ; C.M., Feb. 28, 1846 ; June 29, 1848 ; Crewe Ctee., L.N.W.B., July 18, 1848 ; Feb. 24, Nov. 16, 1852 ; Nov. 15, 1853 ; Jan. 10, May 16, 1854 ; Gen. and Loco. Ctee., L.N.W.B., April 7, 1852 ; Hall : *op. cit.*, pp. 245–6.

[2] C.G., 13.1.72, 19.10.72.

up by the Act of 1816, passed through the railway company's estate, and since it had been planned in order to improve communications between Nantwich, the Grand Trunk Canal and Sandbach, it acted as a feeder to the new railway network. In 1843 an amicable arrangement was made between the Grand Junction Railway Company and the Turnpike Trustees, who obtained a further Act in 1848 (11 & 12 Vict., c. lxix) by virtue of which they borrowed £2,000 in 1849 from Lord Crewe to make a better road to the Potteries in the form of a branch turnpike from Crewe Station along a new " Weston Lane " and through Stowford to join the Nantwich to Newcastle-under-Lyme turnpike at Weston Hall. This tended to diminish the importance of Nantwich as a road centre.[1]

The company bore the whole cost of paving and repairing its private estate roads, which consisted chiefly of those contained in the area bounded by Earle, Lyon and Forge Streets, Coppenhall Terrace, Chester Street and its cul-de-sacs, Delamere and Lawrence Streets, Wellington Square and Victoria Street. They were described as follows in 1848 :—" the streets . . . are . . . much broader than those of Wolverton . . . the footpaths being of asphalt, composed of the company's coal tar mixed up with ashes from the workshops." [2]

As time went on, the contrast between the streets maintained by the company and those under the township surveyor grew, to the disadvantage of the latter. The cost of maintenance formed an appreciable item in the yearly expenses, and in 1857 the directors considered devoting their streets to the public use " in lieu of the company themselves doing the scavenger work and the repair of the streets." [3]   Before the establishment of the Local Board this would have been a retrograde step, and it was not taken.

---

[1] *E.A.* 02, p. 19 ; G.J.B.M., Jan. 12, 1842 ; March 8 and 15, 1843 ; report of *Lord Crewe* v. *Edleston* in *Staffordshire Advertiser*, May 16, 1857. It is said that Lord Crewe's purpose in lending the money was to close, and provide an alternative to, the right-of-way which the public enjoyed through Crewe Gates Farm and past the front of Crewe Hall. The new public of Crewe had evidently made too much use of its rights.

[2] Head : *op. cit.*, pp. 110, 111–12 ; Bagshaw 1850, p. 367.

[3] L.N.W.B., Nov. 14, 1857. The company was still scavenging them in 1922. (*C.G.*, 12.11.20, 7.1.21, 6.1.22) ; Kelly 1857, pp. 103–5 ; 1865, p. 134.

V. The Preservation of Law and Order

The arrival of a large body of mechanics and labourers created problems of policing with which the ancient system of township constabulary could not cope. The constable often had to look on helpless while fights raged between rival gangs of navvies, and in the early 1840's it was " no unusual thing to see two or three men stripped to the waist shouting out and challenging the best man from some other counties to fight."[1] From the census enumerators' books of 1851 some idea of the mixed character of the population can be obtained :—

County or Country of Birth.	Per cent. of Population of Crewe in 1851.	County or Country of Birth.	Per cent. of Population of Crewe in 1851.
Cheshire	38	Yorkshire	1·9
Lancashire	23	Derbyshire . . .	1·4
Ireland	6·2	Warwickshire . . .	1·3
Staffordshire . . .	5·4	Middlesex	1·0
Scotland	3·0	Cumberland . . .	1·0
Wales	3·0	Nottinghamshire . .	1·0
Shropshire . . .	2·8		

The high percentage for Cheshire is partly attributable to the large number of children born to the new settlers since 1842–3. None of the other counties had more than 27 representatives in the Crewe of 1851.[2] The unruliness of the colony and the danger to crops, game and fences became so unbearable that, in 1842, 17 farmers and others " from three or four miles around " founded the second Crewe and Coppenhall Association for the Prosecution of Felons, which filled a real gap in the police organisation of the time.

This body, of a type common in the eighteenth and nineteenth centuries, acted as an unofficial intermediate police-court,

" where persons who were indictable for any offence committed against a member might be brought up, and in the event of confessing their culpability and paying damages sufficient to recoup the injury sustained, they saved themselves from public exposure in

---

[1] *C.G.*, 25.10.84, 9.6.11. The township constable's remedy for the disturbances was as follows : " Let them alone ; they will know when to give over " (*C.G.*, 27.10.83).

[2] P.R.O.,H.O. 107/2169.

being brought before a bench of magistrates for felony or wilful damage or trespass."

The Association prosecuted only in flagrant cases.[1]   In the case of the Crewe body a solicitor was retained, an annual subscription of 5s. was levied, and in 1844 there were 40 members.[2]

Meanwhile, the Rev. Mr. Appleton, company's chaplain at Crewe, had appealed to the Board in 1843 to appoint a police officer " to preserve order especially on the Sabbath," and as a result Crewe possessed two company's policemen by 1846, in which year considerable difficulty was experienced in keeping order during the quarrels which took place among bricklayers and masons employed at the new works in Crewe.   Finally, in 1847, company and Magistrates joined to build a police station in Wistaston [now Eaton] Street;   the company provided a Superintendent.   In addition, there was an office for the railway police in Sandbach Street.   A new County Police Office was erected in Edleston Road in 1876, when the number of police officers maintained in Crewe and the surrounding townships was 14, under an inspector.[3]

After a period of decline, the Crewe and Coppenhall Association for the Prosecution of Felons underwent a remarkable revival, chiefly because Crewe and Birkenhead had by 1876 become " the two great seats of juvenile crime in the county." Shopkeepers and property owners flocked to join the Association,

---

[1] *C.G.*, 10.10.73 ; also *C.G.*, 20.10.82, 21.10.76, 20.10.77 ; S. and B. Webb : *Statutory Authorities for Special Purposes*, pp. 439–40 (which antedates their obsolescence).   The first Coppenhall Association for the prosecution of felons had been founded in 1815.   An advertisement inserted in the *Chester Chronicle* on Jan. 5 and 12, 1816, gave as the reason for its establishment that " horses, sheep, and other cattle, fowls, timber, corn and other valuable kinds of property, have been frequently stolen, burglaries and offences of a like heinous nature committed, in the parish and neighbourhood of Coppenhall . . . and the offenders have hitherto escaped punishment for want of being effectually prosecuted."   Societies of a similar character were established in Haslington about 1789 and at Warmingham in 1815 (*Chester Chronicle*, Nov. 17, 1815 ; *C.G.*, 4.2.82).   The Haslington society was still flourishing in 1882.

[2] *C.G.*, 21.10.76.

[3] G.J.B.M., April 19 and 26, 1843 ; Crewe Ctee., L.N.W.B., Sept. 8, 1846 ; Feb. 23, April 20, 1847 ;   May 2, 1848 ;   Nov. 15, 1853 ; *E.A.* 73, p. 19 ; Kelly 1857, pp. 103–5 ;   1865, p. 134 ;   1878, pp. 160–1 ;   *C.G.*, 30.10.75 ; C.L.B.M., 22.9.75.

so that its membership increased steadily from 35 in 1869 to 144 in 1881. In 1884 the Association, still dealing with over two dozen cases a year, received a severe blow from the death of the man who had been secretary since 1868, and was one of the early farmer-members, Benjamin Mulliner. In 1886 the president of the Association left Crewe, and it apparently ceased to exist after this date ; the incorporation of the town in 1877, and the establishment of a resident magistracy, had removed one of the major reasons for its existence.[1]

VI. The Educational and Religious Policy of the Company

From the first, the directors of the Grand Junction Railway considered it incumbent upon them to provide such facilities for community life as existed at the time. After the letter from the Rector of Coppenhall in January, 1842, hoping that they would " provide in some way for the spiritual wants of the numerous workmen and their families " about to be brought to Crewe, the Board resolved that it was " the duty of the company to contribute liberally towards the supply of spiritual instruction and education." The shareholders were to be asked to contribute not more than £1,000 towards a church and school for Crewe " on the principles adopted by the London and Birmingham Railway." To this sum were added some of the directors' fees and part of the Sunday Travelling Fund, *i.e.* accumulated dividends refused by strict Sabbatarian shareholders.[2] Late in 1842 a committee of directors began superintending building operations, and meanwhile the Bishop of Chester consecrated a room in the coachmaking workshops for divine worship ; a curate of Coppenhall, the Rev. J. Appleton, received £100 to act as first company's chaplain during 1843–4, and from then until the appointment of the Rev. Walter Butler as curate-in-charge (he was made first vicar in 1846), clergymen

---

[1] *C.G.*, 24.10.74, 9.1.75, 22.7.76, 19.10.78, 18.10.78, 18.10.79, 23.10.80, 22.10.81, 15.11.84, 24.10.85 ; *C.Ch.*, 8.1.76, 22.11.84.

[2] G.J.B.M., Jan. 5 and 21, 1842 ; Dec. 7, 1842 ; Jan. 18, 1843 ; Sept. 25, 1845 ; L.N.W.B., Oct. 19, 1861 ; only one shareholder protested by letter against the endowment of Christ Church. See also G.J.B. Rep., Feb. 1, Aug. 1, 1842.

were brought down from Liverpool.   Christ Church was consecrated on December 18, 1845 ; it had cost over £2,300 to build,
and was endowed with £1,000 and a guaranteed stipend of £150.
The patronage remained vested in four directors, who acted as
trustees.[1]

In the case of other religious bodies, the company rarely
refused small favours—the use of a room for divine worship, or
" some trifling assistance " (£10) towards the stipend of a
Presbyterian minister ; but the directors steadily refused to make
large grants towards the erection of churches, chapels or schools
for Wesleyans, Roman Catholics or Presbyterians.   The vicar
of Christ Church enjoyed half- or quarter-fare railway travel,
with some free passes, and the various Nonconformist ministers
and day-school teachers had the same privileges, which were
not abolished until 1897, except in the case of the incumbents
of the company's churches and teachers in the company's
school.[2]

A Government enquiry of 1833 revealed that in Church
Coppenhall there were two Sunday schools, supported by subscription, in one of which there were 61 children, of both sexes,
attending the Established Church, while the other belonged to
the Wesleyan Methodists and boasted 20 pupils.   The first school
can be identified with the one taught by William Roylance,
which was held in Coppenhall Church.   The Rev. John Cooper
later kept a boarding-school in Coppenhall Rectory.

In 1842–3 a barn at the side of the rectory was converted into
a small National school " at a great inconvenience " to the
incumbent, with the help of the Committee of the Privy Council
on Education, the ancestor of the Ministry of Education.   In
1844 the secular instruction of the 40 children in attendance was
said to be " somewhat neglected," but by 1859 it boasted 100
scholars and a schoolmistress.   A dame school existed in Monks
Coppenhall in 1831, and at the time of the Government enquiry
two years later the township possessed two day-schools in which

[1] G.J.B.M., Nov. 2 and Dec. 7, 1842 ; Feb. 8, 1843 ; Aug. 28, 1844 ;
Dec. 10, 1845 ; Church Ctee., March 27, 1843 ; Anon : *Christ Church,
Crewe, a Short History*, n.d ; *C.G.*, 9.2.78.

[2] G.J.B.M., Jan. 3, Dec. 24, 1844 ; Feb. 11, 1846 ; Crewe Ctee., L.N.W.B.,
July 13, 1847 ; Aug. 15, 1848 ; L.N.W.B., Sept. 9, 1848 ; Feb. 9, 1861 ; *C.Ch.*,
7.10.82 ; *C.G.*, 4.9.97, 23.10.97 ; private information.

CHRIST CHURCH AND MOSS SQUARE IN 1845

(*from a contemporary print*)

38 boys and 34 girls were "instructed at the expense of their parents."[1]

The company's educational plan for Monks Coppenhall was therefore a great advance. The room used for divine service, provided with a schoolmistress in 1843 and a schoolmaster in 1844, served the purpose until a separate National school building for infants, boys and girls was completed in 1847. It excited the admiration of Her Majesty's Inspector ; at Crewe he found " excellent buildings and very well-conducted schools " in that year. There were about 300 children in the departments, and the directors' wives, with typical nineteenth-century humanitarian interest in the children of the poor, formed a Ladies' Committee to help in its management. Great care was taken in appointing the first headmistress and headmaster, both of whom came from " normal schools." The company made a small charge per week for each child in attendance.

In 1848 the income from school pence was £150. The fourth child of a family was allowed to attend free of charge and any deficit was made good by the company. The vicars of Christ Church exercised a general superintendence over the school, and in 1847 the Rev. Walter Butler applied, with the directors' permission, to the Committee of Council on Education for a government grant.[2] The application was successful, the school was brought under government inspection and the task began, not only of stamping out illiteracy, but also of training teachers for the great expansion of local elementary education which followed in later years. The work of the school, and of elementary education in Crewe generally, was hampered by the lack of power to ensure compulsory attendance, and by the demands of the works for boy labour. The liberality of the company was partially wasted ; *e.g.* in 1852–3 most of the boys left at the age of 11, and on the average stayed at school

[1] *Trans. Lancs. and Ches. Antiq. Soc.,* vol. lv, pp. 111–12, 128 ; *E.A.* 06, p. 4 ; *C.G.,* 19.11.04 ; *Minutes of Ctee. of Coun. on Educ.,* 1842–3, pp. 802–6 ; 1844, vol. ii, pp. 544–9 ; White 1860, pp. 342–3 ; P.R.O.,H.O. 107/116 (census enumerators' returns, 1841) ; *Education Enquiry,* vol. i, 1833 (abstract of answers and returns relating to the numbers of schools), p. 75.

[2] Church Ctee., G.J.B., March 6 and July 9, 1843 ; G.J.B.M., Feb. 8, 1843 ; Jan. 3 and 10, 1844 ; *Minutes of Ctee. of Coun. on Educ.* (1847–8), vol. ii, pp. 162–3 ; (1848–50), vol. i, pp. 348–9 ; (1852–3), vol. ii, p. 502 ; Crewe Ctee., L.N.W.B., Jan. 26, April 20, 1847 ; *Chester Courant,* Dec. 12, 1843.

only eighteen months. From 1853 the encouragement of apprentices in the works to study at the Mechanics' Institution offset this wastage to a certain extent.[1]

VII. Miscellanea

In the early Victorian age the provision of allotments for farm labourers denoted an enlightened tenant farmer, but Sir John Clapham quotes no example of the same action by industrial firms. At Crewe, however, the railway company, in addition to laying out cottage gardens, considered the problem in 1842, about a year before the migration from Liverpool. After a visit to Wolverton the secretary reported favourably on the subject, and in 1850 the Board instructed Trevithick to let unoccupied land by auction in small lots. The Ordnance Survey map of Crewe dated 1874 shows a considerable number of these allotments.[2]

A savings bank for employees only, under the auspices of the company, was planned in 1845 and appears to have been established in the following year. The receipt and disposal of monies was in the hands of the vicar of Christ Church, with the headmaster of the National schools as actuary. In 1857 money could only be paid in on alternate Saturdays, and to judge by the figures of deposits, as compared with the Nantwich Savings Bank, the Crewe institution cannot be called particularly successful up to that date :—

	Total Deposits (£).	Depositors.
Nantwich . . .	49,384	1,366
Crewe	3,400	160

[1] Crewe Ctee., L.N.W.B., Jan. 24 and Aug. 22, 1854 ; L.N.W.B., Sept. 10, 1853 ; *Minutes of Ctee. of Coun. on Educ.*, (1848–50), vol. i, pp. 348–9, clxviii ; (1851–2), vol. ii, pp. 424–5 ; (1852–3), vol. ii, p. 502 ; *Staffordshire Advertiser*, Nov. 4, 1854.

[2] Sir J. H. Clapham : *Econ. Hist. Mod. Britain*, Vol. 1, pp. 472–3 ; G.J.B.M., April 27, 1842 ; April 5, 1843 ; Crewe Ctee., L.N.W.B., April 9, May 21, 1850 ; Ordnance Survey map, Crewe (1874), 41 feet to 1 inch.

By 1873 control of the bank had passed to the head accountant of the locomotive department. It was at that time open every Friday and paid interest at $4\frac{1}{2}$ per cent.[1]

In 1867 the railway company built the " Engine-men's Barracks," containing 42 beds, on the site of the Crewe flour mills in Mill Street " for engine-drivers and firemen, who, having their homes in other towns, arrive in Crewe in the night, and have to stay till the following morning." There may possibly be some connection between their establishment and the " rationalisation " of train haulage which began in the 1860's. In 1897 they were supplemented by a second " barracks " in Gresty Road.[2]

Dining-rooms for the men in the works " who, living at a distance, bring their breakfast and dinner with them," were opened in 1866, a symptom of the growing urbanisation of the surrounding townships. A description dating from 1873 shows that they were not a canteen in the modern sense of the word :—

" They afford accommodation for over 400, have ranges of steam heating ovens, and are attended by men cooks. When the meal wants warming and cooking, each man places it on a row of tin dishes laid out on the tables, and puts a numbered ticket upon it, and leaves it ; at one o'clock the dinners are served up hot, and nicely cooked."

In 1884-5 a second dining-room was built in Goddard Street to serve the steelworks, and a new one to replace the first was opened in 1892 in Eaton Street ; the two accommodated about 800 men. The preparation and sale of dinners by the company was not undertaken until 1918, when Bowen Cooke established the present canteen.[3]

Another institution founded by Bowen Cooke is the Veterans'

[1] G.J.B.M., April 9, 1845 ; L.N.W.B., March 7, 1849 ; Kelly 1857, pp. 103-5 ; White 1860, pp. 345-6, 370 ; *E.A.* 73, p. 27. Banking facilities in mid-nineteenth-century Crewe were poor. A sub-branch of the Manchester & Liverpool District Banking Company was opened in Crewe from Nantwich on Jan. 3, 1863, and made into a separate branch in 1879. The only other bank in the town in 1873 was a branch of the Midland Banking Company (*Cheshire Observer*, Jan. 10, 1863 ; *C.G.*, 3.8.78, 8.3.79 ; *E.A.* 73, p. 72).

[2] C.L.B.M., 25 and 26.2.67 ; Works, 11.8.96 ; *C.G.*, 9.2.78, 5.9.78, 30.10.78, 5.9.96 ; *E.A.* 73, p. 12.

[3] *E.A.* 73, p. 12 ; Ordnance Survey map (Crewe) 1874 ; *C.G.*, 19.7.84, 12.8.85, 29.8.91, 17.12.20.

Institute.   After 1906, as part of the effort to make Crewe Works an efficient business unit, it became the general practice to discharge all workers at some time between the ages of sixty-five and seventy.   To enable these veterans of the industrial army to meet together socially and enjoy certain recreations, Bowen Cooke established the institute in the disused clothing factory in Sandon Street in 1917.   It proved very popular, and after extensive alterations was reopened by Lord Stamp in 1937. The cost (£3,000) was borne by the L.M.S. Railway Company.[1]

[1] *C.G.*, all December issues, 1906, 17.12.17, 18.1.18, 16.2.21, 14.12.23 ; *C.Ch.*, 24.12.38.

Types of Railway Company's Houses

CHAPTER III

THE HISTORY OF CREWE RAILWAY WORKS AND ENGINE SHEDS

I. Development and Employment

WHEN the works commenced production in March, 1843, the locomotive department seems to have been intended merely for the repair of engines, while the coachmaking and waggon departments were to be used both for repair and manufacture. The original area of the works comprised 2½ acres and in the beginning the number of men employed—" The Pioneers of 1843 "—numbered 161. This formed the nucleus of the " Old Works." Soon it was decided to use the works for the manufacture of locomotives, the first being completed on February 20, 1845.[1] This engine, the " Columbine," is preserved in the Railway Museum at York.

A newspaper reporter has left us the following account of the new railway works as they existed at the beginning of 1846 :—

". . . the workshops . . . cover no less than thirty acres, in the more acute portion of the angle. On the right, you turn into a large apartment fitted up for building new wagons ; it opens into another still larger, and here wagons are repaired. Further on is the forge where the iron work of Mr. [Owen] Owens' department (the wagon-shops) is executed. The fan is used instead of the bellows ; but here, as in all the other smithies, bellows are erected in the event of the fan failing. Turning round from the wagon department, you enter the coach-building room, in continuation of which are the repairing shop and smithy attached. . . .

" The next great wing of the building is devoted to the locomotive department. It presents the aspects of a polytechnic institution : all

---

[1] Supplement to *Railway Gazette*, Sept. 16, 1938, p. 72. Information for this chapter has been found in *Description of the London & North-Western Railway Company's Locomotive Works at Crewe*, 1903, 1913 (official guides) ; *Cassier's Magazine*, Sept. 1903, pp. 393–407 ; Oct., 1903, pp. 19–33 ; Sir. F. B. Head : *Stokers and Pokers*, 1849, pp. 100–12 ; *Chambers' Edinburgh Journal*, Jan. 31, 1846, pp. 77–9 ; June 22, 1850, pp. 391–3 ; *Jubilee of Crewe*, 1887 ; *Times* (*L.M.S. Supplement*), Sept. 20, 1938 ; *Railway Magazine*, Sept.–Oct., 1944, pp. 282–6 ; Nov.–Dec., 1944, pp. 341–3 ; March–April, 1949, pp. 76–8.

the vast implements of engineering science seem gathered together here. Planing machines of all forms and sizes fill up the centre, connected with endless straps to a power-transmitting drum ; while on either side were lathes, punching, shearing and cutting machines. . . . In the extreme wing is the brass foundry and brass work. . . .

" Adjoining is the Locomotive waiting-room . . . where engines are kept always ready under steam pressure in case of accident, and where all undergo examination. A new one was under trial, and it afforded us an opportunity of examining some recent improvements of Mr. Allan's.

" Not the least marvellous thing about this extensive establishment was the fact that the power which moved all the machinery throughout the buildings, covering thirty acres, was transmitted from one steam-engine of 20-horse power, worked on the Cornish or expansive principle. The arrangements secure the most perfect division of labour, and although six hundred men are employed, there was a total absence of bustle, hurry, or confusion. Each man, like the machinery, seemed to fall naturally into his own place."

The demands of the locomotive department for space compelled the removal of the waggon department to Edgehill and Ordsall Lane, Manchester, in 1847, pending final concentration at Earlestown in 1853.[1] Constant factors in the expansion of the locomotive department were the tendency for the various lines to amalgamate, and the construction of branches and extensions to old-established lines. Another factor was the increase in the speed and weight of locomotives generally, which added to Crewe's importance as the central point of a growing system. The following figures illustrate the process admirably :—

	Mileage of L.N.W.R.		Mileage of L.N.W.R.
1846	247	1890	1,877
1870	1,506	1921	2,066 [2]

From 1846 to 1862, however, the triple origin of the L.N.W.R. remained evident from the fact that its lines were divided into three territories. The North-Eastern Division was composed chiefly of the former Manchester and Birmingham Railway, and

[1] G.J.B.M., July 1, 1840 ; Feb. 8, May 31, 1843 ; *Chester Courant*, Dec. 12 1843 ; Crewe Ctee., L.N.W.B., Feb. 9, 1847 ; C.M., Feb. 27, 1847.

[2] Suppt. to *Railway Gazette*, Sept. 16, 1938, p. 29 ; see also G.J.B.M., April 9, 1845 ; C. E. Stretton : *History of the L.N.W.R. Co.*, pp. 5–6.

locomotives continued to be manufactured at the Longsight depot until 1857. The Northern Division, with Crewe as its centre, consisted in 1848 of the lines " from Birmingham to Liverpool ; Rugby to Stafford ; Crewe to Holyhead ; Liverpool to Manchester and Warrington to Preston ; Preston to Carlisle." The third division, the Southern, comprised all the lines south and west of Birmingham ; from 1846 to 1861 the locomotive superintendent of this division, with his headquarters at Wolverton, was the redoubtable J. E. McConnell. At Longsight John Ramsbottom was superintendent from 1842 to 1857, and at Crewe Francis Trevithick held the post of locomotive superintendent from 1841 until 1857.[1]

By 1846 the men employed at Crewe had increased to 600, by 1847 to 1,100, and during the peak year, 1848, the number in all departments reached 1,600, 800 of whom were in the locomotive department. Late in 1848, an observer noted :— ". . . the establishment has turned out a new engine and tender on every Monday morning since the 1st of January, 1848."[2]

In 1848 Head estimated the total population of Crewe at about 8,000, but an observer of 1850, when the local and long-remembered depression was at its height wrote :—" The number of hands employed at present is about eight hundred ; but formerly when railways were more prosperous than now, it exceeded a thousand."[3] Many of the new settlers left the town, and the number of men employed reached its lowest level, 451, in October, 1850 ; by 1851 the total population had fallen to 4,571. Renewed activity in the railway world came in 1852, and in that year Trevithick reported that there were 827 men in his employ.[4]

An additional branch of the railway industry, a rail-rolling mill, commenced production on July 10, 1853. It was topically but unofficially christened the " California Works," presumably

---

[1] *Proc. Inst. Mech. Eng.*, 1897, pp. 236–41 ; Steel : *History of the L.N.W.R. Co.*, pp. 267–70 ; Head, *op. cit.*, p. 100.

[2] Head : *op cit.*, p. 100 ; *cf.* C.G., 27.5.76.

[3] *Chambers' Edinburgh Journal*, vol. xiii (1850), pp. 391–2.

[4] Crewe Ctee., L.N.W.B., Feb. 13, 1849, Nov. 2, 1852 ; for the effect of the depression on the town see A.R.C.M.I. 1849 ; C.C.F.S., Ann. Rep. 1849–50 ; C.G., 2.9.71 (Allman's speech). Whittle said of this period : " Some of the streets were deserted, Manchester Street being nearly all boarded up, as no inhabitants wanted houses " (C.G., 24.4.80).

because it had the same effect locally as did the gold strike of 1849 in the U.S.A. The same year saw wrought iron manufactured at Crewe for the first time. In the 1860's and 1870's the rail-mill was one of the most up-to-date units in the country, in that "cogging" by rollers had been substituted for "cogging" by steam hammers. In 1866 John Ramsbottom, Chief Mechanical Engineer, L.N.W.R., invented a second improvement in rail-rolling practice, and initiated it at Crewe. He applied a reversing engine to the driving of the rollers, so that heavy iron plates which had passed through the rollers could be passed back through them in the reverse direction. This greatly simplified the handling problem, since up to that time the hot metal had been moved back over the top of the rollers to its original position for its second passage through the mill. What is technically known as a "three high" rail-mill, although previously declared to be unsuitable to English conditions of production, was introduced at the Crewe establishment in 1876.[1]

The appointment of John Ramsbottom, the "father of the modern locomotive," as locomotive superintendent at Crewe in 1857 marked the beginning of a period of reorganisation, concentration and bold innovation. By 1859, 700 men were employed in the coachmaking department and 1,500 in the locomotive department. The latter ousted the coachmaking department, which was temporarily moved to Saltley, near Birmingham, in 1859–60, under Ramsbottom's reorganisation scheme. In 1865 the manufacture of L.N.W.R. railway carriages was concentrated wholly at Wolverton, although a carriage repair department, employing about 400 men in 1905, was maintained at Crewe until 1932. Ramsbottom amalgamated the North-Eastern division with the Northern in 1857, and concentrated at Crewe the work of engine construction formerly carried out at Longsight. In 1862 similar treatment was accorded to the Southern Division on Ramsbottom's advice. Henceforward, locomotives were made exclusively at Crewe, although repair shops remained at Wolverton until 1877.[2]

[1] D. L. Burn : *Econ. Hist. of Steelmaking, 1867–1939* (1940), pp. 53, 56-7, 59–60.
[2] Exec. Ctee., L.N.W.B., Sept. 14, 1855 ; Feb. 26, 1857 ; Gen. and Loco. Ctee., L.N.W.B., Aug. 11, 1859, Jan. 25, 1860 ; Steel : *op. cit.*, pp. 267, 270 ; White 1860, p. 344 ; *C.G.*, 27.1.77.

Crewe Works played an important rôle in the early history of the Bessemer process for making steel. Sir Henry Bessemer had invented his new process of steelmaking in 1856, and soon afterwards he suggested steel rails to John Ramsbottom :—" Mr. Ramsbottom, looking at me with astonishment, and almost with anger, said : ' Mr. Bessemer, do you wish to see me tried for manslaughter ? ' "[1] Exhaustive tests, however, convinced Ramsbottom of the new material's utility for the purpose, and the first Bessemer steel rails in the world were laid down at Crewe station on November 9–10, 1861. They proved so satisfactory that in 1864 the company opened its own Bessemer steelmaking plant at Crewe ; this swelled the number of workers on the company's payroll at Crewe to over 3,000, and began the rapid urbanisation of the west end of the township. To establish these works, it was necessary to go outside the " Old Works " to Coppenhall Heyes.

An interesting survey of the workshop organisation at the end of Trevithick's tenure of office, which incidentally reveals that the works were among the most up-to-date engineering establishments in the country, is given in the 1857 edition of Kelly's *Directory of Cheshire* :—

" The increase of traffic and consequent demand for engine-power have caused further buildings to be added ; they comprise two erecting shops, one of which is capable of containing 40 engines undergoing repair at one time ; here are four patent travelling cranes, by which an engine in part, or even when completed, can be removed with the greatest ease and facility to any part of the building ; the fitting shop is of large dimension for the purpose of preparing the work for the erecting shop ; 300 men are employed in this alone ; there are also two turning shops, where the wheels and other machinery are turned, the machinery of which is very valuable, and consists of drilling, planing, shaping and slotting machines, also several turning-lathes, nearly the whole of which are by Whitworth, of Manchester ; the forge . . . contains, besides all the requisite machinery, four of Nasmyth's patent hammers ; the whole of this department is worked by three stationary engines."

The building of a new erecting shop in 1861 marked the end of development in the " Old Works " area. Up to 1864–5 the Chester and Holyhead trains had run through the centre of the

[1] Sir H. Bessemer : *Autobiography*, p. 335.

works, but owing to the increase in traffic this line was then diverted, and the land inside the loop, known as the " Deviation," was utilised for fresh workshops, the first of which was occupied in 1867. This forms the second part of Crewe Works. From 1867 onwards, most of the new buildings were placed in the third portion of the works round the Coppenhall Heyes steel plant. For example, in 1875 the old " California " rail-mill was dismantled and the larger " three high " one, built in its place, was removed to the neighbourhood of the steelworks in 1892. By 1913 the whole works covered 137 acres, of which 48 were roofed over.

It was not until 1872, after F. W. Webb had succeeded Ramsbottom as Chief Mechanical Engineer, that steel was manufactured on a large scale at Crewe. In that year Webb first used steel for locomotive boilers, and in spite of the misgivings of other engineers, the experiment proved entirely successful. Webb was also a practical advocate of steel sleepers (of which he laid the first in 1880) and of steel castings. The 1870's witnessed the installation of equipment for making mild steel by the new Siemens-Martin ferro-manganese process, and in 1901 the Bessemer process was abandoned. As late as 1926, completely up-to-date acid and basic furnaces were installed. Between 1864 and 1932 nearly 3,100,000 tons of steel were produced at Crewe, but in the latter year, faced by an estimated expenditure of £120,000 for a modern rail-mill, the L.M.S.R. Company came to an agreement with the leading firms in the steel industry to close down the two establishments for a period of ten years. The steel manufacturers used their power to transport their products by road instead of rail as a bargaining counter.[1]   The

---

[1] *Illustrated London News*, Jan. 19, 1861, p. 64 ; Bessemer :- *op. cit.*, p. 336 (see also Sir J. H. Clapham : *Econ. Hist. Mod. Britain*, vol. ii, p. 56) ; Morris 1864, p. 74 ; *C.G.*, 6 and 13.10.77, 12.8.85, 31.7.86 ; *C.Ch.*, 17.12.38. In connection with the closing down of the Crewe steelworks, the remarks of the latest historian of the British steel industry are particularly instructive :— " A steel plant which had a secured outlet for part or all of its make would be in a very strong position whatever its production costs if the finishing branch of the concern was occupied in an industry in which competition was not close, or where the cost of the steel was only a minor part in the cost of the finished product. An extreme instance of this occurred where a railway company possessed its own steelworks, as the L.N.W.R. did at Crewe. At the outset this particular integration was part of a far-sighted policy of using

Barrow and Workington works received the Crewe mill's rail-making quota.[1]

F. W. Webb, Chief Mechanical Engineer, L.N.W.R., 1871–1903, carried the principle of concentrating the departments much further than Ramsbottom, but at the same time he diversified the industries carried on at Crewe and endeavoured to manufacture as many of the articles needed on the railway as possible. In 1873 signals, hitherto bought from private firms, were made for the first time at Crewe ; by 1875 this department employed 112 men. A leather works, a soap-works and brick-works, the last with a capacity of over 6 million bricks per annum (1875–6), were all to be found on his domain at Crewe. Even footwarmers for winter railway travel, and artificial limbs for men injured in the company's service, have been manufactured in the works.[2]

One setback, however, occurred at the beginning of Webb's reign. In March, 1876, the private manufacturers of locomotives obtained and served on the L.N.W.R. an injunction restraining it from manufacturing, as *ultra vires*, "locomotive engines or other rolling stock for sale or hire," *i.e.* except those required for its own purposes. The private manufacturers had become alarmed at the facility with which engines could be turned out, and at the resources which the company possessed for undercutting in home and foreign markets during trade depressions. The injunction confined the company's operations within the strict limit of its own requirements and made any fluctuations in railway traffic more keenly felt in Crewe. The manufacturers' fears were fully justified, for in a busy year, the twelve months ending November 30, 1872, Crewe Works could turn out 146 locomotives. In 1878 Webb, to find what could be done in an emergency, caused an engine to be assembled in $25\frac{1}{2}$ hours.[3]

---

steel, and valuable pioneer work resulted. Later the plant had relatively high prime costs, in part, no doubt, because the consumption of a single railway did not warrant the equipment, which fully employed, had the lowest costs ; but no competitor could count on driving the plant out of business " (Burn : *op. cit.*, pp. 245–6).

[1] Burn : *op. cit.*, p. 452, note.

[2] C.G., 20.2.75, 6 and 13.10.77, 28.12.87, 21.9.89 ; Steel : *op. cit.*, p. 352.

[3] C.G., 27.5.76, 9.2.78 ; Steel : *op. cit.*, pp. 341, 446–7 ; injunction printed in *Jubilee of Crewe*, p. 17.

The production of engines has been as follows :—

Year.	Locomotive.	Year.	Locomotive.
1845	1st	1887	3,000th
1866	1,000th	1900	4,000th
1876	2,000th	1911	5,000th

The growth of railway bureaucracy is exemplified by the erection of the locomotive department's new general offices in 1876 and their extension in 1900–1.   George Wadsworth is the first chief accountant of the locomotive department concerning whom there is record.   He held office for the thirty years up to 1885, when the clerical staff in the general offices and the works departments totalled 600.   His successor, Kenneth Macrae, "initiated an elaborate system of accountancy in connection with the locomotive department of the L.N.W.R. Company, which was adopted by most of the principal lines."   He held office from 1886 until 1909.[1]   The first typewriter entered the offices in the early 1890's, but although Webb had installed electric light and a telephone in his office in 1879, the general offices as a whole do not appear to have enjoyed these facilities until 1892.   Later in the 1890's Webb installed an electric power station in the works and by 1903 electricity was "rapidly superseding steam power in all the shops" for driving machinery.[2]

From 1906 onwards persistent efforts were made to apply the principles of "scientific management" to the works, which now appeared more than adequate for the needs of the company. Many workers between the ages of sixty-five and seventy, and some over seventy, were weeded out ; the works could no longer absorb their output of time-expired apprentices, and there existed a state of almost chronic "short time" working.   The war of 1914–18 eased matters temporarily, and men over seventy were re-engaged while the immediate post-war years provided work in plenty which had been postponed on account of military demands. The number of men employed rose to a record height :—

Year.	No. employed in Crewe Railway Works.	Year.	No. employed in Crewe Railway Works.
1861	1,795	1913	7,000
1877	6,000	1920	10,051
1903	7,500	1938	6,520

[1] Works Ctee., 11.9.00 ; *C.G.*, 6.1.86, 13 and 20.2.86, 20 and 23.1.92, 24.5.18, 15.4.21 ; *C.Ch.*, 3.7.86, 23.1.92.

[2] *C.G.*, 9.2.78 ; *C.Ch.*, 6.2.92 ; private information.

The Railways Act of 1921 brought with it problems of readjustment. The Lancashire and Yorkshire Railway, with its works at Horwich, the North Staffordshire Railway, with works at Stoke, and the Midland Railway, with its great Derby works, became, with the L.N.W.R. Company, the London Midland and Scottish Railway from January 1, 1923. Captain H. P. M. Beames, Chief Mechanical Engineer, L.N.W.R., 1920–1, placed the problem before the public thus in 1921 :—" We have lost our monopoly, and I want every man in Crewe to understand that. We are in competition."

After 1923 the Stoke works were closed down and some of the men transferred to Crewe, but the greatest rivalry ensued between Crewe and Derby. A great reorganisation scheme costing £750,000 was therefore carried out at Crewe in 1926–8, and the first locomotive under the new régime rolled out of the workshops on May 5, 1927. The effect of the reorganisation was to place the works on the " belt system," so that in most departments the task now comes to the man, and not the man to the task, as was usually the case before. The speed of repair has also been increased and the claim was made in 1938 that as much work could be done with 6,500 men as was performed in the early 1920's with 10,000.[1]

II. INDUSTRIAL FLUCTUATIONS IN CREWE WORKS

In the earliest days of the railway colony the men started work at 6 a.m., winter and summer, and finished at 5.30 p.m., except on Saturday when the works closed at 4 p.m. Allowing $1\frac{1}{2}$ hours per day for meals, this gives a week of $58\frac{1}{2}$ hours. It must be remembered that this was merely the standard day and that overtime occurred frequently in busy periods. In the 1840's the workers were summoned to their posts by a bell, but on account of the growth of the works and town this became inaudible on the outskirts and was replaced by a " steam gong " in 1862, the ancestor of the present " buzzer." From the beginning the engineering tasks in the works were based on the individual piecework system, under which the worker accepted job and price directly from the foreman, representing the works manager, and was paid through an office, in contrast to the piece-master

[1] *C.G.*, all December issues, 1906 ; 5.7.73, 7.3.11 ; *Times Financial Supplements*, Aug. 23, 1911 ; Feb. 17, 1912 ; *C.G.*, 24.12.20, 19.8.21, 11 and 29.11.21.

system, in which the piece-master accepted job and price, and in some cases paid the engineers. The difference was vividly expressed by the secretary of the Crewe No. 1 Branch of the Amalgamated Society of Engineers who, in reply to a question from the union regarding piece-masters, wrote in 1861 :— " There is nothing of this kind here, every man and boy stands on his own bottom " ! [1]

In 1848 some of the men petitioned to be allowed to cease work at 1 p.m. on Saturdays and to work till 6 p.m. on the other days, but other workers counter-petitioned against the proposal and matters remained as they were until 1858, when the original request was granted.   The works now closed at 6 p.m. on week-days and at 12.30 p.m. on Saturday. The $58\frac{1}{2}$-hour week remained in force till the end of 1871, by which date the Nine Hours Movement was spreading throughout the country.   In the north as a whole the Nine Hours League organised the move-ment, but no evidence exists that this body possessed any influ-ence with the Crewe workers.   They were inspired rather by the example of the engineers at Newcastle-on-Tyne, and sent over £200 to help the successful unofficial strike on the north-east coast.   At a great meeting in the Corn Exchange on October 28, 1871, all grades of men employed in the works helped to pass the following resolution :—

" That . . . the present hours of labour are too protracted and that an earnest effort should be made by us to have them reduced to nine hours per day, and thus give greater facilities for the advancement of our social, domestic and intellectual pursuits."

A representative committee drew up a memorial to the directors on the subject ; this was entrusted to F. W. Webb by James Robertson on November 1, and ten days later the directors announced the granting of the concession, which came into force as from January 1, 1872.   The new hours were arranged as follows:—

Monday to Friday	6 a.m. to 8.15 a.m.
	9 a.m. to 1 p.m.
	2 p.m. to 5.30 p.m.
Saturday	6 a.m. to 8.15 a.m.
	9 a.m. to 12 noon

---

[1] Head : *op. cit.*, p. 109 ; *Cheshire Observer,* March 15, 1862 ; A.R.C.M.I., 1852 ; Exec. Ctee., L.N.W.B., Feb. 26, 1857 ; Gen. and Loco. Ctee., L.N.W.B., July 27, 1859 ; *Economic History Review,* vol. xvii, no. 1 (1947), pp. 39–40.

Many of the labourers seized the opportunity given by the Saturday half-holiday to migrate into the surrounding countryside and supplement their earnings by helping with the harvest. These hours remained unchanged until the beginning of 1919, when the 47 hours week was introduced in lieu of the 54 hours week. The new hours meant the final abolition of the uneconomic and unpopular 6 a.m. beginning to the day's work :—

Monday to Friday	8 a.m.	to 12.30 p.m.
	1.30 p.m.	to 5.35 p.m.
Saturday	8 a.m.	to 12.5 p.m.

With slight modifications these hours still obtained on the outbreak of the second World War, but from 1926 to 1939 the works were rarely open on Saturdays, so that in practice a five-day week of 43 hours existed.

For some years before 1892 it had been the custom to close the works at Whitsun for a week's holiday without pay. In 1892 this holiday was switched from Whitsun to July, and it became a week's holiday with pay in 1938.[1] The granting of unlimited railway tickets to all railway employees at a quarter of the standard fare, in 1890, stimulated a wider use of leisure, and in 1892 this privilege was extended to the North Staffordshire lines. Finally, in 1905, negotiations secured inter-availability of quarter-fares on all lines in Great Britain.[2]

On the whole, the industrial history of Crewe Works has been a peaceful one. In 1848, owing to the incipient depression, wages were reduced, and, in spite of a deputation of fitters and smiths to the directors, the reduction remained. Yet by 1852 overtime was being worked again. A short unemployment crisis occurred in 1855–6, another in 1859–60 on account of the removal of the coachmaking department, and a puddlers' strike

[1] Crewe Ctee., L.N.W.B., March 24, 1848 ; Exec. Ctee., L.N.W.B., March 16, 1858 ; C.G., 4 and 18.11.71, 27.12.18 ; S. and B. Webb : *History of Trade Unionism*, 2nd ed., 1920, pp. 314–15 ; E.A. 91, p. 169 ; E.A. 92, p. 202 ; E.A. 93, p. 213 ; C.Ch., 9.7.38. The Nine Hours Movement spread to the employees of the Crewe Co-operative Friendly Society and to the Local Board's labourers on the Sewage Farm in the course of 1872 (C.L.B.M., Feb. 8, June 20 and 27, 1872).

[2] C.G., 18.6.90, 2.7.90, 14.9.92, 9.11.92, 30.12.05. The negotiations were carried on by committees of the employees which later formed themselves into an organised movement still in existence.

lasted for three months in the beginning of 1864 ; the majority of the men left Crewe for Liverpool.[1]

The prosperity of the early 1870's brought rising prices, especially in foodstuffs and coal.   In August, 1872, the Crewe employees of the locomotive department petitioned for a 10 per cent. increase in wages, but the directors only met some of the demands and succeeded in dividing the fitters, who accepted their offer, from the engine erectors, who did not.   The labourers and other grades remained unsatisfied ; meetings were held, but as strike action was deprecated nothing more resulted than vague talk about a " union," and blame for the skilled mechanics, who had deserted them once they had " got their advance nice and comfortably."   There was also in 1872 a movement among the Crewe station staff, drivers and firemen, for more wages and shorter hours ; this resulted in the formation of a short-lived branch of the new Amalgamated Society of Railway Servants.[2]

The boom conditions of the early 1870's were followed by a slump, of which Crewe felt the effects in the course of 1876. This marked for Crewe the beginning of the period of industrial fluctuation, afterwards labelled in the outside world " The Great Depression."   It lasted with intervals until 1896.   Contemporaries felt compelled to hark back to the well-remembered first depression :—" Never since 1851 has trade been so backward in the Crewe Works as it is at the present time." [3]   The railway authorities decided that the works, for the first time in their history, should be placed on " short time," *i.e.* a five-day week starting at 9 a.m. on Mondays.   The men agreed " through their delegates " to this course, as an alternative to dismissals ; the " short time " started in July, 1876, and ended in March, 1877.

[1] L.N.W.B., Aug. 8, 1848 ; see *supra* ; A.R.C.M.I., 1852 ; *Cheshire Observer*, Feb. 27 and June 25, 1864.

[2] R. Whittle : *Narrative of Events*, p. 14 ; C.G., 24.2.72, 9.3.72, 18.5.72, 10 and 24.8.72, 9.5.74, 13.3.75.   Information about the rates of wages paid in Crewe Works is so scanty that adequate treatment is impossible.   In 1872 a labourer received from 14s. to 18s. a week on full time ; this became 19s. for all labourers in 1906.   Skilled tradesmen received from 25s. to 30s. per week before 1872 ; after this there was a tendency for more men to receive about 30s. and for fewer to remain at 25s.   Thirty shillings per week continued to be the usual wage of a skilled tradesman until 1914 (C.G., 6.11.78, 18.10.79, 3.11.06, 16.5.19).   [3] C.G., 17.6.76.

Unfortunately the revival proved a temporary one and " short time " was resumed in 1878 ; it lasted until the beginning of 1880.[1]

The early 1880's seem to have been extremely prosperous, but in January, 1885, dismissals from the works began, and by the end of the year " short time " was again being worked ; in spite of another revival of brief duration in 1886–7, it continued into June, 1888. 1889 saw demands for wage increases, which were unsuccessful. This led to the formation of the General Railway Workers' Union, and to an increase in the activities of the newly resurrected branch of the A.S.R.S. In 1890 wage increases became general, and overtime was worked for about eight months in 1890–1. Towards October, 1891, we hear of discontent in the works concerning wage-rates, and of dismissals for demanding higher wages. In November a lock-out occurred in the forge on account of the refusal of the men to accept lower piece-rates. The lowering of rates remained a source of great unrest throughout the works during the winter of 1891–2. The coal strike of 1892 interfered with normal working in the forge and rail-rolling mill, but worse was to follow in the winter of 1892–3, when dismissals became alarmingly frequent and brought with them the first local suggestions for old-age pensions.

In June, 1893, almost the entire works went on " short time," after a considerable number of dismissals. In August a further curtailment of hours took place on account of the continued coal crisis, and a four-day week came into operation, *i.e.* the works opened at 9 a.m. on Monday and closed at 5.30 p.m. on Thursday. In addition to this, the chief coal-consuming departments had to be closed down entirely, not only because of the coal shortage, but also on account of certain rearrangements which were taking place at the rail-mills, the steel furnaces and the forge. It was not until January, 1894, that even the five-day week, *i.e.* normal " short time," was restored. Dismissals went on, and full-time working was only gradually restored in the course of 1895. In 1896–7 observers noticed for the first time, with some disquiet, that many young Crewe mechanics were leaving the town and entering cycle and motor-car works,

[1] *C.G.*, 15.7.76, 16.12.76, 21.1.77, 3.3.77, 6.11.78, 11.2.80, 13.3.80, 29.5.80 ; *C.Ch.*, 27.6.76 ; *Co-operative News*, Feb. 14, 1880, p. 108.

chiefly in the Midlands.   Yet it was not generally realised until 1906–11 that the works' annual output of trained young engineers could no longer be absorbed, and that Crewe must either have new engineering industries or stagnate.   The temporary expansion of the personnel in the works during the early 1920's merely masked the real outlines of a problem which had been present since the local " Great Depression " of the 1880's and 1890's. The 47-hour week could have been introduced many years before 1919.

Meanwhile, general overtime succeeded general full time in 1898.   In October of that year the greatest pitch of activity ever known was reached, and general prosperity continued until July, 1899.   Overtime reappeared in 1901, and continued in certain sections for eighteen months.   " Short time " was re-imposed towards the end of 1903, and continued to be the general rule until the winter of 1905–6, when practically full time was resumed.   1906 is noteworthy for a deputation to the chief mechanical engineer and works manager with a view to an all-round increase in wages, which resulted in a definite promise that piece-work and day-work rates should be frequently revised. Dismissals of old men between the ages of sixty-five and eighty were carried out in December, 1906 ; " short time " was staved off until January, 1909, by this weeding-out and by " sacking " time-expired apprentices, but so slack had conditions become by 1910 that some sections of the works were only operating three and three-quarter days per week.   This bout of " short time " lasted nearly three years, full-time working being gradually resumed in 1911, aided by the dismissal of 250 men at the end of that year.[1]   Industrial activity throughout Britain reached its peak in 1913–14, the apex of the great price-rise and export boom which had succeeded the so-called " Great Depression," and this was reflected in Crewe Works, where 1913 was an extremely busy year.   In 1911 the Crewe branches of the various craft unions represented in the works set up the Railway Workers' Joint Committee, in order to put forward more effectively a demand on the management for the higher Manchester district rates of pay.   The Committee proved of great service in wages and hours negotiations during the war of 1914–18, when two of

[1] *Cf. C.G.,* 6.10.11 : " Crewe Works are too large . . . the number of men employed in them is larger than is actually necessary."

its most active members were Councillor W. H. Price, the first secretary, and Alderman Charles Bates, J.P., now of Derby, who left Crewe in 1918.[1]

III. Crewe Station and the Steam Sheds

The Crewe station of 1837 was a very modest affair compared with the labyrinth which greets the passing traveller today. It comprised " a very neat house for the clerk of the Station," together with an " engine-house with a spare engine always ready for use." [2] In 1838 discretionary orders were given to keep " assistant power in readiness at Crewe throughout the night if necessary." A goods station was opened in 1842, and on account of Crewe's growth an entirely new passenger station of the usual early Victorian type had to be built in 1845-6 :—" a magnificent structure . . . with offices, waiting rooms and every convenience. The platforms are covered by an ornamental roof, supported by handsome cast pillars, surmounted by carved oak figures." [3]

Crewe rapidly became one of the most important junctions in the country, but not until the years after 1857 was full advantage taken of its central position :—". . . in Mr. Trevithick's time it was the practice to have as few engines at Crewe as possible but to send them out to Rugby, Chester and Holyhead, and other stations." So said John Rigg, assistant locomotive superintendent from 1857 to 1877. He came from Longsight to Crewe with John Ramsbottom when the latter superseded Trevithick in 1857. In that year Crewe steam sheds contained space for only 16 engines, and employed a mere 64 persons. The completion of a " leviathan " steam shed in 1865 marked the beginning of a process which by 1878 raised the number of locomotives based on Crewe to 140 and the number of drivers, firemen and cleaners employed to 560. This meant that drivers and firemen could be more strictly graded ; the trip system was

---

[1] *Crewe Guardian* and *Crewe Chronicle* newspapers, *passim*, 1880–1923.
[2] See woodcut in *Illustrated London News*, Dec. 23, 1843, p. 405, and map in Municipal Buildings, Crewe ; Osborne : *op cit.*, pp. 216–17 ; G.J.B.M., Oct. 27, 1838.
[3] Bagshaw 1850, p. 368,

introduced in the 1860's and 1870's, and a considerable speeding-up effected thereby.[1]

A new station to replace that of 1845–6 was erected in 1867. Both goods and passenger trains passed through the station itself, so that as early as 1873 " a chronic state of block " existed owing to the enormous increase of traffic.   About 50 acres of land along the line from Shavington to Crewe were purchased in that year for the purpose of adding to the accommodation for goods.   Many improvements to the passenger station were carried out in 1878, and the entrance dates from this year.

In 1890 the first steps were taken towards the construction of large new goods sidings at Basford, but by 1893 congestion had reached such a pitch that it became imperative to reconstruct the whole station.   The plans received approval in 1895, and involved the total separation of passenger from goods traffic. To effect this, a great excavation had to be made to the west of the existing station, and about 35 miles of new lines were laid down for goods traffic.   The work of excavation, known locally as the " Big Dig," lasted from 1896 to 1901, employed well over a thousand men from 1898 onwards, and cost about £500,000. Before this extension the station covered 93 acres, after it, 223 acres. Most of the increase was due to the new goods sorting sidings. The station could now deal more efficiently with the 593 trains which passed through it daily in 1898.[2]

At the same time, a new method of dealing with goods travelling cross-country was adopted, and a new tranship shed came into use in 1901.   Under the energetic management of F. W. West, the local goods agent, the transhipment and sorting of goods was speeded up, and a large number of operating staff brought into Crewe from smaller stations.   For this new method of concentration Crewe provided the ideal geographical centre, and the number of tons dealt with rose year by year.   About 400 men were employed.[3]

After the goods station difficulty had been tackled and solved,

[1] *C.G.*, 9.2.78, 5.9.78, 3.10.78 ; *Cheshire Observer*, July 4, 1863.

[2] *C.G.*, 22.11.73, 11.10.90, 18.4.91, 12.8.91, 2.12.93, 6.1.94, 1.12.94, 5.1.95, 2.1.97, 15.1.98, 8.2.99, 8.4.99, 13.4.01, 4.6.04 ; *C.Ch.*, 5, 12 and 19.9.96 ; Kelly 1878, p. 160.

[3] *C.G.*, 10.8.01, 20.12.02, 24.1.03, 6.2.04, 4.6.04, 27.1.06, 10.2.06, 1 and 15.12.06, 13.4.07, 25.1.08, 6.2.09, 26.1.10.

the enlargement of the passenger station was undertaken in 1903–6. This resulted in the practical doubling of its size by the addition of the present platforms 1 and 2. Few structural changes have taken place since that period, when the area of the platforms became stabilised at 4¾ acres and their total length at 3,790 yards.[1] In 1896, the South Steam Sheds were erected, as part of the reorganisation scheme, to deal with goods engines, while the North Sheds concentrated on passenger locomotives. Mechanical coaling plant was installed in 1913, at which date more than 700 men found employment at the two sets of sheds.[2]

In 1903 the Electric Signal and Telegraph Departments at Crewe were amalgamated, and it was found necessary to build a range of offices for them in Gresty Road, in close proximity to the railway station. These were opened in 1904. Crewe lost the Electrical Engineering Department in 1909–10, when it was removed to London in view of developments in surburban electrification in that area. The constructional work, however, continued to be performed at Crewe.[3]

[1] *C.G.*, 28.3.03, 30.5.03, 4.6.04, 30.6.06, 24.11.06, 5.6.07.
[2] *C.Ch.*, 2.1.97 ; *C.G.*, 26.9.13, 30.1.14.
[3] *C.G.*, 27.6.03, 12.9.03, 20.1.04, 18.1.08, 6.3.14 ; Works Ctee., 8.8.03. In 1914 the staffs of the Central Control, Time and Rolling Stock Departments were brought from various places and concentrated at Crewe.

L.N.W.R. WORKS MANAGERS AT CREWE,
1854–1920

Thomas Hunt	1854–61
F. W. Webb	1861–6
W. H. Kampf	1870–1
T. W. Worsdell	1871–81
Charles Dick	1881–8
H. D. Earl	1888–1903
A. R. Trevithick	1903–10
W. W. H. Warneford . . .	1910–16
H. P. M. Beames	1916–20

CHAPTER IV

THE PROBLEM OF CREWE'S AUXILIARY INDUSTRIES

" The establishment of various Manufactories in Crewe, such as Compton and Co., Rylands and Co., the Fustian Cutting Factories, and the Printing and Publishing Company, are hopeful evidences of Crewe's future greatness. These give occupation to the large surplus female labour, to the daughters of mechanics who object to go to service, and who are unable to learn a trade elsewhere."—EARDLEY'S *Crewe Borough Almanack*, 1878, p. 3.

IN the mid-nineteenth century Crewe was relatively more dependent on the railway company economically than it is now, and the employment provided by the works was then, as it is now, for men only. Crewe differed in this respect from the textile towns of Lancashire, Yorkshire and North Cheshire, where men and women from the same family worked together in the mills. This phenomenon was noted early as 1847 by one of Her Majesty's Inspectors of Schools, who said of the company's National school :—" The girls stop longer than in other schools, as there is no employment for them. The boys are taken away at an early age to the Works." [1] This " surplus female labour," as it came to be called, remained a matter of great concern to the leading men of the town, and there were several attempts to absorb it by attracting the cotton industry to Crewe. A cotton-spinning mill at Nantwich continued to work until 1874, and this project did not therefore appear so chimerical as it would today.[2]

What appears to be the first attempt to make Crewe less of a " one-industry town " was, however, connected with the dairy-farming industry. During the local depression of 1848–51, the tradesmen and farmers of Crewe formed a Cheese and Cattle Fair Committee with the object of making the town the selling and distributing centre for the staple agricultural products of South Cheshire, a position held at that time by Nantwich and Sandbach. When the company laid out the town of Crewe in the 1840's, a large square was left vacant in Coppenhall Terrace

[1] *Minutes of Ctee. of Coun. on Educ.* (1847–8), vol. ii., pp. 162–3.
[2] W. H. Chaloner : *Hist. of the Cotton Manufacture in Nantwich, 1785–1874* (1938).

and came to be called the Market Place or Square. Until 1854 this was the sole market accommodation for the weekly produce sales on Saturday. Following complaints of high prices and insufficient vendors caused by " want of proper shelter," the L.N.W.R. Company caused a roof to be placed over the Square, " like a series of huge square or longitudinal umbrellas built on low pillars." [1] This did not satisfy the leading men of the new colony, and the Cheese Fair Committee pressed for a more substantial market building. Bagshaw gave the programme for the " Great Central Cattle and Cheese Fairs " to be held at Crewe in 1850 for " two consecutive days every three months." [2] In 1852 the directors of the company caused plans to be prepared for a permanent Cheese Market at Crewe, " the cost of which would be about £2,000," besides an additional sum for land and for side lines of rail, making in all about £3,000, and actually obtained tenders for its construction. They finally decided, however, that the project " would not be a proper application of the shareholders' money." [3] Upon this the builder and railway contractor, John Hill, came forward " when others were chicken-hearted, and . . . proposed that it should be done by shares, but the shareholders did not come forward." Hill showed his faith in Crewe's future by undertaking the work himself " upon a plan and under regulations to be approved by the Directors." In spite of the objections of the agricultural interest of the district, which feared a monopoly, John Hill's Cheese Hall was opened with great ceremony on June 2, 1854, and contained accommodation for pitching 2,000 tons of cheese.[4] Later it was provided with a set of rails from the L.N.W.R. main line, " on which covered vans were run on cheese fair days, and thus, with the minimum handling, the produce of the dairy was shipped from the fair to the warehouse of the provision merchant and factor." [5]

[1] L.N.W.B., Aug. 8, 1848 ; Crewe Ctee., L.N.W.B., July 18, Oct. 17, Nov. 7, 1848 ; Feb. 27, March 13, Sept. 25, 1849 ; C.M., July, 1848 ; *Chester Courant*, June 7, 1854 ; *E.A.* 02, pp. 57–9.

[2] Bagshaw 1850, pp. 367, 369.

[3] Sub-Ctee., L.N.W.B., May 7, 1852 ; *Chester Courant*, June 7, 1854.

[4] *C.G.*, 21.9.71 ; Crewe Ctee., L.N.W.B., Sept. 21, 1852.

[5] See full account in *Chester Courant*, June 7, 1854 ; *E.A.* 02, p. 55. The railway company gave " what facilities they could " ; *e.g.* ". . . the late Mr. John Hill, Esqre. never paid anything to the London & N.W.R. Co. for the use of the siding behind the market " (C.L.B.M., Dec. 7, 1871).

About 1860 John Hill and his friends "felt that it was unwise that a town of the growing importance of Crewe should have but one great means of support, namely the Railway Works," and they tried to establish a cotton factory. After Martin Heath had made "minute inquiries" in Manchester, the scheme fell through. Then a Mr. Alfred Whitworth came to Crewe in 1861 to expound the plan of "The Lancashire Cotton Spinning Co.," and offered the small speculators £60,000 with which to build a mill; but even this did not tempt them.

Hill was more successful in 1863, for it was due to his public-spirited move that the L.N.W.R. decided to establish its new Bessemer steelworks at Crewe. It appears that the Edleston Trustees refused to sell the land required, except at a prohibitive price, whereupon John Hill, who had just bought the Coppenhall Heyes estate, "said to the company's officials at Crewe, 'If Edlestons won't sell you theirs, I will give you a piece of mine for your steelworks.'" Hill's gift to the company comprised "some eight or ten acres of land near to Flag-Lane Bridge" in the western portion of the township. The astute railway contractor's display of public spirit reaped rich private rewards, if we may judge by a later laconic announcement in the *Chester Record* newspaper of June 6, 1863, giving a list of important L.N.W.R. constructional works at Crewe "to be carried out by Mr. Hill, contractor." In addition he was "preparing to build 300 tenements."[1] About the same time Samuel Heath made a similar offer of a free site of land for new industries by advertisement in the Manchester and Lancashire daily papers. This scheme was considered for a time by Messrs. John Rylands & Sons of Manchester, but the chief of the firm, Reuben Spencer, turned it down on account of the distance of the land from the railway station. Next, a firm of fustian cutters accepted 1,500 square yards at the end of Richard Moon Street, but, owing to the death of its principal, no development followed.[2]

About the same time the railway company itself moved in

[1] *Cheshire Observer*, Oct. 5 and 26, Nov. 2, 1861; *C.G.*, 17.2.77; *E.A.* 02, p. 55. Hill, "the successful railway contractor," was born in 1810 at Guilsfield, Montgomeryshire. He settled at the Manor House, Wistaston, near Crewe, soon after the establishment of the town, and in Sept., 1853, bought Oakhanger Hall estate, Haslington, from the Rev. J. W. Ready Landon (Hinchliffe: *op. cit.*, p. 108). He died in 1868.

[2] *C.Ch.*, 10.11.77, 2.9.82; *E.A.* 02, pp. 61–3.

JOHN HILL'S MARKET HALL IN 1854
(*from a contemporary water-colour*)

the matter, for in 1865 the directors undertook to build in Sandon Street a clothing factory for John Compton, the head of a
great firm of contractors who made uniforms for the L.N.W.R.
staff. Compton was allowed 25 per cent. discount on the usual
carriage rates, which is noteworthy, because these were a source
of constant complaint from local tradesmen and a major barrier
to the establishment of fresh industries in the town. In 1880
the L.N.W.R. built a new and larger factory for the firm in
Bridle Road, opened with a religious service in that year and
subsequently enlarged in 1890–1 and 1914–15.[1]

To John Rigg must be given the credit of introducing fustian-
cutting into the town. In 1869 he built a factory in Henry
Street at a cost of about £350 in the hope of attracting a new
industry to Crewe, and "speedily let it to a fustian-cutter," a
Mrs. Hall of Warrington. Another industrial experiment made
about this time was the Crewe Cheese Manufacturing
Society Ltd., with a capital of £1,000, of which Rigg was
chairman. The first cheese was turned out in May, 1871, but
the society did not flourish and had to be wound up in 1874–5.
By 1872 the tradespeople of Crewe began to complain that
"female hands" could scarcely be got, and one manager estimated that from 700 to 800 people were employed in the six
factories in the town.[2]

The great stimulus to new industries came in 1876, when the
railway works went on "short time" for the first occasion in
their history. Crewe tradesmen were seriously affected by the
reduction of purchasing power, and the *Guardian* called attention
to the unusually large number of bankruptcies in the town during 1876. On February 14, 1877, a meeting of the "influential
inhabitants," called together by Frederick Cooke, clerk to the
Local Board, debated the problem of new industries for Crewe.
Rigg occupied the chair, and Whittle, the two Heaths, Allman,
Platt, Jackson, Fear and Briggs were present. Many suggestions
were put forward, from cotton-weaving ("a large number of

[1] Estate Ctee., L.N.W.B., March 10, 1865 ; Gen. Stores Ctee., L.N.W.B.,
July 21, 1865 ; C.G., 20.5.71, 28.10.71, 16.10 and 25.12.80, 25.9.13 ; C.L.B.M.,
27.10.68 ; Works Ctee., 13.4.80, 3.9.90, 13.10.14 ; Compton's successors at
the Bridle Road factory were J. Hammond & Co.
[2] *C.G.*, 23.9.71, 19.10.72, 16.11.72, 24.11.77 ; *Return of Ind. and Prov. Socs.*,
1875, p. 66 ; Slater's *Directory of Lancashire, 1871–2*, p. 736.

the people of Crewe, having come out of the manufacturing districts, would be already trained for that work ") to porcelain manufacture, but Martin Heath and Whittle were not enthusiastic, and alleged that the surplus labour, which had existed in the early 1860's, had been absorbed. The sole tangible result was the formation of the Crewe Printing & Publishing Company Ltd., "to erect a typesetting works capable of finding employment for 200 young people." Dr. Alexander Mackie, proprietor and editor of the *Warrington Guardian* and its chain of newspapers, had heard of the movement for industrial development, and had met some of those present at the meeting in February. At the first annual general meeting of the company (August 24, 1877) Dr. Richard Lord was elected chairman and T. E. Gibson secretary. Before the end of 1877 a factory had been built in Camm Street ; in 1880 the company was amalgamated with the newly-formed Mackie, Brentnall & Co. Ltd., and some of the Crewe shareholders became directors of the new company. The Camm Street factory was not a success and closed down in 1884. The movement had failed.[1]

During the acute depression of 1893-4, a sub-committee of Crewe Town Council was appointed to report on the possibility of inducing manufacturers to set up new industries in the town, and later a circular was sent to industrialists in other towns extolling Crewe's industrial advantages. Between 1882 and 1908 several attempts are on record to discover reasons, apart from the obvious one, lack of raw materials, for the reluctance of new industries to settle in the town on a large scale. From these it appears that the absence of canal communication, differential railway rates, and the lack of a municipal water supply frightened industrialists away. The nearest canal basins to Crewe are those at Nantwich and Wheelock, 4 and 5 miles away respectively. As early as 1872, J. J. Bradshaw suggested cutting an extension of the canal from Nantwich so that potteries might be established, and in 1903 F. W. West adduced the old reasons for the slow progress of industrial diversification, *viz.*

---

[1] *C.G.*, from 26.6.76 to 29.1.87, *passim*. In 1877 Rigg helped a young engineer named William Knight to start a small engineering works and a brickyard in Henry Street ; but although a few stationary engines were turned out, no important industrial development resulted.

lack of a canal, and inability on the part of the municipality to guarantee water supplies.[1]

Evidence that railway rates and charges on goods destined for Crewe were either too high or higher than those charged for longer distances between various towns is fairly conclusive, but does not necessarily mean that the railway company fixed these charges with the object of keeping new industries out of Crewe. In 1877 T. E. Gibson announced that a glass-manufacturer friend of his had thought of establishing a works at Crewe, only to find himself " floored principally with reference to the carriage rates demanded by the company." In 1884 Dr. Mackie said in connection with the closing of the Camm Street factory that " the railway companies complained of their inability to charge goods from London to Crewe at as low rates as from London to Warrington." [2] In 1889 Crewe Town Council appointed a standing committee under the Railway and Canal Traffic Act, 1888, to receive complaints " of undue preference given to other towns and persons outside Crewe, in comparison with tradesmen in the town of Crewe." E. R. Hill, grocer, submitted a list of articles ". . . which were carried from Liverpool to Longport *via* Crewe, at a considerably cheaper rate than the same goods were delivered from Liverpool to Crewe, and stating the amount of rates charged." Next year the Corporation received a reply from the Board of Trade to its enquiry concerning the Liverpool–Crewe–Longport case to the effect that " the rates were on a low basis on account of the competition by water from Liverpool, part of which was over a free navigation."

In spite of subscriptions to the Mansion House United Association on Railway Rates, the Corporation could do little. The cost of a local enquiry under the Act of 1888 was considered to be prohibitive, and as no canal was cut, railway tariffs continued to form a hedge round Crewe keeping new industries out, although they were partially reduced by the L.N.W.R. (Rates and Charges) Order Confirmation Act of 1891. The ready-made clothing industry certainly developed considerably after this date.

To many local patriots these railway rates and charges have seemed to be a sinister manifestation of the L.N.W.R.'s desire

[1] *C.G.*, 22.1.76, 24.1.03 ; *G.P.C.*, 11.1.94 ; Sub-Ctee., 16.1.94.
[2] *C.G.*, 28.10.71, 17.2.77, 5.11.84, 23.3.89 ; *C.Ch.*, 22.6.89.

to keep a monopoly of the local labour market and a legend grew up that the company deliberately kept new industries out of the town. This has often been denied by responsible railway officials, and the fact that the company itself introduced the clothing trade into the town counts against it.[1]

There is more substance in the complaint that firms intending to establish factories in Crewe have been deterred when they found that there was no guaranteed municipally-owned water-supply. The Local Board and the Corporation were merely allowed to buy the surplus water not needed by the railway company, which was not bound by section 3 of the Gas and Waterworks Facilities Act, 1870 (33 & 34 Vict., c. 70). For example, in 1872 the Anglo-Swiss Condensed Milk Company decided not to establish a factory in the town because the Local Board found itself unable to guarantee a sufficient supply. In 1908 the findings of a sub-committee of Crewe Town Council, set up in 1904–6 to report on the " probable cost and return of a system of waterworks to be owned by the Corporation," were used in an unsuccessful attempt by the Labour group, led by Councillors Kelsall and Barnett, to remove this obstacle to Crewe's industrial development.[2]

The growing realisation that the railway works could no longer be relied upon to absorb all Crewe's trained mechanics, gave rise to another movement to attract new industries to Crewe. In December, 1908, on the initiative of Alderman Kettell and Councillor Feltham, the Town Council appointed an Industrial Sites Committee to compile a list of pieces of land in or near Crewe suitable for works sites. There was said to be a " large amount of available cheap labour and female workers ; also . . . low rates and taxes," but the attempt evoked no response.[3]   A

[1] *C.G.*, 31.8.89 to 16.1.92, *passim* ; *C.Ch.*, 27.1.94, 7.8.97 ; see also Sir G. Claughton's letter in *C.G.*, 12.1.12 ; Coun., 27.11.89 ; *G.P.C.*, 12.12.89 ; Railway Rates Charges Ctee. for 1890. This committee was reappointed in 1891 and 1892. There is a curious folk-myth, apparently without foundation, that the L.N.W.R. Company gave the site of the Queen's Park to the Crewe Corporation in 1887 in order to keep the Great Western Railway out of the town, and thereby preserve its transport monopoly.

[2] C.L.B.M., 21.8.72 ; *C.G.*, 6.2.04 to 29.8.08, *passim*, esp. 1908 ; Mkt. Ctee., 19.1.04 ; *G.P.C.*, 14.9.05, 11.1.06 ; Sub-Ctee., 12.5.04 to 22.2.06.

[3] G.P.C., 12.11.08, 10.12.08, 12.2.09 ; Ind. Sites Ctee., 12.1.09, 9.2.09 ; 1.3.09 ; *C.G.*, 6.3.09.

more serious proposition was made in 1910–11 by William Irwin of Coppenhall and Bolton, a rag-and-bone merchant of exceptional business ability who had built a bone manure works in Coppenhall about 1906 and was the guiding spirit behind the opening of the Crewe and District Ice Company's Coppenhall Iceworks in 1909. He maintained in 1911 that " a company of iron manufacturers some time ago were in negotiation for the purchase of 150 acres of land in the vicinity of Crewe," but had to abandon the idea " through there being no waterway." [1] To remedy this, he proposed that a company should be formed to cut a branch about 3 miles long from the Grand Trunk canal at Rookery Bridge, Wheelock, to the Cumberland Wharf, Crewe. No locks would be required and the canal would give access to the Potteries, Manchester, Liverpool and Birmingham. Irwin hoped for the subsequent establishment of potteries and an " export " trade in Crewe bricks to other towns. The scheme gained wide publicity, but nothing came of it. Later, in 1911, he proposed an amalgamation of the three rag-and-bone businesses in the town, to carry on wholesale and retail cotton waste, mungo and shoddy manufacturing as a limited company employing " several hundred hands." Here again his Irish optimism led to no result.[2]

In November, 1911, Crewe Town Council resurrected the Industrial Sites Committee in an effort to induce the L.N.W.R. " to give differential treatment to industries that might come into the borough," as several engineering firms were said to be enquiring for works sites. In 1912 several representative local business men were co-opted on to the committee and some systematic advertising began. The last meeting took place on September 2, 1914, during the first encounters of a war which solved Crewe's employment problems for a time. The sole tangible result of the movement was that Councillors Kay and Burrows prevailed on Messrs. Heap & Co., clothing manufacturers of Nantwich, to establish a small clothing works in Buxton Avenue at the beginning of 1912. After the war, when it became clear that unemployment would become even more serious than in the pre-war years, a fresh attempt was made.

[1] *C.G.*, 10 and 24.4.09, 17.7.09, 25.11.09.
[2] *C.G.*, 20.1.11, 24.2.11 (sketch of Crewe end of canal), 3 and 24.3.11, 31.3.11, 8.12.11 ; Works Ctee., 10.5.11 ; Health, 14.6.11.

In April, 1919, a deputation from Crewe Town Council waited on the L.N.W.R. Company " to see if some preferential railway rates could be obtained for the borough," and in the following June, on the receipt of enquiries from Redferns' Rubber Works Ltd., concerning a suitable factory, Crewe Town Council reappointed the Industrial Sites Committee. Nothing is known to have resulted from these moves.[1]

I. Fustian-cutting, 1869–1923

In 1872 Mrs. Hall, after a three years' tenancy of Rigg's factory, moved into a three-storied building in Oakley Street, capable of employing 300 hands. Here she had

" a number of apprentices . . . who were paid so much per piece of fustian which they received from the manufacturers and had to make them into velvet . . . These pieces were not the property of Mrs. Hall, she only received from the manufacturers in Manchester."

Carriage to and from Crewe formed an important item in costs.[2] In 1877 the factory, then closed down owing to the depression, was the property of Meanock & Sons of Congleton and Oldham, who reopened it in the following year. A second three-storied fustian-cutting factory, the Alexandria Mill, was established in 1871 by Thomas Sheppard in Walker Street, and an entire new building was added to it in 1880–1. When Meanock's establishment stood idle in 1877, Sheppard's factory was employing 130 women full time. About 1903 both factories passed under the control of the United Velvet Cutters' Association Ltd., and were still running in 1920, although the Oakley Street establishment provided employment for less than 40 persons.[3]

II. The Ready-made Clothing Industry

The next firm to establish a " sewing-machine " factory in Crewe, after John Compton's company-aided venture of 1865,

[1] G.P.C., 21.11.11 ; Ind. Sites Sub-Ctee., 21.11.11 to 2.9.14 ; Ctee. of Coun., 9.11.12, 2.4.19, 4.6.19 ; C.G., 15.12.11, 9.2.12.
[2] C.L.B.M., 26.10.71 ; C.G., 16.3.72.
[3] C.L.B.M., 17.8.71, 28.9.71 ; C.G., 24.11.77, 30.10.78, 14.8.80, 26.4.93 ; Works, 3.8.80, 9.3.20, 13.4.20 ; Mkt. Ctee., 19.2.07 : S.A. Ctee., 13.5.02. Even the Crewe Co-operative Friendly Society toyed with the idea of establishing a fustian-cutting factory in 1872 (Minute Book, Aug. 13 and 22, Sept. 9, 1872).

was John Rylands & Sons of Manchester, who employed about 10,000 people in various parts of England. George Wallis, a Crewe draper, made goods for them until Thomas Sibley, the first manager, was sent down from headquarters in October, 1871, to organise the new establishment. For about six months workrooms over the " Lamb " public-house in Oak Street served as temporary premises, employing only about 12 persons. After a short spell in Rigg's Henry Street factory, Rylands moved to their own four-storied factory, the Longford Works, near the railway station. Starting with 80 women and girls in 1872, it was employing about 300 in 1877 ; some of these were outworkers who collected the goods from the factory, performed certain operations in their own homes, and then returned the garments to the factory. About 1900, Rylands closed down the establishment, and it was not used for its original purpose until 1903, when Charles Doody & Sons, a Nantwich ready-made clothing firm which had desired to start in Crewe as far back as 1882, reopened it. Under this management it has twice been considerably enlarged (in 1909–10 and 1923–4) until in 1934 it was the largest of the Crewe clothing factories, with 483 employees. The mid-1920's saw the introduction of the " belt system," when suits, overcoats and blazers formed the chief lines manufactured.[1]

Some time after 1887, Coop & Co., Ltd., began the manufacture of ready-made clothing in the deserted printing factory built by the Crewe Printing & Publishing Company in Camm Street. Little is known of the firm's activities, but in 1898 extensive alterations amounting to a practical rebuilding took place, and much new machinery was installed on behalf of W. H. L. Cameron of Manchester. Some skilled garment workers from the expanding Nantwich clothing trade are said to have been imported to staff the newly-christened " Marmion " Works, but only about 80 persons were employed there in 1910. In 1917 Cameron sold the place to the Co-operative Wholesale Society, and production recommenced in June, 1918. Between 1918 and 1933 the staff employed rose from 52 to 220 ; juvenile clothing formed the speciality. In the 1930's this was the smallest

[1] *C.G.*, 16.11.72, 7.2.74, 16.1.75, 31.10.77, 17.11.77, 12.8.78, 19.8.82, 25.1.02, 1.2.02, 10.10.03 ; *E.L.*, 15.9.03 ; Works Ctee., 9.6.09, 13.2.23, 17.4.23 ; Coun., 2.5.23.

of the six C.W.S. clothing factories, with an output valued at £129,000 in 1935, when the "belt system" was introduced. Two extensions have taken place since 1918—in 1931 and 1937-8.[1]

No history of the clothing trade in Crewe would be complete without some mention of the man who developed it in the eastern end of Crewe, C. H. Holmes of Congleton (1857–1913). Holmes came to Crewe in 1891 and set up a small tailoring business at 29–31 Victoria Street. In 1894 he opened a small factory for his workpeople in Buxton Avenue. Soon afterwards he turned over the clothing business to his brother, A. E. Holmes, and concentrated on the development of the Hall o' Shaw estate as a builder. In 1895–6 he built a branch clothing factory in Vincent Street for John Harding & Sons. This Nantwich firm, which had spent some years in temporary premises in Lawton Street, had established Nantwich's second "sewing-machine" factory in 1872. In 1903 the Vincent Street branch was employing 141 people. In 1896 Holmes built what is now known as the "Empire" factory off Hall o' Shaw Street, to which his brother's business was transferred, and the Buxton Avenue building became a printing works. During 1903–5 he built for Smethurst & Holden Ltd., shirt and pyjama manufacturers of Salford, their first Crewe establishment. They occupied it until 1913, when they moved to their present premises. These were extended in 1916 to fulfil war-time government orders. The staff employed has risen steadily from about 40 in 1905 to 420 in 1934.[2]

A. E. Holmes's factory, burnt out in 1901, was soon afterwards taken over by S. & J. Watts of Manchester, who carried on the manufacture of medium-class ready-made suits, flannels and blazers there until 1920, when they moved to a larger disused factory, also built by Holmes and once occupied by F. Whiston & Co., in Chestnut Grove. They were succeeded at the "Empire" Works by J. Mackay & Sons, shirt manufacturers. Watts took over a disused school in New Street as a temporary branch establishment in 1911. In 1912 A. Heap & Co., another

---

[1] *C.G.*, 10.5.84, 12.11.98, 16.11.17 ; Works Ctee., 12.4.10, 7.10.13, 7.4.14, 8.2.16, 8.10.18 ; Carr-Saunders and others : *Consumers' Co-operation in Great Britain*, pp. 423, 431 ; information from C.W.S.

[2] *C.G.*, 15.10.92, 9.12.93, 6.10.94, 5.1.95, 2.11.95, 30.9.99, 1.5.01, 27.12.02, 2.12.13 ; Works Ctee., 9.10.95, 10.2.03, 12.4.05, 9.5.05, 10.12.12, 8.2.16, 12.8.19 ; G.P.C., 12.3.03 ; E.L., 20.6.05 ; *E.A.* 00, p. 28.

Nantwich firm, reoccupied the Buxton Avenue factory, and were employing about 100 people in 1919. Another firm which came into the town in these years was J. Y. Gaukroger & Co., of Manchester and Northwich, pinafore manufacturers, in Queen Street (1914). Besides these larger establishments there existed smaller works of minor importance; *e.g.* in 1905 there were 8 clothing factories using mechanical power, and 13 in 1919. "Plentiful cheap labour" is the usual reason given for the establishment of the industry in Crewe. There are few exact figures showing the total employment afforded; in 1894 there were said to be about 650 tailoresses in the town, and a later estimate (1921) gives the number of women clothing workers as 1,386.[1]

III. Miscellaneous Industrial Developments

In 1878 the Sandbach firm of Button & Brocklehurst established what was later known as the Borough Foundry at the bottom of Market Street. This small foundry, enlarged in 1922–3, subsisted mainly on local orders for castings. The light engineering firm of Messrs. Theakstons, in Gresty Road, which opened works a few hundred yards outside the borough in 1920, failed to realise the high hopes placed in it and left Crewe in 1933 ; the reason given was the pressure of foreign competition. No important industrial development has taken place in the surrounding townships, with the exception of a ready-made clothing business established about 1908 in Willaston, for which a new factory was opened in 1911 by the proprietors, Messrs. H. B. & F. W. Crooks.[2]

Since 1845 there has been a printing and publishing industry in Crewe, the earliest printing works being one founded in that year by Edwin Bennion, who left for Australia in 1853. In 1865 it passed into the possession of Wilmot Eardley (1837–1919), who developed the business considerably, and finally in 1905

[1] Health, 21.1.03 ; E.L., 14.10.02, 11.5.11, 14.5.14, 15.5.19 ; Works Ctee., 10.2.03, 13.7.09, 10.8.09, 7.6.10, 10.10.11, 13.2.12, 9.6.14, 13.10.14, 12.8.19, 9.3.20, 7.12.20, 11.1.21 ; Mkt. Ctee., 11.2.19 ; C.Ch., 5.5.94 and succeeding issues to 6.10.94 (the "Factory Girl" letters) ; C.G., 3.10.94, 6.2.14, 2.12.19, 26.12.19 ; M.O.H. 1903, pp. 20–1 ; 1905, p. 60 ; 1919, p. 27 ; 1923, pp. 9–10.
[2] C.G., 6.4.78, 27.4.78, 13.7.78, 10.10.11 ; Works Ctee., 8.8.22 ; E.L., 11.12.19, 10.2.20, 13.4.20, 8.6.20 ; Coun., 3.3.20.

turned it into a private limited company. He was the Conservative printer, while Henry Taylor was the printer for the Liberal Party. Taylor, who died in 1910, took up printing in the 1870's but it is doubtful whether his business was as extensive as Eardley's. Besides these two, there existed a number of minor printers. For a few months in 1901–2 the *Northern Daily Express* was printed at Crewe, and in 1902, after the collapse of this venture, the Crewe Stationery Co., Ltd., controlled by McCorquodale & Co., printers to the L.N.W.R. since 1846, bought the empty printing works in Frances Street and rapidly extended them. By 1934, 129 persons were employed.[1]

Crewe boasts the distinction of possessing the largest firm in the world manufacturing and selling animal medicines and embrocations only, *i.e.* Day & Sons (Crewe) Ltd., which now commands the British market and has a considerable export trade. It was founded in Shavington-cum-Gresty, near Crewe, in 1840 by J. H. Day (1818–95), who removed his chemical works to Crewe in the 1860's. On the death of his son, A. S. Day (1861–1906), it became a private limited liability company.[2]

The heavy clay of Coppenhall has provided the raw material for a long line of brickmakers, from the anonymous Church Coppenhall farmer whose activities gave a name to the " Brickkiln Fields " of the eighteenth-century land-tax returns and the pioneer John Bunting of Yorkshire who flourished in the 1840's, to John Rigg, T. H. Heath and C. H. Holmes. In 1883, 8 brickmakers were operating within the boundaries of the ancient parish, but after the formation of the Britannia Brick Company, Ltd., in 1906, with the object of developing an existing brickfield in Church Coppenhall, the machine-made products of its plant gradually ousted the small manufacturer.[3]

F. Whiston & Co. Ltd., manufacturers of stamped and pressed metal frames, furniture, perambulators and trays, both for the

[1] *E.A.* 02, p. 4 (d) ; *E.A.* 04, p. 2 (a) ; *E.A.* 06, p. 3 ; *C.G.*, 22.5.10, 15.8.19, 29.8.19 ; E.L., 11.4.01, 9.5.01, 12.6.01, 19.6.01, 14.11.01, 19.8.02, 14.10.02, 15.7.05, 18.11.05 ; Ctee. of Coun., 4.6.02 ; Coun., 2.7.02 ; Works Ctee., 7.4.03, 13.10.03, 9.1.06 ; Mkt. Ctee., 18.8.03 ; G.P.C., 15.5.02 ; *Times, L.M.S. Suppt.*, 20.9.38, p. xxvii.

[2] *C.Ch.*, 27.7.95 ; *C.G.*, 29.9.06, 10.10.06 ; White 1860, pp. 406–7 ; *E.A.* 73, p. 125.

[3] *E.A.* 02, p. 27 ; Slater 1883, p. 142 ; see also *C.G.*, 13.10.77 ; Works Ctee., 1.12.06 ; Mkt. Ctee., 14.1.02.

British market and for export, appear to have settled at 172 Mill Street about 1909 as picture-frame manufacturers ; for some time they operated a branch in the disused Chestnut Grove clothing factory. After the war of 1914–18, however, the firm built a new factory in Mill Street, and in 1934 this employed 120 women and girls.[1]

IV. THE POST OFFICE IN CREWE

The first Crewe post office stood near the railway station at the Royal Hotel, which had been built in 1841. Before this the inhabitants of Coppenhall regarded the arrival of a letter as " a very uncommon occurrence," and at the Rectory " a man was hired three days a week to go to Nantwich for the letters." [2] In the 1840's Crewe town post office moved several times, first to Manchester Street and then to a house in Forge Street, opposite the end of the Iron Bridge, where Joseph Storer, the first Crewe postmaster of whom we have record, lived. In 1855 it was again moved, this time to Henry Wood's business premises in High Street, where for some time the whole of Crewe town postal business was conducted in a box partitioned off an ironmonger's shop.[3] It was on July 26, 1854, that the establishment was split into a town office, under a postmaster, with one lady clerk and two postmen, and a station office under John Matthews, who had the help of two clerks, a stamper, and two mail porters to deal with the postal business passing through the growing railway junction of Crewe. Matthews had been transferred to Crewe from his chief clerkship at Blackburn in December, 1847. Henry Wood (1823–1905), a native of Macclesfield, gradually relinquished the ironmongery business and railway lamp manufacturing as the demands of the postal service increased, and in 1866 had a total staff of twelve. Complaints about the inadequacy of the postal and telegraphic accommodation in High

[1] Health, 11.8.09 ; *E.A.* 11, p. 225 ; *C.G.*, 2.12.13 ; *Crewe Postal Directory*, 1913, p. 87.

[2] *C.G.*, 29.9.77, 31.8.78. On March 23, 1846, Crewe post office was raised from the status of a receiving house to that of a sub-office under Nantwich, with Joseph Storer as postmaster, and on July 10, 1846, Crewe was made a post town. In 1855–6 Crewe was made a Head Post Office. (Information from G.P.O.)

[3] Bagshaw 1850, p. 368 ; Kelly 1857, pp. 103–5 ; White 1860, p. 347 ; *C.G.*, 21.6.02, 17.5.05.

Street began in the 1870's, and in 1882 the District Surveyor from Shrewsbury reported that it was " quite inadequate." The town post office was accordingly moved to the northern side of the Market Square in July, 1883, and in the same year the Crewe station post office was enlarged in readiness for the inauguration of the parcels post. Wood continued as postmaster until 1894. By 1892 the staff employed numbered 79, besides 17 sub-post-masters.[1]

The chief reason for this increase is to be found in the growth of the postal business passing through Crewe, both in ordinary trains and in the travelling post offices. By 1889 it could be said :—

" Crewe is for Travelling Post-office purposes by far the most important junction in the kingdom ; indeed, I may venture to say there is nothing like it in this respect in the whole world. Within three hours—that is, between half-past eleven at night and half-past two in the morning—not fewer than fourteen mail-trains, each with sorting carriages attached, arrive and depart from this station ; whilst the weight of mails exchanged here within the time specified is not less than twenty tons. A great amount of labour is involved in receiving and delivering such an immense weight of bags, the work being all done by hand." [2]

Some idea of the growth of the town traffic may be obtained from the following figures for Crewe alone :—

AVERAGE WEEKLY HANDLINGS

Years.	Letters posted in Crewe.	Letters delivered in Crewe.
1883–5 . . .	15,500	16,000
1905 . . .	55,000	70,000

The increase, more than proportionate to the increase in population, can be attributed to the spread of literacy after the

[1] C.G., 6.7.78, 17.12.81, 16.9.82, 20.9.82, 10.10.82, 7.4.83, 9.6.83, 21.7.83, 28.7.83, 27.4.89, 2 and 9.2.01, 20.5.05 ; C.Ch., 22.12.83.
[2] *Chambers' Journal*, April 13, 1889, p. 236 ; see also C.G., 27.4.89, 1.6.89. Crewe still retains this position—see E. T. Crutchley : G.P.O. (1938), p. 66 :— " In the space of about three hours twenty T.P.O.'s enter and leave Crewe station round about midnight."

educational reforms of the 1870's and the growth of the practice of selling goods by post. In 1905 the present town post office was opened on the Square in " no particular style of architecture." In 1891–2 the sorting offices at the railway station were enlarged, and by 1905, 40,000 mailbags were being transferred daily from one train to another. This did not include the large and growing parcels traffic.

For some years it had been apparent that the postal accommodation at Crewe station needed expansion, and entirely new sorting offices outside the station were opened at a cost of £16,000 in 1912, when it was said that the number of mail-trains passing through Crewe was between two and three times as great as the number reaching any other postal centre, save London. Besides strictly postal business, the telegraph and telephone departments had expanded considerably. An additional opening for Crewe's surplus female labour was indicated by an observer's remark, in 1905, that it was intended " to employ female clerks as telephone operators " in the new exchange. The total staff employed by the post office in Crewe was then 160 ; by 1934 it had risen to 470 ; this number might double during a Christmas rush.[1]

V. Crewe as a Cattle Market and Produce Centre

John Hill's wholesale cheese fairs continued to be held in the Market Hall from 1854 until the 1870's, when they gradually died out. The business of collecting and distributing Cheshire cheese remained with the cheese factor operating from his wholesale warehouse. The first Crewe cheese factor was Richard Pedley of Haslington (1828–1909), who began business in Nantwich Road near the railway station in 1850 and was succeeded by his son, G. A. Pedley. Other important Crewe cheese factors were John Thomas of Burslem (1826–1902), who entered the business about 1862, and Thomas Furber of Weston (1839–1905), manager for Pedley from 1876 onwards. Crewe Town Council attempted to revive the Market Hall cheese fairs in 1894–6, but without success.[2]

[1] *C.G.*, 1.8.91, 28.4.94, 6.5.99, 17 and 20.5.05, 19.4.12 ; *C.Ch.*, 24.12.38.
[2] *C.G.*, 1869–74, *passim*, 14.2.94, 16.6.94, 10.8.95, 8.2.96, 9.12.96, 2.7.02, 29.4.05, 20.10.09 ; *C.Ch.*, 13 and 27.1.94, 17.7.94 ; G.P.C., 11.1.94 ; Sub-Ctee. *re* Cheese Fairs, 27.2.94 ; *E.A.* 02, p. 55.

When John Hill opened his Market Hall he had expressed his willingness to build further warehouses, " to receive any amount of produce which the gentlemen and farmers of the country might be kind enough to bring." In 1857 he opened a Corn Exchange to accommodate the market in grain which had sprung up in the Cheese Hall, but with the growing predominance of dairy-farming and the decline in corn-growing, these corn markets soon died out. The Corn Exchange was then used for miscellaneous public meetings and entertainments. In 1858-9 Hill erected an additional warehouse for the wholesale trade in butter and bacon, and by this time weekly retail markets were being held in the hall on Saturdays for the sale of farm produce.[1]

The Cheese Fair Committee of 1849-54 had been formed to make arrangements for cattle fairs as well, and when Bagshaw compiled his directory in 1850, five were held at Crewe every year. By 1858 the number had been increased to ten and this remained the figure until 1877, when the Crewe Town Council increased the number to one per month. No one appears to have exercised general control over these fairs, which were held in various places in the town—on the vacant plot of land behind the Market Hall, belonging to Martin Heath (whence the cattle overflowed into Earle, Heath and Hill Streets), in the yard of the Adelphi Hotel, and on a piece of land in Oak Street whence they overflowed into High Street and Market Street.[2] That the resulting filthy condition of the public thoroughfares and the obstructions to traffic were tolerated for such a long period of time may well appear surprising to a generation which has come to accept the internal combustion engine, and not the horse, as the mainstay of highway locomotion.

The provision of a municipal Smithfield was a problem of which Local Board and Town Council made a complete muddle. If John Hill had lived a few years longer, the problem might have been settled ; instead, a solution was delayed until vested interests capable of warding off public control had been created. John Hill had begun negotiations with the Local Board for the

[1] *Chester Courant*, June 7, 1854 ; *Cheshire Observer*, July 11, Sept. 19, Nov. 21, 1863 ; C.G., 11.12.69 ; Kelly 1857, pp. 103-5 ; White 1860, p. 346.
[2] Bagshaw 1850, p. 367 ; White 1860, p. 346 ; *Cheshire Observer*, June 6, Nov. 21, 1863 ; C.L.B.M., 1860-74, *passim* ; C.G., 1869-74, *passim* ; Coun., 18.10.77, 8.12.77 ; cattle fair bill (1858) at Adelphi Hotel, Crewe.

sale of a Smithfield in 1867, but the subject had been deferred while the Market Hall was being purchased, a cemetery acquired, and the "Injunction Crisis" developing. Immediately this latter affair had passed over, the townspeople began to demand the removal of the cattle fairs from the streets and the provision of a public Smithfield. The project came under discussion at Local Board meetings in 1873, and in January, 1874, William Hill, auctioneer, informed the members of his intention to form a private Smithfield. The Board gave its permission, and William Hill held his first auction on March 2, 1874, in a field behind Charles Welch's Royal Hotel. These sales were monthly ones, and by the end of the year had become firmly established, attracting buyers from the Potteries, Manchester and the Birmingham district. Helped by Crewe's position as the hub of the L.N.W.R. system, they were the humble beginnings of the town's immense livestock sales in the 1930's.

Meanwhile, the old Crewe cattle fairs continued to pollute the centre of the town, and the *Guardian* began a vigorous campaign to banish them to a properly-regulated Smithfield. The agitation rose to a great height in 1875, when a deputation waited on the Board, and teachers proved by statistics that the open cattle fairs reduced the attendance at the Presbyterian day-schools. Proposals for a municipal Smithfield near the railway station suffered defeat in 1876, and finally an unsatisfactory compromise was reached. Martin Heath agreed first to fence in the land behind the Market Hall and later to sell it for £5,000 to the Corporation (1879). This was not only totally inadequate for the rapidly increasing number of beasts brought into Crewe, but was also too far from the railway station ; the cattle sales here declined rapidly, and in 1896 were said to have "simply died."

Crewe's cattle market centre had by then shifted permanently to the neighbourhood of the railway station. The sales here grew so quickly that in 1882 the Crewe Cattle Market & Abattoir Co., Ltd., was formed, with the object of deflecting as much as possible of the Irish and foreign cattle trade from Liverpool and Birkenhead, by making use of the reconstructed Holyhead Old Harbour (1873–80), with its direct railway communication with the "centrally situated town of Crewe." The new company had a nominal capital of £100,000, the directors of the L.N.W.R. met the promoters in "a very liberal spirit," several railway directors as well as local capitalists were on the Board, and the construction of a large and up-to-date Smithfield, with abattoirs, lairages and a railway siding was begun at Crewe station. The new cattle market was opened in 1883, with the official blessing of Sir Richard Moon and F. W. Webb, who had given the project a great deal of help. Weekly, instead of monthly, sales began in the same year, which was unfortunately marked by the liquidation of Messrs. J. C. & H. H. Etches, auctioneers to the company; foot-and-mouth disease restrictions also hampered operations. In 1884 the promoters admitted that the scheme had been too ambitious, and on November 28, 1885, the company practically leased the market to Messrs. Etches and Henry Manley.[1]

The name of Henry Manley will always be associated with the vigorous growth of the Crewe horse and cattle auctions, which took place in the next twenty years. The son of a wheelwright, Manley was born at Aston, near Wrenbury, in 1828, and became village postmaster, general dealer and chemist. He held his first auction sale on October 21, 1861, at Aston, and was the second auctioneer to open a stock market in Cheshire. After a few months of struggle he gradually acquired a reputation at the monthly cattle fairs of Wrenbury and Whitchurch. His appointment as auctioneer and salesman to the Crewe Cattle Market Company in 1885 gave him his first big chance, and by 1896 he had increased the returns from a few hundred pounds monthly " to nearly £100,000 per annum." When, in 1895, the directors of the Cattle Market Company decided to terminate their agreement with him, he built a Smithfield of his own, opened in February, 1896, to compete for the growing trade of the weekly auctions. This also proved a great success. For example, in 1896 the firm catalogued 2,560 horses; in 1902, 6,750; and in 1908, 7,186. Buyers from Austria-Hungary and Germany became regular attenders of Manley's horse sales, and an observer wrote in 1909 :—". . . it is not an unusual occurrence for a Continental train to be run direct to Harwich, as a considerable number of horses are bought by Continental purchasers."

Manley, who also conducted sales on farms and auctioned

[1] C.G., 1875, *passim*, 1.1.76, 24.3.77, 1878, *passim*, 29.3.79, 24.12.81, 1882–4, *passim*, 30.1.86, 31.3.86, 6.6.96, 20.6.96, 24.10.96 ; C.L.B.M., 27.10.75, 3.5.76 ; Coun., 1.1.79, 29.1.79.

estates, died in 1903, and was succeeded by his four sons. In addition, eight qualified salesmen were employed in 1909, when the normal weekly turnover at Crewe alone was £3,500. Since then the firm of Manley has rented the Crewe Cattle Market Company's Smithfield, and development proved particularly rapid after the war of 1914–18, chiefly on account of the rise of motor transport after the General Strike of 1926. This increased the number of buyers attending, and enabled cattle to be brought in from an ever-widening radius, but caused the decline of the famous horse sales. The weekly turnover of £6,000 in 1926 increased to £10,000 in 1934, in spite of the fall in prices. A smaller market, that of J. M. Barker & Co., was established in 1920, when Crewe could be called the third greatest centre for the sale of livestock in Great Britain.[1]

[1] White 1860, p. 392 ; *C.G.*, 28.12.95, 11.1.96, 18.1.96, 25.1.96, 5.4.02, 23 and 26.9.03, 25.3.05, 14 and 17.8.07, 9.9.10, 31.10.19. Henry Manley was an earnest Wesleyan local preacher. Another result of Crewe's central position was noticed in 1905 :—" Of late years a large number of commercials have taken up their residence in Crewe on account of its being such an excellent railway centre." Crewe branch of the U.K. Commercial Travellers' Association had nearly 70 members in 1907 (*C.G.*, 4.11.05, 9.2.07).

CHAPTER V

THE WORK OF THE MONKS COPPENHALL (CREWE) LOCAL BOARD (1860–77)

BETWEEN 1851 and 1861 a considerable number of houses had been built at Crewe outside the railway company's estate, and to these the company could only extend its public services by separate agreements with individuals instead of collectively to a corporate body. Whereas in 1851 only about 300 of the 825 inhabited houses in the township had been owned by private persons, in 1861 the number of such houses appears to have been about 650 out of a total of 1,473. Counting 5·5 persons to a house, this meant that over 3,500 persons now lived outside the paternal care of the company, and were creating urgent problems of water supply, sewage disposal and highway maintenance.[1] According to the scanty available evidence of persons who had lived through this period, there were less than half-a-dozen gas lamps outside the company's property, all fixed for personal convenience and not for public purposes. Residents used lanterns on dark nights to avoid the mud and ruts of the badly-kept roads, the adequate repair of which was beyond the powers of an unpaid surveyor of highways. Cartloads of cinders and an occasional load of stones were laid on the streets from time to time, and scavenging was done on private initiative. No cheap and swift remedy existed for sanitary nuisances, but those who could afford had their sewers joined up with those of the railway company, provided that these increasingly inefficient installations ran sufficiently close to their property. Other owners of private property began to construct private sewers, which created nuisances objected to by neighbouring farmers, who took a surprisingly prominent part in the movement for the formation of a Local Board. The vestry was incapable of dealing satisfactorily with these matters, entangled as it was in the sectarian controversy between the Nonconformists and the Church Party.[2]

[1] *Census* 1851, pt. i, vol. ii, pp. 20–3 ; 1861, vol. i, p. 561 ; Bagshaw 1850, p. 367 ; Morris 1864, p. 74.
[2] C.P.B., Nov. 4, 22, 23, 1858 ; C.G., 2.9.71, 13.1.72, 19.10.72, 6.10.77.

It was in these circumstances that the landowners and rate-payers of Coppenhall parish held a public meeting on October 3, 1859, at which the Local Government Act, 1858, was adopted by the township of Monks Coppenhall; Church Coppenhall township refused to join in. On December 3, 1859, the Act became law within the boundaries of the township, and an election was held in the following January for the first Monks Coppenhall Local Board. With Benjamin Cotton in the chair as Returning Officer, the first Board meeting took place in the railway company's Town Hall on January 25, 1860.[1] The semi-rural character of Crewe at the time is reflected by the fact that five out of the first fifteen members were farmers. Hill, the two Heaths and Pedley were large property-owners in the district, but only two persons elected were officials of the railway company—Worsdell and Hawkins. This confirms the tradition that the prime movers for a Local Board were the property-owners and farmers of the district, many of whom did not live in the town itself but were among the chief sufferers from its unregulated state. At the first meeting John Hill was elected Chairman in preference to Pedley, who had headed the poll, and the Board began a by no means uneventful career, during which Crewe was endowed with the foundations of its present municipal system.[2]

[1] *Manchester Daily Examiner*, Oct. 15, 22, 29, 1859; *London Gazette*, Nov. 1, 1859, pp. 392–3; C.L.B.M., 25.1.60 (all further references to the Board Minutes are omitted from this chapter); *E.A.* 02, pp. 71–5; White 1860, pp. 347–52. The first fifteen members of the Board were John Hill (first chairman), Richard Pedley, Martin Heath, Samuel Heath, Richard Sherwin, William Walter Higgins, Thomas Beech, John Cope, Nathaniel Worsdell, John Eaton, Joseph Bolshaw, John Yoxall, Henry Hawkins, Benjamin Mulliner and Benjamin Cotton.

[2] From 1860 to 1869 the Board's official title was "The Monks Coppenhall Local Board," but on March 31, 1869, it passed a resolution changing its name to "The Crewe Local Board," and the name of its district to "Crewe," on and from May 1, 1869, due to the "great inconvenience" which arose "in consequence of the two names of Crewe and Monks Coppenhall being applied . . . to . . . the populous part of the township of Monks Coppenhall." It was not so easy to change centuries-old local nomenclature as the Board imagined, for no sanction to this alteration had been obtained from Whitehall, and in 1870 a special clause had to be inserted in a Local Government Supplemental Act (33 & 34 Vict., c. 114) to ratify the new title and remove any doubts as to the legality of acts performed by the Board after May 1, 1869. (See *Index to London Gazette* (1830–80), under *Coppenhall, Monks*; *Staffordshire Advertiser*, Feb. 27, 1869; C.G., 31.12.70—auditor's report.)

The Local Government Act of 1858 (21 & 22 Vict., c. 98) was to be read as part of the Public Health Act of 1848, some provisions of which it repealed. For example, the Act abolished Edwin Chadwick's General Board of Health, and transferred the Board's medical functions to a sub-department of the Privy Council. The Board's supervisory powers (confirmation of by-laws, the right to receive annual reports from the Local Boards, etc.) were vested in the Local Government department of the Home Office. These functions were collected together again in 1871, when Gladstone set up the Local Government Board. The Act of 1858 greatly simplified the procedure by which a district might adopt the sanitary code ; instead of an elaborate system of petitions and government enquiries, a simple resolution of adoption at a public meeting of owners and ratepayers convened for the purpose by twenty or more persons themselves owners or ratepayers—as at Crewe—sufficed. In the case of Crewe the cost of adoption and of the first Local Board election was just under £25.

When constituted, the Board inherited all the powers of the vestry and the surveyor of highways with respect to purely secular local government, except the election of overseers and guardians of the poor. It could construct sewerage works, provide gasworks, light, cleanse (or contract for the cleansing of) its district, and make by-laws concerning the minimum level, width, construction and sewerage of new streets, and the measurements and ventilation of new buildings. Its paid surveyor had the power to order defective cess-pools and water-closets to be put right immediately, and the Board had no need to take its proposed highway rates before Justices of the Peace for approval. It had power to order streets to be made, paved, sewered and channelled at their owners' expense and then devoted to the public use, while it could also adopt or construct bridges. The provisions of the Towns Improvement Acts of 1847 dealing with public nuisances, fires, the naming and numbering of streets, the line of streets, ruinous and dangerous buildings, the provision of a water supply, the prevention of smoke, the control of obnoxious trades, common lodging-houses and slaughterhouses, etc., were included in the Act of 1858, and in addition the Board could establish public markets and cemeteries by adopting the Markets and Fairs Clauses and Burial Acts, and (if it was so desired) establish public baths and wash-houses. It could (under the Lands Clauses Consolidation Act) buy land compulsorily, and borrow money from the Public Works Loan Commissioners or others, but such loans were not to exceed at any one time the whole assessable value of the district, and were to be repaid (with the interest) within thirty years. These loans were made on the security of the rates, upon which the Board could draw to an unlimited extent, but railway, canal and agricultural lands paid at the rate of only 25 per cent. of their assessed value. The Board's accounts had to be audited annually by the District Poor Law Auditor. Members of the Board were elected annually by landowners and ratepayers under the voting system used in the elections for Guardians of the Poor, so that a small ratepayer might have one vote and a wealthy propertyowner a dozen. Taken with the Public Health Act of 1872 (35 & 36 Vict., c. 73), a strangely neglected measure which first made the appointment of Medical Officers of Health compulsory on all urban and rural sanitary authorities, and forced all urban areas to adopt the Local Government Acts, the Act of 1858 marked an advance upon that of 1848. It heralded the beginning of a second stage in English public health legislation, a stage which ended in the extension and codification of 1875, and which has not hitherto received the attention it merits. The history of local boards in general, their problems, the extent to which they used their powers, their place in the preparation for borough status, and the part which they played in the swiftly-developing, complicated pattern of English local life and government in the second half of the nineteenth century, is still unexplored.[1]

A full Monks Coppenhall Local Board consisted of 15 members serving for three years, 5 of whom retired each year in order " to supply the elements both of experience and activity." [2] In the

---

[1] The work of Gladstone's Administration of 1868–74 in the field of public health and local government has been somewhat obscured by Cross' and Disraeli's Act of 1875—the Whigs dished again ! The *Report of the Local Government Board* for 1874–5 noted a " growing disposition, since the passing of the Public Health Act, 1872, on the part of both classes of sanitary authorities (urban and rural) . . . to execute permanent works of sanitary improvement " (p. xliii). For the work of the Local Boards, see Redlich and Hirst : *Local Government in England*, vol. i, p. 149 *sqq.* ; Ensor : *England, 1870–1914*, p. 126, *sqq.*

[2] *Ann. Rep. Loc. Govt. Board*, 1871–2, p. xlv.

course of its history, nearly 50 persons served on it, but a small band of 25 men, Ainsworth, John and William Allman, Beech, Bland, Briggs, Eaton, the two elder Heaths, Higgins, Hill, Jackson, McNeill, Mulliner, Pedley, Priest, Rigg, Teasdale, Thompson, Wadsworth, Welch, Whitting, Whittle and the two Worsdells performed the great majority of the tasks undertaken by the Board.[1]

The passing of the years was marked by the almost total disappearance of the agricultural element so noticeable in 1860. By 1877 John Allman was the last true farmer left. Of the persons who served on the Board, at least 22 had extensive interests either in local land, house-property or building. Yet the Board was by no means tolerant of laxity in enforcing the building regulations. Although badly served by its earliest surveyors in this respect, it took care to prevent infractions after 1868–9, and John Hill's self-announced indifference to the proper enforcement of the building by-laws cost him his seat in 1863. In particular, the jerry-building activities of one William Middlewood of Cornbrook Park, Manchester, were severely dealt with, and proceedings were taken against him on several occasions.[2] This compares favourably with the state of affairs disclosed under the Corporation at the turn of the century.

The railway element in the Board may be divided into two classes; the first contained John Teasdale, Allison, Hawkins, and Bland (who owned land in the township with an annual rental of £260), and was made up of well-to-do working men; the second group consisted of important officials—the Worsdells, Wadsworth and Rigg (the last named owned cottages and land in Henry and West Streets worth nearly £400 a year).[3] Some of the other members of the Board were of working-class

---

[1] See biographical indexes at end of original M.A. and Ph.D. theses in the University Library, Manchester.

[2] *Return of Owners of Land, 1873*, vol. i, under *Cheshire*; for Hill's case, see *Cheshire Observer*, 23 and 30.8.62, 27.9.62, 4.10.62, 20.12.62, 7.2.63, 15.8.63; for Middlewood's, see C.L.B.M., 1868–9, *passim*. Unrecorded building of houses, especially in the 1860's, makes it practically impossible to measure the extent of building at the time, and the passing of plans was no guarantee of the erection of a house. The cessation of building activity during the boom-period of rising prices in 1871–4 was fairly complete, and caused much overcrowding (*C.G.*, 21.3.74, 1.5.75).

[3] *Return of Owners of Land, 1873*, vol. i, under *Cheshire*.

origin ; *e.g.* the Heaths, Whittle and John Allman had risen from the ranks by means of the economic opportunities offered to the ambitious, the hard-working and the lucky in ever-increasing measure in the course of the nineteenth century. Thus, while the complexion of the Board was overwhelmingly middle class, a large percentage of its members had originated in the working class. Those middle-class members who were Liberals in national (and to some extent in local) politics, identified them-selves with the mass of the workmen, who were well-known for their Radical opinions. They combined these opinions with a strong affection for " the company " up to 1880, but after that date the local politics of Crewe underwent a complete and revolutionary change.[1]

By 1877 the Board had built up a committee system which worked well, and in 1871 it could be said that " the work was done in Committee—the Board room was the place where the talking was done." [2] The General Purposes Committee, first set up in 1865 and consisting of a fortnightly meeting of all the members of the Board, soon became the most important. By 1870 it controlled the whole of the money spent. After the setting up of the Farm Committee in 1871 it found an important rival, but it was not until 1877, when the Corporation appointed a Works (Highways and Improvements) Committee, that its work was seriously reduced. In 1877 the four standing com-mittees appointed year after year were for General Purposes, the Farm, Finance, and the " omnibus " committee for Cemetery, Market, Lighting and Water. The Board also built up the rudiments of an efficient administrative staff ready to be taken over in its entirety by the Corporation in July, 1877. Thus, historically considered, the Board may be described as a form of apprenticeship in training men in the practice of self-government before the town attained the dignity of a municipal borough. It is safe to say that an observant inhabitant of Crewe who had left the town in 1860, to return only in 1877, would have noticed a new order in the streets and houses, and the growth of a civic and corporate consciousness which had been in its infancy when he left.[3]

The relations of the Board with the railway company were

[1] *C.G.*, 9.3.72, 6.4.72, 24.3.74, 21.7.77 ; *C.Ch.*, 4 and 25.9.75, 30.10.75.
[2] *C.G.*, 4.2.71.　　　　　　　　　　　[3] *C.G.*, 29.10.70.

generally harmonious, in spite of occasional disputes concerning bridges, unpaid rates and the rateable value of the works, permanent way and steam sheds. In 1855 the company's property was rated at £6,600, while the value of private property in the town only amounted to £3,840, and throughout the period of the Local Board the company paid about one-third of Crewe's rates. Difficulties were smoothed over by the fact that during the rapid expansion of the 1870's, important railway officials usually held the office of chairman of the Board. In Rigg's words :—" I have no more influence with the company than any other member. But I have greater facilities for talking matters over with them." [1]

Although the company could do much by passive resistance to defeat the aims of the Board, as in the case of Flag Lane Bridge, the members of the Board were agreed in 1869 that the company " had never interfered with regard to the regulations they had made." [2] There is no evidence of any conscious official railway policy of " packing," in spite of allegations made in 1873 in connection with an unsuccessful " effort to place more of the company's officials on the Board," when " nomination papers with the names of the company's candidates " were sent to its tenants, and slips containing the same were circulated in the works. This action was probably due to over-zealous foremen. [3] Any serious quarrel between town and company, before 1880, was prevented by tact on the part of the railway officials and a common sense acceptance by the leading men of the town of the company's economic predominance :—" If they reflected for one moment where was the source from which they got their maintenance, they could see that it . . . was one fountain that brought them all their bread and butter, and that was the railway company." [4] When, however, the company's officials started interfering with political opinions, as they did in the 1880's, the Liberal and Radicals took up the challenge with vigour.

I. FINANCE

The task of the Board in raising supplies was lightened by the fact that it governed a district the rateable value of which in-

---

[1] *C.G.*, 29.1.70, 31.12.70, 10.8.72, 30.9.76.
[2] *Nantwich Guardian*, 30.1.69.   [3] *C.G.*, 11 and 25.1.73.
[4] *Nantwich Guardian*, 30.1.69 (Bland proposing Rigg as Chairman).

creased from £11,494 in 1859 to £51,257 in 1874. Notwithstanding this rapid increase, the expenditure of the Board more than kept pace with it, so that the rates levied also rose in amount. In 1860 the only rate levied was 7*d.* in the pound, while the financial year 1876–7 brought a 3*s.* 11*d.* rate plus a 1*s.* water rate.[1]

The Board's finances reveal the extent to which sanitary progress and highway improvement depended on the ability and willingness of local authorities to raise loans on the security of the rates ; these loans were the predecessors of the grant-in-aid, and the chief means by which the central power and local authorities were brought into contact. Crewe's budget for the year ending March 25, 1863, totalled £837, of which only £180 had been raised by loan, but the result of this was seen later in the year when, with only 19*s.* in the bank and the highways in a worse state than in 1859, the chairman had to admit that " the Board would be brought to a standstill before long." [2] Contrast this with the financial year 1874–5, when no less than £17,300 was raised by loans and only £8,752 by rates. By the end of 1868, *i.e.* before the purchase of the Market Hall and the sewage farm expenditure, the town's debt was already nearly £14,000 ; by 1881 it was over £69,000.[3]

In the early period the Board found considerable difficulty in collecting its rates. Between 1860 and 1871 three inefficient part-time collectors mismanaged affairs with disastrous results. Large sums had to be written off as irrecoverable, and the levying of rates was always in arrear. In 1871 the first full-time collector embezzled £73 immediately after being appointed. Henry Warham was thereupon appointed to the full-time position with an assistant. In May, 1873, the Board received a letter from its

[1] White, p. 344 ; *C.G.,* 29.11.73, 24.7.75, 28.10.76, 4.11.76. The 3*s.* 11*d.* levy was made up chiefly by " The Terrible Two-and-Twopenny Rate " required to make good the losses on the Sewage Farm. Wadsworth (chairman, Finance Committee) thought it would " be as good as a Turkish bath for some people."

[2] *Cheshire Observer,* April 18, May 30, 1863. Crewe's first modern budget (for the year ending March 25, 1861) revealed an expenditure of £1,002.

[3] *E.A.* 13, p. 18 ; *C.G.,* 2.5.74, 24.7.75, 28.4.77 ; *Ann. Rep. of Loc. Govt. Board,* 1871–2, pp. lxiv–lxv, pp. 296, 304 ; 1873–4, pp. 683, 687 ; 1874–5, p. 487 ; 1875–6, p. 403. It is interesting to note that the Board's first three loans were from local friendly societies. As the loans became larger it relied on private firms outside Crewe and the Public Works Loan Commissioners.

Treasurer,[1] which showed a bank overdraft of £5,760, but within two years the position had improved so much that the chairman, in presenting a balance of £2,286 at the bank, said :—

"With regard to the rates, I don't suppose that ever within the history of the Board, except perhaps at the very commencement, when its operations were of a very circumscribed nature, such a favourable result as that presented this morning . . . has been . . . attained." [2]

II. Administrative Staff

One of the main services of the Local Board to the development of local government in Crewe was the development of an administrative staff ready to be taken over in its entirety by the new Corporation in 1877. This entailed considerable experiment and trouble, caused largely by the Board's reluctance to offend the ratepayers by paying adequate salaries to its servants. The Board possessed no full-time official whatsoever until 1866. The chief office was naturally that of Clerk to the Board, the head of the municipal civil service. The first clerk appointed was Shearman Sheppard, said to be a friend of John Hill, who served from 1860 to 1868. The first rate-collector was also Hill's market-toll collector, Thomas Bromfield. Sheppard's salary, several times raised from its original £15 per annum, was inadequate. He complained that he had to keep a clerk and neglect his private practice to attend to the Board's ever-increasing business, chiefly rate-levying. In 1869 the District Auditor reported that the accounts " had fallen into a chaotic state of confusion." Sheppard had already been requested to resign. The Board's next choice proved more fortunate, for on December 29, 1868, it selected Frederick Cooke (1841–1912), a young solicitor from Winsford, as Clerk at £80 per annum. Cooke proved a most satisfactory and diligent public servant

[1] The Treasurer's duties consisted merely of holding the balances of funds belonging to the Board, for the Clerk was in reality the " efficient " treasurer. The persons who held the post were the managers of the Nantwich branch of the Manchester & Liverpool District Banking Company, John Mills (1860–3) and F. W. Hobson (1863–78). *C.G.*, 3.8.78 ; Kelly 1857, p. 176 ; Morris 1864, p. 107.

[2] *C.G.*, 27.3.75 ; also 2.9.71, 21.6.73, 5.7.73, 27.3.75, 28.5.77.

throughout the Injunction Crisis, and became the first Town Clerk in 1877, a post which he held until 1909, when he resigned on account of failing health.[1]

In 1872 the Clerk's salary was raised to £200 on condition that he kept a clerk to attend exclusively to the accounts, while Cooke himself devoted more of his time to the strictly legal affairs of the Board. No restriction existed on his extensive private practice as a solicitor, and from the fact that he played an important part in the Incorporation Agitation it will be seen that his position was very different from that of a modern Town Clerk.[2]

The history of the Surveyorship is instructive in that it shows the gradual transition from badly-paid amateurism to high-salaried efficiency. On the formation of the Local Board, Thomas Bromfield, the last of a long line of unpaid Surveyors of Highways for Monks Coppenhall, was automatically superseded by the first paid Surveyor of the new local authority, John Furber, land agent, at £15 per annum. Justified complaints about Furber's " misrule and incapacity " led to his departure in 1862, but in spite of the increased salary given the Board had tried three more Surveyors by 1866, when, in desperation, it advertised for a Surveyor at the unprecedented salary of £150, " being convinced that a competent Surveyor cannot be had for £100 a year." The new surveyor was George Watson, who became the first Borough Surveyor. The salary paid to him, when compared with that of the Clerk, is eloquent testimony to the importance which the Board attached to works of sanitary improvement, and perhaps the best evidence of Watson's superiority over his predecessors is the fact that he managed to retain his office throughout the Injunction Crisis, practically superseded though he was by William Hope, the Chancery

---

[1] White 1860, p. 348 ; *E.A.* 10, p. 24 ; *C.G.*, 1.1.70, 31.12.12 (obituary). *Cheshire Observer,* Feb. 1, 1862 ; petition in Local Board Minute Book under date 28.5.66.

[2] He might be called upon to carry out a task of the following character :— In 1874, when a child dead for seven days from scarlet fever had been discovered unburied in a house in Lockitt Street where from 7 to 14 people usually lived, the Clerk was " requested to send to the Relieving Officer to have the child interred, and if the Relieving Officer neglected to do so, the Clerk was to see to the burial of the child himself " (C.L.B.M., 25.2.74 ; C.G., 28.2.74).

engineer.[1] He was at first allowed to have a private practice, but in 1867 the Board informed him that his salary " was such as to demand his full services," and when it appeared that Watson " was not personally engaged one-third of the time," the views of the Board members are recorded as having been " very freely expressed."   Further cases of neglect occurred in 1868, when he was given the alternative of resigning or giving up his private practice.   He chose the latter, and promised to be in his office at nine o'clock each morning.   An assistant Surveyor, appointed for the first time in 1866, soon became a man-of-all-work.

The Inspector of Nuisances appointed in 1860 was Police-Sergeant Wilson ; this again was not a full-time job, but entailed periodical reports of nuisances to the Board, the inspection of lodging- and slaughter-houses, and (after 1864) of meat.   In 1871 Sergeant Wood, successor to Wilson, received three months' notice for neglecting to report unemptied ashpits, a duty which was especially important on account of the smallpox epidemic of that year.   Inspector Thomas Morris, noted for his zeal in smelling out bad meat, was forced to resign in 1873 on account of a general order from the Home Office prohibiting police-officers from acting as Nuisance Inspectors, and the office became a full-time one at £70 ; the new Inspector, Samuel Stockton, also superintended the road-men, a further illustration of the elasticity of a municipal staff in the process of formation.[2]

III. Roads and Bridges

The adoption of the Public Health Act by the township of Monks Coppenhall eventually made the distinction between the two sections of the town even more marked, whereas up to 1860 there had been no efficient public body in charge of the highways outside the company's streets, after the mid-1860's there was increasing efficiency in road administration under the Local Board.   Two tendencies are traceable after 1860, firstly, spasmodic attempts on the part of the company to devote its private streets to the public use, thereby throwing the cost of maintenance on the township, and secondly, the efforts of the Local

---

[1] *Cheshire Observer*, Feb. 1, 1862 ; C.G., 20.5.82 ; for the Injunction Crisis, see pp. 127–131.
[2] C.G., 13.12.73.

Board, equally spasmodic in 1860–3, to rescue the older highways from the neglect into which they had fallen, to ensure that the rapidly growing new streets should be of the correct width, and to see that new buildings on them should be in a straight line.[1] The Board's reluctance to add to its work by taking over the Company's streets may be partially explained by the extent of its tasks in other parts of the town.

In 1860 the Surveyor had been allotted the duty of cleansing the streets, and a force of from 3 to 4 men was employed in scavenging in 1868. In 1865 the Board bought its first water-cart and in 1870 the first roller appeared on the streets of Crewe. In 1867 the Board, after some hesitation, took over the duty of cleansing the company's streets. The company's efforts to hand over its private streets began in January, 1867, but only in 1869 did the Board decide to adopt Coppenhall Terrace, a main thoroughfare, and Chester Street from the " Golden Canister " on Coppenhall Terrace to Moss Square, together with Prince Albert Street and Liverpool Street, a much-used short cut. These adoptions cut the company's estate into two distinct blocks composed mainly of side streets, the condition of which was not a matter of such concern as that of the thoroughfares adopted. The reluctance of the Board to adopt the remainder naturally increased.[2] In 1867, to save the district from the erection of a toll bar within 2 miles of the Market Square, the Board took over from the Nantwich and Wheelock Turnpike Trustees that portion of their highway which ran through the southern part of Monks Coppenhall.

During the Board's first four years of existence, there was considerable dissatisfaction with the condition of the roads, and a meeting of ratepayers in November, 1862, sent a deputation to the Board on the subject. The Board's unpopularity reached its height in April, 1863, not only on account of the roads, but also because the building by-laws had not been enforced in an efficient manner, and it was rumoured that " charges were to be made

---

[1] *Cheshire Observer,* 1862, *passim,* Jan. 17 and March 7, 1863. It could be said in 1875 that the houses outside the company's estate had been " built for the most part . . . in an irregular line, at least the old ones. Since the Local Government Act was adopted . . . there has been a marked improvement in that respect " (*C.G.,* 1.5.75).

[2] The Board adopted Delamere Street in 1877.

against the officials of the Local Board . . . that body would be thrown out of office *en masse* by the ratepayers petitioning the Secretary of State." [1] This storm passed, but the Board continued to be primarily interested in sewerage throughout the first decade of its existence, and one member later expressed the opinion that Crewe's municipal authorities could have been indicted for the state of the highways in 1866–7. After 1866 much more attention was paid to the roads, and it became the custom for the Board in a body to make an annual tour of inspection of its district (a custom still followed by Crewe Corporation). Not until 1868 was the first road ordered to be made, paved, sewered, and channelled (Station Street), and a large number of central streets which should have been adopted in the 1860's remained unmade until 1875–7. In 1875 it could be said of Market Street, which since 1867 had contained the new Co-operative central stores :—" As the visitor is taken along Market Street . . . he enters a street where civilisation, as far as road-making and paving and asphalting are concerned, is unknown." [2] The constant delays can be explained partly by a desire not to anger the freeholders with heavy road-making expenses, and partly by other tasks which confronted the Board :—" They had plenty to do with regard to their cemetery and irrigation business. . . . The whole subject of permanent works was to be kept in abeyance." [3] After the Injunction Crisis the Board could devote more time and money to the necessary work of maintaining the streets in a condition worthy of a town agitating for incorporation, and in 1874–5 it embarked upon an ambitious programme : " a new street, to be called Richard Moon Street," was to be made, and the arrears from the period 1840–70 were at last liquidated. [4]

By reason of its importance as a railway junction Crewe contains a number of bridges which owe their existence to the demands of the various lines. The most important of these are the Manchester, Liverpool, Chester, Flag Lane and Edleston Road bridges, and the Local Board engaged in a ceaseless war with the railway authorities to decide who should pay, and in what proportions, for their widening and maintenance. The narrow Flag Lane bridge was built by the company in 1867–8, in flagrant

---

[1] *Cheshire Observer*, April 18, 1863.   [2] *C.G.*, 26.7.73.
[3] *C.G.*, 8.10.70.   [4] *C.G.*, 9.1.75, 25.7.75.

disregard of the by-law requiring all roads to be 33 feet wide, in spite of the protests of the Board. The Chester and Liverpool bridges, situated in important central streets, and erected in the early days of the colony, required widening by 1860. In spite of negotiations from time to time, the company did nothing in the matter until 1872 and 1874 respectively.[1]

IV. Public and Private Lighting

The lighting of the streets on the company's private estate was generally considered satisfactory in the early days of Crewe, and the contrast with that part of the town not owned by the company was painfully sharp by the 1850's. Less than half a dozen lamps existed outside the company's estate, and in 1860 none of them was public.[2] It is not therefore surprising to find the Local Board setting up a Gas Committee in August, 1860, and arranging for 25 lamps to be set up by the railway company. The Government of France in the eighteenth century extinguished the street lamps in Paris on moonlit lights, and with the money saved thereby created " pensions in the moon." In nineteenth-century Crewe, the Local Board eased the burden on the rate-payers in the same way ; perhaps the French expedient has aroused an unmerited amount of ridicule. . . . In the early years, the Board did not light its lamps at all during the spring and summer months, and, in addition, from 1860 to 1868 they were not lit for five nights in the month during the period of the full moon from September to February, *i.e.* throughout the winter. Vestiges of these parsimonious customs, a relic of cheese-paring Local Board days, lingered on until the general introduction of electric lighting in 1901.[3] By 1867 the number of lamps under the Board's control had risen to 114, and after several disputes an arrangement was come to in 1874, whereby the local authority took over the lighting of the entire town and bought all the lamps in the company's streets, 79 in number.

[1] *C.G.*, 31.12.70 ; Morris *1874*, p. 252.
[2] Head : *op. cit.*, p. 110 ; *C.G.*, 2.9.71.
[3] *E.g.* as late as 1892 the Town Council rescinded a resolution " That the street lamps in the Borough be not lighted from the 12th May to the 1st August, this year," only to give the Surveyor discretionary powers to *light* the lamps on dark nights.

This brought the number of lamps controlled by the Board to 249, and so disappeared yet another vestige of the early railway community. The lamplighters, three in number, were employed by the gas department of the railway company. One of them, Henry Clarke, an enthusiastic follower of Herbert Spencer and a disbeliever in all forms of corporate control, achieved a local celebrity from his eccentricities and his letters to the *Crewe Chronicle*.[1]

The Local Board interested itself in the supply of gas to the town for other reasons. The company possessed the power to break up the streets in order to lay and repair gas-mains, but its officials often omitted to obtain permission from the Board's Surveyor, and on several occasions the existence of two authorities gave rise to friction and delay, especially as the company's workmen frequently left the streets in an unsatisfactory condition. The Board at various times took up the question of the price and quality of the domestic supply. In 1861 the price had been reduced from 7s. to 6s. 6d. per 1,000 cubic feet, partly as the result of representations by the Board to the directors. In 1863 the directors further reduced the price of what the *Cheshire Observer* called the " worst gas in England " to 5s. 10d. after further pressure from the Board. By 1869 the price had fallen to 4s., although there were frequent complaints about the poor illuminating power. As building operations progressed, the Board would ask the company's gas department to extend the mains into the new streets so that lamps might be installed.[2]

When in 1864 the Board promised the company help " in getting legal powers to make contracts with the Board for the supply of gas . . . to the town," it had made the reservation " without prejudice to the rights and powers conferred upon the Board by the several Acts of Parliament under which they act." In 1870 the company sought additional powers from Parliament to supply gas to Crewe town for another ten years, and interested parties from the Potteries approached the Board to suggest either the flotation of a private gas company or that the L.N.W.R. Company's Bill should be opposed unless a clause were inserted " binding the Company not to charge more than 3s. 6d. per 1,000 feet." Despite this, the company's Bill passed into law

[1] C.G., 2.5.74, 27.3.75, 29.7.76.
[2] *Cheshire Observer*, Dec. 20, 1862, Nov. 28, 1863 ; C.G., 21.11.74.

unamended in 1870. In 1874 began a fresh series of complaints about the quality of the gas, and the agitation for a separate company sprang up again :—" It is high time to cast off the trammels and leading strings of the railway company " . . . " it is high time the public began to talk of a gasworks of their own." Such were among the remarks made in the columns of the *Guardian* on the subject. The matter rested here for two years, but the subject came up again for discussion at a public meeting in 1877, at which Liberal James Briggs and Conservative Wallace Lumb agreed on the desirability of a municipal gasworks. At the last Local Board meeting, McNeill advocated either a private or a municipal works, and a long discussion took place. The subject dropped, however, when early in 1878 the company granted a reduction of 3*d.* per 1,000 cubic feet and effected a great improvement in the illuminating power.[1]

V. WATER SUPPLY

During the first years of the Board's existence the company was preparing to bring water into the town from Whitmore. The first supplies from this new source reached the inhabitants of Crewe in 1864, but those residing outside the company's estate had to wait until 1866 for connections to be made. In the meantime the Valley Brook, scattered pumps, wells and rainwater had to suffice, and in 1865 the Board made an arrangement whereby two persons sold water to the inhabitants at $\frac{1}{4}d.$ per bucket. In the case of the gas-supply the company owned the mains, but when the terms on which the Board was to take water from the company were settled, in 1864, the company made it clear that the Board would have to lay its own water-mains. By 1870 the Board had spent nearly £5,000 under this head. The Board agreed at the same time to pay 6*d.* per 1,000 gallons for all the water which it took for redistribution to consumers outside the Company's property. In 1870 the principle of a rate on the assessed value of the property supplied was decided on, although baths and water-closets bore an additional annual rent. Twelve years later a minimum charge of 8*s.* 8*d.* per annum per house was adopted, in spite of protests from the owners of large blocks of cottage property who generally paid

[1] *C.G.*, 18.6.70, 2.5.74, 17 and 21.11.74, 16 and 30.6.77, 13.10.77, 2.2.78.

the rates.   The Corporation supplied 4,010 houses with water at this date, 2,403 of which were rated at £8 10*s.* or less.   In 1870 it was calculated that about 900 houses out of 3,500 remained without either inside or outside taps.   Figures of consumption are rare, but in 1874 the inhabitants of that part of the town under the Board's control (for the company still supplied its own tenants with water) used 6 gallons per head per day.[1]   The Medical Officer of Health considered this inadequate, but the low consumption was partly due to the bad quality and insufficient pressure.[2]

It was not long before complaints began concerning the water, its quality and its quantity, which were to last with varying degrees of intensity until 1875.   The first concerned the lack of pressure, especially in Hightown.   This district, as its name implies, is above the level of the surrounding district, and the problem could only be solved by erecting a tank in Flag Lane, into which water could be pumped and then released for general consumption, a remedy suggested to the company by the Local Board as early as 1870, but only carried out in 1898.   The other and more serious cause of complaint was the general dirtiness and insufficiency of the supply ; the two conditions were related, for a high pressure automatically cleaned out the pipes and prevented the collection of dirt.   It is also possible that the rapidly increasing population of the 1870's demanded a larger supply than the existing pipe-line from Whitmore could give.   1870 saw the water " very muddy and impure."   Filtration at Whitmore began in this year.   A novel degree of impurity was reached in 1872 :—" It being reported that the town's water was full of centipedes and animalcula, also of green vegetable matter ; it was proposed . . . that the Clerk write to Mr. Webb on the subject."

In 1873 began the period of complaints *par excellence*, and the annoyance became so common that in 1874 Dr. Richard Lord, the Medical Officer of Health, wrote two open letters to the *Guardian* on the subject.   He recommended that the " dirty brownish-looking fluid " should be boiled or filtered, and con-

[1] Compared with 18·9 gallons per head per day in 1937.
[2] *C.G.*, 8.3.75, 15.7.82 ; Coun., 19.7.82 ; *Census* 1871, vol. ii, pp. 390–1. The use of wells and pumps was ordered to be discontinued in 1867, but some continued in use illegally.

sidered that there could be no improvement until the supply was larger and more constant. In his Annual Report for 1874 he advised every householder to buy an animal charcoal filter, and these became as common in Crewe as permutite softeners in a modern "hard-water" district. After a third deputation had been appointed in 1875 to visit Whitmore and Madeley, where the water was found to be excellent, F. W. Webb gave out the welcome news that the company's engineers were proceeding as quickly as possible with a 15-inch main from Whitmore; completion was expected within two months. In March, 1876, the *Guardian* could say :—" . . . we have, during the last year, got an abundant supply of excellent water." [1]

VI. Public Health in Crewe, 1860–77

Public health formed the main preoccupation of the men who made possible the momentous Acts of 1848 and 1858. The first of these had been aided in its passage through Parliament by the threat which insanitary urban agglomerations constituted to their inhabitants, no matter whether they were rich or poor, whether they lived in well-drained dwellings or sewage-infected mansions. Not all the well-to-do lived in sanitary dwellings. Yet many of the Local Boards neglected this aspect of their work, and, in the words of Tom Taylor, " by means of light rates purchased a popularity which was but seldom broken in upon by the complaint of some zealous local reformer who felt sanitary evils more keenly than local taxation." [2] If the case of Crewe is in any way typical, this account of the development of sanitary government takes too little account of the administrative difficulties which the Local Boards had to face in their early years. In Crewe the Local Board, hampered by inefficient Surveyors and by ratepayers who lacked a social sense, did little in its first seven years save attempt to keep the roads in repair, provide the beginnings of a piped water-supply, and sewer a few streets, of which Mill Lane was the most important. An attempt to start the public emptying of ashpits and privies in 1866 failed, and only in 1867 was it successfully restarted with contract labour.

---

[1] *C.G.*, 25.3.76 ; see also *C.G.*, 9 and 30.4.70, 28.5.70, 18.6.70, 2 and 30.7.70, 2.5.74, 11 and 18.7.74, 8.3.75, 1.5.75.
[2] *Ann. Rep. Loc. Govt. Board*, 1871–2, pp. xliv–xlv.

Modern municipal " gas-and-water " socialism has evolved from public and private experiments and the accumulated administrative knowledge of the last century. Such social services could rarely be improvised in the mid-nineteenth century without some loss of financial efficiency.

The Monks Coppenhall Local Board of Health began to take greater interest in the suppression of sanitary nuisances during the cholera scare of 1866. Crewe, a great railway centre with a growing population of what was locally called a " floating character," formed an ideal reception and dispersion centre for the disease. When in July, 1866, Dr. James Atkinson, company's surgeon, wrote to the Board to recommend " immediate attention to the sanitary arrangements in consequence of the approach of cholera in the neighbourhood," he was at once appointed Medical Officer of Health at £20 per annum. He urged drastic action with regard to urban pig-keeping,[1] the laying on of water to all cottages, and the strict control of all lodging-houses. During 1867, however, the scare died down, and Atkinson's appointment was not renewed at the end of his year of office ; it was regarded as an emergency measure only.[2]

The smallpox epidemic of 1871 was a national affair, which caused the deaths of 23,000 people in England and Wales. At this period Crewe was experiencing an industrial boom, coupled with a housing shortage, both favourable to the spread and maintenance of the disease, which manifested itself in Whitegates, a slum area, in March, 1871. Many disquieting facts were discovered by the newly-appointed Nuisance Committee, which had the co-operation of the Crewe doctors. An ashpit in the centre of the town was suppressed ; disinfection and limewashing became the order of the day. Incompetence on the part of the Crewe Relieving Officer in dealing with smallpox cases among paupers led the Board to make representations to the Nantwich Guardians' Clerk, and by the end of April the epidemic was under control. No exact figures can be quoted of total cases and deaths in Crewe, but in one week alone 28 new cases were

---

[1] It is interesting to note that the deep-rooted practice of keeping pigs in the centre of the town was allowed to flourish throughout the Board's history, provided it did not, in the opinion of the Nuisance Inspector, constitute a public nuisance.

[2] *C.G.*, 20.5.71, 24.4.75.

reported. Punctually in March, 1872, the fearsome disease regained its vigour, and identical measures were adopted. To judge from the material examined, most of the cases came from the very poor, those who lived in the worst localities, and had no reserves of money to tide them over a period of sickness. The Board again intervened to request Joseph Pickering, the Relieving Officer, " to deal as liberal as possible " with deserving cases suffering from smallpox. One member of the Board made a spirited attack on the inefficiency and slowness of contract labour in emptying privies ; people were again paying private persons to empty them.[1]

Financial help to the extent of £600 for the poorest victims of the epidemic also came from the men of Crewe works. In March, 1872, a Smallpox Relief Fund Committee was formed to assist " those men . . . prevented from working in consequence of the smallpox." The epidemic continued throughout the summer, so that by the end of August 46 men were being relieved by the committee. A deputation from the committee waited on the Board on August 28 and suggested the opening of a smallpox hospital ; this was the course adopted in 1873, after a committee of workmen had been set up to induce the Board " to establish a smallpox hospital out of the rates." The Board, although hampered by the fact that it had no power to keep persons who were not destitute in a hospital (the place for such cases being the Nantwich Workhouse), decided to convert " the late Mr. William Pym's old farm-house in Pym's Lane into a temporary hospital "—Crewe's first municipal isolation hospital. The outbreak in 1873 proved to be much milder than the previous ones, and although cases were notified, only two persons died.[2] It would, however, give an entirely false picture of Crewe in the 1860's and 1870's to paint it as a smallpox-ridden town, full of overcrowded cottages and lodging-houses. There existed thousands of households which were never stricken by the smallpox however much they might fear it, and which had no need, according to contemporary standards, of the Nuisance Inspector's visits. After 1873–4 the Board was able to resume

[1] *Ann. Rep. Loc. Govt. Board*, 1871–2, p. lii ; *C.G.*, 1.4.71, 29.4.71, 8.7.71, 16.3.72, 1.6.72, 12.9.77, 2.2.78.

[2] *C.G.*, 31.8.72, 14.6.73, 12.7.73, 8.11.73, 24 and 31.10.74. The smallpox epidemic coincided with polluted water supplies.

the task of providing the town with a complete system of sewerage, and as the quality of the town's water improved, the danger of further epidemics diminished.

1873 was marked by an important event in the history of public health in Crewe—the compulsory appointment of a Medical Officer of Health under the Act of 1872 (35 & 36 Vict., c. 79). The Board's choice fell on Dr. Richard Lord at a salary of £50 per annum. Not until 1893 did the appointment become a full-time one. Lord's annual reports, printed in the *Guardian*, contain a great deal of information not to be found elsewhere. From July, 1873, thanks to Lord, detailed vital statistics for Crewe are available. The chief generalisations which can be drawn from them are that about one-half the deaths were those of children under five years old, and that the high birth-rate and the low death-rate were both due to the " almost total absence of old people, and the fact that the majority are newly-married, healthy persons." [1]

VII. Refuse Disposal

One of the most pressing problems which confronted the Board was the creation and maintenance of an efficient sewerage system, a problem aggravated by the fact that the population of Crewe increased by 118 per cent. between 1861 and 1871. It was truly said in 1875 :—" Crewe, without such a Board, would be one of the vilest places in the Midland Counties." [2]

On account of the lack of administrative personnel, the Board issued by-laws in 1860 " concerning the cleansing of privies, ashpits and cess-pools when . . . Local Boards do not themselves undertake or contract with any person for the above purposes."[3]

---

[1] Dr. Richard Lord and his elder brother Dr. John Lord (1820–76), like many of Crewe's doctors in the nineteenth century, came from Scotland. John settled in the town in 1854, and Richard followed him as an apprentice in 1856. They were said to be "sprung from the working-classes." Dr. Richard Lord (1836–1910) was an enthusiastic advocate of sanitary improvement when M.O.H. (1873–8) and a supporter of the famous Coppenhall Spa Pump project. He was for some years a member of the Church Coppenhall School Board. (*C.G.*, 5.2.76, 23.9.76, 4 and 18.11.76, 5 and 13.1.77, 20.1.77, 17.3.77, 7.8.78, 15.11.10.) [2] *C.G.*, 8.5.75.

[3] Before 1865–7 all householders and property owners outside the company's estate contracted privately with local farmers or carters for the performance of this necessary sanitary measure.

These regulations were enforced by the Inspector of Nuisances, who reported bad cases to the Clerk. He in turn would then serve notices on the offenders to cover or cleanse the ashpit or the cess-pool. The organisation of a rudimentary municipal service for emptying ashpits and privies by contract labour took two years (1865–7), at the end of which period the Board and its contractor, who had at last worked out some sort of routine, took over the duty of emptying the ashpits of the company's houses. In these, and in the older houses generally, the custom prevailed of keeping ashes and nightsoil together in " mixens," 280 of which were enumerated in 1873, generally in a badly drained condition. For the year ending March, 1869, the estimate for this service was only £300, and the infrequency with which it was performed may be judged from the fact that some of the ashpits had no openings through which their contents might be easily removed, so that they had to be broken open and subsequently built up again by bricklayers. Most of the pits were emptied less than twice a year.

The contractor was in arrears with the emptyings from 1868 until September, 1872, when the Local Board established a special Nightsoil Removal Committee to undertake the service directly without the intervention of a contractor, and an attempt was made to establish a regular system of collection. Ashes as well as nightsoil were now tipped on the Sewage Farm instead of into places almost inside the town.[1] When, after eighteen months of direct labour, it showed signs of becoming more expensive than under the contractor, the Board promptly returned to the method of contract, after a battle between the " economists," led by Welch and Briggs, and those who desired a healthy town, even if the rates increased somewhat. Complaints about unemptied ashpits, which had almost disappeared under the direct labour system, recommenced, and by the middle of 1875 an unsavoury list of 400 awaited the attentions of Contractor Wood. The Board cut off his supplies, so that he worked " as never man worked before," and reduced the number to 100 by July, 1876, when the Board decided to return to direct labour. In spite of the extra cost this step was warmly supported by the

---

[1] During the Injunction Crisis the inability of the Board to construct new sewers and to allow further entries into existing ones added considerably to the strain on this department.

M.O.H., as the unemptied ashpit constituted " one of the most frequent sources of disease." [1] The real solution lay in the compulsory fitting of water-closets in all new houses. These had first appeared in Crewe in the 1860's, but even in 1875 they were unusual—their installation in a row of cottages in Goddard Street in that year received a warm welcome from Dr. Lord, as affording " an experiment of working." Well might he say in the first Annual Report (1874) : " It will be a grand day for Crewe when the old system of privies has been abolished and water-closets substituted." [2]

VIII. Problem of Sewerage and the Injunction Crisis

Related to the problem of refuse disposal was that of providing efficient sewers. This was rendered more pressing as water-supply by tap came into general use during the 1860's. The first large undertaking executed by the Board (1860–1) was a scheme of drainage for Nantwich Road and Mill Street, then the main shopping centre for South Crewe. The sewage from these two localities was conducted into the Valley Brook, which flowed most conveniently at the bottom of Mill Street. Other streets draining into the brook were sewered between 1861 and 1866. Open drains and private sewers continued to exist in those parts of the town not affected by these reforms, but the Board worked out a general plan for the sewerage of the town in 1863–4, and after protracted negotiations with the directors of the railway company, the Board undertook to construct a main sewer " from a point near the Mill . . . for the purpose of carrying away all the sewage of the place and thus avoiding the pollution of the Brook now much complained of."

Later plans included the provision of two outfalls and culverted sewers (one for each of the two brooks in the township) of which the Board finally decided to bear the whole cost ($£11,600$) ; the Board's and the company's systems of sewerage continued separate. The southern outfall was completed in 1866, the northern in 1868 ; the former had a filter-bed at the spot where

[1] C.G., 8.7.71, 29.6.72, 30.5.74, 8.5.75, 24.7.75, 1.1.76, 25.3.76, 29.7.76, 24.3.77.
[2] C.G., 1.5.75.

it emptied into the brook, but from the subsequent history of the scheme it does not appear to have been very efficient.

The Board imagined that it had reason to congratulate itself upon having devised a fairly cheap system for draining the district, which did away with the nuisances arising from the company's outfall into the Mill dam.[1] Unfortunately the nuisances had merely been shifted downstream, there to offend the inhabitants of Leighton, Woolstanwood and Wistaston Green, to say nothing of the powerful riparian owners. Ultimately Crewe's sewage polluted the River Weaver. The problem was one which had confronted the great towns some years before, but it was now presenting itself to smaller urban communities. These local authorities did not consider that they possessed the resources to solve the problem in a comprehensive manner, and were bewildered by the variety of sewage disposal and purification methods, often both expensive and practically valueless, which inventors and their interested supporters offered them.

The central government passed four Sewage Utilisation Acts between 1865 and 1870, to prohibit the direct discharge of any sewer or drain into a river, to enable local authorities to apply sewage to land, to confer powers on them for the compulsory purchase of the same, and to permit them to borrow money for the purpose under the Sanitary Loans Act from the Public Works Loan Commissioners. Contrary to what was said at the time, Whitehall did not merely confine itself to decreeing that the nuisance should stop, and did in fact give practical advice as to the most practicable system to adopt. In the case of Crewe, for example, Tom Taylor, secretary to the Sanitary Department of the Local Government Act Office, sent down Arnold Taylor in 1867 to advise the Board to adopt " a scheme of sewage irrigation " from the northern outfall similar to that adopted later.[2] His advice was disregarded, and the members of the Board either forgot, or preferred not to remember, that such advice had been given and neglected. The first hint of the coming trouble appeared in the receipt of a letter in 1866 from Broughton & Hensley, solicitors of Nantwich, " on behalf of

[1] *E.A.* 02, p. 57 ; *C.G.*, 25.12.69, 6.10.77.
[2] See esp. C.L.B.M., 9 and 29.10.67 (Enquiry) ; *C.G.*, 6.3.76 ; *D.N.B.* (Tom Taylor).

owners of land in Wistaston," complaining that the Valley Brook had been turned into a public sewer by the Board, and threatening further proceedings if the nuisances were not abated. From the Board's reply it appeared that the brook had been polluted by the sewage from the Company's works many years before the Board existed.

Squire Edward Delves Broughton (1816–89) of Wistaston Hall, about a mile and a half from Crewe, registrar to the Nantwich and Crewe County Court, and clerk to the Nantwich and Crewe magistrates, was a member of the younger branch of the Delves Broughtons of Doddington and a specimen of that dangerous type, the lawyer-landowner. Apart from the fact that he had a just grievance, he seems to have been animated by a personal grudge in his action against the Local Board. He had been in conflict with the Board in matters affecting infringements of the building by-laws and the compulsory purchase of land. Thomas Beech averred later that Broughton had told him the Board would not have been troubled if it had only built him a bridge costing £500 across the brook.[1] The Board delayed taking any action, and continued to hope that no great expense would be necessary. Broughton, however, was not to be appeased. He prevailed upon the Board in 1869 to consult Baldwin Latham, C.E., of Nantwich, " rather a distinguished engineer," as to the best means of irrigation, " as the land-owners are complaining of the fouling of the brook, and threatening proceedings." Latham " could not describe these brooks as anything else but putrid sewers." Broughton waxed lyrical in

---

[1] *C.G.*, 23.10.75. The Board suffered much from the lawyer-landowners of Nantwich. In 1869 R. C. Edleston, solicitor, Clerk to the Nantwich Local Board, to the Commissioners of Land, Assessed and Income Taxes, and to the Nantwich and Newcastle, Nantwich and Woore, and Nantwich and Wheelock Turnpike Trustees, demanded £30 for an easement of sewer from the Crewe Local Board. That body paid, " although . . . of opinion it is most arbitrary and more especially considering the terms on which they have been able to settle with the whole of the landowners . . . with the exception of a gentleman of your own profession." Broughton demanded and obtained from the Board, in 1872, 8s. per square yard for land for a similar purpose, " four times as much as the other landowners . . . accepted without demur." Actions such as these did much to explain Crewe's dislike of Nantwich (Ormerod : *op. cit.*, vol. iii, ed. 1882, p. 523 ; *Return of Owners of Land, 1873*, vol. i, under *Cheshire* (Broughton owned 1,530 acres) ; White 1860, p. 377, Morris 1864, p. 103 ; 1874, p. 294 ; *E.A.* 90, p. 179 ; *C.G.*, 25.11.71).

his wrath concerning Crewe's sewage :—" . . . It not only poisoned the streams and killed the fish, but poisoned the cattle that fed in the meadows adjoining." [1]

On March 17, 1870, the Board received notice that Broughton had caused a Bill to be filed in Chancery, asking for an injunction to deter the Board from emptying any sewage into the Valley Brook. The injunction was granted a few weeks later and gave the Board until May 5, 1872, to construct works which would prevent recurrence of the nuisance, on pain of a fine of £10,000, payable to Broughton, who refused to sell any convenient land for sewage disposal purposes. This galvanised the Board into action ; a deputation visited several towns and returned with a decided preference for irrigation as the cheapest method of sewage disposal in the long run. [2] The decision to adopt it was carried only by the casting vote of the chairman, Bland, and met with stout opposition from the " economist," Briggs. Great credit is due to Bland and Teasdale for their vigorous and successful advocacy of irrigation, as it can be seen from the later history of the scheme that further delay would have caused incalculable harm to the health and finances of the town. As it was, the Chancery injunction contained a clause prohibiting the connection of further sewers to the outfalls ; this certainly contributed to the epidemics of 1871–3. [3]

About half a mile of the southern sewer had to be closed up, and the new pumping station moved from the vicinity of the Queen's Park to a plot of land " adjoining the Chester Railway, near to Merrill's farm." [4] Owing to the nature of the soil, difficulties with landowners and negligent contractors, the Board was forced on May 5, 1872, to apply for an extension to the period of grace. Vice-Chancellor Bacon passed some severe strictures on the conduct of the Board :—" The time was not employed but merely wasted, and no earnest, or sincere, or honest endeavour

[1] *C.G.*, 25.12.69.

[2] Irrigation, the most efficient and popular method of treating sewage at the time, consisted of collecting the sewage in tanks, and spraying or pumping it over a large area of land, on the Chadwickian principle of " sewage to the soil and water to the river." It is still in use (*C.G.*, 20.6.74, 8.5.75).

[3] *C.G.*, 31.3.70, 6 and 9.4.70, 15.5.70, 30.7.70, 15.6.72, 20.6.74.

[4] In actual fact, the completed engine-house and reservoir had later to be moved from Merrill's Bridge to Minshull New Road. This was one of Hope's " special difficulties."

to comply with the order of the Court can I gather from any part of the evidence."

Eventually Bacon modified his views, granted an extension until December 27, 1872, and appointed William Hope, C.E., of London, to superintend the works under the orders of Chancery. Hope's preliminary report may have softened him somewhat :—

" The Board have had special difficulties to contend with. . . . The town of Crewe stands in the centre of a clay district, so that the Board had no choice open to them as to the kind of land to be taken—two shafts sunk to the depth of 30 feet to a bed of clay proved the clay to be so exceedingly solid that it is absolutely dry a very few feet from the surface, and is about as stiff, unyielding and tenacious as any I have ever examined. It is impossible to prepare this land with the same rapidity as that of a light, lump or sandy land. . . . I can testify to the earnestness and intelligence in which the committee, surveyor and farm-bailiff perform their respective duties." [1]

In March, 1871, the Board made the management of the land it had rented as a sewage farm a permanent municipal duty by setting up a Farm Committee to utilise it for agricultural purposes. In 1873 Joseph Jackson, after resigning his seat on the Board, was appointed the first Farm Manager.

The works had by no means been completed by the end of 1872, and an extension was granted until November 9, 1873 ; yet a further extension for four months only became necessary, and was granted in December, 1873, when the Board's counsel could say " . . . the pumping machine is actually got to work." Another successful application was made in March, 1874, this time for eight weeks, and in May the Clerk reported that the Board " was in a position to comply with the orders of the

[1] *C.G.*, 2.7.70, 8.10.70, 15 and 22.6.72, 16 and 30.7.72. Hope's description of Crewe clay will be endorsed by many of Crewe's amateur gardeners. *Cf.* Gladden : *op. cit.*, p. 21 :—" (Crewe) stands upon soil which is a geological freak. In summer it has the composition of granite, and can only be dug with a pick-axe. In winter it combines the consistency of treacle with the specific gravity of lead, and cannot be dug at all." Hope, who was the lessee at £600 per annum of the Romford Sewage Farm, displayed an eager interest in 1872 in the formation of a Co-operative Board or private joint-stock company to manage the Crewe Sewage Farm, since " the machinery of the Local Board was not adapted for managing such a thing as a farm." This project was vetoed by the directors of the L.N.W.R. Co. (*C.G.*, 15.6.72, 18.1.73, 1.3.73).

Court." The whole had cost about £36,800, and the scope had expanded somewhat from the modest 11 acres of 1868 and the estimate of £8,026 made in 1871. The completed Crewe Sewage Farm comprised 269 acres, of which 30 had been purchased outright and the rest secured on long leases. An observer noted in 1875 that the example of the farm had brought about a general improvement in the standard of agriculture in the district.[1]

IX. THE PURCHASE OF THE MARKET HALL

In 1867 John Hill opened negotiations with the Local Board for the sale of the Market Hall, negotiations which were interrupted by his death in February, 1868. June, 1869, saw their completion, with the sale of " the Market Hall, Corn Exchange and yard, chapel and land in front of the two shops adjoining" for £9,355, after a ratepayers' meeting on August 29, 1868, at which the Markets and Fairs Clauses Act of 1847 was adopted.[2] Thomas Bromfield's reign as toll collector for Hill (1854–69) thereupon came to an end. After a few years of direct administration, the Board leased the tolls in 1872 for three years at £612 per annum to James Percy of London, who continued to farm them until 1898, by which date he was paying £1,148 for the privilege. The Local Board's purchase can therefore be considered an extremely profitable one for Crewe. Since 1898 the market has been under the direct administration of the Corporation. A covered outside market has been added and the reconstruction of the Market Hall undertaken. It contributed in 1936–7, together with the tolls from street-hawking and the cattle markets, about £1,100 to the relief of the rates.[3]

X. BURIAL FACILITIES AND THE PROVISION OF A PUBLIC CEMETERY

In 1846 the churchyard of the Company's Christ Church had been consecrated for burials, and the inhabitants of Crewe thus had a practical choice between being buried there or in the ancient

[1] *Ann. Rep. Loc. Govt. Board,* 1873–4, pp. 687, 693 ; *C.G.,* 15.6.72, 18.1.73, 1.2.73, 1.3.73, 9.12.73, 28.3.74, 2.5.74, 30.5.74, 20.6.74, 1.8.74, 12.6.75, 25.12.75, all issues Jan., 1876, 29.6.76, 11.4.77, 28.4.77.
[2] The Board had to borrow £10,500, as the Hall was in a poor state of repair.
[3] White 1860, p. 346 ; *C.G.,* 30.10.69, 4.12.69, 21.1.71 ; *C.Ch.,* 2.9.82 ; Coun., 7.8.95, 1.6.98 ; *Abst. Accts.,* 1936–7, pp. 16–17.

parish churchyard of St. Michael's, Coppenhall. In 1857 an Order-in-Council was issued closing Coppenhall Churchyard to burials from and after July 4, 1857, " except in graves not less than five feet deep, which can be opened without the disturbance of remains, and except in existing vaults and brick graves in which each coffin shall be embedded in charcoal."

At the same time the Order-in-Council laid it down that no further burials should take place in the Christ Church ground, " except so far as is compatible with the regulations for new burial grounds." [1] This was presumably the occasion of the formation of the so-called " Coppenhall Burial Board " under the Burial Boards Act of 1855 (18 & 19 Vict., c. 128), at a well-attended meeting of ratepayers held in the vestry of St. Michael's on October 22, 1857. This meeting appointed a gravedigger, bought harness, and fixed charges for the use of a recently-purchased hearse. In the same year the churchyard was extended. Little is known about this Burial Board, but after it had expired, for some unknown reason, in 1869, the Burial Acts Office discovered that, although notice of the " Coppenhall Burial Board's" formation had been received in London, it had never obtained official sanction and consequently had never possessed a legal existence.[2]

On September 15, 1868, a second Order-in-Council closed the Christ Church ground to burials from December 31, 1869, " except in family graves to be used for the burial of members of the same family, and which can be opened to the depth of five feet without the exposure of the coffin." The operation of this order was twice postponed, on the initiative of the Rev. J. Nadin, incumbent of Christ Church, firstly to the end of 1870 and secondly to October 31, 1871. Thus, with Coppenhall churchyard " getting full," and Christ Church burial ground about to be closed, Crewe presented the spectacle of a growing community of nearly 18,000 without adequate provision for cheap, convenient and speedy burial.[3]

[1] C.M., Feb. 28, March 28, 1846 ; *London Gazette*, June 26, 1857, pp. 2197–8.

[2] C.P.B., Oct. 22, 1857 ; but see Oct. 4, 1855, Oct. 10, 1856 ; new Register of Burials (Coppenhall), 1857 *sqq.*; C.G., 19.2.70; C.P.B., Easter, 1870.

[3] *London Gazette*, Sept. 15, 1868, pp. 4988–9 ; Feb. 8, 1870, pp. 751–2 ; Jan. 17, 1871, p. 168 ; C.G., 8.1.70.

John Hill, " The Successful Railway Contractor "
(1810–68)

To Samuel Heath and John Teasdale belongs most of the credit for the establishment of the Crewe Burial Board and its unsectarian cemetery. In 1869 Heath referred at a Local Board meeting to "the great need there was that a free cemetery" should be made ; his interest in the subject was influenced by a dislike of the "hole and corner business" of vestry government, and by his sturdy Nonconformity :—" . . . it was not reasonable that in a place like Crewe, where there were so many Dissenters, that they should be dragged to the Church." [1]

A certain amount of opposition to the Crewe Local Board becoming the Burial Board for the district manifested itself amongst the "Church Party" and the champions of the "crushed ratepayers," led by Martin Heath, Samuel's cousin, and William Allman, who opposed all improvements involving municipal expenditure. Happily the need for a new cemetery was so evident, and the opinion of the town so set "against another sectarian burial ground," that the Board encountered no difficulty in getting the ratepayers' consent. The Privy Council's consent to the Crewe Local Board becoming the Burial Board for the district was given in May, 1870, and the nucleus of the present Crewe cemetery was formed by the purchase of a six-acre site in Church Coppenhall, opened for use on January 1, 1872. The Board provided the cemetery with two chapels, the one exclusively for the Church of England and the other for the other sects. This annoyed the Roman Catholics of the town, who numbered about 1,000, mostly of Irish extraction, to judge by the nomenclature ; they maintained a small burial ground by the Catholic Church in Heath (Russell) Street, from about 1852 until 1877, under the pit of the present Lyceum Theatre.[2]

Meanwhile, fresh provision was being made for those who preferred to be buried in the shadow of Coppenhall Church. In July, 1871, a vestry meeting for Church Coppenhall decided to form a Burial Board for that township, the first meeting of which took place on December 18 of that year. The Rector of Coppenhall, the gentle Rev. Moses Reid, Richard Whittle and Edward

---

[1] *C.G.*, 2.12.69, 26.2.70. Until 1880 all burials in grounds controlled by the Church of England had to be supervised by the clergy of the Established Church.

[2] *C.G.*, 8 and 29.1.70, 21.1.71, 30.9.71, 7.10.71, 18.11.71, 5.12.74, 9.1.75 ; White 1860, p. 345 ; *E.A.* 73, p. 27 ; Morris 1874, p. 232.

Wilding were among the first members, and Frederick Cooke, registrar to the Crewe Burial Board, was appointed registrar in this case also. It was decided to borrow £600 for a 1½-acre extension to the old churchyard. This was consecrated in 1873.[1]

[1] C.G., 23.12.71, 26.4.73.

CHAPTER VI

INCORPORATION AND POLITICS, 1842–1923

THE Census of 1871 revealed an increase of 118 per cent. in the population of Monks Coppenhall as compared with 1861. The upstart boom town of Crewe had at last outstripped its ancient rival Nantwich. The fact that Crewe was expanding so rapidly gave a feeling of boastful confidence to the inhabitants generally, and created both the need and the desire for a more adequate means of expressing and satisfying their corporate wants. The first recorded mention of a desire to incorporate the town occurs in January, 1872, when John Yates, a local newsagent, said that " Crewe . . . was becoming a very important town . . . and he hoped ere long it would be a borough." [1] Apparently incorporation formed the topic of general conversation throughout 1872, for in September the General Purposes Committee of Crewe Local Board requested the Clerk " to report on the desirability of the district being constituted a Municipal Borough." The *Crewe Guardian* newspaper quoted the example of the Batley (Yorkshire) Local Board, with a population of 18,000, which had petitioned successfully for a charter, and continued :—" Our town is daily increasing in size and importance and its government can no longer be contained in a nut-shell." [2]

Yet when the Clerk read his report in January, 1873, the project was adjourned *sine die*, and the matter dropped until September, 1875. During this period of acquiescence the Local Board took action to secure a larger representation for the town on the Nantwich Board of Guardians, another symptom of Crewe's growing-pains. In 1875 the agitation for incorporation reached its second and final stage. It was not due merely to the desire for " municipal honours " on the part of unsatisfied aspirants to local government, but to the existence of certain definite grievances and certain less-definite hopes. The need for a resident magistracy and a speedier " dispension [*sic*] of justice " were undoubtedly the largest single forces behind the agitation. In 1858 an Order-in-Council laid it down that the " County

[1] *C.G.*, 13.1.72.   [2] *C.G.*, 14.9.72.

Court of Cheshire, holden at Nantwich, shall be holden at Crewe as well as Nantwich," which meant that the tradesmen of Crewe no longer had to travel 8 miles or more to attend petty debt cases and the like. It was arranged that the court should be held at Crewe in alternate months. On May 2, 1870, the seat of the County Court underwent a definite removal from Nantwich to Crewe ; the office was henceforward open on only two days per week at Nantwich, as compared with four at Crewe.[1] Petty sessions have been held at Crewe from 1843 onwards, and in 1860 took place " at the Mechanics' Institute, on the fourth Wednesday in each month." The presiding magistrates at the time were Francis Elcock Massey, a local landowner bearing a Cheshire name famous through the centuries, and the Rev. Thomas Brooke, Rector of Wistaston from 1825 to 1872. The Rector took his duties very seriously. The local press described him in 1862 as being " always at his post," but often he could not proceed owing to the absence of a second magistrate :— " This is not the first time the public have been put to trouble and inconvenience through the irregular attendance of the J.P.'s," remarked the *Cheshire Observer* of December 6, 1862, somewhat tartly, on one such occasion. A year before there had been a demand in the local press for more magistrates for Crewe, and a case was related of a resident in need of a magistrate who had walked out to Wistaston, 2 miles away, only to find that the Rector refused to get out of bed, which is not surprising, as the old gentleman was getting on in years.[2] In 1874 seven J.P.'s were noted as attending the Crewe Petty Sessions on four days per week at 11 a.m., but the frequency of their visits lost much of their usefulness because none of the seven lived in the town. After 1869 the inconveniences of the situation multiplied rapidly, and the *Guardian* commented on the need for resident magistrates. Crewe, unlike Nantwich, had no old-established county families and no merchant aristocracy. Even middle-class tradesmen, who formed the " shopocracy " of Crewe, were rarely

[1] *London Gazette*, Nov. 19, 1858, p. 4904 : *C.G.*, 30.4.70 ; Morris 1864, pp. 74–83. The County Court was held in the Royal Hotel, Nantwich Road, from 1858 until 1906, when it was removed to the police station (*C.G.*, 5.11.98, 17.12.98, 3.3.06).

[2] *Chester Courant*, Dec. 12, 1843 ; White 1860, p. 346 ; *Cheshire Observer*, Nov. 11, Dec. 7, 1861.

admitted at this time to the ranks of the "great unpaid," the
more so when they had the habit of turning out in large numbers,
as in Crewe, to support such a dangerous agitator (in the eyes
of the county J.P. and his tenant, at least) as Joseph Arch.
Working-class magistrates, naturally enough, were unheard of.[1]
Whittle expressed a point of view held by a certain section of
opinion in the town, when he said that the choice lay between
securing a stipendiary magistrate, after the population had
reached 25,000, and incorporation, when the services of a Mayor,
ex-officio a J.P., could be had for nothing :—" Crewe was a new
town, and . . . there were only three or four gentlemen in it."
The rest of the inhabitants were working-men, he continued,
and as J.P.'s, how would they act when administering justice to
their old fellow-workmen ?[2]

In 1872 the Rev. T. Brooke died, and the Rev. J. Folliott of
Stapeley House, Nantwich, became the most constant attender
at Crewe Petty Sessions. During the year ending October,
1876, however, Folliott and two other "Crewe" justices died.
The situation was thereby rendered more intolerable than ever.
Charles Welch, landlord of the Royal Hotel, described the
position as follows :—

"He did not himself see why they at Crewe should have to go to
Nantwich for their magisterial business. Mr. Beech had told them
that two new magistrates would be made for this division of the
county—he believed these two gentlemen would be Baron Schroder,
of the Rookery, which is four miles away, and Mr. Jones of Stapeley,
which is five miles away. It would be most inconvenient for any-
body in the town of Crewe, who had to get a summons, say for a
petty larceny. He knew that from experience ; he would first have
to get a summons and then tramp five miles to the residence of one
of the resident justices, and then it was more than probable he would
find they were engaged at lunch or dinner, and of course he would
be told to wait."

In addition a stipendiary magistrate would mean £1,000 or
£1,500 more on the rates for salary, whereas a borough magistrate would serve for nothing. No property qualification was

[1] The first Crewe working-man magistrate, James Robertson, was added
to the Commission of the Peace in 1893 ; Morris 1874, p. 249 ; *C.G.*, 4.12.69,
9.9.71, 24.3.74.
[2] *C.G.*, 2.10.75.

needed in the case of borough magistrates as compared with the county magistracy.[1]

Several other advantages existed which it was hoped would accrue from incorporation, but they played a smaller part, and were chiefly used as auxiliary weapons in the conflict. For example, the Local Board was elected in the same manner as the Guardians ; this meant that a man might have a maximum of 12 votes, 6 as a ratepayer and 6 as a property-owner. This procedure would not obtain in voting at borough elections and a considerable body of opinion existed in the town hostile to the added influence which this undemocratic system gave to large property-owners.[2] The Poor Law question played a similar part. At the Crewe Local Board meeting on September 29, 1875, members pointed out that the town of Nantwich did very well in the matter of its paupers at the expense of the Union in general and Crewe in particular. It would be easier for Crewe, when a borough, to obtain a separate Union.[3] The supporters of incorporation at first desired quite naturally to include in the proposed new borough that portion of the ancient township of Crewe which contained the highly rated railway station and the urbanised southern portion of Church Coppenhall. This would equalise the rating burden.[4]

It was also felt that the style of Corporation would command more respect fromWhitehall and the Law Courts. In the matter of police, a borough of Crewe would be empowered to keep a separate establishment, and concentrate within the municipal boundaries the 14 county police officers who sufficed for Monks Coppenhall and some of the adjacent townships. Once the movement had been set on foot, additional reasons why Crewe should be incorporated took shape with the greatest rapidity, but most of them had little substance when compared with the great question of the magistracy. One of them, more important than the rest, deserves special notice. The strong Liberal-Radical party in the town supported the movement as the first step towards making Crewe a parliamentary borough, free

[1] *C.G.*, 23.10.75 ; Morris 1874, p. xviii ; *C.G.*, 1873–5 *passim*, and 21.10.76.

[2] *C.G.*, 30.10.75, 30.9.76.

[3] *C.G.*, 2 and 30.10.75. For the whole question of Crewe and Nantwich Board of Guardians see pp. 214–17.

[4] *C.G.*, 30.10.75, 6.11.75, 9.9.76.

from the Tory influences of the local squirearchy. This ambition was partially realised in 1885 when Crewe, made the head of a parliamentary division of Cheshire, returned its first M.P.[1]

The second and successful stage of the incorporation movement received its initial impulse from an unsavoury incident known as "The Cross Street Brothels' Case" or, more facetiously, "The Slaughter of the Innocents." Cross Street and its offshoot Blackberry Street are two small alleys in the heart of Crewe, once respectable, but already in the 1870's on the way to slumdom. By 1875 the cottages of Cross Street and Blackberry Street were nearly all common lodging-houses and often needed the attentions of the Nuisance Inspector.[2] On August 21, 1875, the *Crewe Guardian* contained the following report on the locality and its inhabitants :—

"The chief of the nests of these social rats was to be found in some cottage property in Blackberry Street, off Cross Street, which is the subject of a Chancery suit. . . . The respectable inhabitants of the neighbourhood made frequent complaints, and on Tuesday last, Superintendent Saxton brought Mr. John Caryl, jeweller, and Henry Milton, glazier, High Street, and they made sworn depositions regarding the houses occupied by Joseph Hodgkinson and Alice Bailey, that they were of the worst character. A warrant was issued for the apprehension of the prisoners and on Wednesday they were committed for trial to the Sessions."[3]

The case naturally created a great sensation in Crewe and district, and certain members of the Nantwich Board of Guardians expressed strong disapproval of the Crewe Local Board for allowing such a state of affairs to exist. Beech and Martin Heath sprang to the defence of Crewe and pointed out, in reply to Squire Broughton, that whereas the Board had jurisdiction in the sphere of public health, it had none in matters of morals.[4] The truth was that the fault lay partly with the Local Board, which could have arranged informally for two of its members to make the necessary depositions, partly to the unwelcome publicity attaching to such a necessary duty, partly to the lack of a resident magistracy and partly to the state of the law on the

[1] *C.G.*, 4 and 18.9.75, 25.9.75, 30.10.75, 9 and 30.9.76 ; *E.A.* 87, p. 7.
[2] *C.G.*, 21.3.74, 1.5.75.
[3] Both Caryl and Milton served on the Incorporation Committee.
[4] *C.G.*, 28.8.75.

subject. The Board's Nuisance Inspector had " time after time brought before the magistrates these persons in Cross Street for overcrowding, filthy houses, and admitting casuals," which was all he could do. In fact, the mere existence of the brothels did not constitute a nuisance with which the Board was empowered to deal.

When pursuing the ends of justice on this occasion, Caryl himself had been inconvenienced by the lack of a magistrate in Crewe :—" . . . he went over to Nantwich with another trades-man to see a magistrate, and was kept waiting in his yard for an hour. Then a window was thrown up . . . I had to go a second time over the same job." [1]

The derogatory remarks of Broughton and W. Tollemache aroused an angry feeling among the townspeople generally, which was fanned by the two rival Crewe newspapers. The *Crewe Guardian*, originally a weekly, was one of Dr. Alexander Mackie's chain of *Guardians* centred on Warrington and had published its first number in Crewe on August 29, 1863. Although each issue bore the claim that it was " Neutral in all Matters Political and Religious," there was a noticeable Tory bias in its excellent news-service, and in 1874 the editor of the eighteenth-century *Chester Chronicle* decided to publish a weekly Crewe edition of his Liberal-Radical organ, in response to a visit from two prominent Crewe Liberals, William McNeill and James Briggs. The first issue appeared on March 21, 1874, and while the early *Crewe and Nantwich Chronicle* remained for a long time behind the *Guardian* in lay-out, accuracy and circula-tion, its healthy Radicalism evoked a rivalry which helped in the solution of various local problems.[2]

The first problem was that of incorporation. The *Chronicle*

---

[1] *C.G.*, 30.9.76.

[2] *C.Ch.*, 21.5.92, 22.3.24 ; *C.G.*, 1869–80, *passim*. There had been several attempts to start a Crewe newspaper before 1863. The *Chester Record* gave a few items of local interest from 1860 onwards, while the *Cheshire Observer* contained a great deal of Crewe news from August 31, 1861, until 1863–4, and kept a representative in the town. Birkenhead speculators founded a *Crewe Advertiser and Nantwich Chronicle* early in 1862, as a rival to the *Chester Chronicle*, but the venture proved a failure. A *Crewe Herald* flourished for a short time in 1871–2, and from then until 1874 the *Guardian* could boast that it was the "only newspaper in this crowded town of mechanics" (*Chester Record*, Oct. 3, 1863 ; *C.G.*, 2.3.78 ; Morris, 1874, p. 291 (advertisement).

has the honour of being the first actively to defend Crewe against the aspersions of Nantwich and to mention incorporation as a solution. In the issue of September 4, 1875, appeared the following :—

" Shall we turn Crewe into a Municipal Borough ? . . . we are now convinced that the subject is ripe for settlement. . . . In the first instance . . . Crewe, through its Local Board, has been grievously insulted during the past fortnight and that, too, by persons who have no right whatever to interfere in her local affairs, and who, it transpired, were the persons responsible for immorality revealed . . . we now refer to the astounding accusations made against the character of the Board in the matter of the Cross-street brothels . . . had we our own bench of justices . . . we should have been spared that shameful and most unjust reprimand.   But there is another light in which the subject may be regarded.   Why in the name of reason should the bulk of the police business from Crewe be transacted at Nantwich ? "

The *Guardian*, not to be beaten by its competitor, took up the question on September 11, 1875, but in a more temperate tone. The same issue also recorded the first practical step towards incorporation :—

" . . . a preliminary meeting of tradesmen was held at the Mechanics' Institution on Thursday last.   Mr. Caryl was called to the chair ; several speakers advocated the desirableness of steps being taken with the view of Crewe becoming an incorporated town. . . .   The question of costs having come before the meeting, it was estimated that a rate of 2*d*. in the £ on rateable property would produce £458 and fully cover the expenses . . . ultimately it was unanimously resolved that the chairman of the Local Board be requested to call a public meeting . . . for the purpose of taking the subject into consideration."

Those present formed themselves into a Provisional Incorporation Committee, and the public meeting suggested was held on Tuesday, October 26, 1875, in the Town Hall, William McNeill, Chairman of the Local Board, presided.   The hall was packed, and of the 900 people estimated to be present only between 50 and 60 opposed the resolution :—

" That in the opinion of this meeting it is expedient and greatly to the benefit of the inhabitants of the Crewe Local Board, that a petition should be presented to Her Majesty the Queen, in Council, praying that she will be graciously pleased to grant a Charter of Incorporation to the said district, and also that the Local Board be requested to take all . . . steps for the purpose. . . ." [1]

McNeill stressed the great inconvenience caused by the lack of a resident magistrate when people needed summonses, warrants and remands. In general, the arguments were those indicated above. Some opposition was heard, notably from Thomas Beech, who had said before :—" He had heard persons say ' Never have a Mayor ; if you want your rates increased, incorporate your town.' " [2]

There was, however, no adequate answer to the advocates of a resident magistracy *via* incorporation, and the opposition confined itself to vague generalities and the problematical question of a rate-increase. The majority of those present felt that the town's prestige needed something more dignified than a Local Board, and the pleasure of taking part in a communal agitation outweighed the prospect of monetary loss.

Here the Incorporation Committee met with an unexpected check. The Local Board refused on November 2, 1875, to " interfere further in the matter," and ordered a draft petition to be " handed over to volunteer canvassers for signature by the inhabitant householders of the district." This action represented a coalition of those members who were lukewarm to the project (Martin Heath, Whittle, Whitting) and those who were hostile (Wadsworth, T. W. Worsdell, Beech, Thompson). The Incorporation Committee met later in the day, when McNeill explained that of the 900 people present on October 26 only about 200 were ratepayers, so that the Board felt that a private canvass would be better than a public poll. Canvassers, chiefly local tradesmen, were therefore appointed and laboured for several months gathering signatures for the petition. No counter-petition presented itself, and on June 30, 1876, a notice appeared in the *London Gazette* to the effect that the petition was to be considered by a committee of the Privy Council on August 8, 1876. On August 15, C. L. Peel, Clerk to the Privy Council, wrote to Major Donnelly of the Science and Art Department empowering him to hold an enquiry to " investigate the allegations contained in the petition," and to report on various matters,

[1] *C.G.*, 30.10.75.   [2] *C.G.*, 2.10.75.

including the number of actual householders who had signed the petition, "their several assessments," "the state of the Local Government," its expense, and the boundaries of the proposed borough.[1]

Later, at a meeting of the Incorporation Committee, the desirability of incorporating Henry Street, in the township of Church Coppenhall, and the railway station, in the township of Crewe, was discussed at some length. The proposed inclusion of these two places in the boundaries of the new borough brought the committee into conflict with Church Coppenhall and the L.N.W.R. Company. A deputation accordingly waited on F. W. Webb, Chief Mechanical Engineer, in order to ascertain the directors' views on the subject. At this point, according to Dr. Richard Lord, members of the committee began to lose interest in the subject ; several of its meetings were without a quorum :—

"I believe the unanimous feeling of the Committee was that if the Company intended to oppose we would allow the thing to quietly die away for a few years at any rate. The deputation . . . failed to see Mr. Webb, but had an interview with Mr. [T. W.] Worsdell [works manager], and received the answer . . . ' That the Company were not in favour of incorporation, believing it to be premature ; but that they wouldn't oppose it if a majority of the people wished it, and that they didn't desire the station to be included in the borough boundary.' "

From that time new life was infused into the moribund committee, which at the same time decided not to press further with its plan for the annexation of a portion of Church Coppenhall township.[2]

The Commission of Enquiry was held in the Council Room of the Mechanics' Institution on September 22, 1876. A partner of the firm of the Incorporation Committee's parliamentary agents opened for the resident householders. He said that the rateable value of Monks Coppenhall was £55,934, of which £20,132 stood in the name of the L.N.W.R. Co.[3] Of the

---

[1] *C.G.*, 6.11.75, 8.7.76, 19 and 26.8.76 ; *C.Ch.*, 18.12.75.

[2] *C.G.*, 8.1.76, 9 and 30.9.76, 7.8.78.

[3] In 1855 three-fifths of the rateable value of Monks Coppenhall had been derived from the property of the railway company, but with the growth of the town the proportion tended to dwindle, and remained at about one-third

3,931 ratepayers 2,337, representing £22,318 in the rate books, had signed the petition for incorporation. The passivity of the Company had thus weighted the scales heavily in favour of the borough project :—

" . . . they needed a commission of the peace. Nantwich was the centre of the old petty sessional division. Up to a period not very far distant a county magistrate who liked the work used to come to Crewe pretty constantly for the purpose of signing informations, remanding prisoners, and all that class of magisterial business which was usually done out of petty sessions . . . now that he was dead the nearest magistrate was not less than four miles away, and the inconvenience was very serious indeed. He need scarcely say that the wants of a population of 24,000 were very great indeed. There were very frequently cases of persons being taken up on a charge of drunkenness which could not be remanded, and many other cases which could not be dealt with by less than two magistrates or in petty sessions, and in many of these cases the police were not justified in obtaining a remand. . . . There were a considerable number of gentlemen of position thoroughly competent to perform the duties of a justice of the peace." [1]

C. E. Speakman then appeared on behalf of owners of property to the rateable value of £2,300, and expressed his belief that Crewe " had not a class of people to support a borough." Only one of the many witnesses in favour of incorporation (Dr. Richard Lord) made any reference to larger sanitary powers :—
" He believed the powers of a Corporation were superior to those of a Local Board for public health purposes."

This vague declaration shows the extent to which the magisterial problem overshadowed all others in the minds of the promoters. One of the Company's officials, Bartholomew Kean, gave evidence against the scheme on the grounds that :—
" The great majority of the inhabitants being working-men who lived in houses rented at from 4s. to 6s. a week, and a great part of their rates were paid by their landlords . . . it would be improper . . . to increase the taxes of these people."

---

between 1870 and 1890. In 1906 it had dropped to between one-quarter and one-third, and fell considerably in 1922, when, on account of reduced earning capacity, the company obtained a reduction of nearly £8,500 in the assessment of the works. This lowered the total figure from £43,889 to £35,432 or about one-fifth of the total rateable value of the borough.

[1] C.G., 30.9.76.

Somewhat late in the day the dissentients got up a petition against the grant of a charter; it contained a presumptuous plea:—

" . . . a large proportion of the houses in Crewe . . . have been built on speculation for sale . . . and are of an inferior character . . . your petitioners are the owners of nearly all the land still remaining unbuilt upon, and which has been retained by them with the view of the erection thereon of houses of a superior class."

Incorporation, by raising the rates, would frustrate this public-spirited plan.[1] This did not prevent the Privy Council from granting a Charter of Incorporation dated April 27, 1877. The great news was received some weeks before, on April 7, and on that very Saturday, by a happy coincidence, the works had resumed the five and a half day week after a period of " short time." The Charter laid down that Crewe was henceforward to be governed by a Council of 18 ordinary members and 6 aldermen ; the borough boundary was to be that of the township of Monks Coppenhall. Dr. Richard Lord, M.O.H. to the Local Board, and a prominent member of the Incorporation Committee, was appointed Returning Officer for the first election of 18 councillors and in that capacity presided over the first meeting of the Town Council, until 6 aldermen and a mayor had been chosen.[2]

In 1875 Richard Whittle had prophesied that the men elected to any future Town Council would be the same as those serving on the Local Board. Whittle's judgment proved correct, for in spite of the scramble for seats and the increase in the rates imposed by the Board a few months before, the first borough election on June 30, 1877, resulted in the return of 10 men who had seen service on the former governing body. Although the first Mayor, Dr. James Atkinson, the company's surgeon, had not seen service on the Board, the 5 other aldermen elected at the first meeting of the Town Council—Ainsworth, Martin Heath, Briggs, McNeill and Whittle—were all ex-members of that body. The election of 6 additional councillors on July 21,

[1] *C.G.*, 21 and 28.10.76 ; *C.Ch.*, 28.10.76, 4.11.76. The counter-petition also contained the following gem : " The population consists almost entirely of men employed by the company . . . and there are not in the town sufficient gentlemen and opulent tradesmen of standing and position to support the dignity of a Mayor and Corporation and administer justice without fear or favour." [2] *C.G.*, 11.4.76.

1877, brought 3 more ex-members of the Local Board to the Council Room. In the following November the election of George Wadsworth, Nathaniel Worsdell, T. W. Worsdell and Allen Priest brought the number up to 15. They provided a stiffening of experience to guide the young borough through its first years.[1]

The incorporation agitation had been carried to a successful conclusion by the tradesmen of Crewe, local drapers, newsagents, lawyers, publicans, grocers and insurance agents, mostly of Liberal-Radical opinions, backed by the mass of the workmen. Officials of the company had played a negative part in the agitation, and in the first two elections, with the exception of Dr. James Atkinson, they were defeated. Public opinion felt that this was a " mistake," as the railway officials " were always a welcome medium of communication and smoothers of diffi-culties between the Local Board and the Railway Company." Webb and the directors, also, felt annoyed at this state of affairs ; two of Webb's comments, the first in a private letter, the second publicly issued before the election of November, 1877, ran as follows :—

" I am only sorry that on Saturday last (June 30) they [*i.e.* the men of Crewe works] so far forgot their obligations that they did not exert themselves to return some of the company's officers to watch over their own and the company's interests in this railway town of ours " [2] . . . " if the people of Crewe do not study the Company's interest, I shall not be responsible for what the directors will do in reference to putting on the rates." [3]

Accordingly the Liberals decided to support Nathaniel Worsdell, stores superintendent, T. W. Worsdell, works man-ager, and George Wadsworth, chief accountant, as " Independent Railway Company " candidates in the election of November, 1877 ; they were all elected.[4]

Incorporation led to an intensification of party strife. This first became apparent when, in the voting for the first Mayor, both Martin Heath (Liberal) and Dr. James Atkinson (Con-servative) secured 9 votes each because one of the Liberals,

[1] *C.G.*, 2.10.75, 25.7.77 ; Election Return, June 30, 1877.
[2] *C.G.*, 16.1.14 (letter of Webb to T. W. Worsdell)—see also *C.G.*, 7 and 11.7.77.
[3] *C.G.*, 31.10.77.   [4] *C.G.*, 29.9.77, 6 and 27.10.77, 3.11.77.

A. P. Cotterill, refused to toe the party line. Dr. Richard Lord used his casting vote as Returning Officer, to make Atkinson first Mayor ; before the election, he alleged, pressure had been brought to bear on him to vote the other way. He had been M.O.H. to the Local Board ; it had been hinted to him that his re-appointment to the same post under the Corporation might or might not be automatic. . . . Liberal annoyance with the election of Atkinson is understandable when it is remembered that Martin Heath was the only person who had served on the Board continuously from 1860 to 1877, whereas Atkinson had never been a member and had comparatively little experience of public work. In addition, he was a vice-president of the Crewe Constitutional Association, and had advised the directors of the Company against incorporation. His attitude was summed up by a local wag as follows :—" I object to Corporation, but I don't mind being Mayor." In spite of his lack of experience he enjoyed a certain popularity in the town, which he increased still further by lavish expenditure (about £5,000) during his term of office as Mayor : his re-election in November, 1877, became a foregone conclusion.[1] This incident, and the adoption of the company's officials as candidates by the Liberals, broke down the resolution of the Conservatives not to introduce politics into municipal matters. In October, 1877, it could be said : " The election so far has taken a most bitter aspect on both the Conservative and Liberal sides," while the Tories began to complain that foremen in the works were intimidating their men to vote for the " Independent Railway Company Liberal " candidates. Not until the whole question of the relationship between the Town Council and the Company had been threshed out, was there to be a satisfactory basis for free local government.[2]

I. National Politics and the Intimidation Affair, 1842–92

Although we know that a number of the railway shopmen who founded the Crewe Mechanics' Institution in 1844–5 had

[1] Some of this £5,000 is supposed to have been supplied by F. W. Webb, who was a personal friend of Atkinson.

[2] *C.G.*, 21.4.77, 14 and 18.7.77, 27 and 31.10.77, 16.2.78, 7.8.78 ; *C.Ch.*, 14.7.77. The Conservative Association set up Ward Committees for the first time in 1877.

Chartist sympathies, there is no evidence that any organised branch of the Chartist movement ever existed in the town.[1] There was, however, a vigorous branch of the movement in Nantwich from 1838 onwards, led by Thomas Dunning, the shoemaker-newsagent.[2]

Crewe's importance for Chartism and for the forces of law and order was therefore strategic rather than local. The new railways under construction in the 1830's and 1840's enabled the Government to switch its meagre and overworked force of troops from one part of the country to another with unprecedented swiftness. On August 1, 1842, Charles Lawrence, chairman of the Grand Junction Railway (1841-2), told the tenth annual general meeting of the Company's shareholders at Liverpool that " upwards of 7,000 troops had been conveyed on the line during the half-year, and principally within the space of one week."

On occasion the railways helped the Chartists, too. During the early hours of Tuesday morning, August 16, 1842, Thomas Cooper, the Leicester Chartist, fresh from the great Crown Bank meeting of August 15 in the Potteries which had given rise to serious rioting, trudged along the dark roads from Hanley to Crewe, whence he hoped to take the train to Manchester. It is interesting to note that this meant a journey over a railroad track the final section of which (Crewe to Sandbach) had been opened only a few days before (August 10). He felt that the real control of the movement lay in Manchester, where the " Plug Plot " riots were in full swing. At Burslem he and his two companions succeeded, not without some difficulty and delay, in convincing Mr. Parker, J.P., and the local special constables of their *bona fides* and had time for breakfast at Crewe " before the Manchester train came up." Cooper wrote :—

" When I entered the railway carriage at Crewe, some who were going to the Convention recognised me—and, among the rest, Campbell, secretary of the ' National Charter Association.' He had left London on purpose to join the Conference ; and, like myself, was anxious to know the *real* state of Manchester. So soon as the City of Long Chimneys came in sight, and every chimney was beheld smokeless, Campbell's face changed, and with an oath he said, ' Not

---

[1] See pp. 233-5, *infra*.
[2] See *Trans. Lancs. and Ches. Antiq. Soc.*, 1947, pp. 85-130.

a single mill at work ! Something must come of this, and something serious too ! ' " [1]

For the next six years we hear little about Chartism in connection with Crewe, but in 1848, " the year of revolutions," the new railway junction came into prominence again in connection with the movement of troops. The stationmaster at the time was William Winby, who held the post from 1842 to 1861.[2] The Home Office Papers in the Public Record Office contain a letter dated Friday, June 9, 1848, from General Sir Thomas Arbuthnot, the officer in command of the disturbed districts, requesting the Home Secretary to direct the Commander-in-chief to send seven companies of an infantry regiment to Manchester, and three companies as a reserve at Weedon in Northants. The reasons given for the request were an expected demonstration of Chartists and Irish Repealers in Liverpool on Whit-Monday, June 12, and a public meeting of the Manchester Chartists fixed for the same day. The request for troops was granted.

What followed is graphically described in the words of the *Stockport Advertiser* newspaper of Friday, June 16, 1848 :—

FRIGHTFUL ACCIDENT ON THE LONDON AND
NORTH-WESTERN RAILWAY AT CREWE

" On Sunday last, a railway train, containing a troop of soldiers, was ran into by a train of empty carriages at Crewe. The particulars, as we learn are as follows :—The train containing the soldiers was at a stand-still, and about to turn off to Manchester ; unexpectedly the other train came up, and ran violently into it. The result was that a horse box, containing two horses, was completely smashed, and both animals killed. Several persons were more or less injured. The empty carriages were returning from London, having formed part of the cheap train trip of the previous day."

From General Arbuthnot's letter to the Home Office on Monday, June 12, the day after the accident, we learn that the train contained seven companies of the 9th Regiment on their way from Birmingham to Manchester and that several officers and some N.C.O.s were seriously injured, but no lives lost.

---

[1] *The Life of Thomas Cooper, written by himself* (1872), p. 206 ; Hovell : *The Chartist Movement* (1925), p. 261.
[2] *C.G.*, 9.6.11 ; *Cheshire Observer*, 7.9.61.

The General attributed the accident to "shameful neglect" on the part of the railway company and the Home Office took the matter up with the Railway Board.[1] Thus ended Crewe's connection with the Chartist movement.

Little or nothing is known of national politics in Crewe before 1867, when the Crewe Constitutional Association was formed. The Liberals alleged that the local squirearchy dominated it :—

"The land influence was recognised by everybody, even the Crewe Constitutional Association. Many would remember when that association commenced, all its public meetings had to be presided over by J. Hurleston Leche, Esq., J.P.[2] Not a discussion could take place unless he took the chair, and if he was late, someone could only take his place until he came."[3]

Whatever might be its origins, the association had by 1872 between 500 and 600 members, including practically all the local clergymen of the Church of England, Crewe's only brewer, E. S. Woolf, and the vast majority of the local publicans. Harmonious relations prevailed between the association and the railway company.[4] Henry Platt (1838–1926), wholesale beer and spirits merchant, was one of its founders, and until 1883 acted as secretary and agent. The Liberals and Radicals of the town did not organise themselves until 1872, when the Crewe branch of the West Cheshire Liberal Association was formed. For the first few years of their existence these associations remained little more than committees for ensuring that the names of as many of their supporters as possible appeared on the electoral register.

The alliance between the Established Church and the drink trade arose naturally as a defensive pact against the twin bases

[1] P.R.O.,H.O. bundle 45, O.S.2410 A.B.   For the reference to the Home Office Papers and the *Stockport Advertiser* I am indebted to Mr. F. C. Mather.

[2] Of Carden Park, near Chester (1827–1903), (*C.G.*, 27.6.03).

[3] *C.G.*, 21.12.73 ; *Chester Courant*, July 24, 1867.   Information concerning voters in the county elections of 1714, 1717 and 1727, holding land in Crewe, Monks Coppenhall and Church Coppenhall, exists in the Poll Books of 1714 and 1717 (MSS. in County Record Office, The Castle, Chester) and in the printed Poll Book of 1727.

[4] *C.G.*, 26.11.70, 11.11.71, 12.12.72, 29.9.79, 20.1.83.   In these early years it was said that the Constitutional Association "owed a great deal to the company, for without the company in all possibility there would be no association."

of the Liberal Party in nineteenth-century Crewe—Nonconformity and temperance agitation. Long before 1872, Richard Pedley (1828–1909), the Baptist farmer and cheese-factor from Haslington, who had taken the pledge in his early youth, and Nathaniel Worsdell (1809–86), a Quaker coachmaker and prominent company's official, had been active members of the Crewe Temperance Society, over which Worsdell presided from its foundation in 1843 until 1871. In 1861 these men continued a task begun by the company in its early days when they headed a great movement against the granting of fresh spirit licences for Crewe by the Nantwich Brewster Sessions. A successful petition, bearing 350 names, " amongst them being the signatures of all the clergymen and dissenting ministers of the town," was presented to the Justices, pointing out that 17 licensed houses and 27 beer-houses existed in the railway centre already. During the later 1860's and the 1870's the local clergymen of the Church of England seem to have drifted over to the party of the publicans, and the activities of the multifarious local temperance societies tended to become more and more identified with Nonconformity and the Liberal Party. These activities did not make the Liberal-Radicals popular with the licensed victuallers ; in self-defence the latter banded themselves together in 1873 to found the Crewe, Nantwich and District Licensed Victuallers' Association, with Henry Platt as secretary, *i.e.* practically an annexe of the Constitutional Association.[1] Only one important Crewe publican was an active Liberal during the nineteenth century—Charles Welch of the Royal Hotel (1840–95), of whom it was said in his obituary notice :—

" he resented what he called the ' harassing ' of the Licensed Victuallers' business by the extreme temperance party . . . So that during the last ten years or so, while an earnest and faithful follower of the G.O.M. (whom he greatly admired), he did not regularly attend political demonstrations proper ; though he was frequently found at Committees at the Liberal Club, when municipal contests were being arranged."[2]

---

[1] *Chester Record*, Feb. 4, 1860 ; *Cheshire Observer*, Aug. 31, Oct. 12, Nov. 16, 1861 ; *C.G.*, 28.1.71, 9.3.72, 6.4.72, 3.10.77, 21.9.78, 20.1.83, 18.1.08, 23.5.08, 2.2.26.

[2] *C.Ch.*, 13.4.95 ; *C.G.*, 10.4.95. The " Royal " was not at this time a " tied house " (*C.G.*, 24.9.92).

Other prominent local Liberals included John Eaton (1828–1907), Congregationalist baker and corn-factor from Salford, who, with John Mills, the Christian-Chartist manager of the Manchester and Liverpool District Banking Company's Nantwich branch, brought the Hungarian patriot Louis Kossuth to lecture to enthusiastic Crewe audiences on March 16 and 17, 1857 ; Samuel Heath (1816–82), farmer, builder and local landowner, who led the battle against Church rates and Anglican burial grounds in the interests of religious freedom and Primitive Methodism ; Martin Heath (1810–87) from Manchester, builder and landowner, who had been a Liberal since 1838 ; William McNeill (1832–1917), five times Mayor of Crewe, a Scots travelling draper who settled in the town in 1853 ; and James Briggs (1834–1921), Unitarian pawnbroker and stockbroker. As Church of England clergymen in the town were usually members of the Conservative Party, several prominent Crewe Catholics took an active part in Liberal politics ; *e.g.* Patrick Walsh (1811–84), P. V. O'Connor (1839–1911) and Bartholomew Kean (1818–87). This tendency became more noticeable after Mr. Gladstone's espousal of Home Rule.[1]

In 1877 both Liberals and Conservatives considered that the presence of railway company's officials on the Town Council was a desirable state of affairs, so long as they were not in the majority. John Eaton, presumably excluding Dr. Atkinson, said :—" . . . it had been pretty generally acknowledged that their first election had been a mistake, inasmuch as they had not elected a representative of the L.N.W.R. Company." [2] At the election of November, 1877, three company's officials were elected as Independent Liberals. Of these, Nathaniel Worsdell was well-known for his Liberalism, although his son T. W. Worsdell, also elected, appears later as a member of the Constitutional Association. The complaints of intimidation by works foremen to secure votes for these candidates displeased many Liberals as well as the Tories, and the practice was not repeated in 1878 or 1879.

---

[1] *Staffordshire Advertiser,* March 21, 1857 ; Isabel Mills : *Threads from the Life of John Mills, banker,* pp. 262–5 ; C.G., 14 and 17.5.84, 29.1.87, 18.6.87, 17 and 20.4.07, 18.8.11, 28.12.17, 22.11.21 ; C.Ch., 2.9.82, 29.1.87, 18.6.87, The Rev. W. C. Reid (Rector of Coppenhall 1880–1924) was a Gladstonian Liberal and a High Churchman (C.G., 3.7.86).

[2] C.G., 20.10.77.

After the November elections of 1877 the complete Council consisted of 14 Liberals, 3 Independent " Railway Company " Liberals, 6 Conservatives, and Dr. James Atkinson, a " Railway Company " Conservative.[1]

Dr. Atkinson, who was becoming the accepted leader of the Crewe Conservative Party, retired from the Council in 1880, since he had received the smallest number of votes in the election of aldermen in 1877. When in the course of 1880 it became known that the Liberals would not support his re-election, he persuaded the L.N.W.R. Company's Chief Mechanical Engineer, F. W. Webb (1836–1906), to allow the formation of a committee of works foremen. These foremen were to approach prominent company's officials in the town, obtain their candidatures, and promote their return to the Town Council as " Independents." Webb was undoubtedly a great engineer, but it is equally certain that he made a very poor politician ; he could not refuse Atkinson, who was his personal friend and possessed great influence over him. Webb himself, the son of a Church of England clergyman, had Conservative sympathies and an autocratic disposition. He combined these with a passionate desire to further the moral and material progress of the people of Crewe. In fact, he was a local patriot, pure and simple, wielding enormous economic power over thousands of men and women in a " one-industry " town.[2] This gave rise to a great deal of sycophancy. For example, the Rev. (later Canon) A. H. Webb, his brother, a Conservative and a High Churchman, was in 1879 appointed Vicar of St. Paul's Church, Crewe, a living in the gift of the railway company. His appointment was the signal for the church, which had hitherto been badly attended, to be filled. Throughout the period, Webb had the unstinted support of Sir Richard Moon (1815–99), chairman of the L.N.W.R. Company, whose political opinions were certainly not Liberal.[3]

[1] *C.G.*, 3.11.77, 3.12.81.

[2] *C.Ch.*, 23.10.80 ; *C.G.*, 29.12.80, 31.10.85. Another view of Webb's character was given by the judicious Charles Welch :—" If Mr. Webb was left alone he was a gentleman, but he was so susceptible to influences that had been brought to bear upon him that he did things he must afterwards regret " (*C.Ch.*, 30.11.89).

[3] *C.G.*, 30.11.78, 11.1.79, 26.9.85 ; *Who was Who, 1896–1916* (Moon). Other instances of what was called " the religious screw " are : (*a*) C. Dick, K. Macrae and G. Martlew, all prominent Company's officials, attended the

The first meeting of the committee of foremen seems to have taken place in October, 1880. They claimed to be " independent of political considerations," but the Liberals now found the whole weight of company influence, direct and indirect, thrown into the scales against them, and all those who criticised the Independents were stigmatised as " enemies of the true interests of the town." In the election of November, 1880, George Whale, Superintendent of the running department, Northern Division, L.N.W.R., in harness with J. Thomas, a Conservative, replaced Nathaniel Worsdell in the South Ward, and in the West Ward Charles Dick, Works Manager, running in harness with J. W. Wilding, another Conservative, defeated the Liberal candidate, Allen Priest, who was thereupon " pitchforked " into the Council as an alderman in place of Atkinson. Such was the beginning of the famous Independent Party, which continued to be the dominant factor in Crewe politics until its ignominious collapse in 1891. In 1881 two more Independents secured election, defeating Richard Pedley, Liberal, and WilliamWright, Conservative, but the Liberals of the West Ward returned for the first time Dr. (later Sir) William Hodgson (1854–1940), who eventually proved more than a thorn in the sides of Independents and Conservatives. Some Conservatives felt uneasy at the course of events, especially after the defeat of Wright, but in January, 1882, an alliance was cemented between the Conservative and Independent Parties to fight municipal elections " independent of party politics, which . . . have no real bearing on municipal affairs." To this the Liberals replied that the issue at stake was not party politics but the question of free political life in the town as a whole, and that the railway company had no more " right " to seats on the Town Council because it paid one-third of Crewe's rates than the Manchester Carriage Company had to representation on the Manchester City Council. Charles Welch, speaking for the Liberals, said :—" What they objected to was the statement that the railway nominees had no

---

Congregational Church until they became " Independent " members of the Town Council, after which they attached themselves to the Established Church. (b) William Ellis, foreman of the boiler-makers and " Independent " councillor, 1882–6, was a constant attender at the United Methodist Free Church, Hightown, until the 1880's, when he transferred his patronage to the Established Church, taking with him a large section of the congregation (C.G., 12.5.86 ; C.Ch., 9.6.88, 30.11.89).

politics, for, immediately they got on the Council they were always Tory."[1]   At the meeting of foremen in January, 1882, George Ellis, Webb's secretary, was appointed " to direct operations on behalf of the Company's nominees," and regular committees were set up in the three wards.   In 1883 Charles Ellis, George's brother, became secretary to the Crewe Constitutional Association, and the machine for ruling Crewe stood complete, " a most ingenious idea to make the same establishment a means of manufacturing both locomotives and Tories."[2]

In November, 1882, the Independents gained four more seats on the Council, Eaton and Pedley being defeated in the ultra-Radical West Ward.   November, 1883, saw a short-lived Liberal revival, since the party was now thoroughly alarmed at the trend of events.   Pedley defeated Whale and Eaton defeated a Conservative.   To ensure a majority, the Liberals elected as mayor Henry Wallwork, who had been defeated the year before. They were therefore able to secure two out of three aldermanic seats.   This " pitchforking " into the Council of persons who were not members, although legal, came in for much criticism, but the Liberals repeated the procedure in 1884, when Richard Whittle, defeated at the polls, was " pitchforked " into the Council as mayor.   The Liberals now held 13 seats on the Council, the Conservatives 2 and the Independents 10 ;   the advantages which the Conservatives drew from this alliance are shown by the fact that there is no recorded protest against this practical annihilation of the municipal Conservative Party.[3]

The methods whereby the Independent candidates obtained their votes met with public exposure for the first time in September, 1885, when Albert C. Childs, the able manager of the *Crewe Chronicle* from 1880 to 1922, printed a letter taken from the *Manchester Examiner* on " Intimidation at Crewe," signed by " A Lover of Freedom," a *nom-de-plume* which concealed a member of the Liberal Executive at Crewe.   Childs later formulated a series of charges against Webb.[4]   The question was taken

[1] *C.Ch.*, 30.11.89 ;   see also *C.G.*, 13.11.80, 5.11.81, 28.1.82 ; *Jubilee of Crewe*, pp. 28–32.

[2] *C.Ch.*, 19.9.85.   For C. Ellis, see *C.G.*, 11.10.84.

[3] *C.G.*, 3 and 14.11.83, 5 and 12.11.84, 14.10.85.

[4] *C.G.*, 9.6.22 ;   *C.Ch.*, 19 and 26.9.85, 3 and 10.10.85, 17.10.85 ; *Manchester Examiner*, Sept. 4–18, 1885, *passim*.

up by the national and local press ; letters and leading articles on the subject appeared in the *Manchester Guardian, Daily News, Democrat, Liverpool Echo, Manchester Evening News* and *Liverpool Daily Post*. The best description of Independent electioneering methods came from the Rev. Thomas Naylor, superintendent of the Crewe circuit of Methodist Free Churches, 1882–5 :—

" I can only say that I have seen and heard foremen of the Company stand at the entrance to the various polling booths, and, as the men have passed in to record their votes, patting them on the shoulder, and, with a significant nod, say ' Jim,' ' Dick,' ' Tom,' or as the case might be, ' Remember your bread and cheese ; vote for so-and-so,' so-and-so being the Company's representative brought out in the municipal contest against the Liberal candidates—never in one instance against the Tories. The foremen on such occasions are backed up by a lot of ' seconds' foremen ' and various understrappers, whose business it is to abuse and vituperate the Liberal candidates and their supporters." [1]

Naylor's charges were corroborated by J. W. Williamson of Crewe. He gave the *Liverpool Courier* the names of the Independent foremen and officials, in reply to a letter from " Fairplay " alleging that Naylor was " a political parson of the first water," who during his three years at Crewe had spent " the greater part of each day . . . in the reading–room of the Mechanics' Institution . . . studying the London and provincial daily newspapers for his political sermons." [2] From the revelations it is evident that the foremen habitually asked workmen with Radical opinions and even Liberal Party workers to serve on the Independent ward committees, and, if they refused, either victimised them by reducing their pay, moved them to less pleasant jobs, or discharged them at the first opportunity. The first batch of political dismissals took place in January and February, 1885, among the men affected being " The Blue Ribbon Gang," *i.e.* active supporters of the militant temperance movement of that name, which had made its first appearance in Crewe in 1882. " Blue Ribbonism " attracted many of the Nonconformist Liberals, so that whereas about 150 men were discharged " not a single prominent Tory " received his notice, " with one exception, and he happened to be the Conservative secretary of

[1] *C.Ch.,* 10.10.85 (quoting *Liverpool Daily Post,* 3.10.85), 8.8.85.
[2] *Liverpool Courier,* 6 and 9.10.85, 13.10.85.

one of the Ward committees." He naturally complained and was reinstated. A list of the prominent Liberals discharged during this period was given in the *Chronicle* of October 17, 1885.

The terrorism in the works became so great that of the 125 persons who composed the General Council of the Crewe Division Liberal Association, only four were employed in Crewe Works ; it was impossible to persuade more to serve on it owing to their fear of victimisation.[1] Needless to say, the Liberals were not allowed all the limelight, and after a week's canvassing (or so the Radicals alleged) the foremen organised for October 23, 1885, a meeting of workmen with Conservative sympathies and of those whose allegiance to the company was stronger than their lukewarm Liberalism. This meeting, in order to defend the honour of Crewe, expressed " its entire disapprobation of and indignation at the gross misrepresentations recently made by a local and other newspapers, believing most firmly that the charges of intimidation, tyranny and coercion . . . are entirely without foundation." This could not, however, hide the fact of the discriminatory dismissals ; a Liberal counter-meeting in the Corn Exchange on the same night was quite as well attended and, to crown all, Wadsworth, chief accountant of the Locomotive Department, admitted that intimidation existed. Yet the municipal election of November, 1885, resulted in another victory for the Independents and Conservatives. The state of parties on the Council was now ; Independents 10, Conservatives 3 and Liberals 11. George Whale was thereupon elected mayor, and from that moment until 1891 Crewe was ruled from the general offices of the Locomotive Department.[2]

The history of national politics in South Cheshire during this period must now be traced. Until 1885 Crewe formed part of the West Cheshire division, but local Conservatives and Liberals desired parliamentary borough status for the town ; indeed, many of the Liberals regarded incorporation as merely the first step in this direction, and in 1878 they dropped the " West Cheshire business " (Crewe being the only branch which existed) in order to become the Crewe and District Liberal Association

---

[1] *C.G.*, 6.5.82, 10.10.85 ; *C.Ch.*, 19.9.85, 24.10.85. The names of victims include Richard Dale, John Shone, Thomas Smith and Joseph Bowering. A number of other cases are well authenticated.

[2] *C.G.*, 24 and 28.10.85, 4 and 11.11.85.

on the " Birmingham plan " devised by Joseph Chamberlain
and his lieutenant Schnadhorst.   The president of the association
from about 1880 until 1886 was the Rev. William Mellor, the
local Unitarian minister, who played an active part during the
Intimidation affair.   As the reform of 1878 had abolished
entrance fees the association increased in strength under his
vigorous leadership, while the circulation of the Liberal-Radical
Chronicle rose so rapidly after the revelations of 1885 that by
1892 it sold twice as many copies as all the other local newspapers
combined.   To balance this, the Conservatives now wielded
openly the immense influence of the railway company, the
Established Church and the publicans, while they possessed in
Wallace Lumb (1850–1938), wine and beer merchant, a politician
of considerable acumen, who was dubbed " the mystery man of
Crewe politics." [1]

In 1885 a redistribution of seats made Crewe, not the desired
parliamentary borough, but the head of the Crewe division of
Cheshire, which had a population at the time of about 58,000.
The division included Nantwich, Sandbach and Alsager, together
with the poverty-stricken " Radical villages " of Wheelock and
Mow Cop.   This arrangement had perforce to satisfy the more
ardent of the local politicians.   The Franchise Act of 1884
increased the number of parliamentary voters in Crewe itself
from about 700 to about 5,000, " chiefly artisans."   This Act,
rather than Disraeli's Act of 1867, marked the transition from
middle-class oligarchy to democracy in this part of the United
Kingdom.   In the midst of this political ferment came the
Intimidation affair and the General Election of 1885.[2]

As early as 1879 a comment appeared in the *Guardian* which
showed that the railway officials considered it possible to turn
Crewe into a railway pocket borough :—" Many persons seem
to think that the [proposed] new M.P. will be one representing
the railway interest, and that most probably a director of the
L.N.W.R. would stand the best chance of representing Crewe
in Parliament." [3]

Accordingly in 1885 the Crewe Constitutional Association

[1] *C.G.*, 14.12.72, 21.7.77, 23.2.78 ; *C.Ch.*, 13.4.89, 27.9.90, 16.4.92, 26.11.38.
[2] *C.G.*, 29.3.79, 5.4.79, 12 and 26.4.79, 10.5.79, 9.7.84, 27.8.84, 8 and
11.10.84, 29.10.84, 6 and 24.12.84, 3 and 24.1.85, 21 and 25.2.85, 22.8.85,
10.10.85 ; *C.Ch.*, 22.8.85.   [3] *C.G.*, 29.3.79.

chose a gentleman named Oscar L. Stephen, a director of the L.N.W.R., chairman of the North London Railway Company and " until recently a large partner in the firm of Messrs. Allsopp & Sons (brewers) of Burton-on-Trent," as their candidate for the forthcoming election. The Crewe Liberals, with superior political judgment, brought forward a local landowner who was at the same time well-known for his advanced opinions, G. W. Latham of Bradwall Hall, who had practised at the Bar in his youth. Lord Crewe, a Whig—indeed the only Whig or Liberal landowner on both sides of the road between Crewe and Chester, with the exception of James Tomkinson of Tarporley and the Duke of Westminster at Eaton Hall—thereupon discovered that he could not support " a Radical like Mr. Stephen's opponent." [1] During the contest in November, 1885, the Conservatives blamed Mr. Gladstone's Government for the " short time " in the works, and hinted that Stephen's return would bring back prosperity to Crewe, and *vice-versa*. Latham won comfortably by 5,089 votes to 4,281. When elected he had been suffering from an incurable disease and resigned the candidature for the new Parliament of 1886, a few months before his death in that year.[2]

The intimidation in the works died down somewhat after this signal victory, and the Liberal choice for the General Election of 1886 was W. S. B. McLaren, a Quaker woollen manufacturer from Bradford, and a nephew of John Bright. This time the Conservatives played the " local man " card. Their candidate was F. R. Twemlow of Market Drayton, landowner and barrister. Unfortunately for them, Twemlow spoiled his chances by " cocking the snook " in a somewhat undignified manner at the free and independent electors of Nantwich, an incident never forgotten in the Division. McLaren's majority was 645 ; both sides polled fewer votes than in the preceding year. McLaren continued to represent Crewe until 1895 and proved a cultured and energetic member.[3]

---

[1] *C.G.*, 18 and 25.2.85, 21.11.85. Apparently both Dr. James Atkinson and Sir Richard Moon, chairman of the L.N.W.R., had refused to stand as the Conservative candidate.
[2] *C.G.*, 7 and 31.1.85, 25 and 28.11.85, 2.12.85, 16.6.86, 19 and 26.6.86, 9.10.86 (obituary) ; Latham's great farewell speech is still remembered in the Division.   [3] *C.G.*, 10 and 14.7.86, 17.7.86 ; *C.Ch.*, 10 and 17.7.86.

The majority on the Town Council gained by the Independents in 1885 increased in November, 1886, as a result of the aldermanic elections, when 3 Liberals were replaced by J. W. Wilding (Conservative), B. Kean (Independent), who had been a good Liberal when elected in 1879, and the great F. W. Webb himself. There were now 8 Liberals, 11 Independents, and 8 Conservatives on the Council. Early in 1887 the Liberals were reduced to 7 by the " pitchforking " of A. G. Hill, a Conservative solicitor, and son of John Hill, into the aldermanic seat rendered vacant by the death of Martin Heath. It now remains to be seen what use the Independents made of their victory. No contests took place in 1886. One reason put forward to justify the formation of the Independent Party was that the Corporation Sewage Farm had been making heavy losses under Liberal rule, losses which were partly paid for by rates levied on the company's property. The Independents were therefore likened to a ratepayers' association. This argument was not, however, put forward before 1885, when the Independents made their first attack on the Farm accountancy. An examination of the results of trading at the Farm during the period 1877–93 shows no real improvement under Independent rule, although a new system of accountancy was adopted in 1886.[1]

F. W. Webb became mayor of Crewe in 1887, and was re-elected in 1888. 1887 happened to be the Jubilee both of Crewe and of Victoria's accession, and Webb therefore used his interest with the L.N.W.R. directors to obtain a grant to the Corporation of land for the present Queen's Park, together with £10,000 for laying it out. This magnificent gift seemed to shut out the possibility of a Liberal victory for many years. During his mayoralty Webb kept repeating in his public speeches a pun to the effect that " our Crew(e) " must not be divided, or the barque would be stranded. The *Chronicle* commented somewhat acidly :—

" It is about time that Mr. Webb defined the phrase which he is always trotting out when he gets a few visitors at Crewe. It is possible that he has some very terrible idea in his mind when he talks so feelingly about ' a divided Crewe and our barque being

---

[1] *C.G.*, 9.10.86, 27.10.86, 3 and 13.11.86, 26.2.87, 26.10.87, 13.5.85, 15.8.85, 12.9.85, 10 and 24.10.85, 12.12.85, 27.3.86, 24.4.86 ; *Abst. Accts.*, 1892–3, p. 52 *sqq.*

FRANCIS WILLIAM WEBB (1836–1906)

stranded.' Nobody in his senses wants to divide Crewe, but if the mayor refers to the division between the political parties, which he has evidently tried to bridge over by the introduction of so-called Independents ; if he indulges in the hope that the Tories or the Independents will ever absorb the Radicals, and thus become as one flock having one Tory shepherd, we do not hesitate to say that he cherishes a forlorn hope which can never be realised." [1]

The *Chronicle* had gone to the root of the matter. The issue at stake was not the loss of a few pounds on the Sewage Farm, but the right of the company's workmen to agree or disagree with the politics of the works' officials and foremen, and to be able to take an active part in Liberal politics or temperance propaganda without fear of dismissal.

Liberalism in Crewe's municipal politics reached the lowest point during 1887–8. The Independent majority seemed unshakable, but the Independents had reckoned without the power of the Liberal machine, the personality of Dr. William Hodgson and their own lack of a positive policy in municipal government. Some of the Independent aldermen and councillors began to lose interest in public work, while others found themselves unable to devote sufficient time to Council and Committee meetings (this applied chiefly to the higher officials). In July, 1888, came the beginning of the end—T. H. Heath, a Liberal, defeated H. D. Earl, Works Manager, at a by-election, and signalised his advent to the Town Council by reviving the heated debates which raged in the days of small majorities. The November election of 1888 raised the Liberals on the Council to 10, and great play was made with the fact that defeated Independent candidates were usually elevated to the aldermanic bench.

The Liberal Party found another useful source of strength in the discontent prevalent in Crewe Works in the mid-1880's on account of the company's superannuation scheme for the Locomotive Department (running and works sections) which had been started in 1883. This was commonly known as "The Pension Fund." Pensions at 65 were to be ensured by weekly payments and a substantial annual grant from the railway company. It

[1] *C.Ch.*, 9.7.87—*cf.* "The Tories and Independents have allied themselves together, not so much for the good government of the town, but to crush Liberalism" (*C.Ch.*, 3.11.88).

was an excellent scheme, save for the fact that the majority of the men could not afford to keep up the payments in addition to those they already made to their trade unions and friendly societies, especially during those periods of " short time " in the works so frequent in the 1880's. Control of the fund lay in the hands of annual meetings of delegates from all points on the L.N.W.R. system, and high officials of the company held the key posts in connection with its administration. Membership of the Pension Fund was practically compulsory and stood at 11,828 in 1885. One of the rules laid it down that the man who voluntarily left the service of the company received back only 50 per cent. of his contributions, while he who was discharged received the whole. Not only did this tend to tie the men to the company, but it encouraged insubordination in the works ; cases occurred of men desirous of leaving the company's service deliberately insulting or striking their foremen in order to qualify for dismissal and the full amount of their contributions. The works labourers suffered severely during the " short-time " period, as many of them drew only 14s. 8d. per week without deductions. Employees who grumbled openly naturally became marked as " enemies of the company." The unpopularity of the Pension Fund grew steadily during 1888 and 1889, and was openly used by the Liberals as a means of getting votes. McLaren criticised it severely and asked questions about its legality in the House of Commons, while Chatterton, the prospective Conservative parliamentary candidate, defended the fund as best he could.[1]

By January, 1889, even the *Guardian* admitted that the fund constituted a grievance, a tax on the slender earnings of the men which the majority of them could ill afford, and in February the delegates decided by 51 votes to 15 for a members' ballot on its abolition. Some delay occurred over the holding of the ballot, and on March 2 a public meeting on the Market Square, at which William Urquhart attacked the fund, drew an audience of over 5,000. He stressed the fact that many Crewe branches of friendly societies and trade unions were suffering from the prior deduction of the pension payments and the consequent inability of their members to keep up their contributions to societies unconnected with the works. The results of the voting made public in

[1] *C.G.*, 4 and 24.4.83 to 3.11.88, *passim* ; *C.Ch.*, 15.9.83 to 22.12.88, *passim.*

April, 1889, showed 11,485 for abolition and 1,930 against ; the fund was wound up early in 1890, after an average of about £6 per man had been paid out the previous June.[1]

The activities of Urquhart and O'Connor, both prominent Liberals and trade unionists, in connection with the opposition to the Pension Fund, and the success of the Liberals in defeating Councillor John Bebbington, an Independent foreman, in the first County Council election (January, 1889), led to a recrudescence of the intimidation in the works. The municipal election of November, 1889, did not give the Liberals a majority, and in the aldermanic election on November 9, William McNeill, the last of the Liberal aldermen, was unseated in favour of John Thomas, a Conservative ; considerable excitement manifested itself during the proceedings in the Town Hall, which " were of a somewhat turbulent character, the appointments evidently not being regarded with satisfaction by a portion of the audience."

Since August an agitation had been proceeding in the works for an increase in wages, and as a result the militant " New Unionism " of the time made an appearance in Crewe. At a meeting in October, Urquhart and James Skeldon organised a " mutual defence fund . . . by the payment of 1*d.* and 2*d.* per week . . . to assist any of our fellow-workmen who may suffer by their action in the matter." On November 6 Urquhart presided over a gathering which decided on the formation of a Crewe branch of the General Railway Workers' Union. The hitherto weak Crewe branch of the Amalgamated Society of Railway Servants also took on a new lease of life, but in November, 1889, James Skeldon, Urquhart, and Joseph Jones, president of the Liberal Association, received their discharge from the works. P. V. O'Connor and several others followed soon afterwards. The case of Jones received special attention from Henry Labouchère, the famous editor of *Truth*, who made a special visit to Crewe for the purpose of interviewing the victim of Bebbington's petty spite, and Mr. Gladstone himself, in a

---

[1] *C.Ch.*, 10.11.88 to 9.3.89, *passim* ; *C.G.*, 5.1.89 to 26.2.90, *passim*. Both sides in the controversy ran ephemeral newspapers of a more extreme type than the *Chronicle* and the *Guardian*. The *Nantwich, Sandbach and Crewe Star* (1888–92) was the Radical organ, while the *Crewe and Nantwich Advertiser* (1889–94) gave the High Tory version and interpretation of events. The *Crewe Observer* dates from the Conservative revival of 1908, and expired in 1932.

characteristic letter to the Editor of the *Chronicle*, found the whole episode " so scandalously bad " that he was " compelled to suspend " his belief until he had heard what the responsible officials of the L.N.W.R. had to say for themselves.[1] The *Railway Review* commented :—" Whatever a workman's political opinions may be—from a Communist to a high Tory—he should at all risks be protected in the freest constitutional exercise of them." [2]

At the Council meeting on November 27, 1889, Dr. Hodgson and Pedley moved a long resolution embodying a petition to the next general meeting of L.N.W.R. shareholders, calling their attention to the " state of political serfdom in the works," and to the fact that for " nine long years the Managers of the works and their subordinate foremen have been allied with the Tories of Crewe to crush Liberalism altogether out of the town."

A tremendous debate followed, in the course of which Dr. Hodgson used to the full his oratorical powers to trace the whole course of the Intimidation affair. The resolution was replaced by an amendment deprecating " the introduction of politics into the Council's debates," and this was carried by 11 votes to 9. A reprint of Mr. Gladstone's letter in *The Times* on December 20, 1889, brought Crewe into the national press again, while the company denounced the charges as " absolutely untrue and without foundation." An indignation meeting in the Town Hall, called to state the case for the company, was broken up on January 2, 1890 ; further dismissals added to the popular indignation, especially after the suicide of Thomas Allison, who had been transferred from Crewe to Horwich, a favourite device for quietening dangerous agitators.[3]

Meanwhile, Dr. Hodgson, armed with some railway shares and accompanied by McLaren, McNeill and Pedley, attended the 88th half-yearly meeting of the L.N.W.R. Company's proprietors at Euston in February, 1890, to raise the whole question

---

[1] Mr. Gladstone's letter, together with two other documents on the affair, is printed in full as an appendix ; *C.G.*, 12.1.89 to 1.1.90, *passim* ; *C.Ch.*, 30.11.89 to 28.12.89, *passim* ; *E.A.* 90, p. 181. In October, 1889, Dr. Hodgson somewhat optimistically considered " that much of the interference in its old guise had gone."

[2] *C.Ch.*, 14.12.89.

[3] *C.Ch.*, Nov.–Dec., 1889, Jan., 1890, 1.3.90 ; *C.G.*, 23 and 30.11.89, Jan., 1890, 22.2.90, 29.3.90 ; Caunt : *N.U.R. Souvenir* (1923), p. 9.

there. Their two amendments to the directors' report, the first demanding a public enquiry, the second demanding a declaration inside the works of the company's political neutrality, underwent defeat, but the intimidation subsided and by March, 1890, Crewe Works was described as "a changed place." The company's officials at Crewe apparently received some sort of reprimand from a higher authority, and Charles Ellis resigned the secretaryship of the Crewe Constitutional Association. In August, 1890, F. W. Webb resigned from the office of alderman, followed in September by George Whale, his second-in-command. For some time their attendances at Council and committee meetings had been erratic ; pressure of work formed the official excuse. The alliance between Conservatives and Independents now began to break up. John Allman, a Liberal, was elected alderman in place of Whale because some Independents abstained from voting, but the final victory of the Liberals did not take place until August, 1891, and was gained on a different issue.[1]

In 1879 the railway company had prevented the promotion by Crewe Town Council of a Private Improvement Bill which, among other things, would have extended the borough to include the southern half of Church Coppenhall and the railway station. In February, 1889, the project again came before the Corporation on account of sewerage difficulties in Church Coppenhall. The Liberals wanted the railway station to be included, but the Independents and the L.N.W.R. directors did not. In March, 1891, the Local Government Board approved of the extension northwards into Church Coppenhall, but not the inclusion of the station. The more advanced Liberals, led by Dr. Hodgson, agreed to accept this compromise, only to be faced with bitter opposition from a curious coalition of Independents, Conservatives, and three Liberals (Welch, Jervis and Cotterill), who together formed a majority on the Council. They proclaimed their desire for the total area originally demanded, when at heart they wanted to see the entire abandonment of the scheme. After

---

[1] *C.G.*, 22.2.90, 29.3.90, 30.8.90, 17 and 27.9.90, 4 and 15.10.90 ; *C.Ch.*, 1.3.90, 15 and 29.3.90, 20 and 27.9.30 ; *Times*, 20.12.89, 21.2.90, 22.2.90, 25.2.90. A deputation consisting of A. G. Hill, Dr. Hodgson and Welch pressed Whale to reconsider his decision to resign, for the Liberals would have welcomed the presence of the chief officials of the L.N.W.R. at the council table unaccompanied by their "Independent Party."

several six-hour debates and much wrangling it was decided to settle the matter by a poll of the ratepayers. Dr. Hodgson and his followers found that the ratepayers approved of their policy (the voting being 1,027 for and 825 against), whereupon aldermen A. G. Hill, Wilding and Macrae, and councillors Earl, Martlew and Dr. Atkinson, resigned their seats. From August, 1891, Crewe, then described as " having the most cantankerous of cantankerous councils," came under " the supreme control of a Radical Administration." The election in November, 1891, finally annihilated the Independent Party. The new Council consisted of 20 Liberals and 4 Conservatives. The attempt to " unite " Crewe behind F. W. Webb had ended in utter and ignominious failure. In 1892 the victors appointed two of the discharged workmen, Councillor William Urquhart and P. V. O'Connor, to the posts of assistant Sanitary Inspector and assistant Rate Collector to compensate them for their sufferings in the Liberal cause.[1]

II.　Local Politics, 1892–1923

As soon as the Liberals had achieved their greatest success the first vague movement for " Labour representation " began. During the municipal by-elections of September, 1891, " an ardent believer in working class representation actually went so far as to issue an address to his fellow-employees," while a month later Henry Hallewell, Conservative agent for the Division, made unsuccessful efforts to secure a Conservative-Labour candidate for the November election. Would-be working-men town councillors found themselves hampered in that most of the Council and Committee meetings were held in the morning and afternoon ; evening meetings of the local governing body naturally became one of the planks in the programme of the Crewe branch of the Independent Labour Party, founded in 1894. It was a product of the militant, " New Unionism " of 1888–9,[2] and for the first years of its existence was mainly

[1] Coun., 1879, 1891 ; Fce., 1879 ; G.P.C., 1879, *passim* ; C.G., Nov.–Dec. 1879, 2.4.90, 14.3.91 to 18.11.91, *passim*, 23.7.92, 10 and 31.12.92 ; C.Ch., 31.12.92.

[2] The Amalgamated Society of Railway Servants, the National Union of Gasworkers and General Labourers, and the General Railway Workers' Union all established branches in the town between 1888 and 1894.

occupied in converting an older body, the Crewe Trades Council, to a policy of direct Labour representation. The Crewe Trades Council, which made its first recorded appearance in 1873, had been for the first period of its existence an organ of Radical trade unionism. The first Labour town councillor, William Williams, took his seat in November, 1902, and by 1908 the Labour group on the Council numbered 5. Frederick Manning, returned unopposed in 1900, may be said, as a " Lib-Lab," to mark the transition stage. The Crewe and district branches of the N.U.R. (they numbered seven in 1919), following in the steps of their ancestor, Crewe No. 1 Branch of the Amalgamated Society of Railway Servants, have always played a major part in local politics, while their former rivals, the Crewe branches of the Amalgamated Society of Engineers (now the A.E.U.), remained generally more interested in the industrial side of unionism.[1]

November, 1908, saw a municipal " General Election " as the result of a rearrangement of the ward boundaries and an increase of four in the membership of the Council. Before the contest the state of parties stood as follows :—Liberals 13, Conservatives 10, Labour 5 (the Council had been increased to 28 members on the extension of the borough in 1892). The results of the " General Election," together with the succeeding aldermanic elections, proved disastrous for the Liberal Party, which had made an anti-Labour arrangement with the Conservatives, and even more disastrous for the Independent Labour Party, which failed to secure the return of a single representative. The Conservatives now numbered 20 and the Liberals 12. In belated revenge for the political Corporation staff appointments of 1892, the Conservatives used their majority in February, 1909, to install Councillor H. S. K. Feltham, secretary and organising agent of the Crewe Constitutional Association, as Town Clerk in succession to Frederick Cooke. The Liberals naturally protested vigorously against this " political jobbery," but it is interesting to note that the only serious competitor to Feltham on the short list was Frank Kinsey, who had been until November, 1908, a Liberal

[1] *C.G.*, 14.6.90, 12.9.91, 28 and 31.10.91, 17.6.93, 29.4.93, 10.3.94 (*cf.* G.P.C., 15.2.94), 5.11.02, 9.11.07, 13.11.07, 21.12.07 ; *C.Ch.*, 15.12.94, 29.9.00, 27.10.00, 3.11.00 ; *C.G.*, 19.7.73, 11.4.74 (earliest traces of Crewe Trades Council).

councillor.[1] After November, 1909, the Council found itself equally divided between the two parties, a state of affairs which lasted until the Liberals secured a majority of 2 in 1910. 1911 witnessed the return of the Labour element to the Council Chamber, but party divisions tended to become blurred during the first World War ; the municipal election of November, 1914, was the last to be held until 1919, all casual vacancies being filled by co-option.[2]

Carried forward by the bitter after-effects of the great railway strike and the acute housing shortage, the Labour Party swept all the wards in November, 1919, gaining 8 seats. To fight the next election the Conservatives and Liberals formed in October, 1920, the Crewe Progressive Union, with the veteran Alderman J. Briggs as chairman, for " the good government of the town on sound business lines of progress and development, with due regard for economy." To achieve this end, it was agreed " to sink party politics in municipal affairs, and to support men of moderate views and proved business capacity for seats on the Town Council." This anti-Labour coalition, foreshadowed in the arrangement of 1908, proved successful in that it prevented the Labour Party from winning a single seat in 1920, but economy was not so easy to secure. The total rate levied rose from 11s. 8d. in the pound in 1919–20 to 17s. 0d. in 1921–2, from which height it fell to 15s. 2d. in 1923–4. This failure to reduce the figure to the pre-war level brought into existence another rate-payers' economist organisation, the Crewe Property-Owners' and Ratepayers' Association, founded in 1923 ; it had practically the same leadership and aims as the Crewe Progressive Union, but did not propose to run candidates at municipal elections.[3]

---

[1] C.G., 26.9.08 to 2.12.08, *passim*, Feb., 1909, *passim* ; Ctee. of Coun., 3.2.09 ; Coun., 12 and 23.2.09 ; G.P.C., 15 and 18.2.09.

[2] C.G., 27.10.09, 3.11.09, 9.4.10, 7.5.10, 3.6.10, 19.7.10, 4 and 11.11.10, 3.11.11, 30.10.14, 23.4.15, 3.9.15, 12.11.15. The last councillor elected (unopposed) was C. Alcock (April 24, 1915), the first to be co-opted was Miles Parkes (Sept. 1, 1915).

[3] C.G., 4.11.19, 8 and 26.10.20, 29.10.20, 2.11.20, 25.3.21, 17.2.22, 1.5.23, 15.6.23, 4 and 21.9.23. Crewe has seen four previous ratepayers' associations—1866–70 (?), 1893–4 (?), 1901–4 (?), 1910 (?), all of which proved the essentially negative function of such bodies by " dying from sheer inaction."

III. National Politics in the Crewe Division, 1892–1923

McLaren held his seat with an increased majority against the Conservative candidate, H. W. Chatterton, in 1892. Chatterton was a Protectionist and anti-Home Ruler, a fact which lost him the Catholic vote. This contest gains interest from the fact that the Crown was brought into play for the last time—" Mr. Chatterton's bills were surmounted by the Union Jack and the Royal Standard." McLaren happened to be part-proprietor of a German engineering firm, but this fact, eagerly seized on by Protectionists, did not prevent his return. As a result of Chatterton's defeat, internal dissensions broke out among the Conservatives, and Dr. James Atkinson resigned for a few months from the association. Wallace Lumb, and subsequently A. G. Hill, became the acknowledged leaders of Crewe Conservatism, which now had less intimate connections than formerly with the railway company. The election of 1895 illustrates the growing influence of women in local politics. A Women's Liberal Association had been formed for Crewe in 1886, and in April, 1887, the Conservatives of the town inaugurated the Grey-Egerton Habitation of the Primrose League. In 1889 McLaren presented a petition from the Crewe Town Council in favour of the Women's Franchise Bill, and in 1891 the Liberal women of Crewe attended a lecture on " Women as Guardians of the Poor." In the same year Mrs. Elisabeth Hodgson, the doctor's wife, became the first woman Guardian for Monks Coppenhall. A factor tending towards a Conservative victory was the foundation in 1895 of a Liberal-Unionist Association.[1]

For the 1895 contest the Conservatives chose as candidate the Hon. R. A. Ward, brother of the Earl of Dudley, a young and Ouidaesque Guardee with but a limited interest in politics. The issues ventilated during the contest ranged from the Employers' Liability Bill to Local Option, but Ward's success was due largely to his good looks and soldierly appearance, combined with reckless promises of " full time " for the works in the event of victory. Unfortunately Ward's erratic behaviour ruined the rising hopes of Crewe Conservatism :—

[1] *C.G.*, 5.6.86, 9.10.86, 3.11.86, 15.12.88, 12.1.89, 30.3.89, 18.11.90, 8 and 11.4.91, 18.4.91, 2 and 13.7.92, 20.3.95, 15.6.95, July, 1895 ; *C.Ch.*, 27.7.95.

" In the General Election of 1895 by a strange accident a Tory member . . . was elected, greatly to his own surprise. He had no desire to serve in the House, and early in 1897 it was announced that an election would take place. . . . Election addresses were issued ; a Tory minister came down to support the Tory candidate, but it became abundantly evident that a great Liberal victory was about to take place, when suddenly the Tory Whips issued a statement that Mr. Ward was not going to resign after all, and that therefore there would be no election. Mr. Ward departed for South Africa, and . . . rarely . . . appeared again in the House of Commons, but he remained member until the dissolution in 1900 and thus the con- stituency was disfranchised for three years." [1]

The Liberals profited greatly from this bitter experience ; in 1898 they appointed a paid full-time organising and registration agent, Thomas Darling, one of the Intimidation victims, and from 1894 had the support of the successor to the Crewe estates, Robert Crewe-Milnes, who, as Lord Crewe, held several Cabinet posts in the Liberal Administration of 1905–15 and the first Coalition.[2] On the other hand, the Conservatives were dis- heartened by the Ward fiasco, and on the adoption of J. E. Reiss, railway shareholder and landowner, as candidate in 1899, they lost Wallace Lumb as chairman. From 1899 to 1906 A. G. Hill remained the undisputed leader of Crewe Conservatism. The Liberal candidate, James Tomkinson of Tarporley, local land- owner and bank director, but the holder of advanced Radical opinions, won easily in the " khaki election " of 1900. He represented the Crewe Division until 1910, in spite of an assault on the seat by J. H. Welsford, a full-blooded Tariff-Reform shipowner from Liverpool, and a split in the " progressive vote " in the first General Election of 1910 caused by the appearance of Frank H. Rose, the first candidate of the Labour Representation Committee set up by Crewe Trades Council in 1907. On the death of Tomkinson in a parliamentary steeplechase accident, McLaren was again adopted by the Liberals and in May, 1910, defeated Welsford in a straight fight. Crewe's third contest within the year took place in December, owing to the second General Election, from which McLaren emerged victorious

[1] McLaren in *C.Ch.*, 19.8.11.

[2] Born 1858, created Earl of Crewe 1895, Marquess 1911. He may be regarded as the last of the great Whig landowners to take an active part in politics ; died 1945 (*Times*, June 21, 1945).

with a slightly increased majority over a new Conservative candidate, Ernest Craig, a colliery manager and mining engineer. This year marked the apogee of Liberalism in the Crewe Division, and from then onwards a process of decline set in, unnoticed at first, but hastened by the rise of the Labour vote and the first World War.

McLaren died in 1912, and the constituency prepared for its second three-cornered fight. The Liberals adopted H. L. Murphy, solicitor and secretary to Sir John Simon ; the Conservatives were fortunate in having the only candidate already known to the division, Craig ; the Labour Party brought forward James Holmes, A.S.R.S. organiser, who effectively split the " progressive vote " in revenge for similar action by Liberals in a Potteries division. Craig was thus returned to Parliament by a minority of electors. The Liberal candidate in the 1918 election, Sir Joseph Davies, had been adopted in 1913. A member of Lloyd George's secretariat during the war, he secured the Coalition coupon and Craig retired from the contest. Davies possessed large interests in South Wales coalmines and railways, while his opponent, J. T. Brownlie, president of the Amalgamated Society of Engineers, was possibly the best candidate the Labour Party could have brought forward in the circumstances. Sir Joseph Davies was returned by nearly 3,000 votes, the largest majority known until then in the division, but the Labour vote reached 10,439 as compared with only 2,485 in 1912. In a straight fight in 1922 Sir Joseph suffered defeat at the hands of E. G. Hemmerde, a Labour lawyer, who held the seat easily a year later on a minority vote against Liberal and Conservative opponents. The rise of the Labour Party, deaths among the pre-war Liberal stalwarts, the numerical and qualitative decay of Nonconformity, the decreasing vitality of temperance agitation and the growth in the strength of trade unionism had altered the structure of politics in the Crewe Division. Only Conservatism appeared to be comparatively unchanged.[1]

[1] *C.G.*, 6.1.94, 3.8.95 to 2.8.12, *passim*, 27.6.13, 10.7.14, 26.4.18 to 31.12.18, *passim*, 13.2.20, 16.4.20, 27.10.22 to 24.11.22, *passim*, 12.10.23 to 14.12.23 ; *C.Ch.*, 14.9.95 to 1.7.99, *passim* ; Caunt : *op. cit.*, p. 28. James Briggs and C. H. Pedley both died in 1921.

CHAPTER VII

THE DEVELOPMENT OF SOCIAL SERVICES AND MUNICIPAL ENTERPRISE, 1877–1923

I. Public Order and the Drink Trade.

THE demand for a resident magistracy, which had been the mainspring of the Incorporation Agitation, lost much of its vigour after the charter had been granted, as each successive mayor of Crewe now became an " ex-officio " J.P. for the town. Dr. James Atkinson presided over the first Borough Police Court on July 24, 1877, and in 1878 his name was added to the Commission of the Peace for the county. Many Crewe police cases, however, continued to be tried before the county magistrates in petty sessions, and complaints of unpunctuality occurred in connection with the Borough Police Court. In 1880, therefore, Crewe Town Council petitioned the Lord Chancellor for a separate Commission of the Peace for the borough, which was granted on April 7, 1881. It bore the names of seven Liberals and four Conservatives, not all of whom were residents of Crewe. The Commission did not grant a separate Court of Quarter Sessions, and the new Bench hired a room in the Edleston Road police station for judicial purposes. C. E. Speakman, appointed in 1881, held the office of Clerk to the Borough Bench until 1917.[1]

The question of the appointment of new magistrates inevitably led to political conflict in the Crewe of the 1880's and 1890's. For example, in 1883 the Conservative-Independent coalition prevented the suggested inclusion of Dr. William Hodgson and John Eaton in the Commission. Ostensibly the lack of judicial business formed the excuse, but when we find George Ellis receiving congratulations from the Crewe Licensed Victuallers' Association for his action in the matter, the real reason is not far to seek. The Conservatives did well in the matter of fresh appointments, even after the Liberal victory in 1891, while the Town Council was not consulted by the Lord Chancellor in connection with the new J.P.s made in 1890 and 1892. The *Chronicle* denounced the appointments of 1890 in strong

[1] Coun., 16.6.80, 5.1.81 ; *C.G.*, 28.7.77 to 1.10.81, *passim*, 20 and 23.2.17, 9.3.17.

language :—" This is one of the grossest political jobs ever perpetrated in a town where political jobbery is regarded as a kind of virtue." [1]

In 1893 the creation of six Liberal magistrates, including Dr. Hodgson, redressed the balance somewhat, but when the Duke of Westminster, Lord Lieutenant of Cheshire, enquired concerning the politics of several persons whose names had been sent in by the Town Council in that year for submission to the Lord Chancellor with a view to their inclusion in the Commission of the Peace for the county, His Grace was informed that

" should those gentlemen [Briggs, McNeill, Pedley and Thomas] be appointed there would be an equality of magistrates for both parties on the Crewe County Bench ; but that if the other County Magistrates who occasionally sat at Crewe were taken into consideration there would be a considerable majority of Conservative magistrates for the district." [2]

To James Robertson belongs the distinction of being the first working-man J.P. in Crewe. After his death in 1905 the Crewe Trades Council investigated the position and wrote to the Town Council in 1906 drawing attention to the composition of the magisterial bench, an analysis of which revealed that " the commercial and professional classes were well-represented, whilst labour was entirely unrepresented." The Trades Council suggested that the Lord Chancellor should be recommended to appoint some working-men magistrates. As a result of this, Crewe Town Council moved the Lord Chancellor to add a fresh batch of names to the Commission, including two more Liberal workmen. The Labour Party did not receive magisterial recognition until 1916, on the appointment of Councillor John Williams, a trade union official who had proved his usefulness during the recruiting campaign, when " his services as a working-man speaker were requisitioned in the Crewe division and in various parts of the country." [3]

[1] *C.Ch.*, 16.8.90 ; see also *C.Ch.*, 23 and 30.8.90 ; *C.G.*, 19.12.82 to 3.3.83, *passim*, 28.11.85, 16.8.90, 30.8.90, 29.6.92, 2.7.92 ; Coun., 31.1.83 ; G.P.C., 28.12.82, 25.1.83, 3.12.85.

[2] G.P.C., 14.9.93 ; see also G.P.C., 14.8.90, 10.8.93 ; Coun., 14.8.90, 10.8.93 ; *C.G.*, 28.1.93, 30.9.93, 13.1.94 ; *C.Ch.*, 28.10.93.

[3] G.P.C., 10.5.06 ; *C.G.*, 9.6.06 ; see also *C.G.*, 13.12.02, 4.4.06, 15.8.06, 9.9.10, 25.8.16, and *cf.* G.P.C., 20.7.15 (letter from Crewe Trades Council *re* lack of working-class magistrates).

Before the grant of a separate Commission those Liberals who were enthusiastic advocates of licensing reform and temperance had been obliged to petition the Nantwich Justices at the annual Brewster Sessions in their efforts to check the issue of new licences and the progress of alcoholism. When, after 1881, there existed a Crewe Justices' Licensing Committee and a separate Brewster Sessions for Crewe, their task became simpler. The Liberals did not capture the Licensing Committee until 1893, even though Justices directly interested in the sale of alcoholic beverages could not vote at the constitution of the Licensing Committee. However, between 1877 and 1896 no fresh full licence was granted in the borough. "Blue Ribbonism" and the Sunday closing agitation were particularly lively in the town between 1882 and 1896, several full-dress debates on the latter subject taking place in the Town Council during those years.[1]

During the last quarter of the nineteenth century the great brewery companies began to buy up individual public-houses over wide areas. How far this process had gone in the Crewe of 1892 may be gauged from a list of that date :—

Owner.	No. of Public-houses in Crewe.
Sir A. B. Walker, Ltd. (Liverpool)	8
Greenall & Whitley (Warrington)	8
North Cheshire Brewery, Ltd.	7
South Cheshire Brewery (E. S. Woolf)	6
L.N.W.R. Company	3
Charles Welch	2

The large breweries had reduced the tenants of their tied houses to the level of mere wage-paid managers, evictable in many cases after a week's notice. This system destroyed the sense of responsibility felt by the more liberally treated tenants and the proprietors of "free houses." In August, 1893, the Licensing Committee of the Crewe Bench, with its Liberal majority, fired the preliminary round in a long battle by postponing the renewal of some licences until the Adjourned Brewster Sessions, in order

[1] In 1881 the borough contained 42 licensed victuallers, 44 beersellers and 8 off-licence holders. In 1892 the figures were 42, 40 and 7 respectively (C.G., 20.8.81, 27.8.81, 30.8.84, 29.8.85, 31.8.89, 30.8.90, 27.8.92, 26.8.93, 3.10.94, 29.8.96).

that the applicants might produce their agreements or conditions of tenancy with the brewery companies and thus show whether or not they were *bona fide* tenants.[1] At the Adjourned Sessions the Justices inspected the agreements and refused to renew 10 licences, including all those for Messrs. Walker's houses. Unfortunately their decision was reversed by one vote on an appeal to Quarter Sessions. This skirmish made a great stir throughout England, and resulted in some improvement, especially as the Justices kept up a steady pressure. In 1894 they again refused to renew Messrs. Walker's licences until better terms for their tenants were assured.[2]

The determined attitude of the Crewe Bench inspired reforming magistrates throughout the country, but great vested interests were involved and rendered the task an uphill one. Finally the Licensing Acts of 1902 and 1904 made the production of agreements compulsory and placed all public-houses on a somewhat similar footing to " 1869 beer-houses." If the Justices found other reasons than the unsuitability of the applicant or the premises, the questions of reference to Quarter Sessions and compensation arose. Sir William Hodgson, chairman of the Crewe Licensing Committee from 1900 to 1926, and his fellow-Justices

" all along took the line that the licensee was personally responsible to them . . . Time and time again the companies' Counsel would try to get the Bench to define their criterion of a suitable licensee. In vain was the net spread. Dr. Hodgson was too wary. . . . The Bench might *think* that no man who would sign an agreement which made him the servant of a brewery and put his profit per barrel at a level which left him no working margin of profit *could* be ' a fit and proper person ' to hold a license, but they did not say so. They insisted, instead, upon seeing the agreement ; they modified it to their liking ; they even inserted the prices at which it was agreed the beer should be sold. The actual form of agreement was included

---

[1] Up to 1904 (Balfour's Licensing Act) Licensing Committees could refuse or grant licences practically at their discretion, save in the case of beer-houses licensed before May, 1869. Licences for these could not be withheld except on account of personal unsuitability of the applicants or because the premises were in bad condition.

[2] Anon : *Fasciculus Cestriensis in Honour of Sir William Hodgson* (1934), pp. 18–22 ; C.G., 24.9.92, 16.10.95, *passim* ; C.Ch., 23.9.93, 28.9.95.

in the license. But they enunciated no general criterion. Each applicant was licensed or refused on his own merits. . . . The Licensees were delighted. No longer could the breweries dismiss them on a trivial pretext." [1]

Good results followed—the improvement of the Crewe public-houses, the wide adoption of the " Crewe agreement " as a model, and its quotation in law books on licensing—but the fight with the breweries went on. In vain did the brewers brief such a legal giant as F. E. Smith (later Lord Birkenhead) in an effort to trap Dr. Hodgson, until in 1908 Sir Edward Carson pounced on some words used by the doctor with reference to an application for the Blue Cap Dog Hotel. Thereupon Messrs. Walker instituted High Court proceedings against him for libel. The case was finally abandoned in 1909. Dr. Hodgson apologised and paid £3,529 in costs, £2,500 of which came from his friends, a tribute to the personality of the man who, in a phrase used during this *cause célèbre*, " apparently dominated the Bench." [2]

The brewers eventually reconciled themselves to the limited monopolies presented to them by the steady refusal of the Justices to grant new licences ; as the population of Crewe increased, each licensee gained a larger number of customers. In 1881, there were 259 inhabitants per licence, in 1921, 645.[3]

This refusal, coupled with a ban on fresh singing and dancing licences for public-houses, resulted in a rapid and unforeseen increase in the number of drinking clubs. Clubs attached to the political parties had been a feature of social life in Crewe for some years. The Liberals established one in 1878, while the Conservatives and Liberal-Unionists opened theirs in 1890 and 1896 respectively. The newer type of drinking club eschewed politics ; in 1904 only two existed apart from those mentioned above, but by 1922 the register contained 17, including the political establishments, with a membership of 7,350.[4] Already by 1906 they had replaced the " long pull " (undercutting one's rivals by giving more than a pint of beer for the price of a pint)

[1] *Fasciculus Cestriensis*, pp. 19–20 ; see also C.Ch., 1.10.98 ; C.G., 26.8.99, 1.9.00, 27.12.02, 5.2.26.

[2] C.G., 27.12.02 to 9.4.04, *passim*, 18.1.08 to 21.7.09, *passim*.

[3] C.G., 27.8.81, 29.8.91, 31.8.01, 9.2.12, 10.2.22.

[4] The Licensing Act of 1902 had introduced the registration of clubs.

SIR WILLIAM HODGSON (1854–1940)
(*from the painting by F. T. Copnall, courtesy of the Cheshire County Council*)

as the pet aversion of Sir William, who described their mushroom growth as "most reprehensible" and "an opportunity of evading" the licensing regulations.[1]

Between 1879 and 1905 improvements in the sobriety of Crewe followed a somewhat spasmodic course, and to judge from the statistics of convictions for drunkenness little real progress was made, especially as the police had a reputation for leniency. Only after 1905 did the work of the Licensing Committee begin to bear fruit. Dr. Hodgson acclaimed the General Election of 1906 as the soberest he had known in his thirty years' acquaintance with the town. The decrease in the number of prosecutions became more rapid during the first World War, when shorter hours of opening, the reduced gravity of beer, the dilution of spirits, the shortness of supplies and the absence of men in the armed forces supplemented the Justices' efforts. That the change in habits proved permanent, in spite of the decline in the vigour of temperance propaganda after 1914, is shown by the fact that the decrease continued after the return of the armies and the re-establishment of a more normal social life :—

Year.								Prosecutions for Drunkenness.
1906	.	.	.	.	.	.	.	193
1911	.	.	.	.	.	.	.	105
1916	.	.	.	.	.	.	.	49
1921	.	.	.	.	.	.	.	9 [2]

The police station built in Eaton Street by arrangement between the county and the company, in 1847, soon became inadequate for the growing needs of the Crewe district, and in 1874 the Local Board made successful application to Quarter Sessions for a "new lock-up." The new police station in Edleston Road, completed in 1876, underwent enlargement in 1899, but the population in the western portion of the borough continued to be so unmanageable that in 1910 a branch station had to be opened in Ford Lane. The bouts of fisticuffs

[1] *C.G.*, 28.12.78, 1.10.90, 24.9.92, 26.8.93, 7.10.93, 23.2.95, 25.1.96, 26.5.00, 1.9.00, 28.9.01, 27 and 31.12.02, 28.2.03, 28.3.03, 13.2.04, 11.2.05, 10 and 14.2.06, 9.2.23.
[2] Reports of Brewster Sessions, 1881–1901, in *C.G.*, covering last week in August, then 1902–23, covering first week in February ; *C.Ch.*, 29.8.96.

complained of in the 1840's went on in a more spasmodic fashion, only to be eradicated from Crewe's social life in 1914, when these turbulent spirits found another outlet. Vacant plots of building land, often near to the various works' entrances, formed the favourite stage for these combats.[1]

The Commission of the Peace granted to the borough made no immediate alteration to the Crewe police arrangements, which remained under the control of the county authorities. The Corporation did not press for a separate Crewe police force, as estimates from time to time showed that it would be " cheaper for the borough to continue to be watched by the county police." Crewe Town Council did, however, press from time to time for the removal of the resident superintendent of the police division from Nantwich to Crewe. Not until April 1, 1902, did the Standing Joint Committee elevate Crewe to the headship of a separate police district, including Shavington, Weston, Hasling-ton, Leighton, Rope and Wistaston. The final development came in 1922, when, on the invitation of the Standing Joint Committee, the local magistrates expressed their views on a proposed merger of the Nantwich and Crewe police divisions, and the reduction of the Nantwich superintendency to an inspectorship under Crewe.[2]

II. PUBLIC HEALTH IN CREWE, 1877–1923

The period of acute political strife in Crewe Town Council during the 1880's did not lend itself to the development of a positive conception of local government, and few reforms stand to the credit of these years. The Corporation of 1890 differed very little from that of 1880 in its powers and activities. Precious time was continually wasted in the discussion of comparatively trivial matters, and one of the few administrative advances consisted in the appointment for the first time in 1884 of a permanent Health Committee, " to deal with any infectious disease that may arise, and also with questions affecting the general health

---

[1] C.G., 25.7.08, 27.1.09, 9.12.10 ; G.P.C., 2 and 16.7.74 ; private information.

[2] G.P.C., 14.1.86, 9.2.86, 3.6.86, 15.5.02 ; C.G., 30.1.86, 27.2.86, 19.6.86, 1.9.88, 19.3.02, 8.4.05, 28.3.08, 24.10.22.

of the town." Before this, outbreaks of disease were met by temporary "committees of expediency" and a lavish use of disinfectants. The man behind this move, and first Chairman of the Health Committee (1884–96), was Sir (then Dr.) William Hodgson. He soon came into conflict with Dr. T. C. Bailey, part-time M.O.H. at £50 per annum (1878–93). Bailey, although a would-be sanitary reformer, lacked the patience and tact necessary in dealing with a Council composed in the main of cottage-property owners.[1] No annual reports for 1880 and 1885 ever reached the Council. Dr. Hodgson said of Bailey:—" I hardly remember him to be otherwise than very angry . . . he had [in 1881] condemned the sanitary work of the Corporation . . . and the Corporation had reprimanded him for it, and he stayed away and retired to some obscure corner." [2]   In spite of these and later incidents (a report of his in 1889 was " mainly studded . . . with abuse of the Chairman of the Committee ") Bailey continued to hold office until 1893, when the first full-time appointment was made under the Local Government Board's Order of March 23, 1891.[3]

Between 1893 and 1920 the town benefited from the services of six Medical Officers of Health, all of whom left Crewe to take up posts with better prospects and salaries than the Corporation offered. From 1893 the Cheshire County Council paid half the salaries of the M.O.H. and the Sanitary Inspector (Hodgson had proposed, and almost carried, an application to the Central Government for a similar grant for a full-time M.O.H. in 1882), while the Local Government Board made full use of its powers to increase the remuneration paid to the first of these officials. Before 1893 the Chairman of the Health Committee had performed many of the duties now associated with the staff of the Health Department, and the advantage of a full-time M.O.H. soon became generally apparent, although a proposal to revert to the part-time system (made in 1900) failed to pass by only

---

[1] *C.G.*, 1.3.79, 2.2.78, 8.1.81, 23.7.81, 27.5.82, 12 and 15.11.84, 30.1.92, 25.3.93 ; *cf.* letter dated Dec. 30, 1899, from J. H. Jones, M.O.H. for Crewe, 1893–7, to Meredith Young (M.O.H. for Crewe, 1897–1900) : " I expect you wish as I often did that you could be a member of the Council for a quarter of an hour to give ' adequate expression to your feelings.' "

[2] *C.G.*, 1.6.89.

[3] *C.G.*, 31.8.89 ; Health Ctee., 16.5.89, 15.8.89, 1893, *passim.*

5 votes. After much pressing, the Infectious Diseases Notification Act, 1889, was adopted in the borough from October, 1896, an essential step in the control of epidemics.[1]

Smallpox, the scourge of the 1870's, had by now ceased to be a major preoccupation, thanks to vaccination, a better water-supply, more effective isolation and general sanitary improvement. There have been no deaths in the borough from smallpox since 1884, but on account of an outbreak in 1903, the Pym's Lane Hospital, with accommodation for 10 persons, was extended; fortunately it has not been found necessary to use it since the next (and, up to the present, the last) outbreak in 1920.[2]

The next diseases for which isolation facilities came to be provided were scarlet fever and typhoid, with the opening on October 10, 1897, of the nucleus of the present municipal Isolation Hospital. This, unlike the Pym's Lane Hospital, had a permanent staff, and here again Dr. William Hodgson carried the scheme through its difficult first stages, in spite of opposition from Dr. Richard Lord and other " economists," who favoured either a smaller scheme or none at all. They tended to ignore the fact that scarlet fever had never been absent from the town since 1874, and that the death-rates in Crewe from typhoid and scarlet fever were considerably higher than those for England and Wales. The hospital contained 16 beds for scarlet fever and 10 for typhoid, but while typhoid soon ceased to be a serious menace, scarlet fever proved a more intractable disease. Diphtheria increased rapidly in violence during the decade 1890–1900, after which the Corporation began to supply anti-toxin, first at cost price (1900), then free (1901), to local doctors. A two-ward diphtheria pavilion added to the Isolation Hospital in 1904 did something to check the disease, but bad epidemics occurred in 1910 and 1913 ; the Medical Officer reported that the disease had been " more or less epidemic in Crewe for some years, with

[1] *Fasciculus Cestriensis*, pp. 13–14 ; C.G., 27.5.82, 30.1.92, 3.9.92, 11 and 25.3.93 to 4.8.94, *passim*, 10.8.95, 4.1.96, 8.8.96, 7.4.00. The Infectious Diseases Prevention Act of 1890 was adopted in 1891 (C.G., 20.12.90 ; M.O.H., 1902, p. 6 ; Health Ctee., 18.8.92). For the increase in the work of the Sanitary Department after the extension of the borough in 1892, see Health Sub-Ctee., 16.10.93. William Urquhart became Sanitary Inspector in 1893 and served until 1916.

[2] M.O.H., 1896, p. 17 ; 1903, pp. 27–8, 40, 48–9.

periodic increases in its incidence " ; this remained the position to the end of the period.[1]

The problem of reducing the death-rate from tuberculosis, first noticed in 1898, was not seriously tackled until 1909, when the Corporation provided an open revolving shelter, with assistance from the County Council, in the grounds of the Isolation Hospital. During 1913 all forms of tuberculosis became compulsorily notifiable, and the Insurance Act of 1912 rendered the detection of cases a much simpler task. Movable open-air shelters, provided by the Corporation for domiciliary treatment for the first time in 1916, proved very popular, but the first World War held up negotiations with the County Authority for the joint erection of an open-air pavilion at the Isolation Hospital. This would have supplemented the Pulmonary Tuberculosis Dispensary established in the town by the County Council in 1915.[2] While the death-rates from the above diseases tended to decrease with more or less rapidity, that from cancer gradually rose, and in 1919 was responsible for the largest number of deaths from any single cause.[3]

While public authorities had been gradually building up a municipal health service for infectious diseases, private charity had also been busy providing a Cottage Hospital for Crewe, to relieve the town from dependence on Nantwich Infirmary. Such an institution for the treatment of non-infectious diseases, accident cases and the performance of simple operations had been suggested in 1883 as a " positive necessity," but the matter remained in abeyance until 1893, when A. G. Hill suggested to Webb that he should use his influence with the directors to obtain a free site from the railway company. The site having been obtained, Webb and H. Yates Thompson, director of the Lancashire and Yorkshire Railway, gave £1,000 each towards the building. To this sum was added Martin Heath's " open space " legacy of £500. With these gifts and other public subscriptions it became possible to build in Victoria Avenue a

[1] Ref. Dest. Sub-Ctee., 27.2.94 ; Health Ctee., 3.4.94, 12.3.95, 1.5.95, 5.6.95 ; G.P.C., 11.10.94 ; Coun., 2.5.94 ; *C.G.*, 1895, *passim*, 20.10.97 ; M.O.H., 1897–1916, *passim*.

[2] M.O.H., 1898, p. 44 *sqq.* ; 1907, p. 50 ; 1909, p. 44 ; 1912, p. 50 ; 1913, p. 32 ; 1915, pp. 45, 48 ; 1916, p. 18 ; 1920, pp. 53–4 ; C.G., 24.4.14, 8.1.15, 9.7.15, 3.12.15, 4.2.16.

[3] M.O.H., 1919, p. 14 (*cf.* 1912, p. 57).

three-ward Cottage Hospital, which was opened on August 7, 1895. The hospital was ruled by a body of governors, *i.e.* subscribers who fulfilled certain regulations ; the governors elected a management committee and from time to time filled up vacant trusteeships. The Charity Commissioners regulated the hospital's position as a charity in 1921.

Additions to the hospital since 1895 have been numerous—a mortuary in 1898, living accommodation for the staff in 1900, a children's ward (1901), a new wing (1909), and X-ray apparatus (1920). Some idea of the increase in its scope may be obtained from the number of patients, 24, admitted during the first working year (1895–6) and the number, 620, treated in 1922. As a voluntary organisation the hospital was never free from the necessity of appealing to the public for money, but a substantial Endowment Fund had been built up by the 1930's, and the hospital enjoyed the profits from the Euston Coffee Tavern, Crewe, established by F. W. Webb in 1880, and later handed over to the Committee of Management. Webb also gave £5,000 to the Endowment Fund in 1903.[1]

Another voluntary health service inaugurated in these years was carried out by the Crewe District Nursing Association, founded by philanthropic Crewe women and ministers of religion in 1897. It became redundant and was wound up twelve years later as a sequel to the opening of the Webb Nursing Institute at No. 8, Heathfield Avenue in 1908. This had been made possible by a legacy of £10,000 under F. W. Webb's will, to be used to support nurses to attend on " persons of the poorer classes . . . in the borough of Crewe." [2]

In 1878 Crewe became the scene of a minor piece of sanitary pioneering, when Edwin Whiteman, the company's district estate agent at Crewe from about 1865 until 1905, who had invented a much-improved type of waste-water closet, built the first one in Christ Church day-schools. This " tumbler " or " tip-pan " was gradually installed in many of the company's houses, and, by 1897, 832 existed in the town. Even as late as 1879 only 170 real water-closets were in use in the borough. Fear lest the growth in the number of water-closets might place an undue strain on

---

[1] *C.G.*, 10.1.80, 21.7.83, 13.2.86, 27.10.88, 28.1.33, 4.3.93, 22.4.93 (*cf. C.Ch.*, 25.11.93), 13 and 20.1.94, 26.5.94, 2.3.95, 10.8.95.
[2] *C.G.*, 12.6.97, 22.1.98 ; *C.Ch.*, 8.9.00 ; *C.G.*, 14.12.04, 3.10.08, 9.10.09.

the Sewage Farm and the water-supply often found expression at meetings of the Corporation.   In 1882, after a reprimand from the Local Government Board on the state of Crewe's privy pits, the Corporation amended the by-laws regulating the construction of water-closets, ash-closets with fixed receptacles, and privies with fixed receptacles, but showed a strong dislike for privy pails.   After 1893 every M.O.H. was an enthusiast for conversion to water-closets, but by this time Crewe Corporation and Crewe builders had developed a strange affection for the privy pail, which never failed to find its defenders.[1]

Between 1882 and 1893 no fewer than 2,460 notices were served under section 36 of the Public Health Act, 1875, requiring the reconstruction of privies, or their conversion into water-closets.   Crewe's position in 1897 stood as follows :—

Pail-closets .	2,651
Water-closets	2,614
Waste-water closets	832
Cess-pools .	264
Fixed receptacles	66
Privy middens (mixens)	1,897

An indignant M.O.H., writing in 1899, and recognising that cess-pools, mixens and fixed receptacles were dying out, reserved his strongest language for the privy pail—" a filthy stinking abomination " at the best of times.   He proposed a scheme of wholesale conversion to water-carriage at the expense of the Corporation which could be paid for in the decreased cost of scavenging, and prophesied truly :—" the growth of pail-closets does not promise at all well for the future, as your Council will find out some day."   His scheme came to nothing, but the number of privy pails continued to grow until it reached the maximum in 1910 at 3,104.   Nevertheless, the progress of the water-closet between 1897 and 1911 had been a rapid one, as the figures for the latter year show :—

Water-closets (both types) .	7,099
Pail-closets .	3,053
Cess-pools .	none
Fixed receptacles	2
Privy middens (mixens)	321

[1] " The advocates of the conservancy system appear altogether to leave out of consideration the comfort of those who occupy the houses concerned, quite apart from any question of healthiness " (M.O.H., 1896, p. 46).

The Corporation had no power to enforce the provision of water-closets in new houses until 1920, when, during the privy-pail conversion agitation, sections 39 to 42 of the Public Health Acts Amendment Act of 1907 were adopted and the construction of further privies forbidden. At that date Crewe still possessed 2,787 pail-closets and 106 privy middens. In the same year the M.O.H. prepared a scheme for the systematic eradication of mixens and privy pails. Owing to the " economy campaign " of 1921, the estimate of £600 for the first year's instalment of the scheme (1921–2) was cut down to £100, and this happened again in 1922 and 1923, although in the latter year persistent agitation by Alderman Kettell and the Labour group on the Town Council secured an eventual increase to £200. These monies were used to provide free pedestals, cisterns and piping to persons desiring to pay for the alteration. The Medical Officer's Annual Report for 1923 summed up :—" The Corporation scheme has the advantage of cheapness, but it is by no means expeditious." [1]

The Corporation continued the direct-labour system of scavenging which the Local Board had been forced to adopt. The annual cost trebled between 1879 and 1900. In 1882 an " appalling " list of ash-pits needing reconstruction showed the necessity for the adoption of a system less injurious to property, but no hasty desire to change was observable on the part of Crewe's property-owners :—

". . . these outbuildings . . . are subjected to wear and tear of no ordinary kind. Is a privy pail in use ? then 52 times a year it has to be taken out of the building and replaced. Is an old-fashioned privy or a cesspool provided ? then six or eight times yearly it has to be emptied and the walls of the structure knocked about by the spades or buckets of the labourers, who are working under the worst possible conditions, at night time, with little if any light, in all weathers, and urged on by their foreman to get through their work as speedily as possible " (J. H. Jones, M.O.H., 1894).

With the increasing use of ash-pails and the consequent separation of the two services, it became possible in the 1890's to

[1] *C.G.*, 1879, 1881, *passim*, 7.1.82, 19.8.82, 26.4.84, 28.1.93, 4.5.95, 4.12.97, 9.4.20, 1922, *passim* ; G.P.C., *passim*, 1879, 1882, 10.6.80, 24.2.81, 14.7.81 ; Health Ctee. and Sub-Ctee., 1920–3, *passim* ; M.O.H., 1893, 1894, 1895, 1897, 1899, 1903, 1910, 1911, 1919, *passim*, 1923, p. 21.

organise a more regular system of refuse collection. The work done in this department increased greatly after the extension of the borough in 1892 and the appointment of a full-time M.O.H. in the following year. In 1893 a fortnightly removal of ashes had been the ideal aimed at, in 1895 it was generally inaugurated, and from November, 1900, ash-pails received weekly attention. On account of labour scarcity during the first World War a three-weekly collection had to be introduced in 1916, but on the return of peace a great reorganisation of the department took place. Galvanised iron ash-pails were made compulsory in 1922, and motor transport superseded the last horse in 1923.

After the completion of the Sewage Farm in 1872–4, most of Crewe's refuse from ash-pits and ash-pails and privies was deposited there, until in an unfortunate moment the Corporation leased the New Street pit or " reservoir " (1911) and commenced to fill it with " suitable material," *i.e.* builders' rubbish and old macadam. From 1916 onwards, in spite of its proximity to the recently-erected Borough Schools and the protests of a public-spirited minority on the Council, unsuitable material, *e.g.* general rubbish and ashes, was dumped into it and created a serious nuisance, only suppressed by the erection of a modern refuse destructor in Pym's Lane in 1929–30.[1]

The multiplication of water-closets caused the sewage flowing to the farm to become stronger, and in 1888 the Nantwich Rural Sanitary Authority, after a refusal by Crewe Town Council to take more sewage from Church Coppenhall, applied to the Local Government Board for powers to acquire 16 acres of land near Crewe's Sewage Farm for irrigation purposes. Crewe Town Council, warned in the same year that the Sewage Farm was beginning to pollute the River Weaver, proposed as an alternative that the southern portion of Church Coppenhall should be incorporated in the borough of Crewe, and after a long struggle

[1] C.G., 26.4.79 to 17.3.83, *passim*, 8.12.11, 5.5.16, 2.6.16 ; M.O.H., 1893–1900, *passim* (esp. special report 1899, pp. 12–16) ; 1916, pp. 26–7 ; 1922, pp. 20, 29 ; Health Ctee., Sub-Ctee. and Refuse Dest. Sub-Ctee., 1892–4, *passim* ; Health Ctee., 10.7.07, 14.2.12, 12.4.16 ; Coun., 3.5.16, 10.9.19 ; G.P.C., 19.12.11 ; Sub-Ctee. on Ashpit Scavenging, 27.3.07 ; *Abst. Accts.*, 1882 *sqq.*

this extension came into force on November 9, 1892.   There existed over 22 miles of sewers in the extended borough, through which 455 million gallons of sewage passed in 1896 to the northern and southern outfalls, to be pumped untreated on to the 209 acres of the farm.   The extension of 1892 and the growing number of water-closets soon proved too much for the overburdened and unsuitable soil of the farm ; after further complaints about the pollution of the Weaver from the Nantwich Rural District Council, the County M.O.H. decided in 1897 that the people of Crewe were " not using the best practicable and available means for dealing with their sewage," and during the next few years many veiled threats of an injunction came from the County Rivers Pollution Committee.   The problem was partially dealt with by providing in 1901–3 a septic tank and five pairs of bacteria beds at the pumping station, but as they dealt with only one-fifth of the sewage, *i.e.* that from the northern outfall, a new scheme had to be prepared in 1904 for a subsidiary southern out-fall sewer and sewage works for the treatment of sewage on bacterial principles.   Situated to the south of the Queen's Park, the new works came into full operation in 1913–14.   Not only did engineering difficulties delay them (the slight difference between the highest and lowest altitudes in the borough, 200 and 113 feet, meant that a good fall in the sewers could not be obtained), but in addition certain members of the Council waged in 1908–9 a violent, wrong-headed and unsuccessful campaign against both the site and the methods to be utilised, until one prominent alderman declared he was " sick of sewage."

The completion of these works at a cost of about £50,000 meant that one part of Crewe, north of West Street, Hightown, Victoria Street and Earle Street, and east of the Liverpool line of railway to Crewe station, drained into the northern outfall sewer to the old Local Board works in Minshull New Road, where the sewage was partially treated by the bacteria beds and then pumped over the farm lands by an obsolete engine.   The other part of Crewe, south of the first district, drained to the new works by the modern southern outfall sewer.   In 1922–4 a new sewer was constructed to switch the sewage from the northern outfall to the new works near the Park.   This meant the end of the expensive, inefficient and by now entirely unsatisfactory Local Board works and the abolition of the Sewage Farm, which reverted to its former uses.[1]

From the time when detailed vital statistics for Crewe first became available, the great waste of infant life between birth and the age of twelve months had been generally deplored, but as long as the birth-rate remained much in excess of the crude death-rate little effective action was taken to reduce this " annual slaughter," especially as the infantile mortality rate for Crewe usually compared favourably with that for England and Wales as a whole. Only when the public generally became cognizant of the rapidly falling birth-rate and began to entertain vague fears about a declining population was any serious attention given to the problem of reducing this loss to the community ; *e.g.* successive Crewe Medical Officers of Health called attention to the high infantile mortality rate in the town and suggested measures to lower it from 1896 onwards.[2] Yet not until 1913 were any exceptional measures taken. The major reason for the more energetic interest taken in the subject during the years immediately before 1914 is to be found in a sentence from the M.O.H.'s report for 1911 :—" The steadily declining birth-rate further emphasises the vital importance of conserving the very young." [3]

[1] *C.G.*, 17.3.86 to 23.3.92, *passim*, 5.5.97 to 10.11.98, *passim*, 10.3.00, 14.7.00, 15.7.05, 4.1.08 to 5.3.10, *passim*, 1922, *passim* ; *C.Ch.*, 17.3.88, 30.6.88 ; M.O.H., 1896–8, 1900–2, 1905, 1912–14, 1923, *passim* ; Health Ctee., 27.11.94, 11.11.97 *sqq.* ; Farm Ctee., 13.1.98 *sqq.*, 14.5.08 ; G.P.C., 11.11.97, 9.6.04, 9.2.05, 13.7.05, 14.6.10, 19.7.11, 19.5.14, 17.11.14, 22.7.19, 16.9.19, 16.12.19, 15.1.24 ; Ctee. of Coun., 5.1.16 ; Coun., 18.1.16, 4.1.22, 9.11.23 ; Sub-Ctee. *re* unemployed, 17.11.21 ; Sub-Ctee. *re* Farm leases, 13.9.21, 30.11.21, 19.12.21. The freehold of the Sewage Farm was bought by the Corporation between 1916 and 1923.

[2] Such as the more energetic conversion of cess-pools and privies into water-closets, the better education of mothers and girls in hygiene and baby feeding, and the appointment of a woman health visitor. Many Crewe mothers were said to place " the digestive powers of a baby in arms on the same level as those of an able-bodied navvy " (M.O.H., 1894, p. 12 ; see also 1900, p. 19).

[3] p. 20. *Cf.* M.O.H., 1917, p. 5 :—" The Birth Rate this year, *i.e.* 15·8 per 1,000 . . . is less than half the rate which prevailed up to 1903. When we consider that . . . this means that only 764 children were born in Crewe in 1917 instead of the 1,644 who would have been born if the Birth Rate had been the same as in 1903, the great importance attached to Maternity and Baby Welfare Work is at once explained. We cannot increase the Birth Rate but we can lower the Infantile Mortality Rate, and thus save many children

The connection between deaths from diarrhœa, the number of privies and cess-pools, and the intractable infantile mortality rate, pointed out for years by the M.O.H., received practical confirmation in 1912, when for the first time on record infantile mortality in Crewe, which had latterly manifested a tendency to decline, fell below 100 per 1,000 to 82 per 1,000. It was no coincidence that this occurred two years after the number of privy pails had at last begun to decline, five years after the abolition of the last cess-pool, and at the end of a decade during which mixens had been reduced from 1,720 to 321 (1901–11). Infantile diarrhœa now gradually ceased to be the bugbear of sanitary reformers.

Maternity facilities also needed overhaul. A report dated 1910, made under the Midwives Act of that year, revealed that 12 out of the 35 Crewe midwives (midwives attended nearly 90 per cent. of the births in the borough) were " quite unable to write," and that the majority could not see the mercury in a thermometer. This state of affairs received drastic treatment during the next three years. In 1913 the Health and Education Committees joined to appoint a lady health visitor and dental clinic nurse, and to enable her to follow up all the births more efficiently the Notification of Births Act, 1907, was adopted in 1913.[1]

Between 1915 and 1917 the health visitor began weekly infant consultations at an improvised clinic in Cobden Street, but owing to war activities these were abandoned after a few months. Nevertheless, a great effort to expand the service is observable during the last few years of the struggle. In 1917 a full-time lady

---

who would otherwise die." Crewe's first Health Week (*i.e.* deliberate propaganda to make the public aware of the health services) was held in September, 1920.

[1] The improvement after 1911 is shown by the following figures :—

Year.	Inf. Mort. per 1,000.	Year.	Inf. Mort. per 1,000.	Year.	Inf. Mort. per 1,000.
1900	138	1910	103	1919	54
1901	181	1911	162	1920	85
1902	131	1912	82	1921	91
1903	145	1913	103	1922	78
1904	160	1914	88	1923	69

health visitor was appointed to supplement the work of the first part-time visitor, and in 1918–19, under constant pressure from the new Ministry of Health, a Maternity and Child Welfare Scheme was adopted.   It brought into existence a separate Maternity and Child Welfare Committee (1919), a main Maternity and Child Welfare Consultation Centre in the former Railway Hospital, Lyon Street, opened in 1921, and a branch centre in St. John's Church Room, Stalbridge Road, opened in 1920.[1] The new Committee also organised the distribution of milk free and at half-price to mothers and children under the Milk Order, 1918, greatly expanded the important ante-natal work, and enabled more home visiting to be carried out.   As the culminating point of the scheme, the Committee opened the municipal Maternity House at " Linden Grange," Hungerford Avenue, in 1921, although some time elapsed before the public began to use it at anywhere near the full capacity.   Fifty per cent. of the whole scheme's annual cost came from the national Exchequer, and it is doubtful whether the municipality would have been able or willing to carry out a service of such scope in the absence of the financial stimulus provided by the Ministry of Health.[2]

III. Roads, Bridges and Motor Transport

At an early period in its history Crewe Corporation was smitten with " paving fever," and insisted on the use of stone setts for the streets of the borough.   The expense of this method as compared with macadam led to a long dispute which ended in 1881 with victory for the " macadamisers."   From this date until the making of Edleston Road with Trinidad bitumen in 1921–2 macadam and tar reigned unchallenged.   The decline in the use of macadam for urban main roads was foreshadowed by

[1] It replaced the Wedgwood Assembly Rooms, used 1919–21, and the Cobden Street clinic, used 1918–21.   The latter thereupon became the schools dental clinic.

[2] *C.G.*, 17.4.78 to 25.3.92, *passim*, 1.7.99, 9.5.08, 16.6.14, 7.12.17, 8.8.19, 1920–3, *passim* ; *C.Ch.*, 8.8.19 (scheme) ; M.O.H., 1893–1904, 1907, 1909–23, *passim* ; Health Ctee., 1917, *passim*, 9.10.18, 1919, *passim*, 15.4.20 ; Joint Health and Educ. Ctee., 27.11.17 ; Mat. and C.W. Sub-Ctee. and Ctee., 24.6.19 to 12.1.21, *passim*.

the rapid deterioration of road surfaces during and immediately after the first World War, due partly to unavoidable neglect and partly to the rapid increase in motor traffic.[1]

Until 1882 the only main road in the borough recognised as such by the county was that part of the Nantwich to Wheelock highway which passed through the southern extremity of Monks Coppenhall. This highway had been disturnpiked in 1880-1, and henceforward Quarter Sessions made a 50 per cent. grant to the Corporation towards the cost of its maintenance and improvement. In 1882 the Town Council obtained the recognition by Quarter Sessions of Mill Street, High Street, Market Street to the Adelphi Hotel, and Earle Street to the Market Hall, as main roads on similar terms. In 1883 Market Street to the Grand Junction Inn, Victoria Street, Hightown, West Street to Underwood Lane, and Earle Street to the Manchester bridge, were accorded similar treatment. After the extension of 1892 there were 27 miles of public highway and $4\frac{1}{4}$ miles of county main roads in the borough. Within nine years of the establishment of an elected County Council the joint County and Local Government Board road grant to Crewe had increased six-fold, but it became no easier to secure the recognition of further stretches as county main roads. By 1914 the road grant had decreased so much that a considerable agitation started in the Town Council for a fresh financial agreement with the county authorities on the subject. The first World War merely postponed and aggravated these difficulties. For example, Edleston Road, which had by 1914 definitely replaced Mill Street as the main traffic entrance to the town from the south, had not been declared a main road by the county as late as 1921-2, when its total reconstruction became necessary. The Ministry of Transport made its first grant to the road expenses of the borough in 1922-3.[2]

From January 1, 1881, the railway company had agreed to pay an annual sum to the Corporation for the maintenance of

[1] The first motor-cars to be seen on the streets of Crewe entered the town in June, 1897, at the invitation of Councillor C. H. Pedley (*C.G.*, 19.6.97). See also Coun., 1881, *passim* ; Works Ctee., 12.2.96 ; G.P.C., 16.9.19, 13.1.20 ; *C.G.*, 7.12.78 to 12.11.81, *passim*.

[2] *C.G.*, 17.12.81, 7.1.82, 14.8.86, 6.6.88 to 4.7.91, *passim*, 7.7.94, 3.4.14, 8.5.14, 9.5.19, 5.3.20, 9.4.20, 6.5.21, 1922, *passim* ; *Abst. Accts.*, 1880-1, 1887-8 to 1923-4 ; Works Ctee., 24.8.81 to 7.1.86, *passim*, 29.4.93, 11.7.99, 8.8.99, 8.1.01 ; Coun., 7.12.81 ; G.P.C., 29.12.81.

carriage-ways over the five railway bridges in the borough built after 1845, and the extension of 1892 added three more (in Sydney, North Street and Broad Street) to the eight already within the borough boundary. These additional bridges, together with the Chester bridge, built before 1845, were made the subject of a separate agreement in 1904. One of the Corporation's most difficult tasks has been to negotiate with the company for the widening of these railway bridges. The Manchester, Liverpool and Chester bridges were all widened between 1897 and 1911, but only after delays and haggling extending over many years. In 1923, as part of a public works scheme to relieve unemployment, Flag Lane and Alton Street were connected by a vehicular "New Bridge." This great public improvement had been delayed by the first World War. Crewe still suffers from the inadequacy of Chester bridge and its southern approach, the sole link between two important shopping districts severed by the railways and the natural route for traffic passing through the town. The pressure on Chester bridge is relieved only to a slight extent by the New and Flag Lane bridges.[1]

Although Martin Heath (1810–87) left £500 in the hands of trustees towards the provision of an open space for the town, the L.N.W.R. Company was the first to move in the matter. To mark the jubilee of the Queen and the town, Webb used his influence with Sir Richard Moon to obtain from the shareholders a grant to Crewe Corporation of 30 acres of land, including a 5-acre lake, together with £10,000 to be spent on laying it out (L.N.W.R. Act, 1887, sections 58 and 59). This "Queen's Park," dedicated on July 4, 1887, in the middle of "The Jubilee Mania," was opened to the public by the Duke of Cambridge on June 8, 1888. Although criticised by the Liberals on account of its alleged inaccessibility and of the absurd regulations which marked the first years of its existence, it became a great asset to the town. Under the first curator, George Latimer (1888–1906), who had been a forester, most of the fine trees which grace it today were planted. At first the Valley Brook flowed through the Park lake, but this caused sewage to accumu-

[1] *C.G.*, 25.5.78 to 16.8.79, *passim*, 10.10.85, 2 and 30.1.86, 1891, *passim*, 7.3.96, 6.3.97, 28.8.97, 11.11.99, 1900, *passim*, 16.12.02, 21.8.09 to 29.12.11, *passim* ; Works Ctee., 1880–1, *passim*, 15.10.85, Sub-Ctee., 2.4.09, *sqq.*, *passim*, G.P.C., 20.2.23.

late in the basin and in 1913–14 the brook was culverted to reduce the pollution.

By an agreement dated January 10, 1893, the Market Square, for some years deserted by the produce-sellers, was devoted to the public use by the L.N.W.R. Company, and adopted by Crewe Corporation as a highway repairable by the inhabitants at large. This agreement also provided that the Council " should for ever preserve the Square as an open space, and should not erect any buildings thereon." At the same time the highways abutting on it were adopted by the Corporation, but the company still maintains the rest of its private streets.

The town was still without regular playgrounds in the centre of the town for its large child population (in 1909 the borough contained 9,500 children between the ages of four and thirteen). To commemorate the Queen's diamond jubilee three pieces of land, one in each of the wards, were purchased, largely through the efforts and enthusiasm of Alderman T. Latham and Councillor Peter Swinton, at a cost of nearly £5,000, and eventually laid out as children's playgrounds.[1]

The development of urban passenger transport in Crewe illustrates the extent to which municipal and private enterprise may be hampered by ratepayer "economists" and vested interests. In 1878 Frederick C. Winby of Nottingham, member of a well-known Crewe family, made an agreement with the Corporation to lay down a 3-feet gauge tramway from the Lion and Swan Hotel to the Royal Hotel near the railway station, to be worked by a private company, and in 1879 obtained a provisional order for the purpose from the Board of Trade under the Tramways Act, 1870. As no substantial start had been made on the project by the middle of 1880, Winby's powers lapsed. He had been unable to raise the financial support necessary in order to satisfy the Corporation's requirements in the matter of a paved track.[2] The town continued to depend on Henry Irving's cab service, until about 1882 three brothers, William,

[1] *C.G.*, 2.4.79, 1.11.79, 19.2.87 to 30.6.88, *passim*, 30.8.90, 29.11.90, 6.7.95, 7.9.95, 1897, *passim*, 4.3.99, 1.4.99, 14.3.06, 10.2.00, 10.4.09 ; *C.Ch.*, 9.7.87, 16.6.88, 28.7.88 ; Works Ctee., 27.9.93 ; Coun., 25.1.93, 3.9.13 ; G.P.C., 19.4.10, 17.12.12, 14.1.13.

[2] *C.G.*, 2.11.78 to 25.6.81, *passim*, 26.3.84 ; Coun., 1878–9, *passim* ; G.P.C., 24.10.78 ; Works Ctee., 31.5.81. There was a proposal to resurrect the Winby scheme in 1881.

Thomas and John Adam Ward, established a horse-omnibus service from the George Inn, West Street, *via* Mill Street to the railway station. The earliest available time-table shows 10 departures daily in each direction, with an " extra " on Fridays and Saturdays. By 1901 the Wards were employing 5 omnibuses, and had extended their service to Edleston Road and Exchange Street (1897), and from Hungerford Road to the station (1899), doubtless under fear of competition from the proposals detailed below.[1]

In May, 1896, Councillor C. H. Pedley, who had been in communication with the British Electric Traction Company, brought before Crewe Town Council a plan whereby this firm should lay down and work electric tramways in the borough. Accordingly, in February, 1897, the Light Railway Commissioners held an enquiry at Crewe, under the Light Railways Act of 1896, into the B.E.T. Company's application for a provisional order empowering it to construct a 3 feet 6 inch gauge light railway for electric trams. The system would link the outlying parts of the town with the centre, the railway station, and Haslington, where about 200 company's workmen lived. Alterations made in the draft order by the Board of Trade at the instance of Crewe Town Council, in order to safeguard the road surface, raised the estimated cost of the scheme from £65,300 to £90,500, and as a result the Crewe Light Railway draft order was withdrawn by its promoters in 1898.

Little was heard of the tram project for the next two years, during which time the Crewe Corporation constructed its new electricity works. In April, 1900, the establishment of a municipal tramway came into discussion as a device for utilising electrical energy in the daytime, and thus maintaining a more even load. In November, 1900, the Council resolved to apply for a provisional order to carry out what was practically the 1897 scheme under municipal ownership, at a cost of £90,000 ; the network of lines was to cover 8 miles. The scheme cut straight across party alignments. Progressive Liberals (C. H. Pedley, Briggs and McNeill) found themselves in the same camp with Alderman A. G. Hill, son of the famous John Hill and leader of the Crewe Conservative Party. They were supported by

[1] *C.G.*, 3.1.83, 28.9.87, 5.10.87, 10.7.97, 10.6.99, 13.3.14 ; *E.A.* 83, p. 192 ; Hackney Carriage Sub-Ctee., 16.1.01.

Crewe branch of the I.L.P., whose members supported Hill in his strong advocacy of " municipal socialism." Ranged against them were " economist " Liberals and Conservatives, vested interests (John A. Ward and brothers) and the railway company, whose self-appointed spokesman was Kenneth Macrae, chief accountant of the locomotive department. He discovered practically at the last minute that the scheme would add 1s. 4d. in the pound to the rates, and that the railway company would have to pay one-third of the annual loss, for its property in the town was rated at £42,000. This volume of opposition and the statistics came as a surprise to the supporters of municipal ownership, and the application was refused, after an enquiry on January 30, 1901, lasting seven hours.

In September, 1901, the Corporation, with the approval of a town's meeting, successfully opposed a second application by the B.E.T. Company for a provisional order empowering them to construct 6 miles of track in Crewe and district. In the same month the routes for a municipal scheme less ambitious than the first were approved by the Council, but the scheme itself was never submitted to the Light Railway Commissioners. Disputes broke out in the Council as to whether Mill Street or Edleston Road, or both, should be laid with track. Mill Street had been stagnating as a shopping centre since the construction of Edleston Road in 1882, the consequent development of the south-western portion of the borough, and the removal of the post office from High Street in 1883. Nevertheless, tradesmen from this area viewed with alarm another proof of the district's decay, revealed by the Council's decision to choose the Edleston Road tram-route, and this undoubtedly helped to defeat the scheme. A ratepayers' meeting on March 25, 1902, refused to approve of the Council's decision to make a second application for a provisional order. Macrae and his dependent minions from the L.N.W.R. general offices turned up in force (" It was really a case of the Railway Company versus the town . . . this state of things is becoming a little monotonous," commented the *Guardian*). Although Briggs explained that the second scheme with four tramcars would cost only £35,000, a poll of ratepayers on April 5 decided against tramways by 1,418 votes to 1,076. Whatever the defects of the earlier scheme may have been, there is no doubt, in view of later events, that the modest scheme of 1902, which tapped the most profitable districts, would have paid handsomely. Macrae and those who instigated his opposition must bear a heavy load of responsibility for thwarting its development. The lack of judgment on issues of this character by one who was supposed to be an expert accountant is shown by the fact that he described Hill's successful municipal electricity scheme as a " white elephant " instead of the " milch cow " which it has in reality been. Later, in 1903, he admitted rather hypocritically :—". . . if they were to have tramways they ought to belong to the Corporation. What he objected to was the introduction of a pretentious scheme." [1]

Hardly had the resolutions dealing with the 1902 scheme been rescinded by the Council than several firms began to interest themselves in a private tramway company for Crewe. In spite of protests from the progressive Liberals, Crewe Trades Council and the Crewe branch of the I.L.P. (which received much political publicity from its wholehearted support of municipal tramways), Hewitt and Rhodes of Manchester, electrical engineers, obtained the consent of the Corporation to their scheme in 1903. A proposed draft agreement between the Corporation and the " Crewe and Nantwich Tramways Company," providing for optional municipal purchase after twenty-five years, was actually drawn up, but Hewitt and Rhodes began to evince a desire to turn the scheme into a mere Nantwich to Crewe line, and the Corporation broke off negotiations with them after a well-attended ratepayers' meeting, on October 1, 1903, had resolved by an " enormous majority " that " it is undesirable and objectionable to allow a private company to lay down and carry on a tramway scheme in the town." In November preparations began for a new municipal project, which unfortunately received indefinite postponement in March, 1904. In spite of attempts by Briggs and William Williams to revive it later in the year, nothing further is heard of light railways in Crewe, for " motor omnibuses " of various types had begun to fill the air with alarming noises and noxious fumes.

[1] *C.G.*, 4.5.95 to 10.5.02, *passim*, 31.10.11 ; *C.Ch.*, 7.11.96, 16.10.97 ; Works Ctee., 12.12.82 ; G.P.C., 14.5.96, 1897, *passim*, 9.6.98, 15.6.99, 10.4.02 ; Tramways Sub-Ctee., 9.6.96, 4.9.96, pp. 539–44 ; Ctee. of Coun., 17.11.96 to 20.4.98, *passim* ; Sub-Ctee. of Health Ctee., 11.9.99 ; E.L. and Lt. Rlys. Ctee., 11.4.00 to 8.10.02, *passim* ; Coun., 9.11.00, 10.10.01, 7.5.02.

In 1905 Samuel Jackson of Wistaston, with a few agricultural capitalists and others, floated the Nantwich & Crewe Motor Bus Co. Ltd., with a capital of £5,000, in order to start a 'bus service between the two towns. The two 'buses purchased proved a complete failure, and the company died a natural death before the end of the year. In 1908 Jackson resurrected this service, which was from 1910 owned by J. Gregory. In 1911 Crewe Town Council had advanced from " light railways " to the consideration of municipal " trackless trams " (trolley 'buses), but the proposal changed during 1912–13 into one " to promote a Bill in Parliament . . . to provide and run motor-'buses within the borough and to serve the adjoining district." Had A. G. Hill still been a member of the Council, there is little doubt that a municipal 'bus service for Crewe would have become an accomplished fact. The veteran Briggs and the few remaining progressive Liberals, supported again by the local I.L.P. and Crewe Trades Council, proved no match for the combined forces of Conservative-Liberal indifference and hostility, backed by alert private enterprise. The two remaining Ward brothers, whose horse-'bus service was still without a serious competitor, purchased two motor-omnibuses in November, 1913, " and on Monday afternoon (December 1) they took members of the Council on a trial trip." The aldermen and councillors enjoyed their ride, the Bill was abandoned, and in March, 1914, the Wards floated a company with £12,000 capital to acquire and carry on their business as car, coach and omnibus proprietors, with J. W. Ward as managing director. More motor-'buses were purchased for the Crewe service, but the new company had a short life ; from October 25, 1915, it became part of the Crosville Motor Co. Ltd., of Chester, which was beginning to stretch out its tentacles over Cheshire and North Wales. The operation of the service, hampered by the first World War, extended rapidly after 1920 and stimulated the new suburban development around Crewe. Fierce competition sprang up between the Crosville Motor Co. and a local 'bus proprietor, especially during 1922–3, but it was not until 1934 that the Crosville Company absorbed the last local competitor—Malbank Motor Services Ltd., controlled by Samuel Jackson (1858–1939).[1]

[1] C.G., 7.6.02 to 2.8.05, *passim*, 20.6.08, 5.1.12 to 20.3.14, *passim*, 12.11.15, 7.1.16, 6.4.20, 4.6.20, 1923, *passim* ; E.L. and Lt. Rlys. Ctee., 20.5.02 to

IV. Housing in Crewe

The available evidence suggests that the working-class houses built in Crewe from 1873 to about 1890 were on the average superior in construction to those built in the 1890's and early 1900's, the golden age of the Crewe jerry-builders.[1] The chief of these was the celebrated Jonas B. Potts (d. 1917), who commenced operations in the town about 1877. The furious rate at which housing development proceeded can be judged from the following figures :—

Year.							No. of Houses in Crewe.
1891	.	.	.	.	.	.	6,001 (area of old borough)
							6,817 (,, ,, 1892–1936 borough)
1904	.	.	.	.	.	.	10,041

This competition was probably one reason for the formation in 1897 of the Crewe and District Master Builders' Association, which, as the Crewe branch of the Building Trades Employers' Federation, rendered valuable service in connection with the Corporation's first housing scheme of 1920–2. It comprised in 1900 most of the South Cheshire builders and brickmakers, and was well represented on Crewe Town Council.

Attention was first called to the jerry-building by Crewe's enthusiastic M.O.H., Dr. Meredith Young, in his annual report for 1898 :—

" I cannot help alluding to the character of many of the new buildings constantly being put up in the town. A number of the builders appear to make it their aim, by saving a few shillings here and there, to erect the flimsiest possible structures in the hope that they may get them off their hands before the defects are discovered. . . .

20.12.04 ; Coun., 6.5.02, 2.7.08, 4.10.11, 14 and 20.10.13, 7.10.14, 6.10.20, 4.10.22, 2.5.23 ; Ctee. of Coun., 7.10.03, 27.10.15 ; G.P.C., 21.11.11, 19.12.11, 1913, *passim*, 10.10.17, 14.10.20, 12.4.23 ; Hackney Carriages Sub-Ctee., 12.9.05, 31.8.09, 6.9.10, 2.9.12, 1 and 2.9.14, 1922–3, *passim* ; Mkt. Ctee., 8.12.15 ; Sub-Ctee. *re* Bill, 23.9.13, 10 and 17.7.14 ; Works Ctee., 13.2.23 ; Health Ctee., 21.6.05, 16.8.05, 13.7.10, 1913, *passim*, 10.10.17, 14.10.20, 12.4.23 ; Sub-Ctee. *re* trackless trams, 1.2.12, 16.9.12, 16.7.13 ; private information ; Crosland-Taylor : *Crosville*, pp. 25–7, 40–1, 124–7, 136.

[1] *Cf.* W. D. Chapman, planning officer to the Cheshire County Council :— " Crewe, with its interminable rows of ' 1875 ' houses, multiplied difficulties which actually worsened because the houses were relatively well-built " (*Manchester Guardian*, Sept. 7, 1937).

" Many instances could be produced where working men have invested their life's savings in what they were assured were thoroughly well-built and sanitary houses, only to find out in the course of a few months that they had been, in plain language, swindled " (p. 68).

In his report for 1899 concrete examples can be found, and Young added :—" There are more and uglier facts in connection with these cases which are within my knowledge."   Wholesale infractions of the building by-laws had taken place, for the majority of Crewe builders, determined to live up to the town's motto, " Never Behind," were in the habit of commencing to build before the plans had been passed by the Corporation.   On Young's advice, the Council appointed a building inspector in 1899, but Alderman Briggs, who had a " deeply rooted opposition to the Health Committee, to its officials and its actions," foolishly attacked Young on the publication of his report in 1900, only to find the doctor more than a match for him.   This incident directed the attention of Crewe Trades Council to housing conditions in Crewe for the first time.

The first houses to be condemned and demolished by Crewe Town Council were three in the Coppenhall district in 1899. Whitegates, an insanitary slumlet containing 32 cottages, let at 3s. per week, suffered a similar fate in 1904-6, but was destroyed primarily to make way for a new town's yard and fire-station. Between 1911 and 1919 the Corporation made 553 closing orders under the Housing and Town Planning Act, 1909, and there existed at the end of the period no really bad housing areas.

Owing to the activities of many building societies, and to the fact that the estates existing in 1837 have been gradually parcelled out among thousands of working- and middle-class property owners, Crewe is remarkable for its high percentage of owner-occupiers and for the absence of chief rents.[1]   The only " back-to-back " houses in Crewe were the " block " houses of 1843 owned by the railway company, and called by the M.O.H. " the best type of their kind."   The report of a Board of Trade enquiry into the housing and the cost of living of the working classes in 1905 said of Crewe :—

" dilapidated property is not found and the houses have a cleaner appearance externally than is common with industrial towns. . . .

---

[1] By 1938 5,577 houses, 39 per cent. of the 14,038 dwelling-houses in Crewe, were owned by their occupiers.

In 1901 only 0·5 per cent. of the population were living in houses of less than four rooms, a strikingly low figure for a town which is almost entirely industrial."

Compared with rents in London, which were taken as equal to 100, the rent index number for Crewe was 48, with money figures as follows :—

No. of Rooms per Tenement.	Predominant Weekly Rents including all Rates (Oct., 1905).
4	3s. 6d. to 4s. 9d.
5	4s. 9d. to 6s. 3d.

By 1913 even four rooms did not satisfy the people of Crewe :— " The class of houses built in Crewe during the last 15 or 20 years were very much superior to what they were 40 years ago. The average intelligent working-man was not satisfied now to live in a four-roomed house " (McNeill).

The opening years of the twentieth century saw the beginnings of the modern housing problem in Crewe. The Crewe Trades Council and the Crewe I.L.P. made the question their own in 1903 (when rent increases occurred) and demanded action by the Corporation under the Housing of the Working Classes Act, 1890. The agitation rose in volume whenever the percentage of empty houses in Crewe, in relation to the total number in the borough, threatened to descend below the figure of 2·5 regarded as the minimum by the M.O.H. " Clear the property-owners and house-agents off the Council," became the Labour cry after 1907. In the period 1901–14 Crewe experienced two rapid transitions from slumps in the cottage property market to housing shortages. Between 1900 and 1905 (the latter year was one of acute local industrial depression) the percentage of empty houses in the borough rose from 2·6 to 4·4, and then gradually fell again to 2·7 in 1908, which represented an acute housing shortage. By 1911–12, years of industrial depression, the figures were back again at 4·4 and 4·5, only to fall with great rapidity in the boom year of 1914 to the amazingly low figure of 1·09. During these years (1910–14) very few houses were built in the borough.[1]

[1] During the second of these house property slumps (1910–13), a promising scheme for the development of a garden city on the northern side of the Crewe-Sandbach road by Co-partnership Tenants, Ltd., was turned down by

The genesis of the post-war housing problem can therefore be traced back to 1914 and beyond ; indeed, the first World War may be said merely to have aggravated an already existing problem.   In February, 1914, Crewe Trades Council drew the attention of the Corporation to the " scarcity of suitable housing accommodation in the Borough for the artisan classes " and suggested the adoption by the Corporation of part iii of the Housing of the Working Classes Act, 1890.   A motion calling for the appointment of a committee to consider proceeding with a municipal housing scheme under this Act was on the agenda (in the name of Councillor John Williams) for a Council meeting on the fateful day of August 4, 1914, the events of which effectively dispelled any possibility of such a scheme for five years. The M.O.H. prophesied correctly in his report for 1914 that the shortage would become so acute as to demand action by the municipality.[1]

As early as August, 1917, a circular from the Local Government Board informed the Crewe Corporation that " the Government recognised it would be necessary to find substantial financial assistance from public funds to local authorities," who were prepared to carry out at the end of the war a housing programme for the working classes ; but the members of the Council were by no means enthusiastic, and looked forward to a revival in private enterprise.   In December, 1918, they received a remarkable offer from that public-spirited gentleman, Alderman C. H. Pedley (1863–1921), who

" wished to do everything he could to help Crewe in the great task of reconstruction . . . he had 50 acres of land at Coppenhall which he would let the town have at favourable terms for . . . building ;

---

the Town Council, ostensibly because of inadequate financial terms in connection with the sewerage ; but it is difficult not to suspect that the property-owning aldermen and councillors allowed thoughts of more empty cottages to influence their decision.

[1] C.L.B.M., 15.3.70 ;   C.G., 6.7.95, 10.9.98 to 16.2.01, *passim*, 21.11.03 to 3.12.04, *passim*, 1908, *passim*, 11.11.10, 1911, *passim*, 20 and 25.2.13, 1914, *passim*, esp. manifestoes *re* " breakdown in private enterprise " in 13.3.14 and 19.6.14, 16.11.17 ;   C.Ch., 16.3.95, 4 and 11.6.98, 1.4.99, 28.7.00, 25.8.00 ; Works Ctee., 12.10.80, 8.3.81 to 13.12.83, *passim*, 23.7.85 ;   Fce., 17.6.81 ; G.P.C., 1914, *passim*, 8.5.15 ;   agenda, July, 1914 ;   M.O.H., 1893–1914, *passim*, 1919, pp. 82–5 ;   Works Ctee., 12.10.80, 8.3.81 to 13.12.83, *passim*, 8.12.03, 12.7.04, 8.5.06 ;   Coun., 7.9.04, Housing Ctee., 15.9.19.

. . . he had also a controlling interest in the Britannia Brick Co., which they could also have on favourable terms for the manufacture of the many thousands of bricks which would be needed."

Little appears to have been done to take advantage of this offer, but a housing sub-committee with Alderman Briggs as chairman came into existence in December, 1918. It soon became clear, however, that very little would be done without constant agitation and some violent stimulus. This was provided in November, 1919, when the Labour Party captured the whole of the eight seats in the first municipal election since 1914. Public opinion in the town demanded a forward housing policy ; all manner of shifts were being resorted to in order to obtain a house. The shortage set up considerable social stresses (" Some of the matrimonial difficulties which have of late (1920) engaged the attention of the borough Justices may be traced to the housing difficulty," commented the *Guardian*) ; the Crewe County Court saw many actions for the possession of houses bought at stiff prices in order to obtain accommodation.[1] Between 1910 and 1919 the number of houses in Crewe had increased by 37 only, and in the latter year 736 houses in the borough contained 8 or more occupants. The M.O.H. suggested that 750 houses would be required to meet deficiencies, but this figure suffered a reduction to 500. The L.N.W.R. Company, through the good offices of C. J. Bowen Cooke, Chief Mechanical Engineer, and Mayor of Crewe in 1918–19, provided a partial solution of the problem by erecting 69 wooden Army huts off Victoria Avenue in 1920. Licensed as temporary buildings for fifteen years, they were eagerly sought after at 12s. 6d. per week and most of them are still (1948) in use as dwelling-houses.

Although the first sod of the new Corporation housing estate off Gresty Road had been cut by Sir Gilbert Claughton, chairman of the L.N.W.R., on October 25, 1919, it was a much easier task to buy land and lay out roads and drainage systems than to secure the building of houses by an industry completely disorganised by the war and suffering as a consequence from an appalling lack of materials and skilled labour. The new Labour councillors, in return for their enthusiasm in connection with the problem, were given a majority on the Housing Committee, which

[1] A Crewe Tenants' Defence League (secretary, Thos. Kelsall) existed in 1920–2 to prevent evasions of the Rents Restriction Act.

proceeded to elect the first Labour chairman in the history of the Town Council (E. Yates, 1919–20). The new Housing Committee soon found that the practical difficulties in the way of getting houses built at such a time had not been exaggerated, and when control of the Committee passed from the Labour Party in November, 1920, the first ten houses were not ready for occupation, in spite of all the energy displayed.[1]   The number of houses eventually completed on the Gresty Road site under the Housing Act, 1919, and the Addison Scheme was 216, completed as follows :—

1921	88
1922	123
1923	5

The Government gave instructions that as much as possible of the money required should be raised locally, and in May, 1920, a campaign was launched to sell £150,000 worth of Crewe Corporation housing bonds. A considerable portion of the sum was raised in this manner, but outside borrowing became necessary to complete the £226,000 needed for the first 216 parlour-type houses on the estate. Another 16 houses were finished during 1924 under the Addison Scheme on the second Corporation estate in Alton Street, but with the revival of private enterprise, and the Housing (Subsidy) Act of 1923, fresh obstacles clogged the path of local authorities. Crewe proved no exception ; only with great difficulty was permission to erect 30 more Corporation houses in Alton Street secured, this time under the Housing of the Working Classes Act, 1890. These were completed in 1924. Applications for subsidy under the 1923 Act, to enable private houses to be built, began to flow in during the latter part of the year, and seemed to justify the *Guardian's* complacent comment :—" The Government should . . . stimulate private enterprise, and drop the idea of attempting to create a sort of Elysium . . .   It is a pity such a fanciful picture (' Homes fit for heroes to live in ') was dangled before the people in 1918." [2]

[1] The contract for the first ten houses on the Gresty Road site did not receive the finishing touches until March, 1920. An interesting feature of this project was the appointment of a Women's Advisory Committee to decide on the internal fittings.

[2] M.O.H., 1915–20, *passim*, 1922–3, *passim* ; *Report of the Mid-Cheshire Joint Town-Planning Advisory Ctee.* (1929), pp. 120–1 ; *C.G.*, 3.1.19 to 28.12.23,

V. Suburban Development and Building Trends

Several of the hamlets round Crewe began to develop into satellite communities at an early date ; the compiler of White's *Directory of Cheshire* (1860) noted an interesting phenomenon in the village of Shavington-cum-Gresty, 2 miles from Crewe :—
" Within the last three years many neat cottages have been erected here . . . for the accommodation of the clerks, &c., employed at the works of the railway company at Crewe." The compilers of the census of 1871 attributed the increase of population in Church Coppenhall, Haslington, Willaston and Shavington to the enlargement of the works, and several references are made in contemporary directories to the number of cottages erected in these townships for the workmen from Crewe. Residence in the country meant the opportunity of cultivating an allotment or even a smallholding, of snaring game, and the possibility of casual agricultural employment. The increasing use of the " safety " bicycle from the 1890's onwards, the horse-, and later the motor-omnibus, merely quickened a development which had been proceeding for some time.

Modern sanitary progress in the district round Crewe can be dated from the creation of the Nantwich Rural Sanitary Authority in 1872. This body had the good fortune to appoint as its first surveyor the competent and painstaking J. A. Davenport (1873–1909), who issued a series of reports on the sewerage and water-supply of the various townships. Church Coppenhall appeared to be the most favourably situated in 1873 (the local death-rate was falling rapidly) but the sewers consisted of mere open ditches and no piped water-supply existed in what one might be tempted to imagine was an idyllic rural hamlet :—

" The water-supply is chiefly obtained from pits, which are in many cases to the backs of the houses and which I have too great reason to fear are much polluted. A pit of very pea-soupy appearance was pronounced by the lady of the house to be ' very fair drinking.' "

A small band of reformers, including Rector Moses Reid and Richard Whittle, had secured a Burial Board in 1871, but their

passim ; Coun., 9.7.19 to 3.3.20, 1.6.21, 1923, *passim* ; G.P.C., 14.8.17, 16.10.17, 19.11.18, 20.5.19, 1922, *passim* ; Ctee. of Coun., 4.12.18, 4.6.19 ; Sub-Ctee. *re* Housing, 19.1.19 ; Housing Ctee., 26.6.19 to 20.12.23, *passim* ; Works Ctee., 8.6.20 ; Fce. Ctee., 16.8.23 ; Advisory Ctee., 20.8.20 *sqq.* ; Sub-Ctee. *re* rents, 29.11.20 *sqq.* ; Tenants selection Sub-Ctee., 22.11.20 *sqq.*

efforts to establish a Church Coppenhall Local Board in 1872 met with overwhelming defeat.[1]   The need for a Local Board was lessened by the work of the Rural Sanitary Authority, which provided a piped water-supply in 1872–82, but the sewerage difficulty remained unsolved until 1892, when the southern and more densely populated half of Church Coppenhall became part of the extended borough of Crewe.   The hamlets of Shavington, Willaston and Haslington, the reports on which differed only in detail from that on Church Coppenhall, received Davenport's attention in the course of the following decades.

Men employed in the works lived even further afield than Willaston, as was proved in 1882, when Webb, by enforcing a rule that no company's workman should live more than $2\frac{1}{2}$ miles away from the works, reduced the population of Nantwich and Wybunbury by about 600.   Petitions from the Nantwich Local Board and Nantwich cottage-property owners availed nothing, for a man who was forced to get up at 4.30 a.m. in order to walk the 4 miles to Crewe in all weathers, was not likely to be as capable of working as hard in Crewe Works as the man who resided in Crewe itself.   In 1901 " brakes " ran every day after the works had closed, both to Haslington and Willaston, which were within the $2\frac{1}{2}$-mile radius.

The development of Wistaston township as a suburb of Crewe did not begin until 1911–12 and was delayed by the first World War.   With the re-establishment of the Crewe–Nantwich motor-'bus service in 1919, and the recovery of the building industry, a ribbon development commenced which raised the population of Wistaston from 718 in 1921 to 1,504 in 1931.   This new settlement has been chiefly of middle-class residential type ; it is characterised by the comparative absence of shops and low density of population.[2]

The small increase in Crewe's population between 1901 and 1931 (from 42,074 to 46,061), most of which occurred in the first decade of the twentieth century, can thus be attributed to

---

[1] Similar attempts in 1877 and 1887 came to nothing.

[2] *C.G.*, 23.12.71 to 11.7.74, *passim* ; Sept., 1877, *passim*, 17.6.82 to 23.9.82, *passim*, 13.3.86, 17.3.86, 12.11.87, 9.2.89, 23.3.92 ; *Census 1871*, vol. ii, pp. 390–1 ; *Manchester Guardian*, Sept. 7, 1937 ; White, p. 406.   An observer noted in 1934 that the Crosville Company provided two workmen's 'buses every morning and evening between Sandbach, 6 miles from Crewe, and the works.

three factors. Firstly, although the period 1901–31 was one of immense social progress for the town, it was also an era of economic stagnation, during which many inhabitants of the borough emigrated either to other parts of Great Britain or overseas. The effect of emigration may be judged from the fact that between 1901 and 1911 the population of the borough increased by only 6·8 per cent. or 2,786 persons. This figure came as a great surprise, since the excess of births over deaths in the town during the same period amounted to 6,665. Emigration to Australia took place on a particularly large scale in 1911–12 and a flourishing Crewe and District Overseas Society exists in New South Wales. The second factor, the falling birth-rate, only became serious after 1911. Suburban development outside the borough boundary constituted the third factor.[1]

VI. Gas and Water

The company supplied gas and water to the town of Crewe by virtue of the powers conferred on it by section 75 of the L.N.W.R. (additional powers, England) Act, 1865. These powers were renewed for ten years by section 37 of a similar Act passed in 1870. In 1880 a new Act conferred these powers for an indefinite period, but by section 49 the company remained exempt from the statutory obligations of private gas and water companies. This meant that consumers had no protection, and that no agreement need be made between the company and Crewe Corporation as to continuity of supply, pressure, quality and quantity. The company naturally refused to enter into any such undertaking, and until 1903 the Corporation merely agreed to take surplus water at 6*d.* per 1,000 gallons.

The Corporation owned the constantly growing network of water-mains in the town, with the exception of those supplying the company's property, which continued to receive its supply from the company until the end of the period under review. The 1*s.* per year water-rate levied by the municipal authority had begun to prove inadequate even in Local Board days, and the deficit on the Water Account increased greatly after 1893.

[1] M.O.H., 1911 ; *C.G.,* 7.4.11 to 14.6.12, *passim* ; *C.Ch.,* 11.3.39. *Cf.* " Mr. [Henry] Taylor did a large business in booking passengers for the Colonies " (*C.G.,* 4.4.05).

In 1884 the charges extra to the 1s. rate levied on baths and water-closets were abolished.   Only 42 baths supplied with water by tap existed in the Crewe of 1884, and the attitude of those in authority towards them may be judged from the opinion expressed by Charles Welch, chairman of the Water Committee from 1875 to 1895, that both baths and water-closets were " a great luxury."   In the late 1880's certain members of Crewe Town Council became greatly perturbed at the state of the town's water, and agitated until Webb provided 10 high-pressure filters with carbon media at Crewe station in 1888.   The enthusiasm of Dr. William Hodgson and T. H. Heath for this improvement derived some of its gusto from the fact that the less enthusiastic Independent-Conservative majority could be accused of placing the railway company's interests before those of the town.

The borough extension of 1892, and the rapid introduction of water-closets in the 1890's, caused a phenomenal increase in the consumption of water, both per head of the population and in the aggregate, from 7·25 gallons per head per day in 1891 to 14·2 in 1911 ;   the total annual consumption for the years ending in March, 1887, and March, 1902, was 81·6 and 217·9 million gallons respectively.   On account of this " great pull on the supply, the company duplicated their mains to Crewe, and duplicated their pumping plant at Whitmore . . . without increasing the price of water " ;   but in 1896–8, after further complaints of poor pressure, the existing well and borehole at Whitmore were deepened and two fresh borings made, while in 1899 a new 15-inch water main was laid down from Whitmore to Crewe.   The amount paid to the company for water—never less than £5,000 a year in the 1900's—and the increasing loss on the water account, turned the thoughts of influential members of Crewe Town Council towards a municipal waterworks, the more so because an agreement with the railway company on the water question had only been concluded in 1903 with con-siderable difficulty.   This agreement merely regularised the position, the Corporation being allowed to purchase any surplus not required for works and steam sheds purposes.

In 1904 a sub-committee which included McNeill, A. G. Hill, C. H. Pedley and William Williams, appointed " to collect information and report on the feasibility and probable return of a system of waterworks to be owned by the Corporation," engaged a water expert, T. B. Farrington, who reported verbally in 1905 to a private meeting of the Council.   Farrington appears to have promised a 100 per cent. increase in supply (450 million gallons per annum) for an annual charge of £4,100, but the timidity of the majority on the Council, and " buttonholing " by certain frightened ratepayers, ensured the shelving of the scheme in 1906.[1]   For the next few years the loss on water account fell considerably, so that an attempt by the Labour group on the Council to revive the project, in 1908, ended in failure.   There is no doubt that lack of a guaranteed water-supply tended to make industrialists desirous of establishing new factories fight shy of the town.   Worse was to follow, however, when in February, 1923, Crewe Town Council received a letter from H. P. M. Beames, on behalf of the new L.M.S. Railway Company, concerning the Whitmore water-supply :—

" Recent tests . . . point to the fact that the supply at this place is decreasing. . . .   In the event of the steps we are taking to improve matters at Whitmore not proving satisfactory there would be no option but to curtail the supply to the town."

This letter caused a " mild panic " in the Council, and in the following June Dr. H. Lapworth, water expert, was commissioned to report on the possibilities of an expansion and continuance of the supply from the existing wells at Whitmore, and the possibility of obtaining water for Crewe from alternative sources.   During a conference on the subject on December 19, 1923, Beames told the representatives of the Council that, " assuming that the consumption of water by the company and the town was round about normal, the present supply should be available to 1941, but of course he could not pledge himself to any definite statement."   The levels at Whitmore continued to fall, and in 1929 Dr. Lapworth " expressed the opinion that the area was being overpumped jointly by the L.M.S. Railway Company and the Staffordshire Potteries Water Board."   Unless a fresh municipal supply could be provided, Crewe's industrial position seemed precarious.[2]

[1] This included the interest on capital to be expended, works costs, legal expenses and the repayment of loans in thirty years.
[2] *C.G.*, 1878, July, 1882, *passim*, 26.4.84, 1885, *passim*, 27.2.86, 1888, *passim*, 2.1.89, 27.9.90, 29.8.91, 2.5.96, 1897–8, *passim*, 5.10.01, 15.3.02, 10.5.02, 1904, *passim*, 7.10.05, 10.2.06, 7.12.06, 1908, *passim*, 18.2.13 (lecture by Bowen

The powers possessed by the company with regard to gas were renewed together with those concerning water ; from time to time letters appeared in the local press advocating a municipal gasworks, and in 1890 the Corporation even set up a sub-committee to acquire, if possible, the street gas-mains from the company as a preliminary step towards a Corporation gasworks. Webb reduced the price of gas considerably during his tenure of office as Chief Mechanical Engineer, but lower than 2s. 9d. per 1,000 cubic feet he would not go, since in 1895 " so few houses in Crewe consumed gas at all (that) . . . if it was not for the large quantity they had to make for their own purposes it could not be profitably sold at the present rate." In 1888 only about 1,300 houses out of nearly 6,000 had gas laid on, an amazingly low figure, which points to a lackadaisical selling policy on the company's part. This changed after 1900, as a clause in the L.N.W.R. Act of that year empowered the railway company to manufacture and sell to the public gas cooking and heating apparatus, a local exhibition of which was held under L.N.W.R. auspices in December.

The question of Corporation purchase of the pipes arose again in 1900, when the Council refused the L.N.W.R. gas department permission to break up the streets in order to lay new mains. Complaints of bad pressure had been frequent, and in reply Mr. Whale said

". . . the company did not consider the Corporation had any power or right to deal with a matter of this kind, as they were not conservers of the rights of the inhabitants so far as gas was concerned, and the railway company were not a gas company . . . and simply were suppliers of their surplus gas to the inhabitants."

The Corporation thereupon successfully opposed clauses in the L.N.W.R. Parliamentary Bills of 1900, 1903, 1904 and 1905 giving the company power to break up the streets without the

---

Cooke), 27.2.23, 8.6.23 ; *C.Ch.*, 28.7.88, 29.9.88, 7.8.97, 29.1.38 (Beames' letter and Lapworth's reports) ; M.O.H., 1897, 1901, 1906, 1911 ; *Abst. Accts.*, 1882–3 to 1923–4 ; Coun., 17.7.78, 4.12.78, 19.7.82, 5.5.97 ; Mkt. Ctee., 21.10.79, 29.6.80, 12.4.81, 24.10.82, 9.2.86, 12.4.87, 15.5.88, 11.9.88, 19.2.89, 21.6.92, 7.1.96, 22.4.97, 17.8.97, 1898, *passim*, 18.2.02, 17.2.03, 19.1.04 ; G.P.C., 14.12.04, 14.9.05, 11.1.06, 1923, *passim* ; Conference, 19.12.23 ; Sub-Ctee. *re* water-supply, 19.6.23 ; Sub-Ctee. *re* municipal water-supply, 12.5.04 to 22.2.06, *passim*.

Corporation's consent. The company, on the other hand, steadfastly refused to sell the mains, presumably considering it would be the first step towards a Corporation gasworks. After great preparations for an application to Parliament to become the gas authority in the borough, Crewe Corporation deferred the matter indefinitely in 1906 and accepted the *status quo*.[1]

VII. ELECTRICITY

Electrical energy was first put to practical public use for lighting purposes in Crewe (apart from some experiments by Webb and T. W. Worsdell on Crewe station) on November 18, 1878, when two football matches were played by electric light. Immediately after the passing of the Electric Lighting Act of 1882, four firms announced their intention of applying for provisional orders to supply electricity within the borough, but a special Council meeting called to consider the question in September, 1882, decided to take no action, as the new industry was in its infancy and a general opinion existed that Crewe would be one of the last towns to require a supply. Electricity then ceased to be a practical issue until the light railway scheme of 1896–7 raised the question of motive power for the trams. After this project had fallen into abeyance, influential members of the Council suggested that the Corporation should establish an electricity works " for lighting the streets of the borough," which would also be useful if the tramway scheme were to be revived. The chief enthusiast for municipal electricity was Councillor (from 1902 Alderman) A. G. Hill. Appointed chairman of the sub-committee *re* electric lighting at its first meeting on September 15, 1897, he served as chairman of the Electric Lighting Committee from 1897 until his death in 1906. William Williams, the first Crewe Labour councillor, paid the following tribute to him in 1911 :—" The electric light undertaking of the

[1] *C.G.*, 2.2.78 to 25.10.79, *passim*, 28.4.83 to 21.6.84, *passim*, 28.5.87, 30.6.88 to 1.10.92, *passim*, 29.4.93, 5.5.94 to 7.12.95, *passim*, 6.6.96, 2.12.99 to 15.12.00, *passim*, 13.1.04, 1905, *passim*, 3.6.21 ; *C.Ch.*, 31.5.90, 14.4.00 ; C.L.B.M., 6.8.74 ; Coun., 30.1.78, 25.4.83, 25.5.92, 7.1.03 ; Mkt. Ctee., 21.10.79, 10.2.80, 11.9.88, 12.3.89, 18.2.90, 11.3.90, 18.11.90, 10.4.94, 12.11.95, 18.5.97, 20.2.00, 20.3.00 ; G.P.C., 14.5.96, 12.7.06 ; Works Ctee., 10.1.94, 13.1.03, 9.8.04 to 14.11.05 ; Parliamentary Ctee., 13.3.00 to 15.5.00 ; Sub-Ctee., 18.5.04 ; E.L., 9.1.05, 15.5.06, 14.8.06 ; Spec. Ctee., 27.6.96.

Corporation was due to the far-seeing policy of the late leader of the Tory Party of the Council, the late Alderman A. G. Hill, who was one of the best public men they ever had."

The Bill containing the provisional order empowering Crewe Corporation to supply electricity received the royal assent on August 12, 1898, and supplies of electricity became available late in 1900. The estimated cost of the scheme, £26,000, proved quite inadequate, and by 1907 £50,000 of capital had been sunk in the Corporation's largest enterprise. Between 1901 and 1908 a reserve fund of £3,000 was built up, while over £4,000 of electricity profits went to the credit of the general district rate account during 1908–15.[1] It is important to remember that the supply of electricity for public lighting was the primary purpose of the undertaking, and as late as 1907–8 the number of units used for public lighting exceeded those supplied for private purposes. From this date, private lighting consumed a steadily-increasing proportion of the output. In the years before the first World War the number of private consumers rose very slowly to 606 in 1913, but largely as the result of the systematic canvassing begun in 1923 the figure reached 2,899 in 1925. A clause enabling the Corporation to sell and let for hire electrical fittings had been inserted in the abortive Crewe Motor Omnibus Bill of 1913, but not until April, 1932, was a showroom opened and the sale of electrical appliances begun.[2] The Borough Electrical Engineer from 1900 to 1936 was H. H. Denton (d. 1938), under whose management the Crewe undertaking developed into one of the most successful medium-sized stations in Britain.

In 1918 Crewe Corporation joined the newly-formed Association of Lancashire and Cheshire Electricity Undertakings ; this body watched over the interests of its members during the passage of the Electricity (Supply) Act, 1919. Since 1920 there have been several attempts to form a Joint Electricity Board for

---

[1] Although the rising expenditure on gas formed one of the main reasons for the establishment of the Corporation electricity undertaking, the cost of public lighting rose considerably after the transition from gas-lighting in 1901. The rise was out of proportion to the increase in the number of public lamps. From this and later evidence it is apparent that the Lighting Department has been overcharged for electricity.

[2] The Electricity (Supply) Act of 1919 merely gave the Corporation power to provide, let for hire and connect fittings, but not to sell them.

North Wales and Cheshire, but the medium-sized undertakings, including Crewe, have always been suspicious of a plan which might end in the loss of their independence for the benefit of the North Wales Power Company, Ltd. To this company were delegated in 1923 the powers of the North Wales and South Cheshire Joint Electricity Authority, the first to be formed under the Act of 1919, and it began to supply the L.M.S. Railway Company with power at Crewe immediately. Later in the same year Crewe Corporation agreed to take a supply from the North Wales Power Company *via* the L.M.S. Railway Company. The Crewe undertaking first took bulk supplies from the Central Electricity Board in 1934, and since this date a large reduction has been effected in the amount of power generated in the works.[1]

VIII. Finance

From 1860 until 1895 the ancient and modern systems of rate collection existed side by side under separate control in the township of Monks Coppenhall. The Local Board's (later the borough's) rate collector gathered in the " general district rate " which paid for the highways, refuse disposal, scavenging and sewerage, etc., while the two Overseers, appointed annually from a list submitted by the Monks Coppenhall vestry meeting, collected the " poor-rate " through their assistant overseer. The poor-rate included not only the monies required by the Nantwich Board of Guardians for the service of poor relief, but also the county rate, together with the lump sums levied in the form of " precepts " on the Overseers by Crewe Town Council after 1877. These lump sums for borough fund purposes (as distinct from the general district rate purposes) paid the deficits on

[1] *C.G.*, 23.11.78, 25.10.79, 16.9.82 to 23.6.83, *passim*, 7.8.97 to 27.6.03, *passim*, 26.10.07, 9.5.08, 2.10.09, 7.5.15, 9.6.16, 10.11.16, 4.5.17, 8.6.17, 5.7.18, 9.1.20, 17.2.20 to 7.12.23, *passim*; *C.Ch.*, 21 and 28.5.38; *Abst. Accts.*, 1899–1900 to 1923–4 (annual reports on undertaking); Mkt. Ctee., 26.9.82, 5.6.83; G.P.C., 15.7.97, 14.1.04, 17.4.17, 25.10.22 to 28.8.23, *passim*; Sub-Ctee. *re* electric lighting, 15.9.97, 11.10.97; E.L., 12.5.98 to 15.3.04, *passim*, 16.7.07, 20.4.09, 16.11.11, 11.5.16, 18.1.17 to 13.11.23, *passim*; Coun., 29.10.97, 12.5.98; Fce., 20.12.06, 19.4.17; Ctee. of Coun., 7.2.12 (*cf.* E. L., 15.2.12) 3.12.19; Sub-Ctee. *re* L.M.S. supply, 5.6.23; *Manchester Guardian*, Oct. 29, 1937; *Public Enterprise*, ed. W. A. Robson, pp. 114, 143.

Crewe Cemetery account, the expenses of the School Attendance Committee (1877–1903), the legal charges incurred by Crewe Corporation, the borough magistrates' disbursements, etc. The assistant overseer from about 1871 until 1889 was Thomas Bolshaw, who apparently succeeded his father-in-law, Thomas. Bromfield (1810–97), as the handyman of the township in several minor legal and local government posts. In 1889 the auditor for the Nantwich Union discovered that Bolshaw had about £1,100 outstanding in uncollected rates. Bromfield made this amount good, but Bolshaw resigned the assistant overseership, and the vestry elected Aaron Maywhort to the vacant post :— " His supporters, no doubt, relied on the fact of his being a recognised Liberal, his long connection with the Co-operative Society, and his occupying a prominent position among the Wesleyans and the Blue Ribbonites." [1] The appointment was a full-time one and carried with it a salary of £140 per annum.

In 1895 the Local Government Board, in response to an application under section 33 of the Local Government Act, 1894, transferred to Crewe Town Council the power of appointing the Overseers for the township of Monks Coppenhall, and from that year until their abolition in 1925 these two officers were without exception members of the Council. Later in 1895, a further step in the unification of local government finance in Crewe was taken when the power to appoint or dismiss the assistant overseer underwent a similar transference ; the vestry meeting had at last vanished from the scene.[2]

Owing to the need for a better oversight of the Corporation accounts, Crewe Town Council appointed J. A. Jenkins, from the Town Clerk's private office, to the new post of borough accountant as from January, 1893. On the resignation of Alfred

---

[1] *C.G.*, 10.8.89, 28.8.89 ; *C.Ch.*, 15.6.89.

[2] When the boundaries of Crewe borough were extended as from Nov. 9, 1892, by Order No. P770 (confirmed by the Local Government Board Provisional Orders Confirmation (No. 11) Act, 1892), the boundaries of Monks Coppenhall township remained unaltered, and portions of the townships of Church Coppenhall, Wistaston and Shavington-cum-Gresty were included in the borough. To simplify the process of precept-laying, Crewe Town Council obtained from the Cheshire County Council an order amalgamating these portions with Monks Coppenhall township as from March 25, 1894, thus making the boundaries of borough and township identical again (Elect. Div. Ctee., 10.3.92, 30.11.92, 1893, *passim* ; *C.G.*, 17.12.92).

Williamson, manager of the Crewe branch of the Manchester and Liverpool District Bank, from the position of Borough Treasurer in 1905, the borough accountant (W. Boyle, appointed in 1901) received the title of Borough Treasurer. The final stage in the unification of rate-collecting came in 1918, when Maywhort resigned and the Town Council appointed the Borough Treasurer to be superintendent assistant overseer. Everything was now ripe for the abolition of the Overseers themselves, and for the final amalgamation of the general district and poor-rates.

The rateable value of Crewe for borough fund purposes doubled between 1878 and 1897, from £63,000 to £126,000, but thereafter the rate of increase slackened. The figure of £175,000 was reached in 1924. The borough debt, which in 1879 stood at £72,892, a higher figure than the rateable value, fell steadily during the period of political strife and municipal stagnation in the 1880's, so that by 1891 no more than £33,518 remained to be paid off. This proved to be its lowest point, as the developments in public health and education, coupled with capital expenditure on the electricity undertaking and the new Municipal Buildings, which occupied the Liberal majority from 1891 to 1908, raised the figure of debt to £191,550 in the latter year. Capital expenditure ceased during the first World War, but the post-war housing programme, and the execution of post-poned improvements at inflated prices, caused a rapid rise to unprecedented and, to some ratepayers, alarming figures. By 1925 the borough debt stood at £506,059. In 1904 the new accountant introduced the practice of accepting loans in amounts of not less than £100 from the small private investor ; it proved highly successful and reduced the town's dependence on the large financial houses.

The amount in the pound levied for general district rate purposes followed a similar trend. The exceptional rates of Local Board days were succeeded by lower ones in the 1880's and 1890's, until 2s. 6d. in the pound (levied 1894–5) came to be considered excessive. During the next twenty years the chief rise was not in the general district rate, but in the poor-rate, owing to the increased amounts levied to pay for the Education Act of 1902. The total rate levied grew from 4s. 6d., in 1889–90, to 8s. 5d., in 1913–14, and reached an unprecedented figure in

1921–2 at 17*s*. in the pound. The tendency for Whitehall to thrust fresh duties on the local authorities encouraged the drive towards municipal socialism. C. H. Pedley, the Liberal chairman of the Finance Committee, speaking in 1908, said :—

> There was little prospect of declining rates in any municipality
> . . . and . . . the only chance of relieving this charge was for the
> municipalities to control public monopolies, and so reap for the public
> the benefit of the demand the public created.

Unfortunately, the short-sighted inertia of the majority on Crewe Town Council, and outside interference, prevented any further steps in this direction after the establishment of the electricity undertaking at the beginning of the century, so that apart from the Market it has remained Crewe Corporation's only profit-making department. The excess of expenditure over income in 1901–2 amounted to nearly £23,000 and by 1923 this figure had increased more than fourfold.[1]

IX. THE NANTWICH BOARD OF GUARDIANS AND CREWE

On the formation of the Nantwich Poor Law Union in 1837, under the famous Poor Law Amendment Act of 1834, Monks Coppenhall was still a rural township, and was allotted the single Guardian of the Poor usual in such cases. Later this was increased to two, but the interests of Crewe were still apt to be neglected at Nantwich, in spite of the conscientious attendance at Board meetings of Martin Heath, who was a Guardian for Monks Coppenhall from 1855 until 1881 (except for an interval in 1872–3), usually in partnership with Thomas Beech. In 1873 the Local Board petitioned Whitehall to grant Crewe six additional Guardians, a prayer partially answered next year when the

---

[1] For Crewe Corporation finance generally see :—*Abst. Accts.*, 1877–8, 1879–81, 1882–1924, *passim* (those for 1916–18 were never printed) ; *C.G.*, 17.8.78, 26.4.79, 25.4.85, 13.11.86, 9.8.90, 30.8.90, 26.11.92, 29.4.93 (list of rates levied), 7.4.94, 5.1.95 to 14.5.98, *passim*, 2.3.01 to 23.8.05, *passim*, 4.5.07 ("in comparison with other towns the rates in Crewe were low"), 8.5.09, 30.3.10 to 3.5.12, *passim*, 6.3.14, 8.5.14, 4.5.17, 1918, *passim*, 9.5.19, 7 and 14.5.20, 8.4.21, 6.5.21, 1922, *passim*, 27.4.23 ; *C.Ch.*, 11.5.95 ; Coun., 30.11.92, 2.1.95, 28.3.95 ; G.P.C., 13.3.94 ; Fce., 10.12.93, 22.6.94, 21.2.96, 26.4.96, 21.12.05, 17.6.15, 22.8.18, 17.10.18, 1922, *passim*. There is a marked connection between the periods of sharp rate increases and the formation of ratepayers' associations—1901, 1910, 1923.

Local Government Board issued an order for the appointment of four additional Guardians for Monks Coppenhall; there proved to be no lack of candidates. The interest of the tradesmen and ratepayers of Crewe in the Nantwich Board of Guardians was primarily financial. A strong belief prevailed that the town of Nantwich and the rural portions of the Union did very well in the matter of their paupers at the expense of Crewe. That the Nantwich paupers were to some extent living on the ratepayers of Crewe, seems evident from certain facts published in 1873. At that time the Nantwich Union's rateable value stood at £263,662, of which Monks Coppenhall contributed £47,862 and the town of Nantwich £13,831. The vice-chairman of the Guardians said that with respect to paupers contributed, Crewe "about paid its way," but the figures for Nantwich were "awfully bad"; it contributed as many paupers to the Union as Crewe, and in addition many of the Crewe paupers "came out of the agricultural districts." [1]

The establishment of a separate poor law union for Crewe and some of the surrounding townships had been mentioned as one of the new Corporation's first tasks, but in 1878 the Local Government Board declined to countenance the project and on the whole it appears that Crewe would not have been financially better off with a separate union, a separate workhouse, and a separate administrative staff. In 1881–5 Samuel Heath, a Crewe man, but then resident in Audlem, and Richard Whittle, one of the Guardians of the Poor for Monks Coppenhall, made an unsuccessful attempt to secure the reassessment of the L.N.W.R. Company's property in the Union's area. This again focused attention on the real reason for the interest shown by the people of Crewe in the proceedings of the Nantwich Board of Guardians. No public-spirited interest in the problems of poverty prompted candidates to offer themselves as Guardians, or sustained the efforts made by Crewe Town Council to secure better representation on the Board. It was rather a desire to keep down the cost of poor relief, and to prevent the over-represented agricultural townships from decreasing their rateable values and increasing those of the urban townships by taking advantage of their control of the Union Assessment Committee. Exceptions

[1] Nantwich Board of Guardians minute books, Feb. 20, 1837, 1855–81, *passim*; C.G., 6.12.73, 28.3.74; C.L.B.M., 30.7.73, 21 and 28.8.73.

to this rule occur, but they are few in number ; where they did occur, the Guardians in question (*e.g.* Thomas Beech (d. 1878), and Wallace Lumb (d. 1938)) showed themselves less interested in the problems of poverty than in gaining a local reputation for benevolence by distributing occasional gifts of beer, tobacco and tea among the inmates of Nantwich Workhouse. Even after the election of the first woman Guardian in the history of the Board, and the arrival of the first Guardian who was also a member of Crewe I.L.P., the financial question continued to determine the attitude of the majority of Crewe's representatives, Liberals and Conservatives alike.[1]

The attempt to reassess the railway company's property, brought three railway officials to the Board in 1882 (Bebbington, Dick and Whale). They remained there until after the reassessment of the whole Union had been completed in 1886–7. In 1888–9 Crewe Town Council took up the question of increasing the borough's inadequate representation on the Board, and as from March, 1890, secured an increase of four Guardians for Monks Coppenhall. Crewe now returned ten members to the Board ; at the same time, Church Coppenhall received the right to elect a second Guardian. With the extension of the borough and the amalgamation of the townships it became clear that the position needed reconsideration, and, after a preliminary increase to 11 (December, 1893), the Cheshire County Council decided in May, 1894, to allocate 16 Guardians to Monks Coppenhall. From that year Crewe therefore possessed one-fifth of the seats on the Board, and considerable " interlocking " between personnel of the Crewe Guardians and the membership of Crewe Town Council became possible. The elections of December, 1894, are interesting for several reasons. Three out of the 16 Guardians elected were women, Mrs. Elisabeth Hodgson, Mrs. Betsy Briggs and Miss Ada Nield. The I.L.P. put forward candidates for the first time and secured one representative, but the Conservatives obtained 12 seats out of the 16. Indeed, while Crewe Town Council's complexion was usually Liberal, the Guardians of the Poor for Monks Coppenhall showed a predominantly Conservative complexion after 1881. Some of the

---

[1] Mrs. Elisabeth Hodgson, the doctor's wife, elected Guardian for Monks Coppenhall in 1891, and Miss Ada Nield, elected Guardian for Monks Coppenhall in 1894, respectively.

rural Guardians now began to think that the boot was on the other foot, and considered Crewe over-represented. In 1895 and 1898 they began an agitation with a view to removing Monks Coppenhall from the Nantwich Union and setting up a separate Crewe Poor Law Union. The excuse was that Crewe paupers absorbed more in relief than the borough contributed to the Union's coffers, but, except in unusual periods of industrial depression, such as that of 1894-5, there seems to have been little substance in the loud complaints of these economy-stricken farmers. In 1902-6 a fresh reassessment of the Union took place. This gave Crewe Town Council and the Nantwich U.D.C. ample data on which to base their petitions to the County Council for increased representation on the Nantwich Board. The total population of the Union at the time was almost 73,000, of which Crewe alone contributed 42,000 and Nantwich 7,000, while three-eighths of the Union's rateable value came from Crewe. Yet Crewe and Nantwich together had only two representatives out of the 12 members constituting the Union Assessment Committee, and of the remaining ten, nine were directly interested in agriculture. There is little wonder that the rateable value of much landed property and rural cottage property in the Union had been increased but slightly, and in some cases even lowered, by the reassessment of 1906. This may, in addition, be connected with the decrease of population between 1891 and 1906 in 43 rural townships out of the 69 which went to make up the Union. In the same period Crewe had registered an increase of 13,000. As a result of this petition Crewe obtained four additional Guardians, and now returned 20, or a quarter of the total. This remained the figure until the abolition of Guardians in 1930. The rural districts, with regard both to population and rateable values, were still heavily over-represented.[1]

X. Crewe and the New County Government

Crewe was allotted three representatives on the new Cheshire County Council set up by the Local Government Act, 1888.

[1] *C.G.*, 25.5.78 to 20.7.78, *passim*, 15.9.80, 12.10.81, 15.4.82, 10.3.83, 1884, *passim*, 28.7.86 to 12.7.90, *passim*, 1891, *passim* (esp. 4 and 18.4.91, and corresponding issues of *Chronicle*), 21.1.93 to 27.2.95, *passim*, 18.6.98, 13.7.98, 3.8.98, 15 and 29.10.02, 30.9.05 to 4.8.06, 15.12.09, 15.7.10 ; *C.Ch.*, 15 and 22.12.94.

The Council held its first meeting on February 7, 1889, when Crewe obtained an additional representative by the election of F. W. Webb to an aldermancy. Webb served until 1898 but he took little part in county government. Crewe's first three county councillors were Dr. James Atkinson, Dr. William Hodgson and Charles Welch, one Conservative and two Liberals. After the borough extension of 1892 Crewe's new north ward received the right to return a county councillor, first elected in 1895, while the unannexed portion of Church Coppenhall continued to possess one representative. As on the Nantwich Board of Guardians, the tendency was for political divisions to become blurred and for the real contest to become one between the " urbans " and the " rurals." Dr. Atkinson, county councillor from 1889 to 1910, proved an excellent chairman of the County Finance Committee from its inception until 1907. Dr. Hodgson, councillor until 1908 and alderman from that year until 1940, became first vice-chairman (1903) and later (1907–22) chairman of the County Education Committee. Of his work in this sphere it has been written :—

" During this period the whole of the present fabric of county education received at his hands its shape. Gaps had to be filled ; the patchwork had to be unified . . . the secondary as well as the elementary educational systems of the county are Sir William's work." [1]

Dr. Hodgson, who received a knighthood for his local government services in 1921, succeeded Sir George Dixon as chairman of the County Council, of which he had been vice-chairman since 1908, in 1922.[2]

XI. STAFF AND OFFICES

With expanding spheres of activity came an increased staff of officials. By 1893 salaried posts under Crewe Corporation numbered 23, and in 1907, when a scale of salaries was adopted, 40 posts came within its scope. It included the Education

---

[1] *Fasciculus Cestriensis* (1934), pp. 16–17.
[2] *C.G.*, 29.12.88 to 9.2.89, *passim*, 10 and 13.2.92, 5.3.92, 21.3.94 to 5.5.94, *passim*, 1895, *passim*, 12 and 16.3.98, 27.9.01, 27.2.07, 8.8.08, 26.2.10, 12.3.10, 1919, *passim*, 16.12.21 to 24.3.22, *passim* ; *C.Ch.*, 27.4.95, 19.2.98.

Department's administrative staff, but not schoolteachers. The existence of this scale, and the foundation of a Crewe guild of the National Association of Local Government Officers in 1910, made possible organised adjustment of salaries and conditions with the minimum of friction and public discussion. Yet not until 1900 was the Town Clerk's private staff, consisting of the deputy Town Clerk and two assistants, taken over and paid by the Corporation. The Town Clerkship itself carried with it until 1932 the right to a considerable private practice.

Councillors Manning and Williams tried in 1904 to secure minimum and maximum wages of 21s. and 26s. per week for all labourers in the employ of the Corporation, but had to be content for the time being with an " understanding " that no able-bodied labourer should be paid less than 20s. per week. The Crewe branch of the National Union of Corporation Workers obtained further concessions before the outbreak of the first World War, but did not secure the 47-hour week until 1919, from which date the relations between the Corporation and the manual workers employed in its non-trading services have been regulated by the appropriate Lancashire and Cheshire " Whitley Council." The workers in the electricity undertaking came under a separate district Joint Industrial Council in the same year.

In 1891 Crewe Corporation ordered to be inserted in all its contracts a special clause " binding the contractor to pay not less than the usual rate of wages for work of a similar character in the locality." In 1893 the Crewe Trades Council suggested that " the standard rate of wages as paid to Trade Unionists " would be more suitable, and a year later began an investigation into the rate of wages paid by the Corporation to their employees in skilled and unskilled labour, the hours worked, and other matters. After general complaints that the " Fair Wage Clause " in contracts was " invertebrate " and usually ignored, the progressive elements in the local governing body obtained in 1906 a revised and important clause which provided that the contractor should pay not less than the minimum trade union rate of wages in force in the borough in the respective trades for the time being. Substantial penalties for infringement of the conditions lessened the chances of evasion, and the clause also bound sub-contractors. In 1920–1 the Corporation, in order to reduce contractors' charges, adopted the " direct labour system," and started to employ a number of painters and joiners permanently, chiefly in connection with repairs to corporation property.[1]

The Local Board held its first meetings in various rooms belonging to the Mechanics' Institution in the Town Hall. Later it migrated, first to a room over the *Crewe Guardian* office in Market Street, then to a public-house, probably the Castle Inn, and returned to the Town Hall in the late 1860's. In 1871 the Board settled down in Temple Chambers, Exchange Street, a disused Congregational chapel converted into legal offices in 1869 by their Clerk, Frederick Cooke. The first Town Council meeting took place in the council room of the Mechanics' Institution, and Crewe's governing body met there until 1898, when a Council chamber and mayor's parlour were provided in the new Technical Institute. The needs of a new County Secondary School established in the Institute in 1902 ousted the Town Council again, and after failure to secure an ideal but expensive site for municipal offices on the east side of the Market Square, the decision was taken to build a Council chamber and municipal offices on the site of the freehold property belonging to the Corporation and situated immediately to the east of the Market Hall in Earle Street. These cost £20,000, and were opened in 1905. Built to the design of Henry T. Hare of London, they are considered by competent critics to be by far the best piece of architecture in the town. Unfortunately, this excellence is effectively hidden by the lack of a large open space in front of the building.

Accommodation for the Board's officials and documents did not constitute a serious problem in the early years, and the private offices of the Clerk and the surveyor were used for the transaction of local government business. With the acquisition of the Market Hall in 1869, suitable temporary offices for the surveyor and collector became available in the adjacent Corn Exchange.

[1] *Abst. Accts.*, 1892–3 (list of officials), 1920–1 ; C.G., 28.9.89, March, 1893, 9.7.98, 11.12.01, 8.3.02, 5.3.04, 8.10.04, 4.3.05 to 26.5.06, *passim*, 9.3.07, 10.8.07, 25.7.08, 3.6.10, 7.2.19, 9.4.20, 1.7.21 ; C.Ch., 24.3.00, 28.4.00, 25.6.32 ; Coun., 1.2.05, 3.1.06 ; Ctee. of Coun., 5.3.19, 9.11.20, 26.6.22 ; G.P.C., 12.10.91, 11.7.07 (pp. 401–5), 21.1.14, 14.1.19 ; Works Ctee., 1.3.93 ; Mkt. Ctee., 12.6.94 ; Park, 10.1.06 ; Sub-Ctee., 22.9.04, 20.3.06, 21.6.06, 16.5.13 ; E.L., 1919, *passim* ; Econ. and Ret., 1919, *passim* ; Staffing Sub-Ctee., 27.1.20 to 13.6.21, *passim*.

Additional offices in Temple Chambers were rented from the Clerk in 1869, and in 1871 not only the Board but their surveyor and collector migrated thither. In 1879–80 the Corporation erected a building in the town's yard for the minor officials. The increase of staff during the early 1890's rendered necessary more serious measures, and, after an unsuccessful proposal to purchase a site on the east side of the Square, a public-house in Earle Street, called The Forester's Arms, was converted into a small suite of municipal offices, opened in 1893 and capable of housing the chief departments. This building boasted " no pretensions to architectural design," and soon became hopelessly overcrowded and insanitary. It remained in use until 1903, when, together with the Market Tavern, a disused chapel used as the fire-station, and a hairdresser's shop, it was demolished to make way for the present municipal buildings.[1]

[1] C.L.B.M., 25 and 31.1.60, 25.11.62, 27.1.63, 29.3.64, 26.4.64, 2.5.67, 18.2.69, 22.7.69, 28.10.69, 16.5.71, 25.10.71 ; C.G., 11.10.79, 14.1.93, 17.6.93, 1.1.98, 8.1.98, 15.7.99, 11.11.99, 6.4.01 to 8.12.06, *passim*, 20.12.18 ; C.Ch., 15.4.93 ; G.P.C., 11.2.92 to 14.9.93, *passim*, 11.3.97, 15.7.97, 15.6.99, 25.4.01, 20.6.01, 4.9.02, 4.2.03 ; Works Ctee., 5.4.93, 11.3.03, 8.12.03, 12.7.04, 8.5.06 ; Fce., 19.2.03, 19.7.06 ; Coun., 9.11.92, 7.9.04, 2.8.04 ; Ctee. of Coun., 31.5.93 ; Sub-Ctee., 15.1.02, 11.3.02 ; E.A. 94, p. 7.

CHAPTER VIII

THE TRANSITION FROM DENOMINATIONALISM TO STATE EDUCATION IN CREWE, 1850–1923

I. ELEMENTARY AND SECONDARY EDUCATION, 1850–1903

THE company's National schools in Moss Square sufficed for the educational needs of Crewe for some years, but as early as 1850 a number of private academies and dame schools were in existence. The academies catered for the children of Crewe's small middle class and some of them even took in boarders, but several of the prominent men of the Crewe district sent their sons away from the town to be educated ; e.g. C. H. Pedley, A. G. Hill and T. H. Heath all received their education outside Crewe. The second denominational elementary school to be established in Crewe was a small Roman Catholic one in Heath (then Russell) Street, about 1854, largely through the efforts of the resident priest. In 1860 the L.N.W.R. directors received notification of the necessity for increased school accommodation at Crewe, and in the following year they decided to enlarge Christ Church National schools, in lieu of subscribing towards the erection of day schools by the Crewe Wesleyans and Presbyterians.

The Wesleyans opened their Mill Street school in 1862, probably to accommodate a teaching establishment already in existence ; the building of 1862 is still in use, but has been several times altered and enlarged. The Presbyterians did not establish their day school until about 1869, but these " Scotch schools," as they were called, and the Crewe Presbyterian community in general, filled a place in local educational history out of all proportion to their size.[1] The " Scotch schools " were at first held in the Sunday school room in the Hill Street church, but owing to their overcrowded state the girls' department had to be removed to the Heath Street Hall in 1879. Under William

---

[1] One of the L.N.W.R. directors, and a Manchester member of the " Liverpool Party," Robert Barbour of Bolesworth Castle, Cheshire, subscribed handsomely to the building of the Presbyterian Church opened in Hill Street, Crewe, in 1862 (*Cheshire Observer*, Sept. 7, 1861, Sept, 6, 1862).

Dishart (headmaster, 1869–86) the "Scotch schools" acquired a great reputation and trained many pupil teachers. The rapid increase in the size of Crewe between 1861 and 1871 necessitated the provision of even more school accommodation, and the Rev. John Ashe, ex-stockbroker, curate of Coppenhall and first vicar of St. Paul's, prevailed on the railway company to build a small National school for infants in New Street about 1866, while he himself built a small mixed school for the inhabitants of the "Valley" at the other end of the township. This "Rockwood" school was closed down in 1878. The Wesleyans, fearful lest their children, by attending a National school, should unconsciously imbibe the tenets of an Anglicanism which was becoming increasingly "High Church" in tone, founded a second elementary school in a room over the premises of the Crewe Co-operative Friendly Society in West Street (1869) and in January, 1870, transferred it to a new school-building in Hightown. Under the able John T. Hinchsliff (headmaster, 1869–1912), from the Wesleyan Training College, Westminster, who at one time controlled 140 children single-handed, this school was several times enlarged. It is interesting to note that the Nonconformist day schools usually grew out of the Sunday schools attached to places of worship in the town, at which reading and writing were often taught in addition to religious subjects. Nonconformist men and women mastered the elements of public business while managing these educational establishments, just as the Nonconformist local preachers and Sunday school superintendents received their first lessons in public speaking in the chapels, lessons which later enabled them to come forward as Liberal and Radical orators at political, council and committee meetings.

The Education Act of 1870 wrought a silent change in the situation at Crewe. Whereas before that date religious and educational enthusiasm in about equal proportions had prompted the foundation of elementary schools, after the passing of the Act purely financial considerations carried more and more weight, driving the railway company and the sects forward to establish new schools; for if the town's school accommodation fell seriously short of requirements, a purely secular and non-sectarian School Board, and the consequent levying of a dreaded education rate, would become necessary. This meant the end of the company's disinterested social policy in educational matters, and the new policy was bluntly stated by Lord Stalbridge, chairman of the L.N.W.R., in 1894 :—

" What is done at Crewe . . . in subscribing to schools, is only done after most careful consideration as to whether it is cheaper for the shareholders to pay a subscription or to pay the rate necessary to support a school board, the only consideration moving the directors being the economy which can be effected to the shareholders." [1]

In pursuance of this principle, the company built, furnished and paid the deficits on schools at various points in the town— Adelaide Street (1875), Edleston Road (1875), the Valley, Wistaston Road (1879), and two near St. Barnabas' Church, West Street (1887, 1890) all conducted on the National system.[2] The Catholics transferred their school to a larger building in St. Mary's Street in 1879 with the same end in view. In 1887 the Wesleyan body opened its third Crewe day school in Earle Street. This proved to be the last denominational foundation. All the denominational schools were administered by committees of managers, of which the vicar or minister was an ex-officio member. The link between each set of managers and the Committee of Council on Education (from 1899 the Board of Education) was their corresponding secretary ; expenses were met partly by the school pence, partly from private charity and denominational subscriptions, and partly from the various types of State grant. Any steps taken by the central government to increase attendance, raise the school-leaving age or improve the standard of accommodation, led to growing difficulties for these " voluntary " schools.

In the neighbouring township of Church Coppenhall an entirely different situation existed. Here, through the efforts of the Rector, the Rev. John Cooper, new National schools had been opened in 1862 to replace the barn which had served since

[1] *C.Ch.,* 17.11.94.
[2] Adelaide Street (St. Paul's) school was not, strictly speaking, either a Church of England National school or a railway company's school, but the managers were, until 1904, invariably members of the Established Church and connected with the company. Rev. John Ashe, an enthusiastic educationalist, had sold the site to three L.N.W.R. directors " as trustees of a certain fund which has been collected for the purpose of erecting elementary schools at Crewe." Ashe had collected the money.

the early 1840's, but in view of the increasing population a School Board was formed in 1873. The Board leased the National schools in Broad Street from the trustees, the rector and the churchwardens, at a pepper-corn rent in the following year, and opened a small Board school at Maw Green. From 1872 until 1883 an "unsectarian," *i.e.* Nonconformist, majority controlled the Board, and it was in his capacity as one of its original members that T. H. Heath (1850–1900) first entered public life at the early age of twenty-three. In 1880, however, the Rev. William Cawley Reid became Rector of Coppenhall, and a fierce dispute broke out between this High Churchman and the Nonconformist majority on the subject of religious instruction in the schools. The Church party secured a majority on the Board in 1882, with the rector at the head of the poll, but not before the old Board had made every provision for the erection of new schools, opened in 1883 opposite those of 1862. Coppenhall was therefore well provided with school accommodation, and when, in 1892, Crewe borough annexed part of Church Coppenhall, the Board's district remained intact.

The local governing body exercised no control whatsoever over education in Crewe itself until 1877, when the Town Council appointed the first School Attendance Committee under Lord Sandon's Act of 1876. On its appointment the committee discovered that, although there were 4,073 children of school age in the borough, the average attendance at all the available denominational and private schools was only 2,583 and 727 respectively. During the next two years, being " well supported by the magistrates," for whom better attendance meant less juvenile delinquency, the committee and its active school attendance officer increased the number in attendance by 1,500, and, by bringing the private elementary schools under effective supervision, reduced their number from 20 to 12. The last of these " private adventure " schools, the descendants of the earlier " dame schools," closed down in 1898. Inadequately housed and staffed, they were often little more than unsatisfactory kindergartens. The attendances at the Crewe elementary schools rose above 80 per cent. for the first time in 1883, when the corresponding figure for England and Wales as a whole was 71 per cent.

A census carried out in 1890 showed that there were within

the borough 6,170 children between the ages of five and fourteen,[1] and when the Free Education Act of 1891 came into force problems of accommodation and finance arose in an acute form. The Act made elementary education free, but did not wholly abolish fees, so that the parent who demanded free education for his or her child had to be content with a free place in any designated school. Parents willing to continue paying the school pence could send their child to any school they pleased. The managers of the Crewe schools held a joint meeting in July, 1891, to consider the situation, and decided to set up a joint committee consisting of two managers from every school in the borough. This joint committee interviewed Lord Stalbridge, chairman of the L.N.W.R., and A. H. Holland Hibbert, chairman of the company's education committee. The predominant desire was to avoid the formation of a School Board, and the railway company offered to pay an extra £350 to the joint committee for the first year and £200 every succeeding year. This meant that the company would, after the first payment, be subsidising education in Crewe to the extent of about £850 per annum. Fees were abolished in seven schools in 1891, and at the remaining four (Edleston Road, Adelaide Street, Mill Street Wesleyan and High Street Wesleyan) were reduced by about 50 per cent. The important joint committee of day school managers, for which A. G. Hill acted as secretary from 1891 until 1904, made good the losses from the sums placed at its disposal by the railway company, together with much smaller amounts placed at its disposal by the religious communities and by ratepayers startled at the prospect of a School Board. The Free Education Act, and the raising of the exemption standard from V to VI in 1892, increased the number of scholars on the registers from 5,637 to 6,438 in 1894, while the number of places available fell from 6,156 to 5,977. The managers found great difficulty in paying the teachers' salaries, and the voluntary system appeared to be breaking down.

Again the railway company came to the rescue. In June, 1894, Holland Hibbert convened the joint committee of Crewe day school managers " with a view of preventing the establishment of a School Board." A. G. Hill suggested that company and committee should co-operate to build a new school, as H.M. In-

[1] Children were actually admitted to the schools at four years of age.

spector had condemned the Presbyterian schools in Heath Street. In October, 1894, the Crewe I.L.P. called a town's meeting in an effort to carry a resolution in favour of establishing a School Board, but the proposal was defeated, after a long debate, in favour of an amendment approving the joint committee's scheme. The company's donation towards the new school in Beech Street for 836 children amounted to £2,500, and the joint committee, whose task in raising the remaining £1,000 required was simplified by the " School Board scare," took over the administration of the new factory-like building in 1896. The Presbyterian schools in Hill Street now closed down, and their headmaster, Henry D. Struthers, who had succeeded Dishart, became first headmaster at Beech Street.[1] The company spent an additional £3,500 on another school in Pedley Street, opened in 1897, and on extensions to its other schools, but the M.O.H. reported in 1899 that classes were often held " in the cloakrooms and porches." In 1900 the school-leaving age was raised from eleven to twelve years, and the first mutterings of a fresh School Board agitation made themselves heard. The company accordingly built yet another school in Bedford Street, opened in 1902, for the rapidly-expanding population of the south ward. The joint committee took it over a few months before the passing of the great Education Act of 1902, which for the first time placed Crewe's educational system on a firm and ordered basis.

The Act did not at first find favour with Crewe Nonconformists. Crewe Town Council protested against the measure, and the Crewe Free Church Council, founded in 1897, began to organise passive resistance to its application in the borough, on the ground that the rates levied would go to support schools controlled by the Established Church. When, however, the time came to administer the Act, a definite cleavage of opinion manifested itself. The uncompromising hot-heads founded the Crewe Citizens' League (1903) and passively resisted payment of the education rate, while the more moderate Nonconformists used their power as aldermen and councillors to work the Act as far as possible in accordance with their own views.[2] Crewe Town Council drew up a scheme under the Act in the course of 1903,

---

[1] Struthers became Crewe's first Director of Education in 1903.
[2] Isolated instances of passive resistance to the payment of the education rate occurred until 1909.

and when the new Borough Education Committee held its first meeting on August 25, 1903, Alderman William McNeill, the town's most prominent Primitive Methodist, was elected its first chairman, a position which he held until his death in 1917. Dr. Hodgson, a prominent Baptist and a believer in non-sectarian religious instruction in schools, who had been elected first vice-chairman of the County Education Committee, was one of the county's representatives on the Crewe Education Committee. He played an active part in the violent but constructive disputes of the first few years. The Act came into force within the borough on October 1, 1903, when fees were finally abolished.

The voluntary and denominational character of the education provided in the town up to 1903 raised a crop of difficulties. It was an easy matter to appoint two members of the new Education Committee to serve on the Board of Managers attached to each school, but less easy to arrange for the peaceful purchase or leasing of the 15 school buildings to the new authority. Beech Street school became the property of the new committee without payment in 1904, the Catholic school remained " non-provided " and voluntary, but several disputes occurred before the status of the remaining schools could be settled ; one of these disputes was protracted into 1908. The committee took over the buildings belonging to the Church Coppenhall School Board in 1903.

From the beginning, the Education Committee had made it clear that henceforth all sectarian religious instruction in the schools was to be given at the managers' expense outside school hours, that attendance at such instruction was not to be obligatory, and that teachers were to be appointed without reference to their religious qualifications, except in the case of the " non-provided " Catholic school. As the schools came one by one under the direct administration of the committee, a plan of undenominational religious instruction had to be drawn up (1905), and although " the Education Committee's new religion " provoked mild criticism at first, the religious problem soon ceased to give serious trouble.

The Medical Officer's report on the state of the schools in 1903 showed that most of them were not only badly ventilated and dirty, but positively insanitary. Extensions, repairs and alterations went on continuously until 1914. Dr. Hodgson said in 1905 :—

". . . there never had been an adequate education provided. Sufficient had been done to keep out a School Board, but it had not been possible to keep it out any longer. It had come in since under the new Act, and the Education Committee were doing now what might have been done many years ago under a School Board." [1]

These improvements failed to keep pace with the expanding school population, larger attendances, and the rising standards of the Board of Education. Four sites for new schools were purchased between 1903 and 1913.[2] On the first, in Brierley Street, the committee erected the new Borough elementary and higher elementary schools, at a cost of more than £20,000. A great deal of opposition to this project manifested itself on the Town Council, and threatened to curtail the scheme, but the Education Committee's forward policy was approved by the organised protests of Crewe's trade union branches, and the work proceeded. The new schools, opened in 1908, accommodated 1,525 scholars and made possible the closure of New Street, Earle Street Wesleyan, the Presbyterian (reopened temporarily 1905–8), and Christ Church Schools. The higher elementary school provided a three-year advanced course for selected boys and girls between the ages of eleven and fourteen.[3] Some difficulty was experienced in persuading parents to allow their children to complete the full course, and a prominent Crewe educationalist declared in 1912 :—" The majority of people had received little education, and many looked unkindly on it. Schooling was not looked upon as an ordinary thing."

By 1909 the Education Committee possessed accommodation for 8,155 scholars, when on the average about 8,500 were in attendance at the various schools. From this date the number of children on the registers declined, a fact which was used by

---

[1] *Cf.* Lord Stanley of Alderley, speaking in 1908 :—" The [Crewe] Education Committee came into an inheritance by transfer, and like many people who inherited something they found that their property stood in need of a great deal of improvement."

[2] The average annual attendance rose above 90 per cent. for the first time in 1912 ; the two sites purchased in 1904 have yet to be utilised.

[3] " The considerations which have suggested such special provision for higher elementary education are :—(1) By a good rule at the L. and N.W. Railway Works, no lad is employed before he is 14 years of age, and (2) there is no industry giving abundant and regular employment to girls " (*C.G.*, 6.4.04).

" economists " as an argument for delaying the provision of new buildings :— [1]

	1904	1909	1912
Average number of children on registers	9,196	9,555	9,151
Per cent. of attendances	84·9	88·8	91·3

The lack of public responsibility for education in Crewe before 1903 meant a heavy education rate afterwards. It rose above 1s. 6d. in the pound in 1909–10, and Crewe thereupon became eligible for a special Board of Education grant as " a necessitous school area." The rate did not remain at 1s. 7½d., but soared to 1s. 11d. ; opinion in the town hardened against any further new schools, and pointed to the decreasing child population.[2] The scale of teachers' salaries underwent revision in a downward direction in 1910, and when the Board of Education pressed for a new school building in the Hightown district, makeshifts were resorted to in the endeavour to stave off further capital expenditure. The Technical Institute (1911) and the abandoned Earle Street Wesleyan building (1910–15) had to be pressed into service again. The " economists " even agitated for the total exclusion of children under five years of age from the schools.[3]

Nevertheless, much was accomplished in other spheres. Under the Provision of Meals Act, 1906, free meals were provided every winter from 1907 until 1913, but during the first World War only a few of the worst cases received them, and the practice was not resumed on a large scale until 1922. Kindergarten methods, larger playgrounds, the appointment of a school dentist and the equipment of a dental clinic (1914), occupied the

[1] Whereas more than one-fifth of Crewe's population was to be found on the school registers in 1909, in 1938 the proportion barely reached one-eighth.

[2] The cost per head of average attendance increased from £2 13s. 7d., of which the ratepayers provided only 12s. 4d. in the financial year 1904–5, to £4 5s. 10d. in 1913–14, of which the ratepayers' share was £1 14s. The corresponding figures for 1937–8 were £16 0s. 5d. (ratepayers £7 8s.) per head (*Abst. Accts.*, 1937–8, p. 8).

[3] Councillor F. Manning (Lib.-Lab.), who was later (1918–25) chairman of the Education Committee, even brought forward a preposterous scheme in 1912 for double-shift teaching as a contribution towards the solution of the problem of accommodation, but found himself in a minority of one (*C.G.*, 19.1.12, 22.3.12).

Education Committee and its officials in the first busy years, while certificated teachers gradually replaced the numerous uncertificated ones appointed under the pre-1903 régime. The first woodwork and cookery classes began in the Technical Institute during 1910.

After the stagnation and retrogression of the war years, the Education Committee failed to display much enthusiasm for the progress made possible under the Fisher Act of 1918. The school-leaving age was effectively raised to fourteen years on January 1, 1921, but rather with the idea of relieving the labour-market than as a basis for a fresh educational advance. In spite of the 1920–1 economy campaign, the committee appointed an assistant School Medical Officer, opened two new school clinics (for refraction and minor ailments), and adopted the Burnham salary scale III for its teachers during these years. Physical training, until then somewhat neglected, was taken up with enthusiasm in 1920 on lines laid down in the Board of Education syllabus of 1919, but the town still lacked playing-fields.

In order to assure a supply of adequately trained teachers, the Crewe Technical Instruction Committee had co-operated with the managers of the various schools in the borough to found a Pupil Teachers' Centre for Crewe, Nantwich and Sandbach, opened in 1899 with H. D. Struthers as its first principal and A. G. Hill as secretary. By 1901, 127 pupil-teachers were receiving instruction and the centre was removed from the Mechanics' Institution to the Technical Institute in 1903, to be superseded in 1908 by the Cheshire Education Committee's Training College.

Dr. Hodgson's influence on the present structure of county education has been profound, and in no way more so than in the part he played in the provision for the training of teachers. The Cheshire County Training College at Crewe probably originated in a visit which he paid to the U.S.A. in 1906–7 for the purpose of inspecting American educational institutions and methods.[1] Dr. Hodgson had advocated undenominational training colleges as early as 1900, and when he became chairman of the Cheshire Education Committee it was soon obvious that nothing had

---

[1] Struthers visited Canada and the U.S.A. in 1907 for the same purpose, and reported that American methods of teaching were " in advance of those obtaining in this country " (*C.G.*, 20.4.07).

occurred to cause him to change his views. Crewe's central position marked it out as the headquarters of the new college, which was located for the first four years of its existence (1908–12) in the Crewe Mechanics' Institution. In 1912 it moved to new buildings erected at a cost of more than £33,000 in semi-rural surroundings a few hundred yards from Crewe railway station. Crewe has thus become one of the county's most important educational centres, and a large proportion of Crewe's teachers have received their training at the college.

From 1880 onwards it became increasingly evident that Crewe needed a school which would give a full-time literary and scientific education to those pupils in the elementary schools capable of profiting by it. Louis Hyde's Crewe High School, founded in 1880, and William Dishart's Crewe Academy, founded in 1887, formed the response of profit-making private enterprise to this need ; but admirable as these institutions might be, they catered solely for fee-payers from Crewe's middle class, with a sprinkling of children from well-to-do artisan families. The ancient Grammar schools at Nantwich and Sandbach received some boy-pupils from Crewe, but fell far below their modern degree of efficiency ; girls had to go even further afield. Boys and girls from Crewe who were awarded county scholarships under the Technical Instruction Act of 1889 found themselves seriously handicapped. Again Dr. Hodgson was the moving spirit. A deputation from Crewe Technical Instruction Committee waited on F. W. Webb in 1901 to ascertain whether the railway company would co-operate in the matter, and on meeting with a refusal decided to enlarge the Technical Institute to accommodate a secondary day school. The new school opened in September, 1902, and provided a full-time modern scientific education, although classical and literary subjects were included in the curriculum. County and municipality provided scholarships which enabled working-class children to enjoy, for the first time, educational advantages hitherto restricted to the middle and upper classes. Under its first headmaster (D. H. McCurtain, 1902–38), the school proved a success from the first, and after passing under the control of the County Education Committee in 1903 was provided with new premises in 1909, largely through the efforts of Dr. Hodgson. These are situated in Ruskin Road, and at the time of their opening provided places for 350 scholars.[1] The Ursuline Convent School, Nantwich Road, founded in 1906 by nuns from France, was placed on the Board of Education's list of efficient secondary schools in 1922.[2]

II. THE EARLY HISTORY OF THE CREWE MECHANICS' INSTITUTION (1843-76) AND UNIVERSITY EXTENSION

The first mention of the various organisations which later developed into the Crewe Mechanics' Institution occurs in March, 1843, when the Grand Junction directors were recommended to provide a reading-room for the men employed in the new works, to compensate them for the educational and recreational facilities lost by removal from Liverpool. The fulfilment of the plan was delayed for some months, and in December, 1843, John Moss, chairman of the directors, told the artisans that he " hoped before long to be enabled to establish for them a commodious and well-plenished library and newsroom." Some time before, the company had built a temporary assembly room on the site of the company's schools in Moss Square, and the newsroom and library were established in two rooms attached to this building until they were demolished in 1846. Of these two institutions the library was founded first, at a meeting of workmen on April 4, 1844, called to consider an offer of £25 from the directors of the company. The meeting elected a committee of work-men (including William Allan [3] and Alexander Allan), a treasurer

---

[1] Bagshaw 1850, p. 369 ; White 1860, pp. 345–9 ; Kelly 1857, pp. 103–5 ; 1865, pp. 133–5 ; 1878, pp. 161–2 ; *E.A.* 73, p. 26, 83, p. 185, 87, p. 4 ; M.O.H., 1893, 1898, 1903, 1904, 1911, 1914, 1915, 1917, 1920–2 ; *Fasciculus Cestriensis*, pp. 16–17 ; *Abst. Accts.*, 1904–13 ; *Cheshire Observer*, 5 and 12.10.61, 5.4.62, 23.5.63, 6.6.63 ; C.L.B.M., 21.5.74 ; Coun., 24.7.77, 1.6.04 to 5.4.05, *passim*, 4.9.07, 4.3.08, 2.10.12, 7.1.14, 5.1.21 ; Works Ctee., 19.2.79, 26.7.83, 5.3.90, 15.5.95, 12.2.96 ; School Attce., 13.9.87, 19.8.90, 16.10.90, 1.9.91, 18.10.98, 13.2.00 ; G.P.C., 26.8.86, 10 and 17.1.01, 6.2.01, 1903, *passim*, 10.3.04, 1905, *passim*, 15.3.06 ; Ctee. of Coun., 1.5.02, 4.3.03, 3.6.03 ; Fce., 24.11.05 ; Sub-Ctee., 12.4.07 ; Educ. Ctee., 25.8.03 to 30.9.03 (and joint meetings in same period) ; *C.G.*, 26.1.78 to 1.12.83, *passim*, 18.11.85 to 3.11.88, 30.8.90 to 21.11.96, *passim*, 11.6.98 to 23.2.07, *passim*, 25.3.08 to 21.12.23, *passim* ; *C.Ch.*, 12 and 19.10.89, Sept.–Nov., 1894, 22.10.98, Feb.–Oct., 1900 ; *Report of Ctee. of Coun. on Educ.*, 1878–9, pp. 282–9.
[2] *C.G.*, 13.7.07, 19.5.22.
[3] This was the famous William Allan, afterwards (1851–74) first General Secretary of the Amalgamated Society of Engineers.

and a secretary. A newsroom committee was formed three weeks later (April 24), and contained three members of the library committee, but the two institutions remained distinct. The proceedings of both bodies were submitted regularly for the directors' approval.

The newspapers chosen did not, however, meet with the entire approbation of the directors, who ordered the removal of Feargus O'Connor's Chartist *Northern Star* and the *Weekly Dispatch*, a Radical organ. The effect was disastrous. Thirty-two subscribers resigned (May, 1844) and the newsroom committee's finances had to be subsidised by the Grand Junction directors, who promised " to make up the deficient subscriptions until the numbers again increase to what they were before the withdrawal of the two obnoxious papers." [1] There is no further evidence of a Chartist movement in the town, Crewe's importance in this respect being strategic rather than local.[2]

In November, 1844, the Crewe committee of directors decided to amalgamate the two committees, and at a joint meeting on November 12 railway officials and individual directors played a prominent part. Some of them even became members of the amalgamated library and newsroom committee. This reform did not meet with success, and throughout the winter of 1844–5 the membership continued to dwindle " in consequence of the withdrawal " of the *Weekly Dispatch* and *Northern Star* at the directors' behest. William Allan and John Thow therefore boldly suggested that these two newspapers should be taken again, in view of the fact that " their prohibition from the newsroom does not lessen their reading in this community, but rather the reverse " (June, 1845). The last meeting of this committee before its supersession took place on November 29, 1845. Starting badly, it bore the defects of its origin to the grave.

Were the 32 seceders of May, 1844, content with a passive protest, or did they found an active rival organisation of their own ? Although there is little definite evidence, there may be some connection between the secession and the appearance in

[1] *Chester Courant*, Dec. 12, 1843 ; C.M., 1.7.46 ; C.G., 22.4.71 ; *E.A.* 73, pp. 14–15 ; N.R., April–May, 1844 ; G.J.B.M., May 22, 1844.

[2] See pp. 147–50, *supra.*

April, 1845, of a rival "Mechanics' Institute," which sent a deputation to the joint library and newsroom committee to negotiate for an amalgamation ; this took place in or about September, 1845, when the two bodies united to form the Crewe Mechanics' Institution. Francis Trevithick is said to have played an important part in these negotiations and became the first President, resigning to make way for the new locomotive superintendent, John Ramsbottom, in 1858. The connection thus established between the presidency and the company's Chief Mechanical Engineer or works superintendent at Crewe has been maintained without interruption, and was particularly important for the history of education in the town during the long "reign" of F. W. Webb (1871-1903).

The rules adopted by the new Institution in 1845 provided that it should be governed by an annually-chosen council of 21 members (later increased to 31). "No political or religious subject" could be introduced at any meeting, and the aim of the Institution copied, like the rules, from similar institutions in other parts of the country, was "to supply to the Working Classes of Crewe, the means of instruction in Science, Literature and the Arts." Three members of the council were to be nominated by the directors of the railway company, and nine (later 14) had to be chosen from a list submitted by the directors to the members. This "undemocratic" method of election, whereby a majority of persons acceptable to the company was automatically assured, evoked criticism later, especially after the Intimidation affair had estranged the Liberals from the railway company.[1]

The purpose of the library, an essential part of such an institution, was generally considered to be the supply of instructive rather than amusing books for home reading, but from the first novels formed by far the most popular section. Books on history and biographies came a bad second, with books of a scientific character a bad third. The council several times expressed its disappointment at these features. A standing Library Committee was appointed in 1854, but the popularity of this branch of the Institution did not increase to any large

[1] N.R., 1.5.44 to 21.12.46, *passim*, 22.4.45 to 13.9.45, *passim* ; C.M., 13.9.45, 18.10.45, *passim*, 11.4.46 ; Rules adopted Oct. 25, 1845 ; *C.G.*, 23.10.69 to 11.12.69, 21.1.71, 28.3.91.

extent until after 1871, when the first full-time secretary-librarian, R. C. Stapley, was appointed.[1] Issues rose from 7,191 in 1870 to 18,141 in 1872. · A detailed survey undertaken in 1870–1 showed that the usual picture of a sober, well-instructed artisan with a thirst for useful knowledge, preferably of a scientific character, did not represent the typical British workman, but young students attending the Institution's classes, and apprentices from the works, found the library of great value as a source of text-books. The verdict on the engineer was :—" When he does read, it is for amusement rather than information." Open access to the shelves was not introduced until 1920. The news-room, in such a politically minded town as Crewe, has been assured of constant popularity.[2]

It is safe to say that without the constant financial support given by the railway company the Institution would either have collapsed during the depression of 1848–51, or eked out an inglorious existence, with an attenuated educational department, incapable of making the efforts which later raised it high in the scale of teaching establishments giving technical instruction in England. Not only did the company find shelter for it in the first place, but in 1846–7 the directors saw to the provision of more adequate accommodation in a block of buildings in Prince Albert Street, containing the Town Hall, the library and newsroom, classrooms and committee-rooms, again at the expense of the shareholders. The Town Hall was placed under the control of the Institution's council in 1847, and the monies received from lettings for public meetings and miscellaneous purposes formed an important part of the Institution's revenue.

An even more profitable source of income soon presented itself. One of the perquisites of a master-engineer consisted of the cash premiums received from the parents and guardians of youths whom they desired to place as apprentice-engineers. By a custom which seems to have existed from the first days of the railway colony, the sons of any workman employed in the

---

[1] The honorary secretary now became merely the official channel of communication between the Institution and the railway company.

[2] A.R.C.M.I., 1849–58, *passim*, 1865, 1866, 1868, 1871, 1872, 1873, 1874, 1876, 1935, 1936 ; N.R., 24.5.44 ; C.M., 15.5.65, 10.5.71 ; C.G., 15.7.71, 22.4.71 ; Caunt : *op. cit.*, p. 57.

Locomotive Department of Crewe Works could be apprenticed there without payment of a premium. The first recorded payment of a premium occurs in 1846, when Trevithick handed over £15 to the funds of the Institution ; this he had received from Lord Delamere as payment for apprenticing a lad, William Woods, in whom his lordship was interested. This step was taken at the behest of the directors, and it became the custom for all such sums to be placed to the credit of the Institution. In later years their amount increased rapidly ; *e.g.* in 1930, the year before which the premiums ceased to be devoted to the purposes of the Institution, £250 was received.[1]

In the early 1860's the premises occupied by the Institution became too small for the increasing numbers frequenting them, and constant complaints ensued. A fire which occurred in 1869 hastened the long-awaited reconstruction. Thanks to the efforts of John Ramsbottom, the President, the cost of rebuilding, about £3,500, was defrayed by the railway company. The Institution's new home occupied the old site, but contained a number of new classrooms, and was opened in April, 1871, by Lord Houghton, better known as Monckton Milnes, father of the future Marquess of Crewe. In 1880, through the efforts of Webb, ten new classrooms became available for the students, and a third great extension in 1902 fulfilled Webb's ambitious scheme by bringing the building down to Liverpool bridge. The granting of the nine-hour day at the beginning of 1872 led to a remarkable expansion in all the activities of the Institution, but even after this, members' subscriptions only amounted in 1874 to a little over 25 per cent. of the Institution's income. The financial dependence of the Institution on the railway company throughout its career alone enabled it to achieve a foremost position in education. The question of the ownership of the site and buildings used by the Institution received proper definition in 1905, when they were formally recognised as belonging to the railway company. The company's chief officials at Crewe have almost without exception been connected with the Institution, either as teachers or as

---

[1] *Cf.* A.R.C.M.I., 1853, ". . . the financial affairs of the Institution do not suffer from the same causes as the majority of its contemporaries . . . if it were not for the kindly and continuous liberality of the Directors of the London and North Western Railway Company, it could not sustain its present state of efficiency."

members of the Council, and have often served in both capacities ; *e.g.* Webb himself taught classes between 1851 and 1866.[1]

The original purpose of mechanics' institutions was to provide scientific instruction for the working classes by means of lecture courses, and thereby to stimulate interest in the technical and theoretical aspects of the great industrial changes which were taking place in Great Britain at the time.   The efforts of the Crewe Mechanics' Institution to organise such lectures in the late 1840's and 1850's proved somewhat disheartening, and (to judge from the early minute books) mesmerism, ventriloquism and miscellaneous musical and comic entertainments were far more popular, if also more expensive, than poorly attended talks on astronomy, geometry, optics and physiology.   The general apathy displayed towards these subjects stood in startling contrast to the enthusiasm shown for a series of concerts and balls, one of which lasted until 4 a.m.

Scientific lectures were still occasionally given, and from 1847 to 1851 the Crewe Institution subscribed annually to the Union of Lancashire and Cheshire Institutes, which existed to organise regular courses of lectures by competent speakers ; attendances continued, however, to be " so small and discouraging " that in 1850 the Council considered it " useless to engage any lecturers." Occasionally interest would be aroused by an exceptional speaker or an unusual subject, only to die down again very quickly. The credit for the re-establishment of this branch must be given to two young men from the University of Cambridge, Warren Mand Moorsom and James Stuart, to whose enthusiasm is due the important part played by the Crewe Mechanics' Institution in the movement for University Extension.[2]

Moorsom was the son of Admiral C. R. Moorsom (1792–1861), chairman of the L.N.W.R., 1860–1. After graduation from Trinity College, Cambridge, he entered Crewe Works as an engineering pupil about 1864.   In 1870 Ramsbottom made him manager of the rail mill, a post which he held until his departure

---

[1] C.M., 28.3.46, 1.7.46, 30.6.47, July, 1847, 15 and 22.7.50 ; A.R.C.M.I., 1849–1936, esp. 1859, 1861, 1869, 1930 ; C.G., 22.4.71, 11.9.80, 24.11.80, 30.8.02, 1.3.05, 21.2.06.

[2] C.M., 3.10.45 to 11.3.50, *passim*, and 19.11.55 ; A.R.C.M.I., 1849–55, 1856, 1860, 1861 ; *Prospectus of Union of Lancs. and Ches. Institutes*, 1936–7, pp. 51–3.

from Crewe in 1876. He entered fully into the life of the town, and his interest in popular education is evident from his record of work in connection with the Mechanics' Institution. He became a teacher and examiner in 1864, and a member of the council in 1866. James Stuart (1843–1913) became friendly with Moorsom at Trinity, and in 1875 was appointed professor of mechanics at Cambridge. His interest in University Extension was the product of a desire to found a " peripatetic " Co-operative University, and he occupied the presidential chair at the Co-operative Congress of 1879. Moorsom held opinions which Stuart described as " socialist " ! [1]

The first important step towards University Extension was taken by the North of England Council for promoting the Higher Education of Women, presided over by Josephine Butler, which drew its main strength from Manchester, Liverpool, Leeds and Sheffield. Stuart gave a series of lectures under the auspices of this body in 1867, but the second step was taken by Stuart alone, and his account of it illustrates the occasionally accidental character of historical development :—

" I have now come to the second important step that was taken towards the realisation of University Extension . . . my friend Mr. W. M. Moorsom . . . wrote saying that I ought to come to give a lecture to the workmen there [Crewe] in the mechanics' institute . . . on meteors. . . . I went rather reluctantly and expected an audience of a score or so. But when I arrived I found the hall, which holds about 1,500 people, crowded in every corner. . . . It was, what I had quite forgotten it would be when I undertook to lecture, the night following the great meteoric shower of Nov. 1867. The lecture was the first occasion on which I had addressed any large body of persons. It was a success, and . . . it struck me that this was an opening for a further move in connection with my notion of a peripatetic university. So I said that as they had liked the lecture . . . I would . . . come back in the summer and give them a weekly lecture for a couple of months, going more fully into the subject. In consequence, in the following summer of 1868, I gave a set of lectures on astronomy on the same principles." [2]

---

[1] D.N.B., article on *Moorsom* ; Steel : *op. cit.*, p. 251 ; Stuart : *Reminiscences*, pp. 150, 154, 159, 164, 203 ; *Who was Who, 1896–1916* (Stuart) ; A.R.C.M.I., 1864, 1866–76, *passim* ; C.G., 29.1.76.

[2] Stuart : *op. cit.*, pp. 159–60.

This set of lectures, printed in 1869 as *Six Lectures to the Workmen of Crewe*, was also successful, and Stuart lectured again in 1869. After this the movement languished in Crewe, until in 1871 the council of the Mechanics' Institution, at Stuart's instigation, addressed a memorial to the University of Cambridge, similar to those presented by the Rochdale Equitable Pioneers and the North of England Council. This document is printed in full as an appendix to the Annual Report for that year and asked for the establishment of tutorial classes in the following year. The Institution drew up a plan for itinerant lecturers from the universities " who should go, as it were, on circuit through the various towns," and was particularly definite on the subject of examinations :—

" We wish to state clearly that we are not wishing for more Examinations, but for a better Teaching and Educating power. The months of March, April and May are already largely occupied in Examinations of our students by the various examining bodies in the country, your University included ; and we should not regret to see fewer examinations take place. . . ." [1]

The first courses of University Extension lectures began in October, 1873, at Nottingham, Derby and Leicester. Crewe had to depend upon the unofficial voluntary efforts of several tutors and Fellows of Trinity, solicited by Stuart to deliver a series of scientific lectures. It was the old tale—interest gradually subsided and expenses grew. Moorsom gave a very successful free series of University Extension lectures on political economy in 1875–6, but after his departure from Crewe in the latter year the Mechanics' Institution lost interest in a movement at the birth of which it had played such an important part.[2]

During the winter of 1886–7, the Rev. C. V. Gorton, vicar of St. Barnabas' Church, delivered a series of lectures in connection with the University of Oxford Extension Scheme, but although inaugurated by no less a person than the Rev. Dr. William Stubbs, the famous constitutional historian of mediæval England, the

[1] A.R.C.M.I., 1871, pp. 4–6 ; 1872, pp. 6, 23–6 ; Stuart : *op. cit.*, pp. 161, 163, 167.
[2] Stuart : *op. cit.*, p. 169 ; A.R.C.M.I., 1872–3, 1875–6 ; Adamson : *English Education, 1789–1902*, pp. 341–2.

course was badly attended. It was not until the foundation in 1909 of the Crewe branch of the Workers' Educational Association that organised adult tutorial classes again formed part of the intellectual life of Crewe.[1]

Another of the original functions of mechanics' institutions had been to supply, in their rôle as working-class universities, instruction for those members whose youthful education had been neglected. The evening classes were thus not established primarily for the further education of children and youths, but in fact this became, in the case of those institutions which survived the troubles of early growth, perhaps the most important single branch of their activities. In the case of the Crewe Mechanics' Institution, owing to lack of support from adult members and the emphasis laid upon the need for the instruction of the younger members of an artisan community in scientific and commercial subjects, evening classes for apprentices employed in the works, and for young clerks, ended by crowding out most of the other activities. Boys under fourteen were excluded from the classes in 1873, adults in 1879.

Immediate measures were taken in 1845 to establish classes in the Institution (the three R's, drawing, vocal and instrumental music), but the report on them at the end of the year made discouraging reading. For many years the dancing and " essay and discussion " or " mutual improvement " classes remained by far the most popular. Girls and women were admitted to the classes in 1847. The teachers of these always consisted for the most part of working men whose education was a little better than the average, such as James Ainscow, secretary of the Crewe Co-operative Friendly Society from 1849 to 1852, supplemented by occasional ministers of religion and local schoolmasters. At first payment was at the rate of 1s. 6d. per night for one and a half to two hours' work, but some gave their labours free. In 1875, following the example set by

[1] C.G., 27.1.86 to 23.11.86, *passim*, 25.9.09, 11 and 14.10.10. Among the many "educational societies" which have existed may be mentioned the Crewe Engineering Society (1879–84), the Crewe Scientific Society (1884–1902), and the Crewe Literary and Philosophical Society, founded in 1903. The first two were connected with the Mechanics' Institution ; the Scientific Society promised to achieve more than a local reputation, but was cut off in its prime (C.G., 18.2.80, 4.10.84, 22 and 29.10.84, 18.2.85, 1.3.02, 29.7.03 ; minute books of the first two societies).

Government, the council instituted a system of part-payment by results.[1]

In the course of the 1850's began the slow process of linking up the Institution with the various technical schools, colleges and examining bodies and universities which were developing rapidly at this time to cope with the demand for better scientific education and higher standards of accuracy, and a silent change took place in the character both of the teaching staff and of the subjects taught at the Institution, which ended by becoming an institute of technical instruction. More of the officials and engineers employed in the works took classes in the evenings. Webb described the change as follows :—

" When he came to Crewe first [in 1851] there were no means of obtaining technical education except by employing a private tutor. . . . He afterwards came to the Institution and taught a drawing class for two or three years, and while so engaged, he was teaching himself." [2]

Teachers like Moorsom, Edward Pillow (from 1877 to 1891 " the pioneer of science teaching in Crewe "), W. Davison, T. E. Sackfield and W. Savage, all works officials, helped to raise the standards of the Institution to a very high level. The close connection among the company's staff was illustrated in 1864, when the nucleus of the present Crewe Works laboratory came into existence, and thus made possible the successful establishment of a chemistry class, after several previous failures, " principally for want of a teacher connected with the works." [3]

In the earliest period the efficiency of the teachers and the worth of those taught had not been checked by the examination system, and much of the knowledge acquired by workmen and apprentices in the evening classes after a hard day's work must have been silently forgotten in after-life or during the long summer break, especially as it did not directly improve the economic prospects of the learner. By 1880, however, this had changed ; the last links had been forged in the slender chain which enabled

---

[1] Hudson : *History of Adult Education*, p. lx ; A.R.C.M.I., 1849 to 1859, *passim*, 1864, 1873, 1875–7, *passim*, 1879 ; Rules of 1845, vi, vii ; C.M., 3.10.45 to 25.9.49, *passim* ; Whittle : *op. cit.*, pp. 3–4 ; C.G., 29.1.76.

[2] C.G., 19.2.02.

[3] *C.Ch.*, 23.1.92 ; C.G., 7.19.3 ; A.R.C.M.I., 1864 ; *Times, L.M.S. Supplement*, 20.9.38, p. xviii.

a boy of working-class origin from one of the Crewe elementary schools to climb, *via* an apprenticeship in the works, attendance at the night-classes of the Institution and a scholarship to, say, Owens College or the Royal School of Mines. No doubt the effort, luck and brains required prevented success in many cases where it would have been gained today, but a beginning had been made, and the chain was to be strengthened in the following decades. Webb often promoted those who distinguished themselves at the Institution, while his fame as an engineer, and his many connections with railway and other engineering workshops at home, helped to scatter engineers from Crewe round the globe.[1]

The first step towards encouraging Crewe Works apprentices to study at the Institution in the evenings was taken by the L.N.W.R. directors in 1855, when they placed £20 at the disposal of the council of the Crewe Mechanics' Institution, to be distributed in money prizes among " those boys in the company's works who passed a satisfactory examination before the Government Inspector of Schools," to which the Institution itself added an annual system of prize awards in 1857. Very unfavourable reports on the classes by the examiners continued throughout the 1860's, but certain measures taken in 1868–9 tended to stimulate effort and scholastic competition ; *e.g.* the directors' prizes were thrown open to all young men in the employ of the company in any of the works or steam sheds of the northern division of the railway. The council of the Institution was forced by the public predilection for technical instruction to neglect literary subjects, and to concentrate after 1877 on those " with a special bearing upon the industry of the artisans and mechanics employed in the Locomotive Works, in order to give them the technical training necessary to success in their particular employment, *viz.* mechanical engineering and the manufacture and use of the materials employed in connection with it." [2]

---

[1] C.G., 8.11.02, 27.6.03, 28.11.03, 8.3.05, 15.7.05, 5.8.05, 7.3.08, 7.3.11, 5.5.11. A good example of the work of the Institution in bringing to light undeveloped talent is the case of Charles Dick (1838–88), of Scots peasant stock, who arrived in Crewe " almost destitute," obtained employment in Crewe Works erecting shop, and rose to be Works Manager at Crewe from 1881 until his death (C.G., 9.6.88, 30.6.88 ; C.Ch., 9.6.88).

[2] A.R.C.M.I., 1877 ; also 1855–8, 1866–70, 1872, 1875–6, 1878–1912, *passim* ; *Staffordshire Advertiser*, Nov. 4, 1854 ; C.G., 22.4.71.

Gradually, the Institution became linked with the various examining bodies—the Institutional Association (the revived Union of Lancashire and Cheshire Institutes) in 1855, the Society of Arts in 1863, the University of Cambridge in 1870, the City and Guilds of London Institute for Technological Education in 1879. 1862 saw the establishment of the first Local Committee to conduct examinations under the auspices of the Government Science and Art Department at South Kensington. The examinations of the Science and Art Department proved very popular. Later they were the means whereby the Institution earned substantial State grants. The number and variety of science subjects taught constantly increased until the abolition of the classes in 1912, while standards of teaching and accomplishment gradually rose. Hardly a year passed without the addition of one or more subjects to the curriculum. As a specimen of what was being done by " Crewe's technical college," it appears that even as early as 1875, 21 subjects were selected by the students for examination under the Science and Art Department alone, including chemistry, acoustics, light and heat, magnetism and electricity, theoretical and applied mechanics, steam and the higher branches of mathematics.[1] In the latter years of the nineteenth century the new commercial subjects (shorthand, bookkeeping and typewriting) grew rapidly in popularity. After the reconstruction of the Institution buildings in 1869–71, and the granting of the nine-hour day in 1872, the numbers attending the classes rose rapidly to 516 in 1876. The figure reached 839 in 1895, but in face of competition from the Borough Technical Institute fell to 465 in 1910. By reason of their connection with the Institution several individuals, notably Ramsbottom, Webb and Sir Richard Moon, founded University scholarships for which Crewe students and employees from other points on the L.N.W.R. could compete, while between 1872 and 1909 students from the Institution won 53 Whitworth awards.[2] Webb, the

[1] From the 1880's it became necessary to print, apart from the Annual Report, a special syllabus of classes. The number of examinations taken, the number of successes, and the various authorities under which they were gained, make the Reports themselves bewildering in the solid mass of information they contain.

[2] It became possible from 1902 onwards to organise an annual dinner of old Crewe Whitworth scholars in London (*C.G.*, 15.2.02, 14.2.03, 5.5.11, 19.1.23).

local patriot *par excellence*, calculated that on the basis of population, Crewe was only entitled to one Whitworth award in a century. The labour of the pioneers had borne its fruit, and in spite of immense obstacles the means had been created whereby scientific knowledge and the prospects of personal advancement were placed within reach of all.

When such achievements are borne in mind, the history of the Institution's end as a teaching centre does not make pleasant reading. It is impossible not to feel that had a more conciliatory attitude been shown by Webb and Whale, both of whom desired to make the Institution a permanent College of Technology, a satisfactory arrangement might have been reached which would have ensured the continuance and progressive development of the Institution's work in the sphere of applied science. It was deplorable, but inevitable, that higher education in Crewe should have become involved in the political struggle of the 1880's between the railway company and the town. Webb's autocratic rule at the Institution caused the progressive Liberals, T. H. Heath, Dr. Hodgson and McNeill, to organise and support the opposition Heath Street Hall science classes, established in 1882 with the sanction of the Science and Art Department at South Kensington. Under the direction of J. A. Atkinson, a civil engineer and an ex-teacher at the Mechanics' Institution, these classes proved a success, and many students from them sat for the local examinations held under the auspices of the Institution. The control of the Heath Street classes was said to be " on lines of popular representation," as opposed to the undemocratically chosen council of the Mechanics' Institution, and T. H. Heath claimed in 1891 that the Heath Street Hall " had done better work, earned more money per head [in grants], and did more *pro rata* than the Institution." The Liberals also claimed that " the friendly rivalry " of the two bodies aided that improvement in technical education so earnestly desired by the leaders of Great Britain at the time, chiefly as the means of defeating industrial competition from the U.S.A. and Germany, whose higher educational systems were acknowledged to be better than the British.

The Chancellor of the Exchequer's gift of the " whiskey money " to the County Councils, in 1890, enabled them to begin the administration of the Technical Instruction Act, 1889.

Under the Act borough councils were also empowered to levy a 1*d*. rate for this purpose. The Cheshire County Council received £13,000 from the " whiskey money " in 1890, and in February of that year the progressive section of the Liberals on Crewe Town Council (Dr. Hodgson moved the resolution) made an unsuccessful attempt to secure the levying of the 1*d*. rate. When, however, the council of the Mechanics' Institution later in the year refused a grant of £220 out of the " whiskey money " (the Heath Street Hall gratefully accepted £55 from the same source), the Liberals, who had meanwhile gained a majority on the Town Council, pointed out that the cause of education in Crewe would lose valuable money every year on account of the railway company's refusal to allow four representatives of the County Council to sit on the council of the Mechanics' Institution.[1]

Crewe Town Council thereupon adopted the Act of 1889 and elected a Technical Instruction Committee in September, 1892, notable in that it was the first Corporation committee on which women served as co-opted members. The new committee immediately took over the Heath Street Hall science classes, established four continuation schools and a Women's Institute, and received the grant from the County Council. In addition, the committee built a Technical Institute and School of Art in Flag Lane, opened in 1897 ; besides drawing away a number of students from the Mechanics' Institution, this catered for some not provided for by the older body. It never succeeded in rivalling the Institution in the more advanced scientific courses, for the latter had the advantage of the works officials as teachers. In some respects the Technical Institute acted as a feeder to these classes.[2]

Webb and the Mechanics' Institution Council met the challenge by extending the Institution building (1902) and opening a new physical laboratory (1903), but the Board of Education remained dissatisfied with both the overlapping between the two bodies and the surprising lack of practical equipment at the

[1] There is no evidence to suggest that the temperance wing of the Crewe Liberal Party protested against what might seem to the strict teetotaller an indecent eagerness to obtain money from a tainted source.

[2] In 1903 the Technical Institute came under the control of the County Council's Higher Education sub-committee for the borough of Crewe ; Dr. Hodgson became first chairman of this successor to the defunct Technical Instruction Committee.

Institution.[1] On the other hand, George Whale, who had succeeded Webb as president of the Institution in 1903, openly criticised the theoretical and "unpractical" character of the instruction given at the Technical Institute. In 1906 the Board of Education's inspector, in the interests of co-ordination, suggested the setting up of a Joint Board of Studies, composed of representatives and teachers from both bodies, for the purpose of dividing the subjects to be taught at each school; all art, literary, commercial and pure science subjects were to be handed over to the Technical Institute, while the Mechanics' Institution was to confine itself solely to the teaching of practical subjects for engineers, builders, chemists and metallurgists.

Whale took offence at some of the inspector's remarks concerning "overlapping and wasteful competition, want of modern and better equipment, and more modern methods of instruction," and refused in 1907 to turn the Institution into a School of Practical Engineering or a "miniature edition of Crewe Works" at an estimated cost of £10,000. He imagined that the action of the Higher Education sub-committee in pressing for co-ordination was actuated by "some personal hostile influence at work behind the scenes," with a view to destroying the Institution, whereas by his uncompromising attitude he himself sealed its doom. If Whale and the L.N.W.R. directors had been deeply and genuinely interested in technical education, there is little doubt that the necessary money would have been forthcoming. In 1907 the Board of Education discontinued all subsidies to the Institution for literary, commercial, art and chemistry classes.[2] The Institution, with the support of the directors, continued these classes, but the Board of Education threatened to withhold the grants on the remaining classes if this went on. After submitting in 1910, the Council of the Institution decided to discontinue all classes whatsoever at the end of the session 1911–12, and to hand over this work completely to the Technical Institute. The new Chief Mechanical Engineer, C. J. Bowen Cooke, fifth president of the Mechanics' Institution,

[1] Dr. Hodgson had written of the Mechanics' Institution as early as 1891 : "I am perfectly amazed that so much has been done with so little" (*C.G.*, 14.3.91).

[2] The considerable sum of £470 had been received from this source in the year ending in July, 1907.

proved more conciliatory than Whale.   In his own words, he and the council had decided " that the educational work of the Mechanics' Institution should in future flow through the Board of Education's State-aided channels."   Most of the Institution's teachers accepted appointments in the Technical Institute, where adequate engineering laboratories were opened in 1915.   With the transfer of the library and newsroom to Crewe Corporation as a rate-aided Public Library on April 1, 1936, the last vestige of educational purpose vanished from the Institution which is now merely a body controlling the Town Hall and the affairs of a social club dating from 1913.[1]

[1] *C.G.*, 28.11.82, 9.1.86, 13.2.86, 17.12.87, 2 and 5.1.89, 21.9.89, 17.5.90 to 16.11.95, *passim*, 20.10.97, 22.2.99, 25.3.99, 9.2.01 to 1.8.03, *passim*, 21.2.06, to 26.2.08 (esp. Whale's speech in 29.5.07), 3.3.09, 2.3.10 to 2.12.13, *passim* ; *C.Ch.*, 7.3.91, 5.12.91, 25.2.93, 26.10.95 ; A.R.C.M.I., 1936 ; anon : *Description of the New Engineering Laboratories*, 1915, p. 3 ; G.P.C., 15.9.92, 13.9.94.

CHAPTER IX

THE CO-OPERATIVE MOVEMENT IN CREWE,
1845–1923

INVESTIGATION of the early history of the Crewe Co-operative Friendly Society is hampered by the lack of any record of the committee of management's proceedings from 1845 until 1856. The pioneers of Co-operation in Crewe appear to have discussed the formation of a society in March, 1845, but the final step was not taken until June, 1845, while the dating of the early quarterly reports places the actual commencement of business in the following October. The society's rules were certified under the Friendly Societies Acts of 1829 and 1834 on December 8, 1845, and it is therefore one of the oldest in the country. If we except educational work, the Crewe society has a history as remarkable in its early years as that of the Rochdale Pioneers, as it grew to maturity in a community which numbered less than 25,000 in 1881.[1]

The Crewe Co-operative Friendly Society did not spring up among depression-smitten workers as at Rochdale, but among fairly prosperous engineers and workers in wood and metal. The original rules of 1845, unlike those of the Pioneers, bear no trace of Owenite Socialism, and later accounts speak of the 24 founder-members of 1845, " who placed every penny they were worth in the Society," not in the hope of eventually founding a new Utopian community, but to solve an urgent practical problem. The society can boast as one of its founder-members the famous trade-union leader, William Allan.[2] Many

---

[1] In 1880 it could be said : " . . . there were two great things that really govern Crewe ; first, the great engineering works and second, the great Co-operative Society " (C.G., 14.1.80).

[2] William Allan (1813–74), first general secretary of the Amalgamated Society of Engineers from 1851 until his death, came to Crewe from Liverpool in 1843, when the Grand Junction Railway Company moved its workshops from Edgehill to the raw new colony at Crewe. At Crewe he became secretary to the local branch of the Journeyman Steam Engine Makers' Society, and remained in this post until he left Crewe in 1847 or 1848. His part in the events which led up to the formation of the Crewe Mechanics' Institution has been narrated above. He was said to be inclined to Owenism (S. and B. Webb : History of Trade Unionism, ed. 1920, p. 234 ; C.G., 26.7.73, 5.6.78, 30.1.20 ; Co-operative News, 17.1.80, p.2 ; White 1860, p. 346.)

of the early members came from Lancashire, and it would thus seem that the society was a product of the second wave of co-operative enthusiasm which swept through Scotland and the North of England in the early 1840's.

There exists some interesting evidence concerning the reasons which led the artisans of Crewe to establish a " general fund for purchasing the common necessaries, such as provisions and any commodities . . . required at the best advantage, the retailer's profits thereby being saved," to quote the original rules of 1845. Although the directors of the company had provided houses, schools, gas and water for their employees in the early days of the railway colony, they had not established " tommy shops " but had left the problem of food-supply to private enterprise, with the result that the population suffered for a short period. Under the local conditions of 1842–5 Crewe, the new " boom-town " of South Cheshire, became a by-word as being a place " where working men could not live on high wages without getting into debt." [1] Richard Whittle said in 1863 that the society was " formed chiefly to lower the cost of food, which was kept at monopolist prices by the usual traders " ; the food-supply of the town gave rise to difficulties even as late as 1848, when a number of workmen complained to the L.N.W.R. directors that " they could not buy their provisions economically." This led the company to cover in the market on the Square (1848–9), to supplement the combined shops and dwelling-houses which had been erected on Coppenhall Terrace.[2] More precise and picturesque details about the actual incident which brought this discontent to a head, and led to the foundation of a co-operative store, were provided in 1876 by one of the early members named Nield, who revealed that in 1845

" some butchers brought the carcase of a cow from Shavington, which if they had not killed it . . . would have died of itself and saved them the trouble . . . some of the young fellows of Crewe

---

[1] *The Co-operator*, June, 1863, p. 10. From this point the narrative is partially based on the minute books of the Committee of Management, 1856–80, to which detailed references are not given.

[2] L.N.W.B., Aug. 8, 1848 ; *cf.* Nathaniel Worsdell, speaking in 1863 : " . . . at that period [1845–8] the prices charged by the Crewe shop-keepers were very high, as there was a difficulty to get sufficient supplies for the population of the town " (*Cheshire Observer*, April 18, 1863).

seized the carcase, carried it up Mill Lane and kicked it into the brook. Then a meeting was held and it was proposed that they should bring their provisions from Liverpool. This was the origin of the Crewe Co-operative Society."

The whole business lends support to the view that the much-abused " tommy shop " might be a short-term economic necessity in a new or inaccessible industrial settlement.[1]

The Rules of 1845 contain a series of business-like arrangements for maintaining and running a provision store. Quarterly meetings of all shareholders elected a committee of management consisting of the chairman, secretary, treasurer and nine ordinary members, all elected for six months. A quarter of the committee retired in rotation every three months. The Rules of 1845 provided that the storekeeper should be elected by the shareholders, but this was altered in 1857. From 1847 until 1867 the shareholders' meetings took place in the Town Hall of the Mechanics' Institution. Richard Whittle, in his *Recollections of Events during my connection with the Society*, gives much interesting information about its early history. The first shop, rented from the railway company, was a small grocery store at 17 Earle Street, and for the first year it had " a steady increase in both business and members and made moderate profit . . . on the share capital, for the profits were then divided on the shares and not on purchases." Purchases could be made on credit up to 50 per cent. (from 1848 to 1853 up to 75 per cent.) of a member's share capital, but the shopmen interpreted this rule very generously, even after the tightening-up in 1894. Shares had to be made up to their full value at the end of the quarter, on pain of forfeiting the dividend. The credit system, which remained in force until 1918–19, in spite of various attempts to modify or

---

[1] *C.G.*, 30.9.76. In 1857 the L.N.W.R. directors granted formal exemption to the society's members from the penalties attached to regulations made by the former Grand Junction Board in Oct. 1843 with a view to preventing victimisation of their workmen by employee-shopkeepers, to the effect " That no officer, Agent or Foreman of this Company at Crewe shall be permitted to keep a shop or store, or be a party to or interested in, any such shop or store. . . . That this Board will give no encouragement to any of their workpeople to open shops and will consider their having done so no claim whatever for such persons to be retained in the service in the case of its becoming necessary to discharge any of their workmen " (G.J.B.M., Oct. 23, 1843 ; see also Exec. Ctee. L.N.W.B., Jan. 22, 1857).

abolish it, was originally adopted because the railway company, in the early days, paid its employees fortnightly instead of weekly.[1] While credit tied the members to the society at a time when loyalty and stability were most necessary, few regretted the ending of the system, with its attendant queues at the pawn-brokers and the County Court cases which it entailed four times a year. Dividend on share-capital remained in force until 1853, when a modified " Rochdale " system was adopted ; from this date share capital received 5 per cent interest [2] and the remainder of the distributable surplus was divided according to purchases. The Crewe system differed somewhat from the Rochdale plan in that the dividends were paid out quarterly in cash, and not automatically re-invested in member's share-capital, as at Roch-dale.[3] Each member had to hold at least five non-transferable £1 shares, but in 1863 the chairman admitted that evasion of both this rule and the law prohibiting sales to non-members took place on a large scale. At that time, out of a weekly turnover of between £700 and £800, not more than £1 was received by the society in actual cash :—

" . . . the usual practice of shareholders was to lend their shop-books to non-members, and with these books they got what they wanted and then settled with the shareholders as per agreement . . . in this way the shareholders derived a profit from the amount of goods entered in their books." [4]

The credit system certainly acted as a valuable advertisement and source of outside trade for the society.

During the local depression of 1848–51 the society found itself in trading difficulties and financial confusion. Dismissals from the works were reflected in heavy withdrawals of share-capital. A branch shop which had been opened had to be

[1] This would naturally constitute an additional incentive towards founding a co-operative grocery society.

[2] Reduced to $4\frac{1}{6}$ per cent. in 1885–6.

[3] Whittle : *op. cit.*, p. 3 ; White 1860, p. 346 ; Lucas : *History of the Crewe Co-operative Friendly Society, 1845–1929*, pp. 12, 80 ; see also report of con-ference at Crewe on " Ready money v. credit " in *Co-operative News*, July 27, 1878, pp. 483–4 ; C.G., 14.1.85 ; C.Ch., 17.9.92.

[4] *Cheshire Observer*, Nov. 28, 1863 ; see also strictures of Abel Heywood, the Radical publisher of Manchester, on credit and the Crewe society (*Co-operator*, April, 1863, p. 182).

closed down, members and business fell off, disagreements occurred among those who remained and the £1 shares, up to 1853 the basis on which the profits were shared out, fell in value to between 8*s.* and 10*s.* James Ainscow, secretary from about 1849 to 1852, and a few others, refused to desert the society. Whittle tells us :—" The Fixed Stock, which was a very heavy one, they greatly reduced, and the value of the shares were [*sic*] gradually increased, until the time I became a member [January, 1851] the shares had got back to their old value of one pound per share." [1] The depression reached its lowest depth in 1850, and by 1852 membership had risen from less than 70 to 112, and sales from £2,000 to nearly £3,800 per annum. About 1849 the society had made a start in the bread-baking line, but after a few years this first attempt at co-operative production was abandoned and the committee contracted with a private baker for a supply.[2]

A most important change occurred in the management of the society in October, 1852, when Richard Whittle (1821–86) was appointed secretary at £6 10*s.* per annum. This remarkable man, who rose from the smithy to the directors' Board of the C.W.S. (1877–86), and was twice mayor of Crewe, came from Ashton-in-Makerfield and was descended from good land-owning yeoman stock. When Whittle migrated to Crewe, in 1850, he came to wield the sledgehammer in Crewe works as a blacksmith's striker. Within a month of joining the society the members elected him to the Committee of Management, and he has left us a vivid picture of co-operative organisation in the 1850's :—

" To be a member of the committee in those days meant really to be a voluntary warehouseman, nothing was too rough or too dirty for a member of the committee to do. Going out in the evenings to buy fat pigs, hoisting up flour and hanging up bacon, were some of their chief duties, not to say anything of taking stock every six months,

---

[1] Whittle : *op. cit.*, p. 3 ; Ann. Rep. C.C.F.S., 1849–50 ; *Christian Socialist*, Nov. 29, 1851, p. 344. See also the details *re* the Crewe Committee of the U.K. Society of Coachmakers in 1848, set up to collect information at Crewe concerning " co-operative coachmaking " (Nicholson : *A hundred years of Vehicle Building, 1834–1934*, pp. 39, 41, 50).

[2] *Journal of Association*, May 10, 1852, p. 156, May 31, 1852, p. 179 ; Crewe Ctee. L.N.W.B., April 24, 1849 ; Ann. Rep. C.C.F.S., 1852–3.

when the store rooms were so awkward and inconvenient that it used to take us from shop closing time at night until just about four o'clock next morning, when we had just time to get ready to go into the works." [1]

Whittle's appointment as secretary coincided with a rapid increase in membership, purchases and profits, due partly to the work of Ainscow, partly to the rising tide of economic prosperity in the 1850's and 1860's, and partly to the abilities of Whittle, who was a skilful publicity agent as well as a business man. Endowed with an iron will and great determination, he possessed the art of managing a committee and was not afraid of admitting it :—

" It had been sometimes the tendency to elect for the committee those who were dissatisfied with the policy being pursued. . . . He had seen instances often of committees, like March, coming in like a lion, and going out like a lamb. They were sometimes like lions, ready to devour him. There was something wrong, they said, and they would find it out ; but after a month or two, they had been his fastest friends. . . ." [2]

The society had employed a storekeeper from the beginning. To cope with the rapid expansion of the late 1850's, a superintendent was appointed in 1857 at 28s. a week to purchase and check goods, and also to exercise control over the salesmen and cashier. After two years' trial the committee decided to abolish the post and appoint Whittle as secretary-manager. He thereupon left the works and held these two positions until his death in 1886. An active Radical politician, Whittle was elected to the Local Board in 1872. The reason he gave for the movement's entry into local politics is interesting :—" . . . it was, rightly or wrongly, due to the opinion of their committee that the Local Board committee were throwing obstacles in the way of co-operative members' plans being passed." [3]

The leading offices in the society have usually been held by men prominent in the town's trade union and friendly-society movements, whatever their politics. A surprising number of the men who suffered during the Intimidation affair rose to promi-

[1] Whittle : *op. cit.*, pp. 3–4 ; Hampson : *The Whittles of Horwich*, pp. 25–7 ; C.G., 27.10.77 ; Redfern : *Story of the C.W.S.*, p. 393. Whittle was also a farmer in Church Coppenhall.

[2] *Co-operator*, Feb. 22, 1868, pp. 116–17.   [3] C.G., 24.4.80.

nent posts in it,[1] and it is probable that during the period under review the Liberals and non-political trade unionists possessed a constant majority on the committee of management.

By the end of 1859 the number of members had risen to almost 500 and the sales to nearly £400 per week. This passion for co-operative trading brought into existence the Crewe Working Man's Industrial and Provident Society, founded by the Crewe Working Men's Mutual Loan Society. The Loan Society, which dated from 1859, discovered in 1860 that it possessed surplus capital, and so decided to combine co-operation with money lending. The new society, which carried on business in " food, firing, clothes and other necessaries," registered itself under the Industrial and Provident Societies Act on August 7, 1860, and, as its watchword became " Down with the old Stores," the society of 1845, at first conciliatory, was forced to fight for its existence in " the battle of the dividends." These rose rapidly from 1s. 6d. to 2s. ; but, as Whittle triumphantly recorded, " that was the end, the battle was an unequal one. We had merely to arrange prices, and give any dividend that was required. They had neither standing, capital or business in proportion to ours, therefore they were defeated." [2] In June, 1862, the vanquished organisation was treating for amalgamation with the older society, but the latter refused to entertain the idea and left its rival to expire in the following year.[3]

The phenomenal growth of the town between 1861 and 1881 not only added to the strength of the society of 1845 but gave rise to a crop of smaller co-operatives " . . . from the revival of the old system . . . of selling as near cost as possible . . . No paid servants except the officers, and their places of business being open so many nights in the week and selling goods in certain quantities." [4]

---

[1] Frederick Munroe, vice-chairman 1878–80, chairman 1883 ; Thomas Darling; vice-chairman 1889, chairman 1894 ; John Shone, chairman 1889–90 ; William Urquhart, vice-chairman 1890, chairman 1891–3 (Lucas : op. cit., p. 99). [2] Whittle : op. cit., p. 8.
[3] E.A. 75, p. 90 ; Rules of Crewe W.M.I. and P. Soc., 1860, 1862 (in Registry of Friendly Societies, London) ; Return of Ind. and Prov. Socs., 1872, p. 62 ; Cheshire Observer, Nov. 29, 1862, May 9, 16, and 30, 1863.
[4] Whittle : op. cit., p. 13. The Cobden Society's stores, for example, " were only open one or two nights each week, and on Saturday from twelve until three o'clock " (C.G., 6.12.79).

No less than five of these societies have been traced[1]—the Friends of Industry Unity (1869), the Albert Co-operative Society (1871), the Cobden Industrial Co-operative Society (1870), the Stanley Supply Association (1873), the Second Monks Coppenhall Co-operative Society (1873). Of these, the Friends of Industry Unity, or " Labour Loan " as it was nicknamed from the fact that members acted as shopmen, was the most important, while little is known concerning the last two societies on the list. In the mid-1880's the " Labour Loan " had 133 members, the Albert 66, the Cobden 45. Their share capital rarely averaged £2 per member and even in their best years the amount of trade per member fell much below that of the Crewe Co-operative Friendly Society. Drapery, ironmongery and furniture were handled as well as groceries, or members could obtain these or other lines through private traders holding an agency from their society.[2]

The relations between these new societies were by no means cordial at first. Whittle and his committee feared a renewal of the troubles of 1860–2 and in 1871 held a long conversation " on the decrease in the Society's business and also on so many withdrawals taking place." [3] The competition proved beneficial in the long run; it led to an overhaul of the price list, and after the boom year of 1873 the older society felt safer; its membership now approached 1,200, while the combined membership of its three strongest rivals amounted to just over 400. Its sales were four times as great. In 1871 Lloyd Jones, one of Robert Owen's social missionaries, visited Crewe to lecture on co-operation for the benefit of the new societies, but he soon revealed his preference for the system followed by the Co-operative Friendly Society, and told his patrons " they were scarce fit to be called co-operators." [4] Relations became strained in 1876 owing to some laudatory remarks concerning the Albert which appeared

---

[1] The dates indicate the earliest recorded trace of each society.

[2] *Return of Ind. and Prov. Socs.*, 1870, pp. 2–3, 69; 1872, pp. 2–3; 1873, pp. 2–3; 1874, pp. 2–5; 1875, pp. 4–5; *Report of Co-operative Congress*, 1876, p. 78; 1877, p. 94; 1878, p. 74; C.W.S. *Annual*, 1886, p. 379; Rules of first four societies in Registry of Friendly Societies, London; *E.A.* 73, p. 78; *C.Ch.*, 8.4.76.

[3] C.C.F.S. yearly sales for 1869–73, a period of rising prices, were £45,604, £43,639, £43,863, £46,695, £61,153.

[4] Whittle: *op. cit.*, p. 13; *C.G.*, 1.4.76; Lucas: *op. cit.*, p. 25.

in the *Chronicle*.   Skeldon of the Friendly replied, pointing out that the company's servants were not supposed to engage directly in trade, and enquired whether the grant of the nine-hour day was intended to be used for such activities.   Two years later the Friendly invited the Albert, the Cobden and the " Labour Loan " to an important conference on " cash v. credit " ; two of them sent delegates and P. V. O'Connor, secretary to the Albert, wrote a letter of thanks, " stating that if there had ever been a bad feeling between us, it had now gone, and he hoped for ever." [1] The Albert Society, with a turnover reduced to little more than a £1,000 per annum, ceased business in 1889.   The Cobden struggled on until 1890, and the Friends of Industry Unity came to an end in 1891. [2]

The later 1850's saw a remarkable expansion in the activities of the society of 1845.   After putting up with a good deal of bad bread and inconvenience, the members empowered the committee to erect a bakery behind the Earle Street shop, completed in 1857.   This was the first venture into production since the early bakery, and proved very successful, although the premises had to be abandoned after ten years. [3]   Pork butchery is one of the society's oldest activities, but the beef and mutton trade was not taken up until 1858, and then only to the extent of buying carcases from private butchers.   Then in 1860 the committee built its own slaughter-house, but the profits of the butchery department were disappointing, and not until the late

---

[1] *C.Ch.*, 1 and 8.4.76, 15.4.76 ; *Co-operative News,* July 27, 1878, pp. 483–4 ; during the controversy of 1876, an anonymous controversalist summed up the small societies as follows :—" Nearly all their officers are the leading trade unionists of the town, and . . . are ' knob-sticking ' grocers, drapers, ironmongers, furniture brokers, etc., by working four or five nights a week until ten and eleven o'clock at these so-called co-operative stores."

[2] Miscellaneous rule-books of, and correspondence concerning the liquidation of the Albert, Cobden and Friends of Industry Societies in Registry of Friendly Societies, London ; *London Gazette,* Feb. 3, 1891, p. 636.

[3] Whittle : *op. cit.,* pp. 5–6.   Baking was done at the new central premises from 1867 until 1878, when a large steam bakery came into production. Whittle said in 1882 that many of the members who previously baked their own bread had ceased doing so, with a consequent doubling of the bread trade. The present bakery dates from 1916.   Since the amalgamation of 1896 the society has possessed a smaller bakery at Nantwich (*Co-operative News,* 25.2.82, p. 128 ; 16.3.84, p. 221 ; *C.G.,* 24.11.96, 17.7.97, 24 and 31.3.16, 4.4.16).

1870's could it be considered satisfactory. Tinned beef and mutton made their first appearance in 1869 ; American fresh meat gave a great deal of dissatisfaction from 1877 until refrigerating plant could be installed. New Zealand mutton appeared on the counter for the first time in 1884.[1]

Another line dating from the 1850's is the coal trade. Its history has been uneventful, if we except the period of coal shortage in 1873, when frantic efforts were made to secure adequate supplies for the society's customers, and serious attention to sales development is observable for the first time. In 1873 the society leased a coal wharf, and the value of coal sold in the last quarter of that year was seven times that of the corresponding period of 1872. In 1861 boots and shoes were retailed for the first time, a development quickly followed by the first shoe-repairing workshop. The sale of drapery by the society dates from the same year, while bespoke tailoring commenced in 1862. Ready-made clothing could not be obtained directly from the " Stores " until 1876.[2]

The cataloguing of fresh advances tends to exaggerate the ease with which the system worked and minimises the practical difficulties encountered. Mistakes occurred in other departments beside the butchery. Injudicious purchases of furniture, the sale of which commenced in 1868, led to an enquiry and a permanent Furniture Club.[3] The " club " method of purchase, the parent of " hire purchase " (only introduced into the society's business in 1910) was very popular in nineteenth-century Crewe. In 1873 the *Crewe Guardian* commented :—" As is well-known in Crewe, most of the business is done by clubs. For instance, if a man requires a new suit of clothes, he pays so much a week and joins a clothing club." The article was not delivered to the purchaser until all payments had been made. The same procedure applied to boots, watches, and even portrait-paintings, for which there existed a considerable demand among the workmen of Crewe before the popularisation of cheap photography

---

[1] Whittle : *op. cit.*, p. 7 ; Ann. Rep. C.C.F.S., 1849–50 ; Lucas : *op. cit.*, pp. 37–8, 56.

[2] Whittle : *op. cit.*, pp. 6, 8–9, 14 ; Lucas : *op. cit.*, p. 39.

[3] Whittle : *op. cit.*, p. 20. The committee hoped eventually to manufacture all the furniture required, in a joiner's shop and cabinet department opened in 1891, but the plan proved impracticable (Lucas : *op. cit.*, pp. 42, 55–6).

in the late 1870's. The society's first clothing club opened in 1868, so that local co-operative enterprise cannot be charged with lack of initiative.[1]

Evidence of a rapidly-rising standard of life among the population of Crewe, after the industrial boom of the early 1870's, is provided by a series of agencies distributed to private traders in what were then for the most part luxury goods. The first consisted of an arrangement whereby members could obtain hats and caps from four Crewe outfitters, who paid 15 per cent. of the receipts to the society. This method was then applied to ready-made clothing (1873), jewellery (1873), pianos (1874), photography (1878), and even penny-farthing bicycles (1878). By this system the society obtained for its members the benefit of the dividend without incurring a risk, until the demand for an article rendered it safe to venture into direct trading ; *e.g.* the society opened its own jewellery department in 1885, and the agencies lapsed one by one. Well might Whittle boast in 1877 :—" When I came amongst you grocery was our only business, but now I don't know a single necessity and very few luxuries that you cannot purchase from us. In proportion to our population it is the most co-operative town in the world." [2]

The question of engaging a "co-op doctor" occupied the members during 1869, but a dispute as to whether this scheme should be voluntary or compulsory in character killed an interesting project of health insurance. The society arranged in 1883 for a Crewe dentist to do anything the members might require in connection with their teeth.[3] An optician's sight-testing room was installed on the society's premises in 1914. Services of a rather different kind, which have been inaugurated at various times, include a highly successful Penny Bank (1878), the transaction of business for the Co-operative Insurance Society (1880) and a members' collective life assurance scheme, with benefits according to purchases (1921). The most significant advance for many years was made in 1922, when the society began a

[1] *C.G.*, 26.7.73 (*cf. Cheshire Observer*, March 29, April 12, July 12, 1862—watches sold by private traders, on the instalment system) ; Whittle : *op. cit.*, pp. 11, 20 ; Lucas : *op. cit.*, p. 39.
[2] *Co-operative News*, Oct. 27, 1877, p. 563 ; Lucas : *op. cit.*, p. 38 ; Whittle : *op. cit.*, p. 20.
[3] This service has since been discontinued.

retail trade in milk. Within a few months 13 per cent. of the membership took the whole or part of its daily supply from the society.[1]

The fate of the branch shop opened in the 1840's deterred the members from further experiments in this direction for many years, and the committee of management confined itself to renting four shops adjacent to the original one at No. 17 Earle Street (1856–62). Under the stimulus provided by the establishment of the steelworks, Crewe developed rapidly in the mid-1860's, and none but the staunchest co-operators could be expected to walk miles every time they needed to make a purchase. Accordingly, in 1865 the members decided to establish No. 1 branch in the Mill Street area. The western portion of the township could not be permanently neglected, and in 1866 No. 2 branch opened in West Street. This heralded a period of active building, for in the latter year the railway company gave the society notice to quit its range of shops in Earle Street to make way for an extension to the Town Hall. The society erected new central shops and offices in Market Street, to which the transfer of business took place in December, 1867. Further pieces of land in the neighbourhood were purchased, and the committee developed the site by building cottages, productive plants, and new shops on it. A much-needed Co-operative Hall was opened here in 1900. Besides being used for political and co-operative purposes, this has been leased out as a cinema since 1910.[2]

After the success of the first branches, the society became less chary of extending its trade in this fashion, and by the end of 1924, 26 branches had been established. These were not confined to Crewe. The first venture into the semi-rural districts round Crewe was the Church Coppenhall branch at Cross Green, opened in 1878 after a petition from the inhabitants. The establishment of branches in Willaston, Haslington and Shavington followed between 1881 and 1890, while 1896 saw the absorption of the Nantwich Industrial Co-operative Society,

---

[1] Lucas : *op. cit.*, pp. 34, 35, 36 ; C.G., 13.10.22. The first of the " Shopping Weeks " was held in 1922, after the post-war collapse of sales in 1921.
[2] *Co-operator*, Sept., 1862, p. 74 ; June, 1863, p. 10 ; Feb. 22, 1868, pp. 116–17 ; Whittle : *op. cit.*, pp. 7, 10–12, 13 ; Lucas : *op. cit.*, pp. 22, 32, 36, 51–2, 98 ; C.G., 31.1.00, 7.2.00 ; Works Ctee., 10.4.06 ; G.P.C., 15.3.10.

a concern which had struggled through many vicissitudes since its foundation in 1875. The superior resources of the Crewe society, both in business ability and propaganda, resulted in an immediate increase of co-operative trade and membership at Nantwich. Between 1896 and 1914 there was a lull in extension outside Crewe. In the course of 1914, however, branches at Bunbury and Audlem commenced business, followed by successful ventures at Tarporley and Betley (1916) and Wrenbury (1921). The society now operated over a wide area in south and mid-Cheshire, although the members vetoed in 1924 a proposal to absorb the semi-bankrupt Whitchurch Co-operative Provident Society. These later extensions have been made possible by the advent of the motor-van, of which the society purchased its first in 1914; by 1929 it possessed a fleet numbering 17.[1]

A close connection has always existed between the degree of activity in the works and the fortunes of the society. Membership rose rapidly to nearly 500 in 1859, when it received a temporary check on account of the removal of the coach-making department.[2] The blow did not prove irreparable, and the society passed the 1,000-member mark in the boom year of 1873, to reach 2,000 only five years later. Over 500 new members enrolled themselves in the one year 1889, partly on account of the share-out of money from the liquidated Pension Fund. Whittle's guiding hand had been removed by his death in 1886, and the severe depression of 1893–5 showed up the weak spots in the society's management. Share capital dwindled, and the sales, which had totalled £225,000 in 1892, fell continuously to their lowest point—£178,000 in 1895. The society also suffered serious competition from a private grocer named E. R. Hill, who built up a chain of eighteen shops in Crewe and district during the last fifteen years of the century. Whittle's successor as secretary-manager resigned in 1894 after disagreements with

[1] Lucas: *op. cit.*, pp. 32–3, 47, 62, 66, 83–4, 98 ; Rules of Nantwich I.C. Soc. (1875) ; *C.G.*, 19.4.79, 23.4.81, 8.1.83, 19.4.90, 25.2.91, 4 and 7.3.91, 20.6.91, 23.1.92, 2.4.92, 24.11.96, 17.7.97, 30.3.04, 4.9.14. Sandbach and Winsford possess their own co-operative societies, both dating from 1860, and these have proved strong enough to resist the attractive power of Crewe (*C.G.*, 24.1.03, 1.7.10).

[2] Whittle wrote of this incident : " . . . our largest purchasers and most active members at that time belonged to the coaching department " (*op. cit.*, p. 8).

the committee. Simultaneously the dividend fell catastrophically from 3s. in the pound (1886–94) to 2s. 4d. in the pound for 1894.[1]

A party of reformers, led by William Horabin, secured election to the committee of management (1894), and when the depression lifted a new spirit of efficiency and progress could be observed, due in great measure to the energy of Miles Parkes, chairman from 1896 to 1908, who provided the C.W.S. with its second Crewe director (1907–1919). A scheme of re-development at the central premises, initiated in 1898, was completed in 1916 with the opening of the new bakery. Competition from E. R. Hill diminished when his concern came to grief at the turn of the century. Co-operative membership reached 10,000 in 1905 and 15,000 twenty years later, although this had been accompanied by a decline in the strength of co-operative loyalty. Sales per head per annum decreased from £55 in 1877–8 (when the corresponding figure for the Rochdale Pioneers was only £45) to £34 in 1905. In 1923, with a higher price-level, sales amounted to only £40 per head.[2]

The first World War, with its restrictions on the supply of commodities, brought a number of fresh problems, with some of which the society was in a better position to cope than the one-man business. It secured a representative on the Crewe Food Control Committee, and the predominant position which co-operation gained in the retail trade of the district between 1914 and 1918 can be judged from the fact that in 1917 64 per cent. of Crewe's population registered with the society in connection with sugar-rationing. A summary of the difficulties experienced by 1918 ran as follows :—" There was a difficulty in distribution on account of the shortage of petrol . . . 220 hands had joined the Colours, and their places had had to be taken by girls.[3]

In its early years the society suffered from a chronic shortage of capital, due partly to the credit system and partly to the custom of paying out dividends in cash. In the early 1860's, Whittle, who often held views on financial matters far in advance

[1] Since 1894 the society's accounts have been audited by qualified chartered accountants.

[2] Works Ctee., 10.11.97 ; *C.G.*, 4.4.16 ; *Co-operative News*, July 27, 1878, pp. 483–4. The high figure of sales per head in 1878 was attributed to the large number of Crewe people who took in lodgers.

[3] *C.G.*, 7.5.18 ; Lucas : *op. cit.*, pp. 63–71 ; *C.G.*, 21.9.17, 5.10.17 ; G.P.C., 14.8.17, Coun., 5.9.17.

of those prevailing among the membership, publicly deplored the reduction in working capital by two-thirds which resulted from the practice of allowing a member to obtain goods on the security of his or her share-capital. He also deplored the quarterly division of the trading surplus among the members, when it might have been left to fructify in the hands of the Committee of Management by judicious investment in a corn mill, a cotton mill, or in " no less than from 200 to 250 cottages, which property could have been so arranged that it would have given the franchise to as many members." [1]

After 1865 the situation became somewhat easier ; the shops and cottages erected between that year and 1874 were financed by mortgaging property already owned, but the rate at which the society tied up money in bricks and mortar led it to the brink of disaster in 1870, when a run of capital withdrawals took place. The last of these mortgages was paid off in 1878, and from that time the capital problem became the opposite one of how to put rapidly accumulating funds to a sufficiently profitable use. The society has lent money on the security of houses and land since 1885, but not until 1897 did it adopt the building society clauses of the Industrial and Provident Societies Act, in an effort to employ more of its surplus cash. The society now owns a considerable amount of cottage property in the district, as well as two farms with an area of over 300 acres, purchased in 1918, but the problem of profitable investment still exists. The credit system of trading received its death blow in 1918, when a special committee of enquiry recommended its abolition. The shareholders accepted this overdue reform, which came into full operation the following year ; from that date ordinary dealings have been on a cash basis. [2]

After the *Christian Socialist* ceased publication in 1852 the society lost touch for a time with the co-operative movement in other districts, but a noticeable increase in contacts with other societies occurred in the 1860's. A Crewe delegate was sent to a

[1] *Co-operator*, Sept., 1862, p. 74 ; June, 1863, p. 10. During 1863–5 a mismanaged attempt to build a corn mill nearly split the society, but fortunately its capital remained available for the branch expansions of the 1860's and 1870's.

[2] Lucas : *op. cit.*, pp. 34, 38, 48, 67–8 ; *Co-operative News*, Oct. 27, 1877, p. 563 ; C.G., 14.1.85, 17.6.10, 2.8.18 ; Whittle : *op. cit.*, pp. 9, 10, 13–14.

co-operative conference at Oldham in 1861, and in 1862 the committee ordered 50 copies of the *Co-operator*, a monthly record of the movement, established by Henry Pitman in 1860. This publication remained the sole national publicity organ of the movement until it was superseded by the *Co-operative News* in 1871, and it contains several important documents dealing with the Crewe society. The first of many co-operative conferences to be held in the town assembled in 1863, when several of the neighbouring societies sent delegates.[1]

Crewe's relations with the North of England Co-operative Wholesale Society, founded in 1863, were confined to occasional purchases until 1873, when the society took up shares in it, and henceforth sent representatives to the Wholesale's quarterly meetings. The society of 1845 was not represented at the Co-operative Congress until 1880, when Whittle attended as a delegate from the Wholesale, whereas two of the smaller Crewe societies had been members of the Co-operative Union since 1871–2, and the Albert actually sent a delegate to the Congress three years before the Friendly.[2]

Whittle was extremely interested in the various experiments in co-operative production or " self-governing workshops " established in the course of the nineteenth century, often with unfortunate results. In 1880 he admitted that he had risked some of his private fortune in these ventures, and the entire trade of the Crewe Co-operative Friendly Society in certain lines of goods was carried on in the products of the self-governing workshops. For example, the Crewe society was one of the first to invest in the ill-fated Lancashire and Yorkshire Flannel Manufacturing Society of Littleborough (1872), and all flannels purchased by its members came from this concern. In pursuance of this policy, Whittle's consideration was not always that of buying in the cheapest market. In the mid-1880's the society of 1845 was buying goods to the annual value of £10,000 direct from self-governing workshops, while the figure of its purchases from the C.W.S. for the same period fluctuated between £30,000 and £40,000. The proportion of purely co-operative buying

[1] *Co-operator*, June, 1863, p. 10.
[2] Whittle : *op. cit.*, p. 14 ; P. Redfern : *Story of the C.W.S.* (1913), p. 25 *sqq.* ; *Co-operative News*, 1880, p. 373 ; *Report of Co-operative Congress*, 1872, p. 124, 1878, p. viii, 1881, p. xi.

to total sales for these two years was about 40 per cent., a considerable practical contribution to the establishment of the Co-operative Commonwealth. The figure has been considerably increased since that period.[1]

Attacks on the society for an alleged tendency to monopolise the trade of the town have been made from time to time, and in 1894 it was estimated that about three-quarters of Crewe's retail trade passed through the society's hands ; whatever the exact proportion, it has certainly decreased since the abolition of credit trading and the penetration of Crewe by multiple firms in the period between the World Wars.[2] In 1902 the society guaranteed £500 towards the Co-operative Union's defence fund to combat attacks from private traders, and when, in 1917, the Swansea Co-operative Congress decided to form the Co-operative Party, Crewe voted £2 per 1,000 members to its Parliamentary Representation Fund. During the " khaki election " of 1918 the society addressed a list of questions to both candidates, embodying an advanced programme of nationalisation and egalitarian social reform. Brownlie, the Labour candidate, gave it his unreserved support, but Sir Joseph Davies, the Coalition Liberal, while accepting most of it, made important reservations. Being a coalowner, he could hardly be expected to support nationalisation of the coalmines.[3]

The society's educational efforts in the early period of its history leave much to be desired. Small donations to the Crewe Mechanics' Institution were excusable when every pound was needed for capital development, but even these ceased after 1862. The backwardness of such a rich society in the field of education gave rise to complaints from co-operators in other towns, and for their benefit Michael Reilly (chairman, 1875–82) explained that the existence of the Crewe Mechanics' Institution relieved the local co-operators from the necessity of efforts in the same direction. A newsroom established in 1868 at the central premises had to make way for a furniture shop four years later,

[1] *Co-operative News*, Jan. 17, 1880, p. 42 ; April 11, 1885, p. 317 ; Jan. 23, 1886, p. 81 ; Redfern : *op. cit.*, pp. 99, 270–1.

[2] *C.G.*, 23.10.75, 12.5.94, 3.11.06, 6.10.09. T. E. Gibson said in 1877 : " Were it not for the Co-operative Stores, he did not know of another town in England where the trading community would be more likely to prosper " (*C.G.*, 30.10.77).

[3] *C.G.*, 13.12.18 ; Lucas : *op. cit.*, pp. 54, 68–9.

and the members remained notoriously indifferent to the charms of the gospel of mutual aid as propounded by the *Co-operative News*, even when it was sold at $\frac{1}{2}d.$ per copy.

The position improved after 1887, when the society resumed its annual donation to the Mechanics' Institution and gave a similar one to the Heath Street Hall science classes, although no co-operative subjects were taught there. In 1896 twenty free places in the courses at the Borough Technical Institute were offered to the sons and daughters of members, and when the Crewe Secondary School was opened, in 1902, the society endowed two free places for the first three years. Nothing of a systematic or co-operative character was attempted until in 1903 some of the more ardent women co-operators formed the first Crewe branch of the Women's Guild. Even this collapsed after nine years of existence.[1]

It is typical of Crewe that the first regular classes organised by the society were of a strictly practical character—on salesmanship (1912, 1916), apprenticeship and book-keeping (1916). The special committee of enquiry (1917–18) which recommended the abolition of the credit system also advocated the development of education in co-operative principles, and as a result the first Crewe Co-operative Education Committee came into existence in 1919, supported by grants from a fund created by appropriating £1 out of every £800 net profit made by the society ; the society now possessed an adequate instrument for spreading the theory and practice of co-operation among members, employees and their children. Much stress has been laid on social events, not strictly educational in character, but the members of the Educational Committee were able in their first year's report to point to the fact that in all " the places they had visited during the winter there had been an increase in trade." [2]

The labour problem first arose soon after the society began employing more than one storekeeper ; in the late 1850's complaints of irregularity and drunkenness among the shopmen were frequent, and numerous dismissals took place. A code of regulations for the government of shop and salesmen promul-

[1] *Co-operative News*, Jan. 17, 1880, p. 42 ; *C.G.*, 14.7.77, 14.1.80, 6.10.86. 14.7.88, 2.3.89, 12.9.96, 6.9.02, 6.1.04, 3.2.06 ; *C.Ch.*, 19.1.89, 2.2.89, 9.2.89, 26.9.96 ; Lucas : *op. cit.*, pp. 39, 58 ; A.R.C.M.I., 1849 ; E.A. 12, p. 183,
[2] Lucas : *op. cit.*, pp. 89–93 ; *C.G.*, 13.1.20, 27.2.20, 20.8.20.

gated in 1856 fixed the hours of work at 72½, a not unreasonable figure for the time. This had been reduced to 69 by 1861, when the first recorded early-closing movement in Crewe occurred. In that year the drapers of the town " agreed to close their shops four nights in the week " ; but not until 1871 do we find a general movement to close on one afternoon per week. It began among those tradesmen who sold clothing, and by October, 1871, had spread to all classes of shopkeepers. A well-attended meeting in that month elected a committee to enforce, as far as possible, early closing on Thursday afternoons. James Briggs, clothier and pawnbroker, describing the over-work in retail shopkeeping, said :—" They must have their assistants behind the counter, or be behind themselves, and that way they were working twelve hours a day in the week and on Fridays and Saturdays . . . 14 or 15 hours." [1]

Whittle, representing the Crewe Co-operative Friendly Society, which introduced the 58-hour week into its shops the following year, thought that the meeting's proposals did not go far enough. The society had already begun to close its shops on Saturday afternoons. The general half-day closing movement collapsed after less than a year's trial, chiefly on account of " the petty meanness and little-mindedness of a few . . . shopkeepers in trying to overthrow it," and an attempt by Wilmot Eardley and J. Blackhurst to revive it in 1877, during the summer months, had a purely transitory effect. Only compulsory State legislation would induce the anti-social small shopkeeper to forgo a chance of stealing the trade of his early-closing rivals. Even State legislation on this subject was apt to be laxly administered by a Town Council which depended to a large extent on the shopkeeper vote.[2] The Crewe Tradesmen's Association and the Early Closing Association of shop assistants, founded in 1891 and 1898 respectively, were but the last and most nearly successful of these spasmodic attempts to make early closing on one day a week a general social habit. By the 1890's the better

---

[1] *C.G.*, 28.10.71 ; see also *C.G.*, 8.7.71 and *Cheshire Observer*, Sept. 14, 1861 ; April 18, 1863. The employees of the Co-operative Society obtained a 48-hour week in 1919 (40 in the offices) by a regional agreement between the A.U.C.E. and the societies in the district (*C.G.*, 22 and 26.8.19).

[2] Although it merely fixed a maximum of 74 hours' work per week, the Shops Act of 1892 remained a dead letter in the borough.

class of shops closed regularly on Wednesday afternoons, but the Tradesmen's Association admitted in 1909 that it would be useless for the Town Council to go further and enforce the Shop Hours' Act of 1904, " owing to the fact that there were so many small shopkeepers who did not even recognise the weekly holiday." Even after the passing of the Shops Act of 1912 Crewe Town Council, torn between conflicting interests, did not make an early closing order for the borough, even though it was backed by an energetic branch of the Shop Assistants' Union, founded in 1901. The matter remained in a very unsatisfactory state until a war-time Government order imposed uniform hours of closing in 1916.[1]

The early difficulties experienced by the Crewe Co-operative Friendly Society in recruiting suitable shopmen were lessened between 1862 and 1877 by the gradual elaboration of a system of apprenticeship and the fixing of a maximum standard wage-rate of 24s. in 1859. This was increased to 25s. in the 1880's, and remained around this level until the outbreak of the first World War.[2] The number of persons employed by the society numbered about 20 in 1867 ; by 1901 it had risen to the neighbourhood of 400 and in 1929 was 619, of whom 394 were classed as " distributive," and 225 as " productive." Those employed in the bakery, shoemaking and tailoring departments naturally presented special wage-problems, since they were for the most part skilled craftsmen connected with trade unions, and could claim a higher wage than the man behind the counter. Later, the claim of the Amalgamated Union of Co-operative Employees to negotiate for all grades and occupations in the movement simplified the task of the management in dealing with such matters, a fact not at first realised. The Crewe branch of this trade union dates from the very foundation of the A.U.C.E. itself—1891, but even in 1897 it contained only 32 members.

---

[1] *C.G.*, 4.11.71, 16.12.71, 6 and 13.1.72, 24.2.72, 3.3.77 to 29.9.77, *passim*, 29.6.78, 26.4.79, 29.5.80 to 18.9.80, *passim*, 22.4.82, 5.1.84 to 26.1.84, 22.3.90 to 19.4.90, 11.4.91, 9.5.91, 13.6.91, 20.6.94, 8.9.94, 10.10.94, 21.9.98, 23.7.98, 1899, *passim* ; 5.4.12 to 8.12.16, *passim*, 8.6.23 ; *C.Ch.*, 2 and 9.1.97, 23.1.97 ; Health Ctee., 13.9.94, 10.2.15, 12.5.21, 14.9.22 ; G.P.C., 14.1.09, 16.4.12, 20.3.17, 14.12.20 ; Corporation proceedings, 1912 to 1915, *passim* ; Whittle : *op. cit.*, pp. 13–14.

[2] Head salesmen in charge of departments received commission on sales up to 1889, when a fixed weekly wage was substituted.

Membership increased considerably during the first World War and in the immediate post-war years, when the question of wage increases demanded continual discussion and negotiation. An impending strike and lock-out of the society's employees in August, 1919, arising out of a dispute between the A.U.C.E. and the society, led to a general settlement which secured a minimum of 60s. for adult male shopmen (instead of 46s. at 21, rising to a maximum of 52s. at 27). The special committee of enquiry of 1917–18 reported in favour of employees being represented as such on the committee of management, but this was not granted within the period under review. Instead, employees made use of their rights as members under the society's rules. On the growth of the influence of employees in the conduct of the society, S. and B. Webb comment as follows :—

" The eligibility of employees for election to the committee of management is less widely accepted [than their eligibility to vote as shareholders] and may be more open to question. A few societies (like the Crewe Co-operative Friendly Society, Limited) have never had any disqualifying rule, though members who were also employees were not often nominated. They are now (1921) beginning to be nominated and elected—the Crewe Society had its first employee member in 1918 and its second in 1920." [1]

---

[1] *The Consumers' Co-operative Movement* (1921), pp. 40–1 ; *C.G.*, 16.4.15, 26.8.19, 29.6.23 ; *C.Ch.*, 19.1.89, 2.2.89, 9.2.89, 14.3.91 ; Lucas : *op. cit.*, pp. 40, 69, 75, 77, 81–3 ; *E.A.* 98, p. 157. In 1924 the society established a superannuation fund for the benefit of its employees. The fact that there had been only three mild examples of strike action in the society's history up to 1924 bears eloquent tribute to the cordiality of the relations between employers and employed.

CHAPTER X

UNEMPLOYMENT IN CREWE, AND THE FIRST WORLD WAR

" The political economy of war is one of its most commanding aspects. Every farthing, with the smallest exception conceivable, of the scores and hundreds of millions which a war may cost, goes directly and very violently to stimulate production, though it is intended ultimately for waste or destruction."—W. E. GLADSTONE, review of Tennyson's *Maud*.

" We always become wise after the event ; but only until the next event. The tears and blood of the old wars leave no trace upon our memories. The Great War is passing away from the minds of the new generation. Unless something entirely unprecedented enters quickly into the hearts of mankind, the orphans we are now bringing up will in their turn go to war as if it was a game and find it, as we found it, a grave."—GENERAL SIR IAN HAMILTON'S speech at the unveiling of Crewe War Memorial, as reported in *Crewe Guardian*, June 17, 1924.

DURING the latter part of the nineteenth century the poorer sections of the working class in Crewe experienced several spells of severe distress, when the seasonal employment of winter was aggravated by stoppages in the building trade caused by bad weather and frost. The worst winters in this respect were those of 1878–9, 1886–7 and 1890–1. Crewe Town Council tried to meet the problem by setting up in 1879 a Relief Committee, later (1881) split up into separate ward committees. These committees·received gifts in cash and kind from the local middle class and tradespeople, and distributed them to the needy in the form of money, meals for starving schoolchildren, coal, soup, clogs, boots and shoes. Such distress swelled the numbers on the books of the Guardians of the Poor at Nantwich, and was naturally worst amongst labourers not organised in trade unions, for the skilled artisan could fall back for a time on his union's unemployment benefits. This is one of the reasons for the rapid growth of trade unionism in the town after 1889. From 1879 onwards it became the settled policy of the Corporation in winter to set the able-bodied unemployed working for a short time on the roads, the stone-heaps, or the sewage farm.

The distress caused by the prolonged " short time " of 1893–5 taxed the capacities of the Relief Committees to the utmost.

Total unemployment, as distinct from " short time," extended for the first time since 1848–51 to the skilled artisan class, and during the worst months between 500 and 600 families in the borough suffered acute distress. Between 1895 and 1903 Crewe enjoyed a period of comparative prosperity, but even in the financial year ending in March, 1903, over £4,000 in outdoor relief was distributed in the borough by the Guardians, and this figure remained about the same until 1909. During the same period, an average of 500 persons from Crewe received relief in Nantwich Workhouse every six months.[1]

In the winter of 1904–5, unemployment aggravated by the town's incipient industrial stagnation returned in an acute form, and was met with the traditional method of appointing Relief Committees and undertaking minor public works. In December, 1904, the Town Council ordered the Borough Surveyor to open a labour register wherein the names of unemployed residents might be enrolled. Prospective employers of labour were invited to make use of the register, which thus served as a primitive type of labour exchange. The limited value of such public works as the council could undertake as a cure for the problem is seen from the fact that the £800 spent in six weeks, during December, 1904, and January, 1905, the equivalent of a 1½d. rate, only provided 167 men with employment of from two to four days' duration. In 1905 the various Corporation Committees received instructions for the first time to keep back work until the winter, when unemployment normally reached its highest point. Meanwhile, the public of Crewe began to demand State assistance for local authorities in their efforts to combat what was beginning to emerge as a permanent problem. Parliament had passed the Unemployed Workmen Act of 1905 which provided for the establishment of distress committees in the worst areas, and set aside a certain sum to be spent on public works in such places.

The chief sympathisers with the plight of unemployed were the advanced Liberals and the more active members of the Crewe I.L.P. In December, 1905, Councillors W. Williams and C. H. Pedley sponsored an unsuccessful attempt to induce

[1] *C.G.*, Jan.–Feb., 1879 ; Jan.–Feb., 1881, 1886–7, *passim*, 24.12.90 to 14.2.91, *passim*, 1892–5, *passim*, 1.7.99, 23.3.01, 28.3.03 ; *C.Ch.*, Jan., 1891 ; Coun., 29.1.79, 2.2.81, 31.12.90, 25.10.93 ; G.P.C., 14.1.86, 7.3.89, 13.4.93 ; Works, 4.3.86 ; M.O.H., 1897–1905, 1908, 1911.

the Local Government Board to apply the Unemployed Workmen Act to the borough. During the winter of 1905–6 the Crewe I.L.P. organised an " Unemployed Committee," interviewed the Mayor, and agitated for a vigorous policy of public works. A second unsuccessful attempt to obtain a distress committee under the Act of 1905 was made in 1906–7, immediately after the railway company had begun to discharge its older hands.[1] The Unemployed Committee thereupon denounced John Burns as a " traitor," and there was a renewed demand for old age pensions. The Unemployed Committee also staged a march of Crewe unemployed to Nantwich Workhouse—at that time a novel form of political demonstration (February, 1907). There can be little doubt that vigorous campaigns on this general pattern in all parts of the country must have had a powerful influence on the Liberal Government's decision to pass the first Old Age Pensions Act in 1908.

Distress in the borough was sensibly diminished during the winter of 1909–10 by the award of old age pensions to 512 persons resident in the borough. The removal of the pauper disqualification in 1911 added to the beneficial effects of the measure, and the amount of outdoor relief dispensed by the Guardians in Crewe fell gradually from over £4,000 in the year ending March, 1909, to less than £2,000 in the year ending March, 1915, although the general economic prosperity of the boom-years 1911–14 must also be taken into consideration. Another measure calculated to lessen the friction with which the economic machinery of the district functioned was the establishment of Crewe's Employment Exchange. In 1911 Crewe Town Council, at the request of Crewe Trades Council, and " having regard to the recent discharges of workmen by the L.N.W.R. Company," petitioned the Board of Trade to set up one of the new Labour Exchanges in the town. This petition was granted in the following year. In the interim, the town's trade unions made use of the Labour Exchange at Macclesfield.[2]

---

[1] Alderman McNeill made a third unsuccessful attempt in 1908–9.

[2] *C.G.*, 3.12.03 to 7.6.12, *passim*, esp. 11.1.11 (238 cases removed from the Crewe Relieving Officer's books by old age pensions) ; *C.Ch.*, 9.11.12, 19.9.31 ; M.O.H., 1908, 1912, 1913, 1914 ; Coun., 5.4.05, 6.2.07 ; G.P.C., 12.2.03, 10.11.04, 14.12.05, 13.12.06, 14.2.07, 12.2.07, 13.8.08, 10.12.08, 12.2.09, 17.10.11, 21.11.11 ; Works Ctee., 13.12.04, 10.1.05, 9.1.06.

Crewe possesses something of a military tradition. The French invasion scare of 1859 stimulated the Volunteer Movement in Cheshire, and after a public meeting on the subject in 1864, sanction was received in 1865 permitting the formation at Crewe of the 36th Cheshire Rifle Volunteer Corps. The officers were drawn for the most part from the railway company's officials ; in 1878 it consisted of 401 men, but it was disbanded in 1880. A more useful piece of military organisation appeared in 1887, when F. W. Webb and his subordinate officials, together with prominent local Conservatives, became pioneers in the new art of mechanised warfare by forming a Railway Engineer Volunteer Corps. Within one year of its inception it consisted of six companies with 24 officers and 610 men, all employed by the railway company, and comprised engine drivers, firemen, cleaners, boilermakers, riveters, fitters, smiths, platelayers, shunters and pointsmen. Later it became known as the 2nd Cheshire Engineer (Railway) Volunteers ; 245 of its members enlisted as a matter of form in the regular army for one day, in order to pass into the Royal Engineers Railway Reserve, where they remained for six years, liable for active service at any time. This unique force proved exceptionally useful during the Boer War (1899–1902), when 285 of its officers and men saw service in South Africa, driving armoured trains, building and repairing bridges, working the heavy traction engines of the Steam Road Transport Company, and putting up wire fences round the blockhouses.[1]

It is interesting to note that of the 26 Crewe men who died on active service during this war, the Boers killed only 4, while 19 died of disease and 3 from accidents. The Liberals held aloof from the Volunteers, and McLaren (M.P. for Crewe, 1886–95, 1910–12), who was a Quaker, helped to found a branch of the Peace Society for the Crewe district in 1888. During the struggle in South Africa, many of the Crewe Liberals remained pro-Boer.[2]

In accordance with Haldane's army reforms, the Corps became

[1] A. Terry : *Historical Records of the 5th Administrative Battalion of the Cheshire Rifle Volunteers*, p. 86 ; G. R. S. Darroch : *Deeds of a Great Railway*, pp. 22–3 ; *C.G.*, 20.9.02.

[2] For the Peace Society and the pro-Boer attitude of the Liberals, see *C.G.*, 11.2.88 to 10.4.89, *passim*, 16.9.99, 1900, *passim* ; *C.Ch.*, 25.8.00.

part of the Territorial Army in 1908, and after dwindling to about 200 officers and men was disbanded in 1912. Later in the year, however, a Territorial battery of artillery was formed at Crewe under the style of the 3rd Cheshire Battery, 3rd Welsh Brigade, R.F.A., together with a section of the ammunition column.[1]

The outbreak of the war of 1914–18, in which 526 Crewe men were killed or died of wounds and disease, speedily solved the unemployment problem for the time being, and by October, 1914, the manager of the employment exchange could report that only 42 names remained on his books. The rush to enlist in the new armies became so great that even in September, 1914, the works officials expressed alarm at the depletion of their labour force. Local recruiting campaigns proved so successful that even the War Office paused. The railway company thereupon began to re-engage men over sixty-five years of age and to take on boys of twelve, as the School Attendance Officer soon discovered. The rising cost of living proved an important factor in this rush to seek employment. By July, 1915, munitions and not recruits had become the paramount consideration, and Craig, the M.P. for the division, held a series of meetings in the works (July, 1915) with the object of increasing the output of war material. He helped to create an atmosphere favourable to the relaxation of trade-union standards and to " dilution " by the introduction of unskilled labour.[2]

The war of 1914–18 wrought a remarkable industrial transformation in the works. New locomotive construction practically ceased, but a number of engines and waggons, together with complete workshop equipment, had to be sent to the various fronts. Many boilermakers received their notices of discharge, and migrated to the shipbuilding yards at Birkenhead; some returned in 1919–20. By 1917 materials for maintaining even the existing rolling-stock ran short, and extensive purchases from the U.S.A. became necessary. Under the supervision of the Railway War Manufacturers' sub-committee of the Railway

[1] *C.G.*, 15.3.79, 5.4.79, 15.5.80, 12.6.80, 9.4.81, 28.5.81, 10.5.82, 11.12.86, 1887, *passim*, 14.3.88, 11.10.99, 18.10.99, 9.2.01 to 12.8.03, *passim*, 15.2.08, 1.5.09, 19.3.10 to 13.9.12, *passim*, 21.8.14; Sub-Ctee. of Coun., 12.5.88.

[2] *C.G.*, 14 and 21.8.14, 25.9.14, 6.10.14, 13.11.14, 4.12.14, 1.1.15, 9.7.15, 3.9.15, 27 and 30.7.15, 3.8.15; Darroch: *op. cit.* pp. 25–6, 36–7, 135–8.

Executive Committee (the instrument whereby the State exercised war-time control over the railways) Crewe Works became "a private arsenal, subsidiary to the Royal Arsenal at Woolwich." [1] Armoured trains, gun carriages, carriage limbers, waggon limbers, ammunition bodies, 4-in., 5-in., 6-in., and 8-in. howitzer guns, 12-pounder quick-firing guns, high-angle anti-aircraft guns, cable-wire and tractors were only a few of the more important articles connected with the war effort manufactured in Crewe Works between 1914 and 1918. Girls and women appeared in the works for the first time in March, 1915, when the production of graze-fuses commenced. The output of this highly important component, thanks to a system of three consecutive eight-hour shifts, rose rapidly from 150 to a steady weekly average of 3,000. In another portion of the works women turned out approximately 100,000 6-in. shells. Altogether about 500 women were employed and the Works Manager admitted in 1918 that "he had been absolutely staggered" by the jobs the women had done in Crewe Works with the greatest of ease. [2]

On account of its strategic position, Crewe acquired immediate importance, not only as a troop-train centre but also as a depôt from which munitions from government and other factories in the North-Western Area were sent south. Crewe depôt handled during the war 9,700,000 shells, 17,200,000 small components, and 27,000 tons of raw material, mostly during 1917–18. [3] In view of the above activities, it is probable that Crewe's comparative freedom from air raids was due to the embryonic character of air warfare at the time. Crewe Town Council took certain elementary precautions in 1915 to ensure a black-out,

---

[1] Darroch : *op. cit.*, p. 38. The Railway War Manufacturers' sub-committee consisted of the chief mechanical engineers of the main railway companies, together with representatives of the War Office.

[2] *C.G.*, 5.3.18 ; Darroch : *op. cit.*, pp. 55–6, 60–3, 68–9, 75–82, 87–8, 103–4, 106–12, 115–6, 119, 128–30, 132–4, 148, 178–81. Women also worked in the town and engine sheds as bus-conductors, engine-cleaners and postmen (*C.G.*, 3.12.15, 31.12.15, 7.3.16, 8.9.16 : Coun., 5.7.16 ; Health Ctee., 14.9.22).

[3] *C.G.*, 8.1.15, 10.1.19 ; *Times*, 6.1.15, and *cf.* 6.2.40 ("Crewe station in war-time") ; Darroch : *op. cit.*, p. 172. The voluntary helpers in the Forces' canteen on Crewe station achieved nation-wide publicity in a popular song of the time as "the girls at Crewe."

but as these failed to operate during a threatened Zeppelin attack on the night of January 31–February 1, 1916, they had to be overhauled. Most of the town's street lamps were henceforward extinguished $1\frac{1}{2}$ hours after sunset, and a second "nocturnal aerial raid" on November 27, 1916, passed off quietly. The nearest bomb fell several miles away from the borough.[1]

During the first months of the war few realised that the struggle would finally demand the complete concentration of the nation's productive resources, and with more or less vague memories of the Crimean and Boer campaigns in their minds, many Crewe people, misled by the cry of "business as usual," imagined that 1915 would admit of peace-time activities being carried on without interruption. For example, as late as May, 1915, one of the Crewe branches of the N.U.R. asked the Town Council "to move in the direction of providing sufficient housing accommodation for the working-class inhabitants," and in the following September the Works Committee passed plans for a large block of offices for the Prudential Assurance Company which the builders managed to complete two years later. On the other hand, municipal capital expenditure received an immediate check; plans for a badly-needed new school in Newdigate Street had to be dropped. Urgent government orders necessitated extensions to two of the town's clothing factories in 1914–16.[2]

1915 saw the beginning of the manpower "comb-out." An all-party campaign under the auspices of the Crewe Division Recruiting Committee (E. Craig, Sir Joseph Davies and John Williams) in the spring met with a disappointing response, and although men came forward more briskly for a time after the *Lusitania* incident, Crewe Town Council had already passed a resolution in favour of "some form of compulsory military service" (May 5, 1915). Some of the Liberals, headed by the aged McNeill, opposed the motion. After this events moved

[1] E.L., 11.3.15, 15.4.15; G.P.C., 22.2.15, 20.4.15, 15.2.16, 20.11.17; Ctee. of Coun., 2 and 10.2.16; Coun., 1.3.16, 6.2.18; Mkt. Ctee., 10.2.16, 10.10.18; C.G., 7.5.15, 4 and 25.2.16, 3.3.16, 7.4.16, 5.5.16, 9 and 16.11.17, 7.12.17, 8.2.18.

[2] G.P.C., 15.9.14, 18.5.15; Works Ctee., 13.10.14, 7.9.15; E.L., 10.2.16; Coun., 1.8.17; C.G., 18.6.15. (*Cf.* Fce. Ctee., 22.4.15—Local Government Board circular *re* municipal capital expenditure).

quickly. Crewe Borough National Registration Committee compiled a national register for the area, and in December, 1915, about 6,000 men attested under Lord Derby's scheme. In February of the next year the local Military Tribunal appointed under the Military Service (No. 2) Act met for the first time. It consisted of one representative each from the Crewe Trades Council and the Railway Workers' Joint Committee, two Liberals and four Conservatives. Five cases of conscientious objection to service under the final compulsory Military Service Act of May, 1916, occurred, and of these three secured exemption on religious grounds. Altogether Crewe contributed between 4,000 and 5,000 men to the armies.[1]

Towards the end of the war the public services of the Corporation began to suffer seriously from the manpower shortage. The Borough Surveyor died in 1916, and for two years the town remained without a successor. The Medical Officer of Health was absent on military service for the last two years of the struggle, and the War Office attempted to secure the services of his deputy. As early as June, 1916, the Corporation decided to cut down the refuse disposal services drastically, and in the same year the Sanitary Inspector resigned on grounds of ill-health. In the sphere of trade, the operations of the Military Tribunal closed down numerous one-man businesses. When the owners of these businesses began to trickle back from the war, their disgust with government restrictions on re-opening, and allegations of a bias against the small trader, found vent in the revival of the Crewe Tradesmen's Association in 1917.[2]

No sooner had the question of conscription been settled than the food question came to the fore. After the first frantic rush on the food-shops which began on Tuesday, August 4, and lasted throughout the week, Crewe, in common with the rest of the country, settled down to a period of rising prices unaccompanied by any particularly acute shortage. Crewe was, in fact,

---

[1] *C.G.*, 6.2.15 to 16.5.16, *passim* ; G.P.C., 16.3.15, 20.4.15, 15.6.15 ; Coun., 5.5.15, 10.2.16 ; Nat. Reg. Ctee., 21 and 28.7.15, 16 and 18.8.15, 9.5.16. A National Service Committee was set up in 1917 in connection with recruiting for munition workers.

[2] Health Ctee., 14.6.16 ; G.P.C., 20.2.17, 17.4.17, 7.5.19 ; Ctee. of Coun., 2.5.17 ; M.O.H., 1916 ; *C.G.*, 19 and 30.10.17, 14.12.17, 11.1.18, 29.3.18, 26.7.18, 29.11.18, 17.1.19. Retail business licensing orders remained in force until December, 1919 (Ctee. of Coun., 5.2.19 ; G.P.C., 14.5.18, 20.1.20).

saved by its situation in the middle of a rich food-producing plain from the worst effects of the war-crisis. In January, 1915, the Town Council urged the Government to take " immediate steps to control the food-supply of the nation," but not until the end of the following year did the Corporation itself make any move to promote food production. Then, aided by the stimulus of the unrestricted submarine campaign, the Land Cultivation sub-committee, under the energetic chairmanship of Alderman J. H. Kettell, took over a large number of private allotments and ploughed up vacant pieces of Corporation land. The County War Agricultural Committee provided seed-potatoes. The sub-committee's labours, and the growing shortage of foodstuffs, increased the number of allotments in Crewe from 165 in 1914 to 2,233 in August, 1918, in spite of the fact that some of the land had to be broken up with pick-axe and mattock. This meant one allotment for every four families in the borough. The potato queues of April and May, 1917, when the Market Inspector had to deal with " as many as 2,000 people," who " waited hours to obtain a few," became a thing of the past, and after the cessation of hostilities the allotments movement received recognition as a permanent feature of the town's social life.[1]

In the middle of 1917 an acute sugar shortage developed ; one of the first tasks of the newly-appointed Crewe Food Control Committee (August, 1917) was to institute a voluntary rationing scheme for this commodity, followed by similar measures for margarine and meat in January and March, 1918, respectively. When compulsory rationing came into force on April 1, 1918, much useful spadework had thus been done. Thanks to the efforts of J. C. Manley on the Crewe District Auctioneers' Committee and of Councillor R. P. T. Darlington on the Food Control Committee, Crewe enjoyed constant, if restricted, supplies of meat, and when the Food Control Committee was wound up in 1920 the members admitted that, as regards food generally, there had been very little trouble. One lesson of the

---

[1] *C.G.*, 7 and 11.8.14, 4.9.14, 6.10.14, 5.2.15, 15.9.16 to 8.11.18, *passim*, 9.4.20 ; Coun., 2.9.14 ; G.P.C., 19.1.15, 18.6.18 ; Ctee. of Coun., 6.12.16, 4.12.18 ; Land Cultivation Sub-Ctee., 15.12.16, 9.1.17, 22.5.17 ; Mkt. Ctee., 10.5.17 ; Health Ctee., 10.1.17. In the interests of food production the Corporation relaxed the by-law prohibiting pig-keeping within 60 feet of a dwelling-house.

first World War Crewe refused to learn—the clear demonstration of the need and value of a public abattoir. In 1897 not one of the borough's 14 private slaughter-houses was entirely satisfactory, and most of them were " buildings utterly unsuited for the purpose." In the following year the Crewe Butchers' Association elected a vigilance committee to co-operate with the M.O.H. in the detection of " slink " meat, but efficient meat inspection was said in 1905 to be " an impossibility." During the winter of 1917–18 the Food Controller accepted the offer of the Crewe Co-operative Friendly Society to place its abattoir under Government control as the sole slaughter-house in the borough, and the deputy M.O.H. reported that this centralisation made possible a much greater amount of meat inspection, a gratifying state of affairs at a time when, owing to the suspension of the Tuberculosis Order, 1914, and rising prices, tubercular cattle were appearing on the market in increasing numbers. The figures he quoted constituted an overwhelming argument for the establishment of a public abattoir, with a qualified resident meat inspector, but with the end of food control, the old system of private slaughter-houses returned.[1]

The power of organised labour to enforce its demands for higher wages, to cope with the rising cost of living, increased as more men were drained away to the armies. The Crewe Railway Workers joint committee gained in 1917 the Manchester district rates of pay for which it had pressed since 1911. Many new trade union branches came into existence and those already established grew rapidly ; perhaps the most striking case was that of the Crewe branch of the National Union of General Workers, which counted 86 members in 1914 and 558 three years later. Similarly the Crewe Railway Clerks' Association had one Crewe branch in 1914 and three at the end of 1919, with 1,200 members. In 1917 Crewe Trades Council, on the advice of Professor G. W. Daniels of Manchester University, started a campaign to organise the unskilled labourers and female workers in the town, with the co-operation of the Federation of Women Workers, the Garment Workers' Union and the Paper Workers' Association. Most categories of organised workers secured sub-

[1] G.P.C., 18.1.98, 14.8.17 ; Food Control, 22.8.17 ; Coun., 3.10.17 ; C.G., 8.6.17 to 12.4.18, *passim*, 3.1.19, 21.2.19, 8.4.19, 9.7.20, 23.11.20, 9.12.21, 18.4.22 ; M.O.H., 1897, 1898, 1905, 1917–20.

stantial wage-increases in 1917–19, sometimes after a threat of strike action. 1919–20 saw the fairly general introduction of the 47- or 48-hour week in occupations with strong trade union membership. For example, the Crewe branch of the A.U.C.E secured the 48-hour week in 1919, while their badly-organised fellow-workers in the Shop Assistants' Union had to rest content with vague declarations in favour of the measure from individual members of the Crewe Tradesmen's Association.[1]

The growing power of the unions, unaccompanied by any change in a Town Council composed predominantly of trades-men, led to a great deal of friction during the last two years of the first World War. The struggle became one for more adequate labour representation on the various war-time Corporation committees (the Military Tribunal, the Food Control Committee, the Fuel and Lighting Committee) which regulated communal life to an ever-increasing degree from 1916 onwards. A particular bitter wrangle developed in the winter of 1917–18 over the appointment of three additional representatives of the consumer to the Food Control Committee, with the Corporation ranged against the Crewe Co-operative Friendly Society and various local working-class organisations headed by the Crewe Trades Council. The latter body told the civic fathers that it was of the opinion that they " did not know, in any matter, who was the person to represent labour." Finally the Food Controller allowed an increase of three co-opted members, to the satisfaction of everybody but the Co-operative Society, which had to rest content with a single representative. The preponderance of private trading interests had nevertheless been somewhat reduced.[2]

In the sphere of war finance, the people and institutions of Crewe, at first through voluntary associations and later through the efforts of the semi-official Crewe War Savings Committee, established in July, 1916, purchased 277,000 War Savings Certificates and £690,000 worth of War Bonds up to December, 1918. The movement continued after the armistice, and some of the

---

[1] *C.G.*, 18.7.16 to 16.10.16, *passim*, 2.2.17 to 26.4.18, 17.1.19 to 22.8.19.
[2] *C.G.*, 14.9.15, 18.1.16, 22.2.16, 31.8.17, to 6.9.18, *passim*. G.P.C., 18.7.16, 14.8.17, 19.2.18, 19.5.18, 23.7.18 ; Coun., 10.2.16, 5.9.17, 6.2.18, 3.4.18, 1.5.18, 10.7.18 ; Health Ctee., 9.8.16.

funds required for the first Corporation housing estate came from this source.[1]

The war drew to a close amidst a severe epidemic of influenza, which resulted in 186 deaths within the borough during the winter of 1918–19, equivalent to 35 per cent. of Crewe's war fatalities at the fronts. The violent strain which had been placed on the social and economic structure of the town soon manifested itself. In the " khaki election " of December, 1918, the unsuccessful Labour candidate polled 10,439 votes as compared with less than 2,500 in 1912. The men serving in the armed forces drifted back to the town in the course of 1919, and there was much talk of " reconstruction." By November, 1919, about 900 unemployed presented an awkward local problem, and the Ministry of Labour replied to an anxious Crewe Town Council's request for public works grants that the Government was relying to a great extent on " the encouragement of private enterprise for the absorption of the unemployed " (December, 1919). The Ministry's optimism seemed justified during the short post-war boom in 1920, when the number of unemployed fell from 1,241 in February to its lowest point, 290, in September. After this a gradual increase took place. The work of the new Crewe Employment Advisory Committee, active from 1919, now acquired increasing importance in connection with the employment exchange. The Juvenile Advisory and After-care Committees, established in 1919 and 1920, also did valuable work in persuading members of the public to keep their children off the labour-market pending the raising of the school-leaving age to fourteen in 1921.[2]

Crewe Town Council became fully aware of the serious position in September, 1921, when the public began to demand

---

[1] An immense amount of voluntary work by private individuals alone made possible the steady functioning of civilian life and the operation of charitable and social service committees for the armed forces. See *C.G.*, 28.2.19 (social work of L.N.W.R. Employees Committee) ; *C.G.*, 9.5.19 (Red Cross Hospital at Crewe 1915–19) ; also work of the St. John Ambulance Brigade —*C.G.*, 20.6.19 ; E. J. W. Disbrowe : *History of the Volunteer Movement in Cheshire, 1914–20* (for Crewe battalion see pp. 86, 91, 97, 100) ; *C.G.*, 3.11.16, 25.7.16, 9.2.17, 1.6.17, 17.8.17, 3.1.19, 28.3.19, 4.1.21, 20.1.22.

[2] *M.O.H.*, 1917–19 ; *C.G.*, 28.6.18, 25.10.18 to 7.3.19, *passim*, 6.9.19, 14 and 21.11.19, 5.3.20 to 3.12.20, *passim*, 26.8.21 to 29.8.22, *passim*, 27.4.23, 3.7.23, 4.9.23 ; Coun., 5.12.17 ; G.P.C., 18.4.22.

the starting of a large-scale public-works programme to relieve unemployment, especially as the expenditure on housing was drawing to an end. An extensive programme of public works took time to prepare, and it was not until three months later that work began on the first important scheme, the reconstruction of Edleston Road. Crewe's trade union branches distributed about £50,000 in unemployment benefit to their members in the course of 1921, a fact which helps to explain their vigorous support of a public works policy, and much blame accrued to the Corporation for its alleged dilatoriness. Apart from those totally unemployed, many men were working various degrees of short time.

State assistance was forthcoming from the Unemployment Grants Committee from 1921 onwards, which undertook to pay from 50 per cent. to 65 per cent. of the interest for some years on money borrowed for the schemes, provided that the unskilled labour employed received only 75 per cent. of trade-union wage-rates. The main schemes executed under this scheme, at a cost of £100,000, were the reconstruction of Edleston Road and Market Street (1921–2), the Alton Street bridge (1923), the new northern outfall sewer (1922–4), and the straightening of the Valley Brook (1923–4). It must be said that the policy of undertaking public works proved somewhat expensive, and its supporters exaggerated the extent to which it would alleviate unemployment directly. For example, in February, 1923, when most of the schemes were in progress, only 232 men could be found employment on alternate weeks.[1]

[1] G.P.C., 14.10.19 to 18.12.23, *passim* ; Sub-Ctee. *re* unemployment, 2.2.21, 12.9.21, 27.4.22 to 14.12.23, *passim* ; Coun., 5.10.21, 4.10.22 ; C.G., 29.4.21 to 7.12.23, *passim*.

EPILOGUE, 1923–46

CREWE continued to stagnate industrially until 1938. The Census of 1931 revealed that the population within the borough area had begun to decline, although considerable surburban development was taking place. The number of men employed in the railway works fell from over 10,000 in 1920, the peak point, to 6,520 in 1938. This reduction was due to the rationalisation of locomotive repair and construction in the 1920's, and the closing down of the steelworks, the rail mill, and the carriage repair department, in 1932.[1] Fustian cutting has died out, and considerable changes have taken place within the ready-made clothing industry. Messrs. John Hammond & Co. left the town in 1931, but both the C.W.S. and Charles Doody Ltd. have enlarged their factories. In addition, there are two newcomers to the clothing trade of the borough—County Clothes, Ltd., a firm from the U.S.A., with two factories (1936, 1938), and F. Coupe Ltd., from Northwich (1936). Both these firms are expanding rapidly. The Crewe clothing trade is therefore definitely increasing in importance and may soon rival that of Nantwich.

During the great depression of 1929–34 the leading towns-people reacted to events in much the same fashion as their fore-bears. In 1931 they formed the Crewe Industrial Development Association, with the Town Clerk as secretary ; the association's object was to induce manufacturers to take advantage of Crewe's central position by establishing new industries in the borough. The Corporation placed a considerable amount of money at the disposal of the association, and systematic advertising was under-taken in France and Germany as well as Britain, but little or nothing resulted. The decision to wind up the association was taken in 1938, after the most important event in the economic history of Crewe since 1843 had occurred—the announcement, in June, 1938, that owing to the rearmament programme the Air Council had decided

" to establish at Crewe a new factory for the production of com-plete Rolls Royce aero engines to meet the requirements of the

[1] C. S. Lake : *Reorganisation of Crewe Locomotive Works, L.M.S.R. Co.* 1929.

Royal Air Force expansion and to increase the capacity for rapid production . . . in emergency. The new factory will be financed and owned by the Government, but its operation and management will be entrusted to Rolls Royce Ltd." [1]

While the original suggestion that Crewe's unemployed engineers should be found work in their home town by locating the new factory at Crewe, came from Amalgamated Engineering Union circles at Derby, where Rolls Royce Ltd. has its headquarters, the actual establishment of the new industry in the town was only made possible by the progressive policy of Crewe Town Council in deciding to promote a Bill in Parliament empowering the Corporation to construct municipal waterworks at Eaton in Cheshire. The levels at the L.M.S. Railway Company's bore-holes at Whitmore had continued to fall after 1923, and it became imperative that the town should possess an alternative source of supply. The Bill received the Royal Assent on June 23, 1938, and a promise that the water project would be proceeded with immediately was a vital factor in determining the location of the Rolls Royce factory at Crewe. Rapid housing development took place round the new factory from 1939 onwards, as the original estimate of 4,000 employees rose in actual fact to a peak figure of 10,000.

Crewe's area was extended to 4,414 acres by the Ministry of Health's County of Chester Review Order of 1936. Together with portions of the surrounding townships, Crewe railway station (at long last) and the remaining portion of Church Coppenhall (again owing to the imminent need of a general sewerage scheme) became part of the municipal borough of Crewe as from April 1, 1936. The extension has proved to be a very unsatisfactory compromise, as it did not include the major portion of Wistaston, Crewe's garden suburb, and in all probability a further readjustment will become necessary within the next few years.

From 1931 until 1933 more than 20 per cent. of the insured population of the Crewe district was unemployed, but the figure had fallen by 1939 to between 8 per cent. and 9 per cent. In April, 1939, the railway works, after many years of " short

[1] Report of 31st Annual General Meeting of Rolls Royce, Ltd. (*Sunday Times*, 3.7.38 ; see also *Daily Telegraph*, 7.6.38 ; *Staffordshire Evening Sentinel*, 10.12.38).

time " (*i.e.* the five-day week), commenced opening on Saturday morning. Considerable social progress has been made since 1923, both before and after the Crewe Trades Council and Labour Party's nominees secured a majority on the Town Council in November, 1930, a majority which has been maintained ever since. It must be admitted, however, that the speed of social reform increased considerably after 1930. By March, 1938, the local authority owned 1,463 houses, and the obnoxious privy, deplored by successive Medical Officers of Health since 1874, has now been practically exterminated, most of the remaining ones being in the recently-added and outlying parts of the borough. The long-awaited refuse destructor was opened in 1930, followed by the equally long-awaited Ludford Street central school in 1932, and a new maternity and child welfare centre in 1935. A town-planning scheme for the borough was ordered to be prepared in 1926, and much was done between the wars to tidy up the town and soften its worst asperities. Much remains to be carried out under the Crewe Corporation Act of 1938—central town improvements, extensive street widening, a new bus station, and a new sewerage scheme. Crewe's prosperity during the second World War rested on the uncertain basis of armament manufacture, and on the cessation of hostilities the staff employed at the Rolls Royce factory underwent considerable reduction, although it was estimated in 1946 that about 2,000 men would still be employed in manufacturing the firm's Bentley motor-cars. Large sections of the factory have been turned over to County Clothes Ltd., and Kelvinator Ltd., refrigerator manufacturers of London. It was estimated in 1946 that these two firms between them would employ at least 2,000 workers. Meanwhile a firm of chemical manufacturers decided about the same time to base itself on Crewe Hall, and the Post Office authorities were said to be pressing for the speedy development of Crewe's proposed municipal airport at Minshull Vernon, a few miles north of Crewe, in order to speed up the Irish mail traffic. Crewe's industrial future seems assured. Derby and Coventry have shown that, given the right facilities, comparatively light industries will establish themselves in a " heavy industry " town, and Crewe appears to be at the beginning of a similar phase of economic development.

APPENDICES

THE POPULATION OF THE
TOWNSHIP OF MONKS
COPPENHALL AND THE
BOROUGH OF CREWE 1831–
1931

FIRST PERIOD OF GROWTH
Probable set-back during
depression of 1848–51

QUIETER PROGRESS
Rail-mill in 1852-3, but removal
of Coach Dept in 1859-60

PHENOMENAL INCREASE
(a) Locomotive manufacture concentrated
at Crewe 1862
(b) Steel Works 1864
(c) Railway extensions

QUIETER PROGRESS
(a) Webb's policy of concentration of Departments
(b) Natural increase   ("A floating Population"
(c) but depressions   T.W. Worsdell in 1935)
in 1876-7, 1878-80

BETWEEN Jan. 1881 and Dec. 1890
9520 births & 4347 deaths took place
in Crewe, but the population grew by
only 4376. The deficit due to
emigration & suburban develop-ment

BOROUGH
EXTENSION (1892)
Railway centralisation
& expansion 1895–1901

STAGNATION
(a) migration to other
towns, or emigration
(b) Suburban
developments
(c) Falling birth-rate

50,000
45,000
40,000
35,000
30,000
25,000
20,000
15,000
10,000
5,000
0

1831 1841 1851 1861 1871 1881 1891 1901 1911 1921 1931
148   203   4571 8159 17810 24385 28761 42074 44960 46497 46061

APPENDIX I

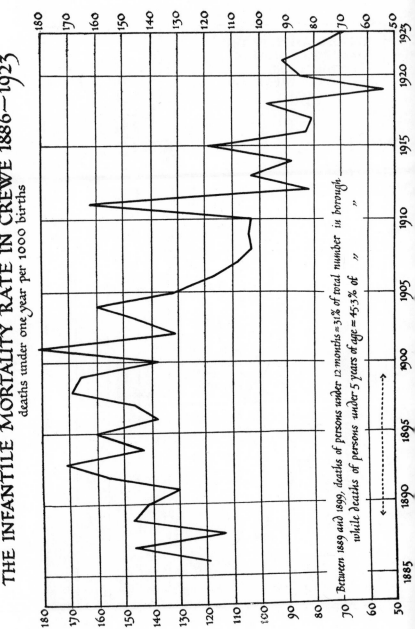

THE INFANTILE MORTALITY RATE IN CREWE 1886—1923
deaths under one year per 1000 births

Between 1889 and 1899, deaths of persons under 12 months = 31% of total number in borough
while deaths of persons under 5 years of age = 45.3% of "   "   "

APPENDIX NO 3

POLITICS IN THE CREWE PARLIAMENTARY DIVISION, 1885–1945

1885
(10,815 electors)

G. W. Latham (L.) . . .	5,089
O. L. Stephen (C.) . . .	4,281

Liberal majority 808

1886
(10,815 electors)

W. S. B. McLaren (L.) . .	4,690
F. R. Twemlow (C.) . .	4,045

Liberal majority 645

1892
(11,412 electors)

W. S. B. McLaren (L.) . .	5,558
H. W. Chatterton (C.) . .	3,990

Liberal majority 1,568

1895
(12,018 electors)

Hon. R. A. Ward (C.) . .	5,413
W. S. B. McLaren (L.) . .	4,863

Conservative majority . . 550

1900
(13,447 electors)

J. Tomkinson (L.) . . .	6,120
J. E. Reiss (C.)	4,921

Liberal majority 1,199

1906
(15,051 electors)

J. Tomkinson (L.) . . .	7,805
J. H. Welsford (C.) . . .	5,297

Liberal majority 2,508

January 1910
(15,866 electors)

J. Tomkinson (L.) . . .	7,761
Sir John Harrington (C.) .	5,419
F. H. Rose (Lab.) . . .	1,380

Liberal majority 2,342

April 1910
(15,866 electors)

W. S. B. McLaren (L.) . .	7,639
J. H. Welsford (C.) . . .	6,041

Liberal majority 1,598

December 1910
(15,866 electors)

W. S. B. McLaren (L.) . .	7,629
E. Y. Craig (C.)	5,925

Liberal majority 1,704

1912
(15,925 electors)

E. Y. Craig (C.)	6,260
H. L. Murphy, K.C. (L.) .	5,294
J. Holmes (Lab.)	2,485

Conservative majority . . 966

1918
(34,818 electors)

Sir Joseph Davies (Coal. L.) .	13,392
J. T. Brownlie (Lab.) . .	10,439

Coalition Liberal majority . 2,953

1922
(37,159 electors)

E. G. Hemmerde, K.C. (Lab.)	15,311
Sir Joseph Davies (L.) . .	14,756

Labour majority 555

1923
(37,959 electors)

E. G. Hemmerde, K.C. (Lab.)	14,628
Sir Thomas Strangman (C.)	8,734
R. Montgomery, K.C. (L.).	8,068
Labour majority	5,899

1929
(51,448 electors)

J. W. Bowen (Lab.) . . .	20,948
D. B. Somervell, K.C. (C.)	11,732
W. C. Llewelyn (L.) . .	9,076
Labour majority	9,216

1935
(52,744 electors)

Sir Donald Somervell, K.C. (C.)	21,729
J. W. Bowen (Lab.) . . .	20,620
Conservative majority . .	1,109

1924
(38,583 electors)

E. Y. Craig (C.)	18,333
E. G. Hemmerde, K.C. (Lab.)	14,705
Conservative majority . .	3,628

1931
(51,892 electors)

D. B. Somervell, K.C. (Nat. C.)	25,141
J. W. Bowen (Lab.) . . .	18,351
National Conservative majority	6,790

1945
(62,768 electors)

S. S. Allen (Lab.) . . .	28,416
Sir Donald Somervell, K.C. (C.)	18,468
Labour majority	9,948

Note : The population of the Division in 1885 was 57,721, in 1931 76,269.

APPENDIX NO. 4

THE MEMBERS OF PARLIAMENT FOR THE CREWE DIVISION, 1885–1929

LATHAM, *George William* (1827–86), Liberal-Radical M.P. for Crewe Division 1885–6, barrister and landowner, of Bradwall Hall, near Sandbach ; educ. Oxford University, called to Bar 1852, inherited his estates 1853, active County J.P., was vice-chairman of Knutsford Court of Quarter Sessions for more than twenty years ; fought four unsuccessful Parliamentary contests 1868–83 (*C.G.*, 28.11.85, 6 and 9.10.86, 13 and 16.10.86) ; Churchman, estab. Bradwall Reformatory.

MCLAREN, *Walter Stowe Bright* (1853–1912), nephew of John Bright, advanced Liberal M.P. for Crewe Division 1886–95, 1910–12, member of the Society of Friends (Quakers) ; woollen spinner of Bradford, had interests in South Wales coal, director of Bolckow, Vaughan & Co. of Middlesbrough, shipbuilders, and part-owner of Petzold Co., engineering firm, Germany ; staunch Free Trader (*C.G.*, 14.7.86, 15.3.12, 2.7.12).

WARD, *Hon. Robert Arthur* (1874–1904), Conservative M.P. for Crewe Division 1895–1900, brother of Earl of Dudley ; little interest in politics ; captain in the Horse Guards, 1900 (*C.G.*, 9.6.94, 9.3.04).

TOMKINSON, *James Raymond*, of Willington Hall, Tarporley, Cheshire (1840–1910), landowner and director of Lloyds Bank, member of an old cavalry family. " Save for his pronounced Liberal opinions, he was a typical representative of a county which has sent a long succession of native landed proprietors to Parliament " ; M.P. for Crewe Division 1900–10 ; killed while riding in Parliamentary Steeplechase (*C.G.*, 2.1.04, 3 and 16.4.10) ; Churchman.

CRAIG, *Sir Ernest*, b. 1859 at Houghton-le-Springs, County Durham, mining engineer, coalowner and colliery manager, Churchman, M.P. for Crewe Division 1912–18, 1924–9, d. 1933 (*C.G.*, 12.7.12, 26.11.18).

DAVIES, *Sir Joseph*, South Wales coalowner, director of Cambrian Railway, member of Lloyd George's secretariat during Great War, Coalition Liberal M.P. for Crewe Division 1918–22 ; b. 1866 (*C.G.*, 13.3.14).

HEMMERDE, *E. G.*, K.C., b. 1871, Recorder of Liverpool, 1909–48, Labour M.P. for Crewe Division 1922–4 ; d. 1948 (*C.G.*, 17.11.22 ; *Times*, 25.5.48).

APPENDIX NO. 5

RELIGIOUS BODIES AND THEIR PLACES OF WORSHIP IN CREWE

1. CHURCH OF ENGLAND

    (a) *Coppenhall* parish church (St. Michael's) ; date of foundation unknown, but it existed in the 13th century ; new church buildings in 1821–2 and 1884–1910.

    (b) *Crewe*

    services began in 1843 in a portion of the Grand Junction Railway Company's Coachmaking Works.

        1. *1845 : Christ Church* (L.N.W.R.), opened.

        2. *1869 : St. Paul's Church*, Hightown (L.N.W.R.), opened. It originated in a mission by the Rev. John Ashe, curate of Coppenhall, between 1865 and 1869.

        3. *1885 : St. Barnabas' Church*, West Street (L.N.W.R.), opened. It originated in a mission from St. Paul's.

        4. *1896 : St. John's Church*, Stalbridge Road (L.N.W.R.), opened. It originated in a mission from Christ Church, started in a corrugated iron building on the site of Edleston Road schools, about 1867.

        5. *1900 : St. Andrew's Church*, Bedford Street (corrugated iron) opened. It originated in a mission begun about 1889.

        6. *1912 : All Saints' Church*, Wistaston Road (corrugated iron), opened. It originated in a mission begun about 1891.

        7. *1923 : St. Peter's Church*, Earle Street. It originated in a mission started about 1889.

(C.G., 9.2.78, 6.4.78, 9.3.78, 3.11.83, 1 and 26.3.84, 20.9.84, 24.10.85, 27.2.86, 6.3.86, 31.5.84, 1.10.84, 15.12.96, 18.6.04, 21.1.05, 10.3.09, 16 and 20.10.09, 6.9.12, 7.2.13, 6.6.13, 9.2.23, 8.5.23 ; C.Ch., 13 and 20.11.97 ; E.A., 89, pp. 58–9, 90, pp. 9–10, 91, p. 17, 92, p. 18, 93, p.17.)

2. WESLEYAN METHODISM

    (a) *Coppenhall Society*. The district was missioned from about 1805 to 1825 or 1828.

        1. *1825* or *1828 :* Remer Street chapel opened (closed 1869).

        2. *1869 :* North Street chapel opened.

    (b) *Crewe : Mill Street* (Trinity) *Society*

        preaching commenced in 1842.

        1843 : temporary building opened.

        1848 : second Mill Street chapel opened on same site.

        1877 : third Mill Street chapel opened on same site.

        Hightown Society

        the district was missioned 1864–8.

        1868 : Hightown chapel opened.

        Earle Street Society

        the district was missioned 1875–81.

        1881 : Earle Street chapel opened.

        West Street Mission 1883–7

        1887 : West Street school-chapel opened.

(C.G., 16.2.78, 28.12.78, 4.5.87, 23.7.87, 5.3.02, 9.12.19 ; Rev. C. Caine : *History of Wesleyan Methodism . . . Crewe Circuit.*)

3. PRIMITIVE METHODISM
- (a) *Heath Street Society*
  - preaching commenced about 1841–2.
    - *1846*: first chapel opened in Market Street (closed in 1855).
    - *1855*: second chapel opened in Heath Street (" Heath Street Hall ").
    - *1865*: third chapel (" Wedgwood ") opened ; this replaced the one opened in 1855.
- (b) *Mill Street Society*
  - the mission commenced about 1861.
    - *1863*: first chapel opened in Wesley Street (closed in 1865 or '66).
    - *1865*: second chapel opened (Mill Street).
- (c) *West Street Society*
  - the mission commenced about 1865.
    - *1866*: Ramsbottom Street school-chapel opened.
    - *1874*: Ramsbottom Street " Heath Memorial " chapel opened.
- (d) *Coppenhall Society*
    - *1868*: Warmingham Road chapel opened.
- (e) *Henry Street Society*
    - *1877–80*: services held in John Rigg's Henry Street factory.
    - *1880*: Henry Street chapel opened.
- (f) *Sydney Society*
    - *1896*: Herbert Street chapel opened.
- (g) *Bradfield Road Society, Coppenhall*
    - *1899*: school-chapel opened.
- (h) *Ruskin Road Society*
    - *1904*: chapel opened.
- (i) *Minshull New Road Society*
    - *1905*: school-chapel opened.

(C.G., 15.2.73, 16.3.78, 12.7.79, 18.2.80, 26.7.93, 5.3.04, 1.6.07, 26.3.15, 15.10.15 ; E.A. 90, p. 19 ; *Primitive Methodist Magazine* 1855, pp. 557–8 ; Anon : *Memoir of the Life and Labours of Mr. John Wedgwood* (1870).

4. UNITED FREE METHODISM (WESLEYAN ASSOCIATION)
- (a) the cause was started about 1841.
    - *1843* (October 8) : Earle Street chapel opened [1]—(closed in 1860).
    - *1860*: Market Terrace chapel opened.
    - *1883*: Hightown chapel opened, and Market Terrace chapel closed.
- (b) *1906*: Stewart Street mission chapel opened (offered for sale in 1920).

(C.G., 4.5.78, 17.10.82, 10.5.02, 15.9.06, 17.12.20 ; C.Ch., 28.7.83 ; Slater : *Chronicles of Lives and Religion in Cheshire*, pp. 290–2.)

5. INDEPENDENT METHODIST (" FREE GOSPEL ") CHURCH
- the cause was started about 1869.
    - *1871*: old Baptist chapel rented in Oak Street.
    - *1901–9*: temporary premises.
    - *1909*: Flag Lane chapel opened.

(C.G., 22.6.78, 3.10.82, 25.8.09, 8.12.09.)

---

[1] This was the first building expressly designed for public worship to be opened in Crewe (Slater : *op. cit.*, p. 290).

6. METHODIST NEW CONNEXION
mission started about 1875.
1881 : Edleston Road chapel opened.

(*C.G.*, 8.1.81, 10 and 14.9.81, 21 and 29.9.81.)

7. ROMAN CATHOLIC CHURCH
services first held about 1844.
1852 : Heath Street (then Russell Street) church opened.
1879 : removal to upper storey of a new Catholic school building in St. Mary's Street.
1891 : St. Mary's Church opened.

(*C.G.*, 11.1.79, 20.8.90, 29.7.91.)

8. THE BAPTIST CHURCH
(" General " and " Particular " Baptist congregations are no longer distinguished in Crewe.)
(*a*) *The " Particular " congregation*
cause first started either in 1844 or 1849.
1854 : small chapel opened in Newdigate Street (closed in 1860).
1860 : Victoria Street chapel opened (closed in 1895).
1895 : West Street school-chapel opened.
1901 : West Street Tabernacle opened.
(*b*) *1863 :* Schism—part of this congregation broke away and formed a new body.
1865 : Baptist Mission chapel opened in Oak Street.
This congregation came to an end about 1869–71.
(*c*) *The " General " Congregation*
cause started in 1882.
1884 : Union Street Tabernacle opened.

(*Cheshire Observer*, 31.5.62, 26.7.62, 27.6.63, 25.7.63 ; *C.G.*, 18.5.78, 22.6.78, 14.7.78, 25.4.83, 12.5.83, 13.9.84, 16.3.95, 28.4.00, 19.1.01 ; *C.Ch.*, 23.11.95.)

9. PRESBYTERIAN CHURCH OF ENGLAND
Presbyterian station opened, 1844.
1862 : Hill Street Church opened.

(*Cheshire Observer*, 7.9.61, 6.9.62 ; *C.G.*, 29.1.81, 2.10.97.)

10. WELSH PRESBYTERIAN (CALVINISTIC METHODIST) CHURCH
preaching commenced 1843.
1868 : St. Paul's Street chapel opened.

(*C.G.*, 8.6.78, 4.7.83 ; Owen : *Hanes Methodistiaeth Sir Fflint*, pp. 579–88.)

11. WELSH CONGREGATIONAL CHURCH (" UNDENOMINATIONAL ")
1900 : Derrington Street corrugated iron chapel opened (there had been a former short-lived revolt against the Presbyterians, *c.* 1880–3, by the " Wesleyans ").

(*C.G.*, 12.5.00, 4 and 11.8.00 ; Owen : *op. cit.*, pp. 579–88.)

12. CONGREGATIONAL CHURCH (INDEPENDENTS)

cause started in 1841.

1847: Oak (Exchange) Street chapel opened (converted into legal offices—Temple Chambers—in 1869.)

1870: Hightown chapel opened.

(*C.G.*, 30.3.78, 11.12.97; *E.A.* 02, p. 47.)

13. FREE CHRISTIAN (UNITARIAN) CHURCH

cause started about 1862–3.

1865: Beech Street chapel opened.

14. SALVATION ARMY

" invaded " Crewe for the first time in 1882.[1]

1883–9: temporary " barracks " in Camm Street.

1889: Market Terrace Citadel opened.

15. THE CHRISTADELPHIANS

commenced about 1882.

1908: Sandon Street Hall taken.

(*Cheshire Observer*, 27.6.63, 25.7.63, 1.8.63, 26.9.63; *C.G.*, 11.5.78 (Unitarians); *C.G.*, 8.2.82 *sqq. passim*, 14.3.83, 24 and 31.7.89, 26.10.89 (Salvation Army); *E.A.* 83, p. 8, 89, p. 66, 09, p. 111.)

16. SPIRITUALISM

Crewe Spiritualist Society commenced about 1905.

1921: premises in Mill Street opened.

(*C.G.*, 13.1.06, 27.1.06, 23.2.07, 6.3.07, 29.3.18, 3.12.20.)

17. RAILWAY MISSION

1894: first hall acquired.

1909: new hall opened.

(*C.G.*, 16.6.94, 3.5.09; *C.Ch.*, 16.6.94.)

Only those bodies are listed which, by 1923, had acquired permanent headquarters. The Latter Day Saints (" Mormons "), the Plymouth Brethren, and the Catholic Apostolic Church have at various times boasted organised bodies of adherents in Crewe.

NOTE (A) The strength of Nonconformity, and of Primitive Methodism in particular.

(B) The Presbyterians and Unitarians, through their prominent members, have exercised an influence on the life of Crewe out of all proportion to their numerical strength, *e.g.* William Dishart and H. D. Struthers were Presbyterians (" Scotch schools " influence), while James Briggs, the Rev. William Mellor and the Rev. H. Bodell Smith (Unitarian minister, *c.* 1890–5, founder of Crewe Independent Labour Party), were all Unitarians and politicians.

(C) The early date of the Welsh Presbyterian congregation.

(D) The extent of church and chapel building activities in the 1860's.

---

[1] The intention of the Salvation Army was to " drive the Devil out of Crewe." T. H. Heath commented in 1899 : " Notwithstanding the erection of citadels, and much demonstrating in force in sight of the enemy, the object sought to be attained not only by the Salvation Army, but by others equally as enthusiastic, is still far from realisation " (*E.A.* 02, p. 49).

APPENDIX NO. 6

TRADE UNIONISM IN CREWE, 1843–1939

CREWE DISTRICT SECRETARIES OF THE A.S.E. AND A.E.U.

1880–9	Wm. Urquhart
1889, May–Dec.	G. Dentith
1889–1901, June	Eli Beard
1901–5, March	A. E. Dinan
1905–10, Jan.	J. E. Dideridge
1910–17, July	W. H. Price
1917–18, May	W. G. Elvy
1918, May 4–18	L. E. Skellern, *pro tem.*
1918, May 18–1923 . . .	G. T. West
1923, Aug.–	Thos. Talbot

Former Name of Union, with Dates of Existence, if Available.	Former Name, with Dates of Existence if Available.	Name of Union, and Number of Branches in 1939.
Journeyman Steam-Engine Makers' Society.	*Amalgamated Society of Engineers.*	*Amalgamated Engineering Union.*
CREWE BRANCH, 1843–50 (*Rules*, 1843, p. 54)	CREWE BRANCH, No. 1, 1851–1920	CREWE No. 1 BRANCH, 1920–
	CREWE BRANCH No. 2, 1866–1920 (Annual Report, 1866, p. 47)	No. 2, 1920–
	CREWE BRANCH No. 3, 1875–1920 (*C.Ch.*, 4.3.76)	No. 3, 1920–
	CREWE BRANCH No. 4, *c.* 1884–1920	No. 4, 1920–
	CREWE BRANCH No. 5, 1903/4–1920	No. 5, 1920–
	CREWE BRANCH No. 6, 1914–1920	No. 6, 1920–
	CREWE BRANCH No. 7, 1917–1920	No. 7, 1920–

Former Name of Union, with Dates of Existence, if Available.	Former Name, with Dates of Existence if Available.	Name of Union, and Number of Branches in 1939.
Steam-Engine Makers' Society. " No. 1," *1843* or *1850* to 1920 (*Christian Socialist*, Dec. 7, 1850, p. 46)		No. 8, 1920–
" No. 2," 1873–1920		No. 9, 1920–
" No. 3," 1917–1920		No. 10, 1920–
Amalgamated Society of Metal Planers, Shapers, Slotters, Horizontal Borers and Milling Machine Workers. Crewe branch (earliest mention 1889 —*E.A.* 90, p. 33) –1894	*United Machine Workers' Association.* Crewe branch 1894–1920	No. 11, 1920–
Various mentions of *Brass Founders' and Finishers' Society* occur—earliest 1860, but the branch appears to have collapsed *c.* 1910 (*Chester Record*, 28.1.60 ; *C.G.*, 21.9.78).	*Associated Brass Founders', Turners', Fitters' and Finishers' and Coppersmiths' Society.* Crewe branch *c.* 1914–20.	No. 12, 1920–
	Scientific Instrument Makers' Trade Society. Crewe branch 1906–1920	*Amalgamated Engineering Union.* No. 13, 1920–

(There is frequent mention of engineering unionism at Crewe in J. B. Jefferys : *The Story of the Engineers*, 1946.)

| | *Friendly Society of Boiler-makers.*

Crewe branch 1843–   became | *United Society of Boiler-makers and Iron and Steel Shipbuilders.*

Crewe No. 1

Crewe No. 2 1912–
(*C.G.* 7.10.13) |

Former Name of Union, with Dates of Existence, if Available.	Former Name, with Dates of Existence if Available.	Name of Union, and Number of Branches in 1939.
		United Pattern-Makers' Association. Crewe branch 1903–
	Friendly Society of Iron-founders. Crewe branch 1864–73 (collapsed) refounded 1876–1920	*National Society of Foundry Workers.* Crewe branch 1920–
	Amalgamated Society of Coremakers. Crewe branch (?)–1920 (earliest mention 1916 —C.G. 23.6.16).	Became part of above.
	British Steel Smelters', Mill, Iron and Tinplate Workers' Association. Crewe branch 1906–17	*British Iron, Steel and Kindred Trades Association.* Crewe branch 1917–
		National Amalgamated Tin, Iron Plate, Sheet Metal Workers and Braziers. Crewe branch 1906– (C.G. 9.3.07)
	United Kingdom Society of Coach-Makers. Crewe branch in existence 1848, but probably dates back to 1843. c. 1848–1919	*National Union of Vehicle Builders.* Crewe branch 1919–

Former Name of Union, with Dates of Existence, if Available.	Former Name, with Dates of Existence if Available.	Name of Union, and Number of Branches in 1939.
	Amalgamated Society of Railway Servants. Crewe No. 1 1872 to *c.* 1875 (collapsed : C.G. 2 and 9.3.72, 9.5.74, 8.5.75) refounded 1888–1913.	*National Union of Rail- waymen.* Crewe No. 1 1913–
	Crewe No. 2 1896–1913	Crewe No. 2 1913–
	Crewe No. 3 1905–13	Crewe No. 4 1913–
	General Railway Workers' Union. No. 1 Crewe branch 1889–1913 (C.G. and C.Ch. 14.12.89) No. 2 Crewe branch 1891–1913	Crewe No. 3 1913–
	United Pointsmen's and Signalmen's Society. Crewe branch 1908–13	
		Crewe No. 5 1916– (from 1913 until 1916 was sub-branch no. 1 : Caunt, pp. 8–10).
		Crewe No. 6 1919–
		Crewe No 7. 1919–
		Crewe No. 8 1924–
	About 1903 the Crewe branch of the A.S.L.E. and F. absorbed " the old Enginemen's Society " (C.G. 27.5.03).	*Associated Society of Loco- motive Engineers and Firemen.* Crewe branch 1889 or 1890 (C.G. 5.4.93, 6.4.04)

Former Name of Union, with Dates of Existence, if Available.	Former Name, with Dates of Existence if Available.	Name of Union, and Number of Branches in 1939.
		Railway Clerks' Association. Crewe No. 1 1903–4 (collapsed) refounded 1911– (C.G. 19.1.12)
		No. 2, 1919–
		No. 3, 1919–21 "Professional and Technical" collapsed, refounded as
		No. 4 "P. & T." 1937–
		No. 3, 1921–
		National Union of Clerks. Crewe branch 1910– (C.G., 2.12.10)
United Kingdom Postal Clerks' Association. Crewe branch 1887–1914	*Postal and Telegraph Clerks' Association.* Crewe branch 1914–19 became	
		Union of Post Office Workers. Crewe branch 1920–
	Postmen's Federation. Crewe branch 1891–1919 } became	
	National Union of Gas Workers and General Labourers. Crewe No. 1 branch 1893– collapsed (C.G. and C.Ch., 28.10.93) refounded 1906– became	*National Union of General and Municipal Workers.* Crewe No. 1
		Crewe No. 2 1934–

Former Name of Union, with Dates of Existence, if Available.	Former Name, with Dates of Existence if Available.	Name of Union, and Number of Branches in 1939.
	National Union of Corporation Workers. Crewe branch 1912–28	*National Union of Public Employees.* Crewe branch 1928–
		National Association of Local Government Officers and Clerks. Crewe Guild 1910– (C.G., 2.4.10)
	National Union of Elementary Teachers. Crewe branch 1872–1890 (C.G., 21.3.08)	*National Union of Teachers.* Crewe branch 1890– (Nantwich split off 1908 —C.G., 5.12.08, 17 and 20.2.09)
United Garment Workers' Union, founded in 1912 as Crewe branch of the *Amalgamated Union of Clothiers' Operatives.* Crewe branch 1915–20 (first mention 1917— C.G., 19.6.17)	*Amalgamated Society of Tailors* (from 1894 " *and Tailoresses* "). Crewe branch about 1867–1933 became *Tailors' and Garment Workers' Trade Union.* Crewe branch 1920–33	*National Union of Tailors and Garment Workers.* Crewe branch 1933–
		National Amalgamated Union of Shop Assistants, Warehousemen and Clerks. Crewe branch 1891–1895 (?) (collapsed) refounded 1901–

Former Name of Union, with Dates of Existence, if Available.	Former Name, with Dates of Existence if Available.	Name of Union, and Number of Branches in 1939.
	Amalgamated Union of Co-operative Employees (after 1918, " *Commercial Employees and Allied Workers* "). Crewe branch 1891–1922	*National Union of Distributive and Allied Workers.* Crewe branch 1922–
		Journeymen Butchers' Federation. Crewe branch 1922–
	Union of Saddlers and General Leather Workers. Crewe branch 1914–	*National Union of Leather Workers.* Crewe branch
		Amalgamated Union of Operative Bakers and Confectioners. Crewe branch about 1867– (C.G., 13.3.75 ; C.Ch. 4.3.76)
	Amalgamated Society of Carpenters and Joiners. Crewe branch 1865–1921	*Amalgamated Society of Woodworkers.* Crewe branch 1921–
		Amalgamated Society of Woodcutting Machinists. Crewe branch 1918–
		Electrical Trades' Union. Crewe branch 1916– (from 1914 to 1916 was a sub-branch of Withy Grove branch, Manchester).

Former Name of Union, with Dates of Existence, if Available.	Former Name, with Dates of Existence if Available.	Name of Union, and Number of Branches in 1939.
		National Amalgamated Society of Operative House and Ship Painters and Decorators. Crewe branch 1893–
		National Association of Operative Plasterers. Crewe branch 1892–
	United Operative Bricklayers' Society. Crewe branch in late December 1892 or early 1893 to 1921.	*Amalgamated Union of Building Trade Workers.* Crewe branch 1921–
	United Operative Plumbers' Association. Crewe branch or lodge 1884–	*Union of Plumbers, Glaziers and Domestic Engineers.* Crewe branch
		National Federation of Building Trades Operatives. Crewe branch about 1918
London and Provincial Union of Licensed Vehicle Workers. Crewe branch 1919–20	*United Vehicle Workers' Union.* Crewe branch 1920–2	*Transport and General Workers' Union.* Crewe branch 1922–
	Workers' Union. (Crewe Rail Shops 867) 1923–9	*Transport and General Workers' Union.* (Crewe Rail Shops 6/127 branch)
	Amalgamated Association of Tramway and Hackney Carriage Employees. Crewe branch 1897– (?) (C.G., 4.9.97)	

Former Name of Union, with Dates of Existence, if Available.	Former Name, with Dates of Existence if Available.	Name of Union, and Number of Branches in 1939.
	United Carters' Association. Crewe branch 1893 (*C.G.*, 20.9.93) re-formed in 1901 as the Crewe and District branch of the *Carters' Association* (*C.G.*, 4.9.01) at one time affiliated to Crewe Trades Council (*C.G.*, 3.10.08)—now extinct.	
		Typographical Association. Crewe chapel 1919–
		Society of Women employed in the Bookbinding and Printing Trades. Crewe branch 1919–
		National Union of Journalists. Crewe district branch 1912–
		National Amalgamated Union of Life Assurance Agents (or " *Workers* "). Crewe branch 1897–
		Amalgamated Society of Farriers and Blacksmiths. Crewe branch 1917–22 (?) extinct
		" *Wheelwrights' and Blacksmiths' Society.*" Crewe branch 1894– (?) (*C.G.*, 20.6.94) extinct

Former Name of Union, with Dates of Existence, if Available.	Former Name, with Dates of Existence if Available.	Name of Union, and Number of Branches in 1939.
		National Amalgamated Furnishing Trades' Association. Crewe branch 1906–10 (extinct)
(Information from the Crewe branch secretaries and the general secretaries of the various unions, also from Messrs. W. Smedley and W. R. Boughton.)		
		Amalgamated Railway Vehicle Workers. Crewe branch (in existence in 1912— extinct ? C.G., 12.1.12)

In 1939 the three chief unions in Crewe were :—

	Members
Amalgamated Engineering Union	4,123 (April)
National Union of Railwaymen .	3,258 (Feb.)
Railway Clerks' Association .	1,023 (March)

Next came the National Union of Tailors and Garment Workers, with just under a thousand members. The remaining branches ranged in membership from the 551 of the Associated Society of Locomotive Engineers and Firemen, to the 4 or 5 members of the Crewe branch of the Amalgamated Society of Woodcutting Machinists. The total number of trade unionists in Crewe and district was probably not far short of 12,000 in 1939.

APPENDIX NO. 7

OCCUPATIONS IN CREWE ACCORDING TO THE CENSUS OF 1921

MALES

Metal workers	6,502
Railway workers	2,241
General labourers	1,062
Clerks and draughtsmen	1,021
Commercial corporations	887
Woodworkers	536
Builders, bricklayers	536
Painters	299
Road transport	228

FEMALES

Tailoring, dressmaking	1,386
Domestic servants	735
Commercial occupations	631
Clerks and typists	288
Teachers	225

" Even after deducting the 10,053 married women from those neither retired nor gainfully employed we are still left with 3,926 females apparently without occupation, and it seems evident that there is an ample supply of female labour available for new industries in the town " (*Annual Report* of the Medical Officer of Health for Crewe Borough for 1923, pp. 8–9).

APPENDIX NO. 8

OCCUPATIONS IN CREWE ACCORDING TO THE CENSUS OF 1931

(N.B.—Only categories employing more than 100 workers are given here)

1. MALES

Total number in Crewe . .	22,916
Number over 14 years . . .	18,027
Number occupied	16,148, of which 12,730 were in work and 2,237 out of work
Number unoccupied . . .	1,879 *i.e.* retired, etc.

OCCUPATIONS

5,114 metal workers.

1,875 railway transport workers.

1,288 commercial and financial workers, including 449 proprietors and managers of retail businesses and 450 shop assistants.

1,021 clerks and draughtsmen.

758 builders and bricklayers.

524 water and other transport workers, including 259 messengers and porters.

469 workers in wood and furnishing.

411 road transport workers.

409 personal service.

318 painters and decorators.

275 drivers of stationary engines.

261 warehousemen and packers.

247 makers of textile goods and articles of dress, including tailors and shoemakers.

243 electrical apparatus makers.

238 professional occupations, including teachers.

186 agricultural workers.

2,060 other and undefined workers, including 1,224 general and undefined labourers and 713 unskilled workers in factories and other works.

2. FEMALES

Total number in Crewe . .	23,153
Number over 14 years . . .	18,352
Number occupied	4,888, of which 4,096 were in work and 297 out of work
Number unoccupied *(sic)* . .	13,464 *i.e.* housewives, retired, etc.

OCCUPATIONS

1,564 makers of textile goods, including 935 tailoresses and 512 milliners, embroiderers and sewers.

1,420 personal service, including 892 domestic servants and 138 charwomen.

746 financial and commercial workers, including 231 owners and managers of retail shops and 466 shop assistants.

409 clerks and typists.

304 professional occupations, including 203 teachers.

(From *Census*, 1931 (England and Wales, Occupations), p. 432, where categories employing less than 100 are given.)

APPENDIX NO. 9

THREE DOCUMENTS ON THE "INTIMIDATION AFFAIR" 1885, 1889

1. FROM "THE CREWE CHRONICLE," SEPTEMBER 26, 1885

The Editor made the following charges against F. W. Webb :—

" 1. That through the action, direct and indirect, of Tory railway officialism, the political life of Crewe is cramped and hindered beyond description.

2. That after incorporation for four years the Liberals possessed a great majority in the Town Council ; that then a leading official, then and now a prominent Tory, called a meeting of foremen to control the then pending elections ; and that the ' works ' were deliberately canvassed *against* the Liberals.

3. That as a consequence not a single foreman and not a single workman in the Railway Company's employ dare openly act on the Committee of the Crewe Liberal Association while they may and do join the Conservative Association with impunity.

4. That the Tory cry now is that they are for the Company and the Liberals are against the Company, thus throwing the enormous influence of officialism into the scale against the Liberal candidate.

5. That Mr. Webb has encouraged and permitted foremen in the works to canvass, and therefore insult men on the Executive of the Liberal Association and ward committees by asking them to serve upon canvassing committees of works (i.e. Tory) candidates.

6. That according to ' A Lover of Freedom's ' letter in last week's *Chronicle* ' gross intimidation ' was used by these men in fulfilling Mr. Webb's behests ; and that he personally was admonished by his foreman for taking a ' foolish interest in politics,' and warned that he would ' get into trouble ' if he did not give it up.

7. That the Tories were cognisant of this intimidation, telling ' A Lover of Freedom ' that he was among a number of other Liberals who would be discharged.

8. That eventually ' A Lover of Freedom ' and fourteen others were discharged, and that when he went to receive his back pay with his doomed companions he found *every one were Liberals* !

9. That out of more than 100 men discharged there was only one Tory, a Conservative secretary of one of the ward committees, and he was reinstated.

10. That the panic is so great at Crewe, that while the Crewe Liberal Club is unable to post a list of its members, the brother of the private secretary of Mr. Webb, a clerk in the Railway Company's offices, is the hon. secretary of the Conservative Association for the Crewe division of Cheshire."

2. FROM "PROCEEDINGS OF CREWE TOWN COUNCIL," 1889, p. 135

General Council Meeting, November 27, 1889 :—
" It was moved by Councillor Hodgson,
Seconded by Councillor Pedley,
That the following memorial be passed under the Corporate Common Seal,

and sent to the next general meeting of the Shareholders of the London, and North-Western Railway Company for their approval, viz. :—

Your Memorialists desire to call your attention to the fact that the Chief Officials of the Railway Company residing in Crewe, have for some years been using their official influence as Managers of the property of the Shareholders, to create the impression in the minds of the Railway Company's Employees, that their association with Liberal Organisations will jeopardise their prospects of promotion, and even of their permanent employment under the Company.

They therefore strongly urge that political liberty should be secured to the workmen in your great workshops located here.

For nine long years the Managers of the Works and their subordinate Foremen have been allied with the Tories of Crewe to crush Liberalism altogether out of the town. First, as regards the town, they have never during the whole of that time supported a Liberal for membership to the Town Council, but they have on the contrary under the guise of ' Independents ' joined in supporting Tory candidates.

They have moreover turned every Liberal Alderman off the Council, and put Tories in their places. Secondly, by intimidation and persecution of your Liberal workmen, and by making the chances of promotion depend upon subserviency to the Tory political demands of the Management, they have created a state of political serfdom in the works, which is simply intolerable to some of your best and most faithful servants now in your employ.

Your Memorialists therefore pray that your Directors may be instructed to declare once for all that the men in Crewe Works shall not be interfered with in the exercise of their political rights.

As an amendment,
It was moved by Alderman Whale,
Seconded by Alderman Macrae,
That this Council deprecates the introduction of politics into its discussions, and declines to assent or pass under the Corporate Common Seal any memorial for furthering the interests of any political party."

Amendment carried by 11 votes to 9.

3. W. E. GLADSTONE'S LETTER TO THE EDITOR OF " THE CHRONICLE " (*printed in " The Crewe Chronicle," December 21, 1889*)

" Dear Sir,—The case at Crewe, as it is set forth in your letter and in the *Crewe and Nantwich Chronicle*, is so scandalously bad that you must forgive me for saying I am compelled to suspend my belief until I know what any such among the local officers of the London and North Western Railway Company as are included in the charge have to say upon it. They, the paid servants of a great commercial company, which is not, I apprehend, a Primrose League, are accused of allowing their own political opinions to weigh, and to weigh penally, in the employment and promotion of workmen ; which IF IT BE TRUE, IS NEITHER MORE NOR LESS THAN A SHAMEFUL MALVERSATION IN A PUBLIC TRUST. Such proceedings are bad enough, when unhappily any landlord or employer is tempted by a selfish fanaticism ' to do what he will with his own,' so as to inflict SUFFERING UPON HIS FELLOW SUBJECTS. But when this is done by persons who are themselves only servants, against their fellow-servants who happen to be a degree lower in the scale, when they do what they will, not with what is their own, but with what is not their own, either to indulge their passions, to promote their interests, or to propagate their opinions, THEIR CONDUCT IS IN THE LAST DEGREE SHAMEFUL AND UNWORTHY. Therefore as I have said, I suspend my opinion until these very grave and quite sufficiently particular allegations have been answered. Should there however be an apparent intention to withhold a reply, and should you consider it desirable, you will be quite at liberty to publish this letter.

Yours very faithfully,
W. E. GLADSTONE."

HAWARDEN, *Dec. 5th*, 1889.

INDEX